Building Trust

*Developing the
Russian Financial Sector*

THE WORLD BANK
Washington, D.C.

© 2002 The International Bank for Reconstruction and Development / The World Bank
1818 H Street, NW
Washington, DC 20433
Telephone 202-473-1000
Internet www.worldbank.org
E-mail feedback@worldbank.org

All rights reserved.

First printing September 2002
1 2 3 4 05 04 03 02

The findings, interpretations, and conclusions expressed here are those of the author(s) and do not necessarily reflect the views of the Board of Executive Directors of the World Bank or the governments they represent.

The World Bank cannot guarantee the accuracy of the data included in this work. The boundaries, colors, denominations, and other information shown on any map in this work do not imply on the part of the World Bank any judgment of the legal status of any territory or the endorsement or acceptance of such boundaries.

Rights and Permissions
The material in this work is copyrighted. No part of this work may be reproduced or transmitted in any form or by any means, electronic or mechanical, including photocopying, recording, or inclusion in any information storage and retrieval system, without the prior written permission of the World Bank. The World Bank encourages dissemination of its work and will normally grant permission promptly.

For permission to photocopy or reprint, please send a request with complete information to the Copyright Clearance Center, Inc., 222 Rosewood Drive, Danvers, MA 01923, USA, telephone 978-750-8400, fax 978-750-4470, www.copyright.com.

All other queries on rights and licenses, including subsidiary rights, should be addressed to the Office of the Publisher, World Bank, 1818 H Street NW, Washington, DC 20433, USA, fax 202-522-2422, e-mail pubrights@worldbank.org.

Library of Congress Cataloging-in-Publication Data
Building trust: developing the Russian financial sector.
    p. cm.
    "This book was produced by a World Bank team led by Michael Fuchs who planned, coordinated, and edited the book."
    Includes bibliographical references.
    ISBN 0-8213-5161-3
    1. Finance—Russia (Federation) 2. Banks and banking—Russia (Federation) I. Fuchs, Michael J. (Michael Joseph), 1951– II. World Bank.

HG186.R8 B75 2002
332'.0947—dc21   2002027221

Contents

Foreword   ix

Acknowledgments   xi

Abbreviations and Acronyms   xiii

Executive Summary   xv

Chapter 1   Building Trust for Financial Sector Development: An Overview   1
     Introduction   1
     Trust, Financial Sector Development, and Growth   3
     Legal and Accounting Infrastructures   6
     The Banking System: Structure and Performance   13
     Regulation and Restructuring of Banks   21
     Improving Enterprise Financing   33
     Conclusion   42

PART I   **Legal and Accounting Infrastructures**   **49**

Chapter 2   Creditor Rights   51
     Introduction   51
     The Framework for Secured Transactions   53
     Enforcement Mechanisms   56
     Information Mechanisms   64
     Other Obstacles Related to the Use of Pledged Assets   67
     Annex 2.1. Creditor Rights: The International Experience   70

Chapter 3   Framework for Corporate Insolvency   83
     The Role and Function of Insolvency Systems in Market
         Economies   83

Overview of Russian Corporate Insolvency Practice   86
Legal Framework for Corporate Insolvency   91
Implementation of the Insolvency Regime   97
Assessment of Key Features of the Bankruptcy Regime   102
Framework for Corporate Workouts and Restructurings   106
Conclusion   107

Chapter 4   Disclosure and Transparency   115
Introduction   115
Accounting Standards and Disclosure   116
Auditing Standards and Disclosure   118
Enforcement and Disclosure   120
Recommendations   121
Comparison of Russian and International Accounting and Auditing Standards   122

PART II   The Banking System: Structure and Performance   127

Chapter 5   The Role of the Financial System   129
The Importance of the Financial Sector for Economic Development   129
The Key Role of Banking System Reform   131
Size and Structure of the Russian Banking Sector   133
Domination by State Banks   136
Roles and Ownership Structure of the Banking Sector   137
Conclusion   139

Chapter 6   Analysis of Banking Practices   143
Introduction   143
Asset Structure and Quality   145
The Structure of Bank Liabilities   150
Schemes That Distort the Structure of Liabilities   152
Assessing Bank Capital   153
Profitability   153
Conclusion   155

Chapter 7   Reforming the Role of State Banks   159
Influence of State-Owned Banks on Performance and Growth   160
The Trend Away from State Banks   161
State Banks in the Russian Federation   162
The Role of Sberbank   164
The Government's Management of Sberbank   165
The Strategic Review of Sberbank   171
Restructuring Sberbank   175
Vneshtorgbank   176

                    Vnesheconombank   178
                    New Development Banks   179
                    Conclusion   181
                    Annex 7.1 Reforming State Banks   184

Chapter 8   Encouraging Foreign Entry to the Banking Sector   205
                    Introduction   205
                    The Presence of Foreign Investment and Foreign Banks
                        in Russia   206
                    The Regulatory Environment for Foreign Investment
                        in Banking   208
                    The Survey and Opinions of the Foreign Bank Subsidiaries
                        in Russia   211
                    Future Plans   215
                    Conclusion   216

PART III   **Regulation and the Restructuring of Banks**   227

Chapter 9   Building Trust through Effective Banking Supervision   229
                    Improving the Enabling Environment   231
                    Political Will   232
                    Role of the Banking Sector   234
                    Establishing the Role of Banking Supervision   235
                    Improving Supervisory Effectiveness   238

Chapter 10   Does the Russian Federation Need Deposit Insurance?   249
                    Introduction   249
                    Deposit Insurance in Other Countries   252
                    The Benefits and Risks of Deposit Insurance   252
                    Introducing Deposit Insurance in Russia   255
                    The Design of Deposit Insurance Schemes   257
                    Leveling the Playing Field?   258
                    Creating Trust through Incentives   259
                    Conclusion   260

Chapter 11   Bank Restructuring and Liquidation   263
                    Legal Protection of Depositor Interests   263
                    Depositor Preference   264
                    Effective Resolution of Troubled Banks   266
                    Restructuring of Banks in Bankruptcy Proceedings   271
                    Compromise of Depositor Claims in Restructuring   276
                    Judicial Bank Liquidation   277
                    Administrative Aspects of Bank Liquidation   281
                    Conclusion   284

Chapter 12 ARCO   287
            Introduction   287
            Overview of ARCO's Operations   291
            ARCO's Experience in the Rehabilitation of Banks   294
            ARCO Deposit Insurance Scheme   297
            ARCO's Experience of the Bank Liquidation Process   301
            Privatization of ARCO Banks   303
            Conclusion   305

PART IV   Enterprise Financing   311

Chapter 13 Enterprise Access to Financing   313
            Commercial Credit   313
            Bank Financing   316
            Veksels   318
            Leasing   320
            Other Financing Instruments   321
            Conclusion   321

Chapter 14 Capital Market Development   327
            The Mass Privatization Program   327
            Reform of the Russian Banking and Payments System   334
            Developing the Government Debt Market   335
            Mobilizing Savings   338
            Improving Corporate Governance   340
            Legislative Initiatives   345
            Enforcement of the Law   348
            Capital Markets Supervision   351
            The Role of the Capital Markets Supervisor   354
            Transparency and Disclosure   356

LIST OF BOXES

Box 1.1   Financial System Development and Economic Growth   4
Box 1.2   Consolidation of the Banking Sector: The Government/CBR Joint Strategy   16
Box 1.3   Sberbank and Its Restructuring   18
Box 1.4   Restructuring of State Banks Other than Sberbank   20
Box 1.5   Strengthening Banking Supervision: The Government/CBR Joint Strategy   23
Box 1.6   Problem Areas in ARCO's Approach to Bank Restructuring   34
Box 1.7   Overcoming Constraints on Lending to the SME Sector   35
Box 1.8   Summary of the Joint Government/CBR Program for the Development of the Russian Banking System   43
Box 1.9   Priority Trust-Building Measures   46

CONTENTS   vii

Box 2.1   Positive Features of Pledge under Russian Law   55
Box 2.2   Recommendations for Expanding Access to Credit   71
Box 2.3   Principles and Guidelines for Effective Insolvency and Creditor Rights Systems: Secured Transactions Recommendations (Extract)   72
Box 2.4   EBRD Core Principles for a Modern Secured Transactions Law   74
Box 5.1   The Main Functions of the Financial Sector   132
Box 5.2   The Post-1998 Crisis Period: A Missed Opportunity for Consolidating the Banking System?   135
Box 5.3   Consolidation of the Banking Sector: The Government/CBR Joint Strategy   139
Box 7.1   State Export Credit Agencies   180
Box 8.1   Where Is Russia in Foreign Bank Presence?   209
Box 8.2   Large Foreign Bank Entry during the 1990s: Some Case Studies   217
Box 8.3   The Generally Accepted Guidelines for the Supervision of Foreign Banks   221
Box 10.1   The Design of the Proposed Russian Deposit Insurance Scheme   250
Box 12.1   ARCO's Deposit Insurance Scheme   298
Box 13.1   Arrears and Noncash Settlements   314
Box 13.2   Safeguards in Managing Credit Risks   323

LIST OF FIGURES

Figure 1.1   Sequencing of Financial Sector Reforms   45
Figure 5.1   Number of Operating Banks   136
Figure 7.1   Development of the Brazilian Financial System   188
Figure 7.2   Development of the Chinese Financial System   191
Figure 7.3   Total Deposits of Sectors within the Chinese Banking System   195
Figure 7.4   Development of the German Financial System   197
Figure 12.1   Impact of the Introduction of Deposit Insurance on Member Banks   299
Figure 14.1   Sources of Corporate Finance in Russia   331
Figure 14.2   Enterprise Use of Equity Finance   332

LIST OF TABLES

Table 1.1   Financial Market Depth (2000)   5
Table 3.1   Number of Bankruptcy Cases   91
Table 4.1   Rules Missing in RAS and Present in IAS   122
Table 4.2   Discrepancy between RAS and IAS Disclosure Requirements   123

Table 4.3	RAS Rules That Differ from IAS	124
Table 4.4	The 39 Approved Russian Standards on Auditing and the Equivalent International Standards on Auditing	125
Table 5.1	Monetary Survey Data on the Russian Banking System	134
Table 5.2	International Comparison of the Banking System Depth	134
Table 5.3	Number of Credit Organizations by Paid-in Capital	134
Table 6.1	Key Statistics on the Asset Composition of the Russian Banks	146
Table 6.2	Loan-loss Provisions as Percentage of Gross Loan Books	149
Table 6.3	Share of Nonearning Assets in Total Assets	150
Table 6.4	Key Statistics on the Composition of Liabilities	151
Table 6.5	Key Statistics on the Profitability of the Reviewed Banks	154
Table 7.1	Government Ownership Stake in the 10 Largest Banks	160
Table 7.2	Data on Various Segments of the Banking Market	163
Table 7.3	Sberbank Share of the Russian Banking System (according to RAS)	167
Table 7.4	Market Share within the Chinese Banking System	194
Table 7.5	Comparison of Market Share of Assets in Public Banks, 1995	196
Table 7.6	Market Share of Different Bank Groups in Germany, 1999	198
Table 7.7	Comparison of Banking System Structures	199
Table 7.8	Comparison of Public Bank Structures	200
Table 8.1	Foreign Banks Operating in Russia, as of October 2000	207
Table 8.2	The Size of Some of the Foreign Banks in Russia	209
Table 8.3	Major Assets and Liabilities of Some of the Foreign-owned Banks in Russia, as of December 2000	213
Table 12.1	Banks in ARCO's Portfolio as of December 31, 2000	291
Table 12.2	ARCO Amicable Settlements in which Corporate Depositors Benefited	297
Table 12.3	Insurance Coverage of Deposits in the ARCO Scheme	299
Table 12.4	Deposit Growth per Quarter in Insured Banks Relative to the Region as a Whole	300
Table 13.1	The Role of Commercial Credit	315
Table 13.2	Credit to Private Sector	317
Table 13.3	Interest Rate Spreads	317
Table 13.4	Structure of Payments for Goods, Works, and Services in Russia	319
Table 14.1	Financial Market Depth, 2000	330
Table 14.2	Reasons for Inability to Attract Outside Investors	333
Table 14.3	Corporate Governance Scorecard for Russia	341
Table 14.4	Fines for Administrative Offenses in 2001	349

Foreword

The Russian financial sector has come a long way in the first years of transition. At the inception of the transition process 10 years ago, there was virtually no functioning financial system. Since then, the foundations of the legal, regulatory, and institutional infrastructure have been established, and the system has had to adapt and evolve under the weight of periodic economic, financial, and political instability.

Key to developing the financial sector in a market economy is the process of building trust among market participants. This process was severely tested during the 1998 financial crisis, which revealed many shortcomings in the implementation of financial sector reforms.

Since the 1998 crisis, the authorities have succeeded in stabilizing the financial system, but much remains to be done to reap the potential benefits of market-based intermediation in promoting efficient resource allocation and enabling the Russian economy to achieve stable and sustainable growth. Savers need to gain confidence in the solidity of financial institutions and entrust them with their financial savings. These financial institutions need to improve their intermediation skills and be comfortable lending to productive enterprises without being the controllers or owners of those enterprises.

In December 2000, the Government and the Central Bank approved a joint strategy for the reform of the banking system. This initiative, along with other initiatives—such as enactment of important amendments to the banking legislation and publication of a corporate governance code by the Federal Commission for Securities Markets—provides a welcome sign that a new era of financial reform is about to begin.

This book, a product of the World Bank's ongoing work in support of the Russian financial system, assesses current developments within the financial system and provides a road map for implementation of high-priority improvements. The book's purpose is to support the process of creating a broader understanding of and consensus on high-priority reform measures among interested parties within the Government (the Federation Council and the Duma), regulatory authorities, the judiciary, and the financial community at large.

Cesare Calari
Vice President
Financial Sector
World Bank

Acknowledgments

This book was produced by a World Bank team led by Michael Fuchs, who planned, coordinated, and edited the book. Contributors were Noritaka Akamatsu, Laura Ard, Thorsten Beck, Sally Buxton, James Foster, Marina Frolova, Richard Hands, Gordon Johnson, Cliff Isaak, Andrew Lovegrove, Jo Ann Paulson, Susan Rutledge, Sergei Shatalov, Phil Smith, Mark St. Giles, Esen Ulgenerk, Marius Vismantas, Kirill Vorobiev, Mark Walker, and Igor Yashenko.

We express our special gratitude to the peer reviewers: Lajos Bokros, Millard Long, and Larry Promisel, who made valuable comments and suggestions. In addition, Christof Ruehl provided substantive inputs. Particular thanks are also due to Patrick Honohan and Alexander Fleming, who reviewed the entire text prior to its completion.

The team gratefully acknowledges the support of the Central Bank of the Russian Federation and Government officials without whom production of this book would not have been possible. Comments provided by the Central Bank and Government agencies on an earlier draft of the book—which have been incorporated in the current text—are also most gratefully acknowledged. Considerable credit is also due to background material and analyses provided by the staff of the European Bank for Reconstruction and Development and other donor representatives.

Several people provided invaluable assistance: Anahit Adamyan, Zeynep Kantur, and Irena Tchoukleva, data analysts; Frank Kenefick, Tatiana Segal, and Anna Sukiasyan, technical editors; Marina Kuznetsova, team coordinator; Susan Graham, developmental editor; Melissa Edeburn, production editor; and Bennet Akpa, print coordinator.

Abbreviations and Acronyms

AMC	Asset management companies
ARCO	Agency for Restructuring of Credit Organizations
BIS	Bank for International Settlements
CBR	Central Bank of Russia
EBRD	European Bank for Reconstruction and Development
EU	European Union
FCSM	Federal Commission for Securities Market
FIAC	Foreign Investor Advisory Committee
FIDP	Financial Institution Development Project
FIG	Financial-industrial groups
FSFR	Federal Service on Financial Rehabilitation and Bankruptcy
GATT	General Agreement on Tariffs and Trade
GDP	Gross Domestic Product
GKO	Short-term Federal Government Securities
IAPC	International Auditing Practices Committee
IAS	International Accounting Standards
IASB	International Accounting Standards Board
IBRD	International Bank for Reconstruction and Development
IFAC	International Federation of Accountants
IFC	International Finance Corporation
IMF	International Monetary Fund
IOSCO	International Organization of Securities Commission
ISA	International Standards on Auditing
IPA	Institute of Professional Accountants
KPB	Kuzbassprombank

LLP	Loan-loss provisions
MoF	Ministry of Finance
NCS	Noncash settlements
NPL	Nonperforming loans
OECD	Organisation for Economic Co-operation and Development
OTC	Over-the-counter markets
RAR	Russian Audit Rules
RAS	Russian Accounting Standards
RDB	Russian Development Bank
RSA	Russian Standards on Auditing
RTC	Resolution Trust Corporation
SME	Small and medium-size enterprises
SoE	State-owned Enterprise
TACIS	Technical Assistance to Commonwealth of Independent States
USAID	United States Agency for International Development
VEB	Vnesheconombank
VTB	Vneshtorgbank
WTO	World Trade Organization

Executive Summary

A sound, efficient financial sector does not necessarily guarantee long-term growth, but long-term growth is difficult to achieve without a sound, efficient financial sector.

In the immediate aftermath of the financial crisis in August 1998, the Russian authorities focused their efforts on macroeconomic stabilization and the consolidation of government finances. Because these efforts were so successful, and because the devaluation of the ruble and the rise in raw material prices provided an economic impetus, the Russian Federation's economic growth in 2000 and 2001 was impressive.

Although certain sectors of the Russian economy—especially those related to raw material exports and import substitution—have experienced impressive growth in recent years, this growth has a narrow base, which is vulnerable to raw material price and exchange rate fluctuations. Broadening this base depends upon improving the availability of financing to a much wider group of enterprises—many of them small or medium-size enterprises that are unrelated to larger industrial groups. While considerable effort has gone into stabilizing the Russian financial sector since 1998, a lengthy agenda remains regarding the restructuring of the sector.

Trust is key to promoting the growth of market-based financial intermediation—to encourage savers to entrust their financial savings in the form of deposits to financial institutions and to encourage financial institutions to lend to enterprises without being the controllers or owners of those enterprises.

The fundamental theme of the Russian financial system's recent history has been that of lack of trust. Trust has been undermined by both market participants and government authorities. Those in control of failed banks have shifted assets to avoid obligations to creditors, including depositors; financial disclosure has been weak; enforcement of contract rights has been unpredictable; state banks have received preferential treatment; corporate governance has lacked accountability; and regulatory oversight has been insufficient. Banks currently are undercapitalized, and their lending is primarily with connected parties. The essential function of financial systems in market economies—to support the process of resource allocation—has gone unfulfilled. In building greater trust, special attention will need to be paid to maintaining the confidence of those providers of funds—be they retail depositors or minority share owners—who are at present provided with the least legal protection and information.

Any comprehensive strategy designed to enhance trust in Russian banking will need to focus on four major themes: (1) encouraging financial intermediation by improving the legal and accounting infrastructure for financial sector development; (2) improving the current structure and performance of the banking system; (3) improving the effectiveness of bank regulation, bank restructuring, and liquidation; and (4) enhancing enterprise access to finance.

LEGAL AND REGULATORY INFRASTRUCTURE

Russian banks are currently unable to engage in sufficient lending to an enterprise sector that is starved for working capital and long-term finance. Most enterprises rely on intragroup finance and on various forms of informal finance, such as payment and tax arrears, and veksels as sources of working capital finance. On the whole, banks—be they domestic or foreign—are reluctant to expand the scope of formal intermediation, given the weak protection afforded to them as creditors.

Strengthening creditor rights depends in part on improving the legal framework that protects creditor interests and ensures effective discipline. Needed legislative improvements include establishing greater clarity in the priorities of creditor claims as well as introducing simplified enforcement procedures (both judicial and nonjudicial). Also necessary is the introduction of better notification procedures, such as a centralized register of collateral on movable property and a credit-reporting system.

Creditor rights are also closely linked to the insolvency system, which provides an orderly and equitable debt collection mechanism for failing or failed enterprises. The key issues related to the insolvency system are connected with the system's implementation, particularly taking measures to avoid the manipulation of claims to the advantage of management or particular creditors. Resolving these implementation issues will require improving the quality of judges and creating specialized insolvency judges, strengthening insolvency criteria to avoid bad-faith filings, and providing for more creditor participation in the insolvency proceedings.

Market-based financial systems depend on the timely exchange of reliable information to third parties. Current disclosure, accounting, and auditing standards in Russia provide insufficient insight into the financial and governance situation of enterprises and banks. Weak accounting and disclosure requirements allow enterprises and banks to camouflage financial and nonfinancial information with the purpose of evading taxation, minimizing harassment, undermining the position of minority shareholders, etc. Consequently, phased implementation of International Accounting Standards (IAS) is imperative, as is the need for corporate financial and nonfinancial disclosure in compliance with international standards (e.g., information about ownership based on effective control rather than nominal ownership).

STRUCTURE AND PERFORMANCE OF THE BANKING SYSTEM

Creating greater trust in the Russian banking system depends on taking steps to consolidate the banking system and to improve the structure and performance of Russia's state banks. The performance of the sector could also be enhanced by greater entry on the part of foreign banks.

Many of Russia's 1,300 licensed banks are not financially viable or adequately capitalized, at least when measured by IAS. Also, the majority of Russian banks do not actively solicit deposits from the public; they are essentially "pocket banks" that exist to perform certain convenience functions for their owners. However, as licensed deposit-taking institutions, these banks are authorized to accept deposits from the public; if these banks are not financially sound, trust in the banking system will be undermined. The danger to system stability could be accentuated by the introduction of a deposit insurance system that would support even the weaker banks in attracting household deposits. Under current circumstances, supervising such a large number of deposit-taking institutions may be impossible for the Central Bank of Russia (CBR). Thus an important step toward improving trust in the banking system would be to consolidate the banking system by: (1) encouraging bank mergers,

(2) gradually increasing the minimum capital threshold for all banks, and (3) removing banking (i.e. deposit-taking) licenses from the many institutions that have no intention of soliciting deposits from the public.

Reform of the state banks is the first priority in creating greater trust in the financial system. Assisted by liquidity and the capital support provided by the authorities, the share of new lending provided by state banks in Russia has increased significantly since the 1998 crisis. Worldwide experience suggests that state banks cannot be expected to allocate resources efficiently in the long term, and this in turn hampers growth. State bank lending tends to be politically motivated rather than based on sound market principles; it tends to be concentrated on large influential or state-owned enterprises, thereby depriving credit to small and medium-size enterprises. As a result, state banks tend to accumulate significant losses that can ultimately become a serious fiscal burden.

Although the medium-term focus should be to ensure an orderly privatization of state banks to reputable strategic investors, poorly executed privatization may exacerbate—rather than resolve—governance deficiencies. In particular, the pivotal role played by Sberbank, by far the largest of the Russian state banks, in the payment system and in the provision of social payment services means that any immediate, radical change in its operations could have negative and far-reaching consequences. The authorities will therefore need to proceed with caution.

In the interim, measures can be taken to improve state bank operations so that the playing field is leveled between state and private banks. Many of these measures involve dismantling the privileges enjoyed by Sberbank and the other larger Russian state banks, Vneshtorgbank and Vnesheconombank. Sberbank enjoys a number of financial advantages, such as deposit insurance for household deposits and ready access to financial support. Sberbank's disclosure requirements regarding the bank's governance and finances are minimal and need to be enhanced. Strategic choices for Sberbank's future role—whether it be a fully commercialized bank or a savings bank investing in a narrow set of safe assets—will have an impact across the country. While the strategic options are being explored, quantitative limits should be placed on Sberbank's rapidly expanding, and potentially risky, corporate lending portfolio.

Vneshtorgbank (VTB) does not have a pivotal position in the banking sector, nor does it perform critical agency or social functions on behalf of the government. VTB should be prepared for privatization to a reputable strategic owner as soon as practicable. Although Vnesheconombank (VEB) does perform some banking functions, its main role is the administrator of the government's foreign liabilities. Recently VEB has considered taking on a new agency function for export/import guarantees. Although current plans are to make VEB into a fully fledged state bank, little would be gained by establishing yet another state bank. Channeling subsidies through state banks—such as the Russian Development Bank and the Russian Agricultural Development Bank—confuses the business of banking with the provision of state subsidies. Subsidies would be better and more transparently administered by government agencies than through banks.

One means of jump-starting lending to the private sector and instilling greater trust in financial intermediaries might be to allow foreign banks to use their expertise, technology, and capital to expand the availability of credit to Russian enterprises. Foreign banks have, however, demonstrated a reluctance to increase their lending exposure to enterprises in the current Russian credit environment. Thus foreign entry depends crucially on improving transparency and disclosure for banks and enterprises, and on improving the implementation of the legal framework, especially as it relates to protection of creditor rights and the process of corporate insolvency.

REGULATION AND RESTRUCTURING OF BANKS

While a banking license provides bank owners and managers with the privilege to solicit deposits from households, retail savers do not have the capacity or knowledge to understand the condition of the banks in which they place their deposits. Creating trust in banks therefore depends on developing the banking supervision function.

Although the legal foundation for banking supervision and banking regulations are generally well developed in Russia, developing trust in the banking system depends on the willingness of the authorities to enforce disciplinary action. Improvements in the effectiveness of banking supervision are needed regarding on-site supervision, bank licensing requirements (including scrutiny of financial structures and business plans), enforcement of "fit and proper" requirements for shareholders and management, stricter enforcement of capital requirements, and supervision of banking groups on a consolidated basis.

While it is true that introducing deposit insurance in private banks—even if only partial insurance—would go some way toward leveling the playing field between state-owned and private banks, it would be premature to introduce deposit insurance before steps are taken to upgrade the structure and performance of the banking industry, the CBR's supervisory effectiveness, and the overall environment for information and contract enforcement in the economy. One crucial precondition to introducing deposit insurance is the capacity of the banking supervisor to limit the risks of the insurance scheme: to prescreen banks for entry into the insurance scheme and provide ongoing monitoring of insured banks. If deposit insurance is introduced for weakly supervised banks, some reckless or dishonest bank owners/managers may take advantage of enhanced access to insured deposits to fund dubious banking ventures, which when they fail result in bailouts to be paid from the insurance fund. Such behavior would undermine rather than build trust in the sector.

Building procedures and rules for bank restructuring and liquidation that protect the position of creditors are also crucial. Currently, retail depositors lack adequate protection because of delays in restructuring efforts, liquidation efforts, or both; the adoption of restructuring efforts based on weak assessment of true business viability; and ineffective judicial liquidation proceedings. All of these factors can compromise depositor interests. Problem banks should be identified sooner (for instance, by using IAS); restructuring plans should be based on an evaluation of business viability rather than on conformance with formal criteria; liquidation proceedings should be streamlined and administrative processes introduced; and liquidation of banks should not be side-tracked into efforts to reach settlements that compromise the legitimate rights of certain classes of creditors.

FINANCING ENTERPRISES

The small and medium-size enterprise sector is normally the locomotive of growth in transition economies. It is therefore important that banks are encouraged to channel a larger part of their lending to this sector. While this process can be assisted by measures designed to enhance collection of debts—such as those adopted by foreign credit lines—as well as measures (outlined above) to improve the functioning of the financial system, a significant contribution will also come from developing the capital market.

The basic framework of capital markets exists in Russia, but these markets remain underdeveloped, in part reflecting a lack of trust in the banking industry, which has responsibility for services such as custody, payment, and settlement functions related to capital market transactions. Underdevelopment of capital markets also reflects poor corporate governance, particularly a failure to honor minority shareholder rights;

an underdeveloped market for government debt, a key benchmark for other financial markets; complicated and diffuse legislation, which results in confusion as well as overlap and conflict between regulatory agencies; and a lack of credible enforcement of legal rights and obligations.

The focus of capital market reforms in the coming period should be to develop the domestic government debt market; to create specialized securities courts, or arbitration proceedings; to improve judicial enforcement of minority shareholder rights; and to improve coordination among regulatory agencies.

* * *

The task of building trust in the Russian financial system is a difficult and complex one involving the interaction of many interrelated variables and players in the financial, governmental, and judicial sectors. The issues of financial sector reform are highly interdependent. The subsequent chapters illustrate this interdependence and expand on and develop in detail measures that support the reform process. Although reform of the Russian financial sector will be a long-term task, measures can be taken today to strengthen the sector so that its role in supporting sustainable growth in the Russian economy can be enhanced.

CHAPTER 1

Building Trust for Financial Sector Development: An Overview

INTRODUCTION

In the immediate aftermath of the financial crisis in August 1998, the Russian authorities focused their efforts on macroeconomic stabilization and the consolidation of government finances. As a result of the success of these efforts, as well as the impetus provided by the devaluation of the ruble and the rise in raw material prices, economic growth in 2000 and 2001 has been impressive.

Sustained economic growth in the Russian Federation, just as in other market economies, will depend on the development of a sound financial sector. While certain sectors of the Russian economy—especially those related to raw material exports and import-substitution—have experienced dramatic growth in recent years, this growth has a narrow base and is vulnerable to raw material price and exchange rate fluctuations. Broadening this base depends on improving the availability of financing to a much wider group of enterprises—many of them small or medium-size and unrelated to larger industrial groups. Although considerable effort has been made to stabilize the financial sector since the crisis, much remains to be done if the sector is to better support investment and growth in the next phase of Russia's transition.

The demise of the financial sector in 1998 was accompanied by a complete loss of confidence and trust. Trust in the Russian financial system has been repeatedly broken during the last decade, most notably by hyperinflation in the early 1990s, and by the government's default on its own liabilities in 1998. Trust has remained low in the period following the 1998 banking crisis, in which failed banks avoided obligations to depositors and other creditors by shifting and hiding assets. It has been damaged by the lack of transparency in banking operations, resulting from vague or incomplete financial information. It has been weakened by a legal environment that is unpredictable with respect to enforcement of contract rights. It has been further weakened by favored treatment for state banks, inefficient capital markets, inadequate corporate governance, and insufficiently vigorous financial market supervision. Building trust takes time in any environment, but establishing trust in Russia will be especially difficult against the backdrop of the current situation. At issue now is how to instill trust in the financial system.

Establishing trust requires working on several dimensions of the financial sector. First, developing the financial system depends on establishing the basic legal and accounting infrastructure to support transactions on market-based terms (i.e., between unrelated third parties); participants (intermediaries and customers and providers of finance) must have confidence that their interests will be adequately protected. Second, establishing trust depends on improving the structure and performance of the financial sector to ensure that financial services are provided reliably and efficiently. Third, especially to protect the interests of the weakest participants (small depositors and minority shareholders), regulation of the financial system will need to be strengthened to ensure that imprudent and illegal behavior by participants is detected and effectively inhibited, and that steps are taken to restructure nonviable institutions. Finally, the process of building trust will need to encompass broader aspects of enterprise financing, including the development of the Russian capital market. Success in all these dimensions will be needed to deepen financial intermediation and improve its efficiency. These various dimensions of trust-building will be crucial for the necessary reconfiguration of the financial system.

This chapter, which summarizes the book, first explores the relationship between trust, financial sector development, and economic growth. It then summarizes the four parts of the book, which focus on measures that will help build trust by (*a*) encouraging financial intermediation by improving the legal and accounting infrastructures for financial sector development, (*b*) improving the current structure and performance of the banking system, (*c*) improving the effectiveness of bank regulation and restructuring, and (*d*) enhancing enterprise access to finance. The chapter concludes with a summary of the measures that should be taken to rekindle trust in the financial sector so that it can more ably support the restructuring of, and investment in, the enterprise sector.

TRUST, FINANCIAL SECTOR DEVELOPMENT, AND GROWTH

Development of financial systems requires building trust in institutions, an exercise that takes time even under the most favorable circumstances. While it does not necessarily guarantee long-term growth, such growth is difficult to achieve without a sound, efficient financial sector.

The benefits of developing the financial system are likely to be considerable, especially in circumstances such as those in Russia, because lack of trust in the Russian financial system has stimulated the development of value-detracting and inefficient activities (see Box 1.1). The challenge going forward will be to engineer a change from the negative to the positive contributions of the financial system, to escape from the vicious to a beneficial cycle, and to reap the benefits of reversing the substantial capital outflows of the past decade.

Trust in, and development of, the Russian financial system was severely jolted by the crisis of August 1998. Even prior to the crisis the system was small, and growth since then has only returned it more or less to its pre-crisis level. The total deposit base (M2) of the country's banking system at end-2001 amounted to no more than 23 percent of gross domestic product (GDP), and claims on the private sector amounted to only 15 percent of GDP. All 1,300 Russian banks together have assets equivalent only to those of a medium-size Western bank. Table 1.1 provides an international comparison for year 2000 of the size of financial systems in various countries, including Russia.

One response to the small size of the current financial system might be to argue that it is just as well that the system is no bigger. A bigger system could have posed a greater threat to economic stability during the crisis of 1998 and might have delayed or dampened the subsequent economic revival. In as far as banks are conduits for value-subtracting activities, such as directed lending, shrinkage of the banking system may have resulted in less lending to economically nonviable enterprises and thus have benefited the post-crisis economic expansion.

But the question now arises as to the sustainability of this economic growth in the absence of a more effective financial system and a broadening of the economic base. While the ruble depreciation and rising raw material prices provide a welcomed one-time growth stimulus, their effect was most markedly felt by narrow segments of the economy—especially the exporting and import-substituting sectors—and they have already both been partially reversed. Currently the Russian economy is characterized by a dual structure. The flow of savings is concentrated in a small number of large companies, which rely on raw material production and

Box 1.1 Financial System Development and Economic Growth

A well-developed financial system promotes growth in the following ways:
- It ensures a more efficient allocation of resources by increasing investment in growing industries and decreasing investment in declining industries. Rather than increasing the savings rate in the economy, a better-developed financial system would foster growth in the fastest growing segments of the economy and those industries most heavily dependent on external finance.
- It lowers the volatility of economic growth by helping to diversify the production base and moving away from heavy dependence on natural resource industries.
- It works to alleviate poverty by raising the level of economic growth, reducing the impact of economic shocks (by providing households and small entrepreneurs safe institutions in which they can place their savings and access credit) and reducing the potentially onerous fiscal cost of financial crises.

Well-functioning financial systems in market economies also contribute to economic growth by lowering transaction costs, improving the allocation of scarce resources and thereby increasing productivity, and reducing system vulnerability. In particular, they effect this through:
- *Payments intermediation*. Lowering the cost of transactions by providing cost-efficient payment service.
- *Savings mobilization*. Providing households and enterprises with financially sound and trusted savings vehicles.
- *Resource allocation*. Facilitating the collection of information about enterprises and allocating capital to sound, productive investments.
- *Governance*. Monitoring enterprise managers so that funds allocated will be spent as envisaged and result in timely repayments.
- *Risk transformation*. Transforming risks through aggregation and ensuring that they are carried by those most capable of bearing them.

In all of these functions, financial systems perform as agents working on the behalf of others to support economic growth. On the other hand, the absence, or abuse, of these functions in a poorly functioning system can detract from growth. Some examples of negative functioning are:
- *Lack of payments intermediation*. Encouraging nontransparent and costly payments processes and preserving soft enterprise budget constraints through inefficient forms of noncash payments, such as barter.
- *Poor savings mobilization*. Stimulating insecure and inefficient savings forms (mattress savings) and capital flight, often amplified by tax evasion and money laundering.
- *Resource misallocation*. Preserving inefficient enterprise structures through noncommercial, intragroup lending and lending by state-owned banks (on other than transparent and commercial terms), resulting in less-than-optimal allocation of resources and mounting fiscal liabilities.
- *Malfeasance in governance*. Allowing bank and enterprise managers to manipulate results and maintain patronage (pocket banks), thus preserving the influence in enterprises of shareholder groups.
- *Concentration of risk*. Hindering the financing and growth of firms and, because other agents are unwilling to take on the burden of risk transformation, concentrating risks with state-owned banks, resulting in the accumulation of contingent fiscal liabilities.

For further discussion of the potential contribution of the financial system development to economic growth, see Chapter 5.

Table 1.1 Financial Market Depth (2000)

Country	M2 (money and quasi-money) US$ billions	M2 % of GDP	Bank claims on private sector US$ billions	Bank claims % of GDP	Total bonds* US$ billions	Total bonds % of GDP	Total equity US$ billions	Total equity % of GDP
Russia	55	22	31	12	9	4	39	16
Czech Republic	37	76	25	50	8	15	11	23
Hungary	20	44	11	26	13	28	12	26
Slovak Republic	18	94	6	31	2	13	1	4
Poland	68	41	41	26	20	12	31	19
France	656	51	942	73	716	55	1,475	114
Germany	1,179	63	2,280	122	1,178	63	1,432	76
Italy	599	56	775	72	941	88	728	68
Netherlands**	326	89	501	137	197	54	695	190
United Kingdom	1,570	111	1,899	134	565	40	2,933	207
Japan	5,797	126	5,175	112	4,967	108	4,547	99
United States	6,084	61	4,846	49	10,768	108	16,635	168

*Bonds are defined as debt securities with maturities of greater than one year. Total bonds comprise Government Bonds and Corporate Bonds. For all developed countries and Russia, bonds data are as of September 2000.
**Data for the Netherlands are for bank claims on the private sector for all residents of the Euro Area.
Sources: IFC Emerging Markets Bonds Electronic Database; IFC Securities Market Development Group Database–2001; IMF–International Financial Statistics (IFS) January 2001; IMF–IFS Electronic Database (SIMA); BIS Quarterly Review, March 2001; IMF–Report on Post Program Monitoring Discussions; Deutsche Bundesbank Monthly Report–April 2001; EIU–Country Profiles–Russia (2000); Central Bank of Russia electronic database.

processing as their main source of earnings and then re-deploy considerable resources abroad—in the form of capital flight. Based on the recent resurgence in their earnings, these companies have also broadened their domestic interests by, inter alia, acquiring stakes in related sectors of the economy. Experience from other settings suggests that vertically integrated companies are notoriously inefficient in allocating resources. At present, other sectors outside these large groups—often dominated by smaller companies—have only very limited access to external financing. Thus, if Russia is to experience sustainable growth based on a diversified industrial and service economy over the coming years—as opposed to "islands of growth" financed by a few large conglomerates—the authorities need to focus on developing an enabling environment for broad-based intermediation between savers and investors.

So sustained economic growth in Russia will depend critically on the development of a sound financial system. Development of financial systems requires building trust in institutions, an exercise that takes time even under the most favorable circumstances. A start should now be made to kindle this trust through implementing measures to strengthen the legal and accounting infrastructures, improve bank performance, strengthen bank regulation, and lay the foundations for capital market development.

LEGAL AND ACCOUNTING INFRASTRUCTURES

Financial intermediation among unrelated third parties depends on the existence of a supporting enabling environment. Only when the enabling environment is conducive to financial intermediation among unrelated third parties would it be reasonable to expect a deepening of the intermediation process. There are three key aspects to improving the enabling infrastructure: strengthening creditor rights, establishing sound corporate insolvency and workout practices, and improving disclosure and transparency.

Enhancing Trust by Strengthening Creditor Rights

A modern, credit-based economy must be supported by a legal framework that provides for the creation of security interests in all types of property: immovable and movable; tangible and intangible; present and future; and on a global basis, by all types of borrowers in favor of all manner of lenders. In turn, the effectiveness of this framework is predicated upon straightforward, inexpensive registration mechanisms; the predictable, swift, and affordable enforcement of secured claims outside of insolvency; and a sound insolvency system that provides an orderly and equitable debt collection mechanism for failed or failing enterprises. When these elements are in place, borrowers gain broad access to credit on more favorable terms, lenders are able to reach informed credit decisions based on more accurate assessments of the risk inherent in the underlying transaction, and financial discipline is generally instilled in market participants.

However, a number of major shortcomings in the Russian legal framework have been identified and must be addressed in order to capitalize on the gains already achieved, to unlock the potential economic benefits of the reforms implemented to date, and to enhance the trust of market participants. Current shortcomings (which are further discussed in Chapter 2) include:

1. *Problems with the enforcement system.* Russian law generally does not allow creditors to enforce collateral security through nonjudicial self-help remedies, but instead generally requires enforcement through court or arbitral proceedings, followed by sale at public auction. The process is lengthy and expensive and is used by debtors for delay. It is unpredictable due to inconsistencies between courts (general as compared to commercial courts, and regional variances) and a lack of qualified court bailiffs to execute the court orders.

    As a result of these problems, creditors generally seek to limit their risk by reducing the supply and availability of credit ("credit rationing"), requiring additional collateral ("over-collateralization"), increasing the applicable rate of interest, and/or reducing the term of the credit.

2. *Shortcomings of the system of priorities of claims.* Upon liquidation or bankruptcy, both secured and unsecured creditors' claims are equally satisfied from the aggregate proceeds of sale, in the order of priority established by law. Secured creditors are not paid in relation to the value of the security they hold; they are simply lumped into a single creditor class and paid pro-rata as members of that class. This unfairly favors creditors who are under-secured. Another problem is that while as a class secured creditors are given priority over unsecured creditors, they are nevertheless subordinate to wage claimants. In many instances these wage claims are significant. The result is that secured creditors can easily receive payment on their claims in an amount less than the value of their collateral. As a result, creditors are, when considering a decision to lend, unable to rely on the collateral security that debtors may provide.

    In addition, under Russian law, the precise ranking of the preference of a secured claim will depend upon the timing of when the claim is enforced; the result will be different depending upon whether it takes place during the ordinary course of the pledgor's business, in the context of a liquidation of the pledgor, or in bankruptcy proceedings relating to the pledgor. A consistent approach ought to be taken in each of these circumstances. In addition, the number of claims ranking ahead of those of secured creditors should be reduced to the absolute minimum, and their claims should be capped.

3. *Absence of a registration system for collateral security in movables.* Russian law does not provide for the registration of

nonpossessory pledges of movable property. Security in movable property is critical for the financing of small and medium enterprises (SMEs). By the nature of their businesses, SMEs will own movable property such as equipment, inventory, and receivables. Currently, the only means of publicity of nonpossessory pledges on movable property in Russia is through manual entry in a pledge record book that must be maintained by pledgors themselves, if they are either a company or a natural person registered as an entrepreneur. This system is rife with abuse and is viewed with widespread and justifiable skepticism by creditors generally.

4. *Absence of a credit reporting system.* There has never been a credit reporting system in operation in the Russian Federation. Without access to reliable information on the financial condition of a debtor, a creditor is unable to properly assess the credit risk that it would assume in the context of the proposed debtor or transaction. In the absence of reliable financial information, a creditor is likely to implement one or more of the risk mitigation measures mentioned above (such as over-collateralization or credit rationing).

Establishing Sound Corporate Insolvency and Workout Practices

The second aspect of strengthening the enabling infrastructure for financial intermediation relates to the restructuring and exit mechanisms applied to enterprises. Insolvency systems, like general systems for debt recovery and enforcement, stabilize commercial relationships by enabling market participants to more accurately price, manage, and control risks of default and corporate failure. While general noninsolvency enforcement systems (creditor rights) provide a vehicle for resolving individual disputes between creditors and debtors, insolvency procedures offer a means for collective resolutions when failures in an enterprise's performance raise questions about that enterprise's viability. Consequently, an insolvency system plays a vital role in maintaining commercial and market confidence and in stabilizing the financial system, serving as a disciplinary mechanism for both the financial and corporate sectors. An effective insolvency process encourages prudent lending and a sound credit culture by (*a*) establishing a mechanism (such as rehabilitation) for the financial restructuring of firms whose going-concern value exceeds their liquidation value, thus preserving both value and employment; (*b*) providing an orderly exit mechanism for failed enterprises; (*c*) ending unproductive uses of business assets and transferring them through liquidation to more efficient market participants; (*d*) providing a final and equitable debt collection mechanism for creditors; and (e) improving the enforcement of creditor rights to expand credit flows.

Sufficiency of the legal framework/implementation for corporate insolvency. Following the adoption of a new bankruptcy law in 1998, the legal framework for corporate insolvency law in Russia is now fairly well conceived, relatively comprehensive, and generally consistent with international standards of best practice. The 1998 bankruptcy law replaced and improved upon the 1992 legislation, which was poorly designed and drew on a mix of different legal systems. In recent years, the increase and efficiency in cases handled has demonstrated that the new system is better conceived and understood. Nevertheless, the regime does not perform as it should, with one major criticism being the lack of consistency in its implementation (rather than in its content). Implementation problems center upon manipulation of the system to inequitably favor management or particular creditors to the detriment of creditors in general, and include: "stacking" representation on creditor committees and disenfranchisement of other creditors; wrongful disallowance of valid claims and allowance of fraudulent claims; collusion between external managers and management/judges; use of bankruptcy proceedings as a form of hostile takeover; corrupt/irresponsible external managers paying no heed to demands/interests of creditors.

The institutional framework for implementing the insolvency regime remains fragmented and inconsistent with respect to its capacity for handling insolvency cases. Cases are handled by the arbitration courts, which have a wide range of responsibilities. In a few jurisdictions (including Moscow) where there is generally a high caseload and relatively sophisticated matters are dealt with, certain judges have been designated insolvency specialists and are handling proceedings with greater consistency. Most complaints about implementation relate to practices outside Moscow, where court capacity and sophistication vary dramatically. The abuse of discretion has been cited as a key problem.

There should be a focus on the criteria for selection, qualification, and training of judges as specialized insolvency judges; there should also be an enhancement of continuing education programs. Emphasis should furthermore be placed on developing greater transparency within the system, on improving creditor access to information, and on establishing legitimate creditor involvement as a necessary counterbalance to the discretion of judges and administrators/external receivers.

The lack of regulation and potential for arbitrage in the system has continued to foster distrust of the process. The primary agency involved in a regulatory capacity is the Federal Service on Financial Rehabilitation and Bankruptcy (FSFR). The FSFR has been responsible for training, qualifying, and supervising the activity of external receivers. To date, it has issued more than 12,000 licenses—a major achievement, but one that suggests that licensing standards are low and that there is a glut of poorly trained and unqualified receivers. Given the ratio of licenses to the number of cases filed, one can in fact reasonably conclude that many licensed receivers are inactive in the bankruptcy process. More importantly, the process for weeding out and delicensing incompetent receivers, or for addressing abuses in the system, is poorly implemented and developed. Finally, in light of alleged abuse in many areas, the system must be examined to ensure that independence and impartiality are maintained between the courts and administrators and receivers, and to ensure that conflicts of interest are avoided.

Impediments to rehabilitation and corporate workouts. With respect to enterprise rehabilitation in the context of court insolvency proceedings, the process is being abused to keep insolvent businesses out of bankruptcy and to enable hostile takeovers of solvent ones. A more legitimate rescue culture is needed, directed toward the salvaging of viable businesses.

The weaknesses and unpredictability in the current environment generally discourage all parties, with few exceptions, from relying on formal insolvency proceedings. Lenders in Russia consequently prefer self-help measures, such as direct repossession of collateral, although this repossession is done outside the legal framework. Also, lenders favor out-of-court workouts, because such workouts are viewed as providing the path of least pain and uncertainty. However, the legal environment currently is inadequate to allow participants to develop consensual arrangements that can restore an enterprise to true financial viability. The result is that most, if not all, of the informal workouts amount to no more than restructurings of debt. This limited result can only postpone the inevitable day of the enterprise's failure, because the parties have not been able to take advantage of a number of other restructuring options commonly available in international practice. An enabling environment for legitimate restructuring should include laws and procedures that

1. Require disclosure of or ensure access to timely, reliable, and accurate financial information on the distressed enterprise
2. Encourage lending to, investment in, or recapitalization of viable, financially distressed enterprises

3. Support a broad range of restructuring activities, such as debt write-offs, reschedulings, restructurings, and debt-equity conversions
4. Provide favorable or neutral tax treatment for restructurings.

Although informal workouts are accomplished outside of a formal judicial setting, for these workouts to succeed, there must be an adequate formal backup in terms of effective legal enforcement of the mutual rights agreed upon in the course of the workout. If the plan fails, then there must be a reliable framework of insolvency procedures. In Russia, where creditor rights and insolvency systems can be broadly categorized as weak, legitimate consensual resolutions of troubled enterprises are difficult if not impossible to achieve. (Strengthening corporate insolvency and workout practices is the subject of Chapter 3).

Disclosure and Transparency

In addition to establishing a sound legal and judicial system that provides protection to creditors, a crucial component of the enabling infrastructure for market-based financial intermediation is the disclosure of information about banks and their enterprise customers. Unless outside, nonrelated third parties have access to timely, reliable, and comparable information about the financial and governance structures of corporations and banks, it will be impossible to establish any trust in the financial system, and the basic functioning of a market economy will remain thwarted.

Russian enterprises and banks have been reluctant to apply internationally recognized financial reporting and disclosure standards, in part because of the perceived costs associated with compliance, as well as the inherent fear that disclosure and transparency would lead to a loss of power—an understandable concern in an environment where parties have historically used access to information as a means to maintaining their power base. However, the economic costs of camouflaging financial and nonfinancial information about enterprises and banks are enormous. Lack of transparency results in inefficient resource allocation in an economy where risk capital is in particularly scarce supply. A few Russian enterprises and banks are improving their transparency and reporting since they now realize that their access to external funding is improved. Disclosure and transparency, however, need to be greatly enhanced, even if only based on Russian accounting standards.

Strengthening regulatory requirements. A concerted effort by a broad-based constituency of regulators, shareholders, board members, and corporate managers, together with accounting and auditing professionals will be required to change the historical concerns about disclosure. In the Russian environment, the lead in imposing broader and more reliable disclosure will have to be taken by two key regulators, namely the Federal Commission for Securities Markets (FCSM) and the Central Bank of Russia (CBR). In addition to ensuring that financial reporting is in compliance with international standards, these bodies will need to insist on detailed compliance reporting, and must be prepared to impose severe penalties on directors and management for material misstatements and omissions.

Disclosure. Insufficient disclosure of financial and nonfinancial information remains one of the main deterrents to investment by nonrelated parties—be they shareholders, creditors, or depositors—in Russian enterprises and banks. Current Russian disclosure requirements are inadequate. For example, the "lower of cost or fair market value" principle is not applied to all categories of assets, barter transactions are often not recorded at fair market value, and inter-company or non–arm's length transactions are often concealed. The rules and standards of reporting must be strengthened to ensure that reporting is based on effective control rather than ownership, thus protecting shareholders, creditors, and depositors from loss of value incurred by incomplete or inadequate disclosures.

Accounting and auditing standards. The quality of financial information is directly affected by the quality of standards under which it is compiled and disclosed. The Russian Accounting Reform Program, adopted in 1998, envisaged a gradual move to International Accounting Standards (IAS), but the process has stalled. Issues related to professional capacity, legislative and taxation barriers, as well as fears about the effects that adoption of full IAS would have on the Russian economy are some of the reasons for the delay. The policy of rewriting Russian Accounting Standards (RAS), rather than adopting IAS in full, has diverted scarce resources away from the actual implementation and training needs. It is worth noting that a number of transition countries have already moved to IAS rather than go through the protracted process of gradually modifying national accounting systems based on Soviet-era concepts. Financial statements according to IAS should be adopted as the starting point for any tax computation with a limited number of reconciling items in those areas where tax rules and IAS differ. The implementation of IAS should be phased, focusing first on publicly listed companies and all banks.

An important component in ensuring that the financial reporting requirements under IAS are effectively and correctly implemented will be to require the full support of the auditing profession. The opinion of a professional and independent auditor, and their liability for their audits, will be a key part of adding assurance to the users of financial reports. International Standards of Auditing (ISA) provide the auditor with standards to guide the audit process as well as professional ethics related to professional conduct.

Accounting for banks. While the CBR has agreed in principle that IAS guidelines and reporting formats will be introduced for all banks starting January 1, 2004, there are many hurdles to full implementation, including tax and legal impediments, training, preparation of guidance and conversion procedures, regulatory changes, and, of course, the pressure from banks unwilling to adopt IAS. Many banks already produce IAS audits and the question is to what degree the CBR will implement corrective and other actions based on these numbers. The reality of the situation is that the transition to IAS may reveal that a significant number of Russian banks do not meet the CBR capital adequacy ratios and are not safe institutions in which Russians can deposit their money. On the other hand, unless the authorities are willing to fully recognize the financial fragility of many banks in the system and take action regarding the weak banks, it is inconceivable that outside parties will gain trust in the financial system. (Transparency and disclosure and the transition to IAS are discussed in greater depth in Chapter 4.)

THE BANKING SYSTEM: STRUCTURE AND PERFORMANCE

Developing trust in the banking system is critical for broader-based financial sector development. It would, for example, be difficult to conceive how investors will gain confidence in securities markets when banks are not trusted to deliver reliable payment, custodial, and settlement services. The development of a well-functioning banking sector will need to precede the development of other parts of the financial system. While a banking system may be able to function efficiently without a capital market, it is impossible to conceive that a capital market could function efficiently without the services of a well-developed banking system.

Any comprehensive strategy for improving trust and spurring development of the banking system in Russia needs to be based on a solid understanding of current trends and practices in the banking industry. An integral part of the strategy for developing the banking system will be (a) improving the structure and viability of the banking sector, including removing privileges/burdens available to or imposed on state banks, and (b) consolidating the private banking sector by imposing higher supervisory standards and greater supervisory stringency. Finally, consideration should be given to the role that greater participation by foreign banks might play toward building trust in the banking system.

The Structure and Viability of the Banking System

A World Bank analysis done immediately following the 1998 crisis confirmed that, even before the government's default on its obligations and on the devaluation losses attributable to uncovered currency forward positions, the biggest factors contributing to the crisis of the banking system were the poor quality of loan portfolios, large concentrations in lending, and disproportionate exposures to related parties (a fallout of the loans-for-shares privatization auctions). Remarkably little has changed since 1998 in the business attitudes and substance of many Russian banks, and the actions of the authorities have had an insufficient effect on them.

Consolidation of the banking system. The Russian banking system is highly concentrated, with just 30 banks accounting for more than 67 percent of system assets and 53 percent of system capital. Given the aggregate size of the system, it is clear that the overwhelming majority of Russian banks are very small: at end-2001 (based on their submissions to the CBR developed under Russian Accounting Standards) only 230 banks have capital above 150 million rubles, which is slightly below the EU minimum capital requirement of 5 million euros (equivalent to 170 million rubles).

Although the financial situation of banks has generally improved since 1998 and the system is more stable, most banks are still caught in a vicious cycle: their capital is too small to generate sufficient earnings to fund the investments needed to help them grow independently. Thus, the future viability of Russia's many banks depends on being able to attract new capital and/or becoming party to mergers to form more viable banking institutions.

It is difficult to conclude that many of these banks are anything but clearing and settlement centers, which primarily perform treasury functions for enterprises or for local and regional governments. Their work also commonly includes activities that clearly cannot be regarded as "legitimate" banking business, such as the issuance and discounting of veksels for such purposes as avoiding reserve requirements, tax evasion, money laundering, and facilitating capital flight. The continued presence of these entities as "banks" stifles the process of building trust in the Russian financial system.

The CBR's difficulties in supervising such a large number of banks would be aggravated if the authorities introduce even a minimal general deposit insurance scheme. Such insurance would augment the ability of the many small, inadequately monitored banks to attract deposits from the public, which would create potentially sizeable fiscal liabilities. Thus an important step toward improving trust in the banking system—and an important precondition for introducing deposit insurance—would be to take decisive action to expedite consolidation of the banking system by replacing full banking licenses with limited ones for institutions that do not actively solicit deposits from the public. Several complementary measures should be implemented:

1. Allow those institutions that do not actively solicit deposits from the public to continue functioning, but only as regulated and supervised finance companies.
2. Introduce a higher minimum capital threshold for those institutions wishing to maintain a license for the provision of the full spectrum of banking services.
3. Tighten the accounting and disclosure requirements and implementation of supervision as a means to identify nonviable institutions for delicensing.

The authorities have recognized the need to undertake measures to promote the consolidation of the banking sector, although current proposals would appear to result in undue delay (see Box 1.2). The current situation of the Russian banking industry and a review of measures to encourage consolidation within the industry are discussed in Chapter 5.

The results of an analysis of the performance of a sample of Russian banks—including many of the top 30 banks—since the 1998 crisis are provided in Chapter 6. This analysis is based on information published by the CBR and provided by banks under the auspices of the World Bank's Financial Institutions Development Project. The analysis raises concerns regarding the (a) viability of many of the banks included in the sample (especially if international rather than Russian accounting standards were applied to such items as their loan loss provisioning); (b) rapid expansion of the banks' loans portfolios—especially those of state banks—and their high levels of loan concentration; (c) inadequacy of the banks' internal risk management systems; (d) widespread use of schemes

> **Box 1.2 Consolidation of the Banking Sector: The Government/CBR Joint Strategy**
>
> The joint GoR/CBR program* for the development of the banking system recognizes that there is a need to consolidate the sector. A step was taken in this direction in the fall of 2001 when the minimum capital level for newly licensed banks was raised to 5 million euros (the minimum capital level applied within the European Union). The joint strategy recognizes the need to establish "nonbanking lending institutions," thereby allowing the authorities to limit the licenses of certain banks so that they can no longer solicit deposits from the general public. Nonetheless, the joint strategy in effect *further delays* the implementation of actions for the existing 1,300 banks. The following measures were proposed in the joint strategy:
> - As of 2005 a rule will be applied whereby the licenses of banks below 5 million euros are automatically revoked if their capital adequacy falls below 10 percent. Currently similar action can be applied to all banks, but only if their capital adequacy is below 2 percent (see Chapter 9).
> - In 2007 a minimum capital requirement of 5 million euros will be applied to all banks irrespective of the size of their capital, which in effect removes any "grandfathering" of current lower capital requirements for existing banks.
>
> The joint strategy states clearly that any reorganization of banks—including any merger with other banks—must be *"based on the principle of voluntary participation."* In this respect the strategy reflected continued hesitancy on the part of the authorities to use the powers already at their disposal to consolidate the banking system. These powers include stricter accounting and reporting requirements, more effective use of supervisory powers, and full implementation of the recently tightened legal framework for bank liquidation.
>
> *Joint Government/CBR Strategy for the Development of the Banking Sector of the Russian Federation (finalized in December, 2001).

designed to evade the CBR's supervisory regulations; and (*e*) the opaqueness of current corporate governance structures in the banking industry. In addition to drawing attention to the fragility of the banking system, this analysis lays out the agenda for many of the actions related to reform of banking supervision (discussed subsequently in Chapter 9).

Reforming state banks. The relative importance of the state banks in Russia expanded in the aftermath of the 1998 crisis because of the government's preferential treatment of state banks and the decline of the private banking sector. The increased share of new lending undertaken by the state banks raises serious concerns about the viability of these banks going forward and about the possibility of increasing contingent fiscal liabilities. In fact, managing and containing the role of state banks is probably the most important aspect of any concerted effort to build trust in the Russian financial system.

International experience shows that relying too much on state banks to provide financial intermediation generally hampers growth. Countries with relatively large state ownership of the banking sector experience less financial sector development, lower growth, and smaller gains in productivity than countries in which private bank ownership predominates. The reason for this lower growth is that state banks do not generally allocate capital to its most economically efficient use. As lending by state banks tends to be concentrated on the largest (often state-owned) or most influential firms, they do not support more efficient, diversified distribution of credit. In recent years the combination of politicized lending and weak management operating under greater regulatory forbearance —reflecting weaknesses in the oversight exercised by government supervisors of the banks owned by government—have led to cases of spectacular fiscal loss in such countries as diverse as Brazil and France. The findings from international studies also confirm that the negative effects from state ownership are greatest in low-income countries with poorly developed financial sectors and weak protection of property rights— countries not unlike Russia.

If trust is to be instilled in the financial system, the government must move to contain the detrimental impact that these state banks can have on economic growth and financial sector development. As illustrated in Box 1.3, and elaborated further in Chapter 7, Sberbank—which controls 75 percent of the market for retail deposits—poses a particular challenge for the stability of and balance in the banking sector.

Although the medium-term focus should be to ensure an orderly privatization of relevant state bank functions to reputable strategic investors, given the public policy functions played by state banks, any such strategy needs to be carefully conceived and implemented. Ill-conceived privatization may exacerbate, rather than resolve, governance complexities. When privatization is not a near-term prospect, the immediate focus should be to ensure effective governance and a more level playing field between state-owned and private institutions. These issues as they relate to state-owned banks other than Sberbank are summarized in Box 1.4 and further discussed in Chapter 7.

The dominance of state banks in Russia is likely to persist unless concomitant measures are taken to strengthen the institutional framework for private banking and financial market development. Any restructuring of the banking system will thus require a broad-based and concerted effort. Measures will need to be taken to improve the effectiveness of banking supervision, implement improved accounting and disclosure practices, and strengthen the rights of creditors to support lending by banks to unrelated third parties. Additionally, financial markets will need to be deepened—in the first instance the interbank and government debt markets—to provide alternative asset disposition options for those state

Box 1.3 Sberbank and Its Restructuring

Before the 1998 crisis, Sberbank invested most of its assets in government securities, but since the crisis it has aggressively expanded its lending to the corporate sector. The bank has established itself as the dominant source of loans to large Russian corporations, such as oil, gas, electricity, chemicals, construction, and trade enterprises, and to state and municipal bodies. In the year 2000 alone Sberbank expanded its loan portfolio by 60 percent and by January 2001 Sberbank accounted for almost 30 percent of aggregate outstanding loans extended by the banking sector. On a regional level, the dominance of Sberbank in lending operations might sometimes be even higher.

Sberbank currently has several operating advantages: a large, geographically dispersed retail branch network; state guarantee of household deposits; the status of being "too big to fail"; a strong internal payments system; and a key role in the distribution of state pensions.

These advantages, however, come with significant costs to the efficiency of the banking system as a whole, including a possible detrimental impact on competition resulting from Sberbank's dominance of the retail market; the conflict of interest inherent in the CBR's roles as bank owner, regulator, supervisor, and authority responsible for monetary policy; and the risk inherent in being "too big to fail"—i.e., that the bank through complacency may accumulate contingent fiscal liabilities and need to be rescued by the government. While there may be an argument for keeping a state savings bank as a transitional institution, international experience demonstrates that state banks, like Sberbank, hamper the ability of the financial system to contribute to efficient resource allocation and thereby reduce the economy's growth potential.

Key strategic issues need to be addressed: Given Sberbank's dominant position in the Russian banking sector, key issues related to its business strategy, interest groups, and ownership urgently need to be addressed. Unless these issues are addressed, Sberbank will continue to dominate the sector in an unfair way and the role of private agents in the financial system will remain peripheral, thus undermining the processes of building sustainability and trust.

The government needs to decide what type of medium-term business strategy Sberbank is to pursue. Some options are discussed in Chapter 7. While the final decision will need to be based on more information than is currently available—based on international experience with the restructuring of state banks—a medium-term option for restructuring Sberbank would be:
- To preserve Sberbank's functions as the nationwide savings bank,
- To reduce the risks associated with the public service function of the bank as a savings institution for small savers by requiring the bank to invest in safe assets such as government securities, and
- To carefully privatize the bank's corporate lending portfolio as a separate commercial operation.

In implementing such a medium-term option it would be important that the privatization and/or restructuring plans be carefully and thoroughly prepared before being put into effect. The strategic plan for Sberbank needs to consider the bank's future competitive position—such as the need for the government to level the playing field by equalizing any financial or other privileges and obligations enjoyed by or imposed on the bank, and the possibility for attributing monetary value to such privileges and obligations.

Alternative ownership structures and their influence on the various interest groups also need to be considered. Among the alternatives to be considered are maintenance of the status quo, with the CBR as majority shareholder as an interim solution, despite serious concerns regarding

(Box continues on next page)

> **Box 1.3** *(continued)*
>
> conflict of interest which this entails; a return to full government ownership; appointment of an independent board of trustees to manage the government's interest in the bank; and possible partial or full future privatization.
>
> *Immediate safeguards and next steps:* Privatization of at least parts of Sberbank should be a medium-term goal, and while strategic options are prepared and considered, interim measures—including placing constraints on the growth of the bank's lending portfolio—urgently need to be taken to minimize the damage that Sberbank's operations potentially could inflict on the economy and the financial system. These measures are essential to setting in motion the self-reinforcing process of building trust.
>
> It is important that these safeguards are put in place immediately, to contain unsound business practices and to provide time for a thorough evaluation of the bank's plans for future business development. In the short-term the appropriate emphasis would be on strengthening the governance of the Sberbank and ensuring that the bank is run according to commercial principles, thereby allowing more emphasis to be placed on the return on capital and gradually reducing the need to monitor such factors as the bank's lending growth and interest rates. At the same time, however, plans for the medium-term restructuring of Sberbank need to be identified and carefully designed with a view to their staged implementation.

banks that are rapidly expanding their loan portfolios. Of particular significance will be the institutional reform of the market for domestic government borrowing. As discussed further below, reforms in government debt management are crucial, not only for the development of financial markets, but for the structural reform of the banking sector as well.

Encouraging foreign bank entry. One means of jump-starting lending to the private sector and instilling greater trust in financial intermediaries might be to allow foreign banks to use their expertise, technology, and capital to expand the availability of credit to Russian enterprises. Foreign banks have, however, demonstrated a reluctance to increase their lending exposure to enterprises in the current Russian credit environment. The Russian authorities could take steps to encourage the expansion of foreign interest in the Russian banking sector by formally removing limitations on the share of foreign capital in the banking sector and by actively seeking foreign strategic investors for state-owned banks. Implementation of the supervisory reforms—placing less emphasis on observance of supervisory norms and more on proactive assessment of bank viability—will also be important in providing a more level playing field for competition by foreign banks. Foreign banks, which are already subject to stringent supervision by their home countries, stand to benefit from

Box 1.4 Restructuring of State Banks Other than Sberbank

Vneshtorgbank

Vneshtorgbank (VTB), Russia's second-largest bank, has received several sizable capital injections from its owner, the CBR, since the 1998 crisis. Like Sberbank, VTB has expanded the sphere of its activities beyond its traditional business—of providing trade credits—to providing commercial lending to large Russian corporations. The government has announced its intention to privatize the bank and is considering a proposal by the European Bank for Reconstruction and Development (EBRD) to provide some initial outside capital with a view to prepare the bank for further privatization to strategic investors. Unlike Sberbank, VTB does not fulfill agency or social functions on behalf of the government. This bank is thus well-suited for privatization to a reputable strategic owner. Sale to a reputable foreign bank would provide capital, experience, and reputation in governance, and technical know-how. In preparation for privatization to strategic investors, VTB will need to prepare a strategy regarding its future business plans, thus increasing its value to future prospective owners. Even if full privatization is a few years away, this strategy should be announced soon so as to provide the foundation for an assessment of VTB's ongoing business decisions. It is, for example, far from clear that VTB's acquisition of international banks formerly owned by CBR, or its plans to expand its domestic branch network, would enhance the bank's value in privatization.

Vnesheconombank

Vnesheconombank (VEB) manages the government's foreign debt and—although it does not have a banking license—performs some banking functions, including taking deposits and lending to some large Russian corporations. This situation needs to be resolved and various options are under consideration. The government has announced its intention to establish a debt management agency to manage domestic and foreign sovereign liabilities, and has announced also that a strategy for VEB will be decided in the near future. One plan being considered is to transfer VEB's banking operations to another government-owned bank, such as Roseximbank, and provide additional capital to the newly consolidated bank.

Once the process of separating VEB's debt management business and other government-related transactions has been completed, the key issues that still need to be assessed are (*a*) whether VEB should continue as a government agency providing export/import guarantee support to Russian enterprises and whether it should receive a banking license and (*b*) whether the stand-alone commercial activities of VEB provide the foundation for a viable business operation. A case might be made for supporting foreign trade through partial guarantees provided by a government agency, but this business does not require the agency to have a banking license. Given that there has already been considerable expansion of the role of state banks in Russia in recent years, and the need to create a more level playing field, any step toward expanding VEB's role as a banking institution should be taken with caution, and be preceded by thorough analysis and justification.

New State Banks

Two new state banks have been established since the 1998 crisis: the Russian Development Bank (RDB) and Rosselkhozbank (the Russian Agricultural Development Bank). Both banks inherited bad assets from the government or other institutions (notably SBS-Agro), and the incentive within these institutions to operate according to commercial principles is therefore already compromised. Government intervention to subsidize interest rates or guarantee credits should not be allowed to compromise the functioning of financial markets. Where such transfers can be justified, other instruments, such as transparent budgetary subsidies, should be considered rather than interventions that tend to distort financial markets.

measures bringing supervisory practices in Russia closer to international standards.

A survey of foreign banks already active in Russia revealed that the main factor inhibiting greater foreign investment in the Russian banking industry is the risk associated with making credits in an environment characterized by weak legal enforcement. While foreign banks have on the whole been able to collect on their credits, they have also had to invest considerable resources in managing their credit risks. In seeking to contain those credit risks, foreign banks, like their domestic counterparts, have focused on lending to the leading, large Russian corporations.

Recent international studies have confirmed the economic benefits of admitting foreign-owned banks, and identified their capability both to stimulate operational efficiency and competition and to eventually help stabilize the financial sector. The entry of foreign banks has generally been associated with improvements in the quality of both regulation and transparency, particularly where the entry of those banks is accompanied by the introduction of international standards of accounting and auditing. While the pressure of competition from foreign banks can encourage local banks to take higher risks, the entry of disreputable foreign banks could weaken the banking sector. Both risks emphasize the urgent need to strengthen prudential regulation of the banking sector. (The survey of foreign banks and issues related to encouraging foreign entry are the subject of Chapter 8.)

REGULATION AND RESTRUCTURING OF BANKS

Building trust in the financial system depends on developing banking supervision with the primary goal of protecting the financial standing of the weakest participants in the financial system, the retail depositors. Building trust in the Russian financial system will also depend on establishing a reliable framework for bank restructuring and liquidation. Here again a key concern is that trust is defrayed due to the less than full satisfaction of depositor claims. Only once effective bank regulation, supervision and resolution mechanisms are in place would it be advisable to introduce deposit insurance, thereby formally protecting smaller depositors.

Banking Supervision

A banking license provides bank owners and managers with the privilege of soliciting deposits from households. Retail savers, however, do not have the capacity or knowledge to understand the condition of the banks in which they place their deposits. In addition, troubled banks are often able to maintain their liquidity (by generating new deposits) for some time after they have eroded the cushion of security provided by their capital base. Thus, creating trust in the financial system depends crucially on developing a banking supervision function with the primary goal of protecting the financial standing of the weakest participants in the financial system, the retail depositor.

The status of banking supervision. The CBR has made significant progress in establishing a bank supervision role, particularly considering that the principle of bank supervision has been introduced into and built in Russia only within the last decade. All the key functions of banking supervision are in place, and they are supported by a comprehensive set of laws, regulations, and internal rules, providing the supervisors with broad powers of enforcement. The bank supervision staff has had to learn how to apply new laws, regulations, and procedures. Furthermore, although the CBR's reputation for supervision was savaged by the 1998 banking crisis, it has survived the experience, and all the key staff will have gained valuable practical experience from it. These are formidable strengths on which to build. Moreover, improvement in the overall economic environment has helped the banking sector to somewhat improve its viability, which should make dealing with weak banks and toughening the supervisory system easier. In addition, the continuing low usage of banks (by international standards) should enable the taking of hard decisions on weak and problem banks without significant economic consequences.

However, despite the strengths and opportunities listed above—as well as the significant effort that has gone into upgrading the banking regulation and supervision framework—banking supervision still has quite a number of weaknesses that need to be addressed. This is especially important if a deposit guarantee system is to be introduced as planned by the authorities, since such a system would not be capable of providing reasonable protection for depositors, without accumulating disproportionate contingent fiscal liability, unless underpinned by strong and effective supervision. Unsafe and unsound banks should be kept out of a system underpinned by deposit insurance. As noted in Box 1.5, the Russian authorities are committed to strengthening the banking supervision function in the coming period.

The enabling environment for bank supervision. In the final analysis, everything rests upon the willingness of the major market players (both

> **Box 1.5 Strengthening Banking Supervision: The Government/CBR Joint Strategy**
>
> A joint GoR/CBR program* for development of the banking system has put together a comprehensive program for improvement of the bank supervision function, which includes the following main areas:
> - Improvement of the licensing process, including tightened requirements for financial strength and fitness and properness of bank owners;
> - Continued introduction and implementation of Basel Core principles of effective bank supervision, focusing on assessment of risk management systems and internal controls in banks rather than on compliance checks;
> - Development of proactive approaches to bank supervision and improvement of early warning systems;
> - Tightening of prudential requirements with a view to a better reflection of risk profiles;
> - Strengthening definition and role of capital adequacy;
> - Strengthening oversight of banking groups on a consolidated basis;
> - Increasing emphasis on on-site supervision (inspections), focusing inspection efforts on problem banks, banks involved in high risk-taking and/or those with inadequate risk management systems and weak internal controls;
> - Improvement of bank supervision process through transition to international accounting standards and adjustment and streamlining of bank reporting requiring amendment of the Law on Accounting as well as adjustment of laws regulating taxation;
> - Reorganization of the bank supervision function, with a view to finding an optimal balance between centralization and decentralization of the supervision process;
> - Enhancing bank rehabilitation and liquidation procedures;
> - Improvement of corporate governance in banks, including enhancement of the role of bank external auditors in line with best international practice.
>
> Recognition by the CBR of the need to improve banking supervision along these lines is an important step forward. Implementation of such improvements is in line with the recommendations that the World Bank and IMF have previously proposed to the Russian authorities. A high-level assessment of the effectiveness and efficiency of CBR supervision function, which was carried out by the World Bank at the request of the CBR in autumn 2000 may have contributed to the development of such plans by the CBR, especially regarding the enhancement of the role of the on-site inspection process.
>
> *Joint Government/CBR Strategy for the Development of the Banking Sector of the Russian Federation (finalized in December, 2001).

state and private banks) to conduct their business in a prudent and trustworthy manner. They must be willing to submit to rigorous supervision in the interests of the market as a whole. In addition, development of the enabling environment depends very much on support from the political system, as represented by constituents including the government, the Duma, the management of the CBR, the court system, and large corporations. The support of all these parties is needed if banks are to evolve into a position of financial and economic strength. The failings of this "enabling environment" in Russia have been well documented but include:

1. *Lack of transparency.* Weak application of accounting standards, and deliberate "window dressing" of regulatory reporting make it difficult to ascertain the financial condition of banks and enterprises, and leave the supervisor without adequate information on which to act. There is little acceptance among banks that such behavior is inappropriate.
2. *Confluence of stakeholder interests.* While ownership links continue to exist between banks and enterprises, the ties to government interests remain so strong, and disclosure regarding these entangled stakes remains so weak, that it would not be possible to establish the foundation for a market-based banking system that is dependent on monitoring by outside stakeholders.
3. *Limited enforcement of responsibility and accountability for imprudent banking behavior.* There is a lack of willingness within the business environment to make bank managers, controllers, and shareholders answerable for their misdeeds and mistakes, the costs of which continue to be forced on depositors and creditors. It has been accepted that many individuals associated with failed banks, for example, have resurfaced in bridge banks or newly chartered banks.

These shortcomings are well understood by the Russian authorities. However, until the issues are fully addressed, it will be impossible for good banks to effectively and profitably perform their key functions of intermediating savings and of contributing to the efficient allocation of resources and growth of the economy. The efforts of banking supervisors to support the development of a safe and sound banking system and to protect trust in the system will similarly continue to be thwarted, unless the recommended changes are made.

If banking supervisors are to play a leadership role in protecting depositors and ensuring the stability of the banking system, their mandate will need to be changed and strengthened. Given the current condition of the banking system and the established behavior of many bank managers, controllers, and shareholders, which focuses on circumventing laws and rules, the nature of banking supervision will need to shift. Staff and management of the supervisory function must be able to switch the emphasis of their supervisory efforts from an exhaustive and bureaucratic verification of compliance with technicalities, to a more forward-looking assessment of the current financial condition of the banks, the integrity of their operations, their vulnerability to shocks, and their capacity to manage risk. The supervisors must be able to implement timely and effective actions to correct shortfalls. They will need to be able to exercise greater authority in requiring swift corrective actions in cases of bank abuse (including inaccurate reporting), financial deterioration, and capital insolvency; and in identifying and assigning responsibility to bank owners, controllers, and managers. Now that need for these further changes has been recognized in the joint strategy of the government of Russia and the CBR, the urgent priority is for effective implementation of the declared principles.

Implementation of bank supervision. Effectiveness in implementation depends primarily on the content of supervision—less on the organization of that supervision. Effectiveness cannot be achieved without a sustained shift in the attitudes and working culture of both the supervisors and the banks. This shift will need to be repeatedly confirmed and demonstrated by senior CBR management. As part of this cultural change, a start should be made as quickly as possible on advising noncompliant banks that action will be taken against them, and on subsequently taking action against continuing abusers. As many cases as possible must be brought into the public domain: nothing will boost public confidence (and improve supervision itself by encouraging conformance by other banks) as much as seeing action being taken against banks—particularly high-profile ones—that violate banking laws and regulations.

As appropriate, the international financial institutions and donors can assist in supporting key efforts to improve the effectiveness of banking supervision—in particular as regards protecting the savings of retail depositors and supporting the process of building trust in banks—in the following areas:

1. *Increased emphasis on on-site supervision.* It is important to improve the accuracy and truthfulness of regulatory reporting and this will involve the introduction of improved reporting and accounting standards. However, while compliance with accounting procedures and regulatory ratios are important—and skills in these areas were to some extent inherited from the Soviet period—going forward, much greater emphasis needs to be placed on developing on-site supervision in order to verify asset values, assess the operational capacity of individual institutions, and prepare timely and effective supervisory interventions.
2. *Strengthening bank licensing requirements.* Given that the banking system is burdened with an abundance of severely distressed banks, increased supervisory attention should be devoted to preventing the entry of new problematic banks and ensuring the suitability of new managers and shareholders. When licensing banks

—rather than just ensuring that the bank meets certain minimum requirements and that its shareholders and managers meet fit and proper criteria—the CBR should place much more emphasis on evaluating a bank's ongoing business strategy, internal controls, and risk management systems, and safeguard margins on capital and liquidity to ensure that the bank is viable and therefore depositors can withdraw their funds in full and on a timely basis.

3. *Fit and proper requirements.* Increased effort is needed to hold shareholders, controllers, and managers of failed institutions accountable for their actions and to prevent them from reentering the banking sector. Requirements regarding the regular disclosure of shareholders and the granting of approvals for share acquisition should be tightened and expanded to include indirect as well as direct shareholder interests. Consideration also needs to be given to tightening the definition of imprudent activities and strengthening enforcement actions against criminal misconduct.

4. *Strengthened definition and role of capital adequacy.* The focus on preserving bank capital as a readily available cushion to absorb potential losses needs to be strengthened. Measures need to be taken to (*a*) improve due diligence on the true nature and availability of bank liabilities qualifying as bank capital, (*b*) strengthen the ability of supervisors to charge equity capital down to the value ascertained as part of on-site bank inspections, and (*c*) substitute capital insolvency for illiquidity as the criterion for bank bankruptcy. Legislative amendments addressing the last two of these points were enacted in 2001. Their effectiveness now depends on how they are implemented.

5. *Strengthened oversight of banking groups on a consolidated basis.* Oversight of banking groups is particularly important, given that so many banks are parts of groups. The recently enacted amendments to the Law on Banks and Banking have introduced the notions of "banking groups" and "bank holding." Although the advantages of consolidation should be considered when assessing the potential risks arising within a financial-industrial group, the fact of its consolidation should not be used to camouflage the capital weakness of an individual bank within a group simply because of the strong standing of the industry balance sheets within that group.

6. *More expeditious bank rehabilitation process.* The current rehabilitation process is highly procedural, involving long delays and allowing even badly distressed institutions to continue operations.

To engender depositor and public confidence, the supervisor will need to be much more proactive in evaluating bank safety and soundness and, faced by a deteriorating institution, should act rapidly to implement corrective action. In its supervisory function, the CBR should focus its activities on (*a*) obtaining and analyzing information related to the core elements of bank distress, (*b*) encouraging mergers among banks to reduce the number of nonviable or only marginally viable banks, and (*c*) where appropriate, targeting its rehabilitation efforts only on potentially viable banks.

In all of these areas, bank supervisors will need to continue the process of learning how to take prompt corrective actions and will need the political backing to take such actions. Clear guidelines will be needed for the delegation of the exercise of judgment to designated on-site supervisors and for ensuring the collective endorsement by senior management of final decisions. A commitment to continued training is also essential to upgrade knowledge of best practices and to ensure even-handed implementation of the revised supervisory practices in the diverse regions of the Russian Federation.

Finally, banks themselves should have primary responsibility for legal compliance, monitoring, and responding to changing risk profiles. Trust in banking systems in a market economy does not depend on an extensive system of monitored controls. It depends instead on the acceptance and application of a set of supervisory standards (applied to bank owners and managers themselves), good business plans, strong internal risk management, and legal and policy compliance systems. (Strengthening the effectiveness of banking supervision is further discussed in Chapter 9.)

Deposit Insurance

In 1999, a Deposit Insurance Law was passed by the Duma, only to be turned down by the Federation Council. At the same time, the Agency for Restructuring Credit Organizations (ARCO) introduced a deposit insurance scheme modeled on the rejected 1999 law for a subset of the banks under its administration. Recently the authorities are again seriously considering the introduction of deposit insurance.

The motivation for such proposals seems to be an attempt to increase trust in the financial system and attract more deposits into the formal banking system by formally protecting small depositors with the hope of fostering banking sector stability. By guaranteeing the savings of small depositors, the authorities might hope that deposit insurance would encourage small savers to entrust their savings to banks, discourage bank runs in times of crisis, and thereby promote stability and the long-run development of financial intermediation. Furthermore, in the Russian context it has been argued that if deposit insurance were available to private banks, the competitive advantage currently enjoyed by state-owned banks could be expected to diminish and a more level playing field would thus emerge.

These are laudable *goals*—fully consistent with the theme of this book regarding instilling trust in the financial sector. However, the question is whether deposit insurance is likely to be an effective means of achieving those goals. There are significant risks associated with introducing deposit insurance; controlling these risks requires a sufficient regulatory and supervisory infrastructure, which is still in its developmental stages in Russia. Introducing deposit insurance can exacerbate risk-prone banking behavior by reducing the incentive of large as well as small creditors to monitor banks' fiscal soundness. A banker can rely on deposit insurance, not the quality of the bank itself, as a marketing draw for attracting new deposits. If the bank is unsound, meaning it has little if any capital, the owners have nothing at stake, and they will use the newly acquired deposits for high-risk lending. This undermines the benefits of deposit insurance for developing financial intermediation.

Creditor/depositor complacency about the bank's financial condition can result even if the deposit insurance guarantee is only limited to cover the funds of small retail depositors. Large depositors may well perceive implicit coverage extending to them in times of crisis. This is particularly true for the most recent proposals in Russia, which provide for an explicit government guarantee of the deposits. This guarantee is not delimited by moneys available in a deposit insurance fund, and so the tendency is to believe that its coverage will, in other respects, extend beyond its explicitly stated limits. Given the lesser role played by creditors in monitoring their risks, the introduction of deposit insurance places a greater onus on the supervisory and regulatory authorities.

In order to reap the benefits of deposit insurance and minimize the risks—including the potential fiscal liabilities faced directly by the government associated with paying out insured depositors in a systemic crisis—the authorities will first need to upgrade other aspects of the banking system safety net as well as wider elements of governance. This will in particular involve reforming the current regulatory and supervisory environment, implementing expeditious bank failure resolution mechanisms, and introducing a commercial framework for the operation of state banks. The agenda related to reforms in these areas is considerable and will take time to implement.

The design of a deposit insurance scheme is also essential to its success. A poorly designed deposit insurance scheme can undermine rather than contribute to trust in the banking system. The authorities should not look to deposit insurance as a "quick fix" to instilling trust in the banking system. At this stage, introducing deposit insurance would likely create a sizable fiscal liability and increase banks' appetite for risk-taking, thereby contributing to bank fragility. (The issues relating to deposit insurance are further elaborated in Chapter 10.)

Bank Restructuring and Liquidation

Rebuilding trust in the Russian financial system will depend in part on a framework for bank restructuring and liquidation that first and foremost protects the savings of retail depositors. There are, under the current Russian legislation, sufficient measures to provide depositors with adequate protection of their interests in the event of liquidation. Retail depositors are classified by law as first-priority creditors, and if a failed bank is liquidated promptly, there should likely be sufficient assets to satisfy their claims. However, depositors have often received less than full payment of their claims or have had to wait for years before receiving payment.

The key problem of Russian bank liquidation and restructuring is that depositors are often not afforded a sufficient capital cushion in the bank for satisfaction of their claims. In a liquidation setting, this is caused by ineffective execution of existing bank liquidation procedures, resulting either in depriving depositors of their full share of bank assets, or else in diminishing those assets due to delays. In the context of restructuring, the cushion can also be undermined; Russian accounting standards, used to measure the success of restructuring efforts, do not provide an accurate picture of the bank's capital structure. Also, existing regulatory criteria do not allow for a sufficiently broad evaluation of the bank's financial health or the overall viability of a bank's rehabilitation plan. Consequently, banks that should realistically qualify for liquidation are considered "rehabilitated" and remain open. As a result, and by the time such banks fail, their assets are more than likely depleted to the point where they are unable to satisfy the claims of their depositors.

Bank restructuring framework. Two entities in Russia are currently responsible for bank restructuring. One is the CBR, which is responsible for overseeing the provisions of the bank bankruptcy law relating to measures to avert bankruptcy. The other is ARCO, which is governed by the provisions of the Law on the Restructuring of Credit Organizations.

The credibility of both institutions in their restructuring actions is critical to rekindling trust in the banking system at large. The CBR and ARCO have differing mandates in their responsibilities for bank restructuring. The CBR is required to become involved in the rehabilitation of a bank at the first sign of financial difficulty. The CBR is responsible for overseeing the development of a rehabilitation plan by the bank, or if the bank fails to develop a plan on its own initiative, to order the bank to develop such a plan. If the bank still fails or refuses to undertake rehabilitation efforts, the CBR can appoint a temporary administrator. The objective of the rehabilitation is to bring the bank back into compliance with regulatory guidelines relating to—among other factors—capital adequacy and liquidity. This process does not provide for a sufficiently early or effective intervention by the CBR, because the criteria for initiating the process and for measuring its success are calculated using RAS. Banks usually fall below capital adequacy thresholds long before they become illiquid, but the meaningfulness of the law's 10 percent capital adequacy standard is undermined by the lax standards applied under RAS and weak supervisory stringency in applying these standards. These weaknesses are compounded by the fact that the regulatory criteria used to measure the success of the rehabilitation tend to focus on discrete aspects of the bank's condition, rather than on the overall financial viability of the bank. Thus a "rehabilitated" bank may in reality still be in financial trouble. The likely result is that depositors will be inadequately provided for in the event that the bank fails and is liquidated.

The CBR should adopt a revised approach—undertaking early intervention, based upon IAS, and using an approach that considers the interrelation of the bank's financial fundamentals as a whole, thus evaluating each bank restructuring for its realistic business viability. Given the excessive number of banks in Russia, the CBR should wherever possible facilitate the restructuring process by exploring and supporting restructuring options that involve bank consolidation or merger.

Bank liquidation practice. The Russian legislation basically provides a sufficient framework for bank liquidation, and this framework has been enhanced by recently enacted amendments to the banking laws. However, there have been a number of stumbling points when bank liquidation is carried out in practice. The problems have been the net result of actions of the many parties involved in bank liquidation/bank bankruptcy proceedings, and the effect of these actions is a diminishment of the retail depositors' ability to recover their funds. Problems include:
1. *Judicial backlogs and delays.* There are many delicensed banks awaiting liquidation through the courts, in cases that are being

delayed by judicial docket congestion and a shortage of experienced and licensed arbitration receivers. Compounding the delay in many instances is the use by bank owners of procedural loopholes and redundancies to challenge CBR action in multiple appeals. For instance, it has been possible for bank owners to appeal the CBR's delicensing decision in the bank bankruptcy proceedings, as well as in separate arbitrage court proceedings at any point up to several years later. The recently enacted legal amendments should provide some relief for the court system by reducing the possibility for repeated legal challenge of CBR actions. Pursuant to these amendments, a delicensing decision must be appealed within 30 days of the announcement of that decision.

2. *Inadequate level of expertise.* Members of the judiciary and arbitration receivers alike suffer from a lack of experience and/or knowledge of the pertinent laws and procedures. There have been some calls to establish specialized commercial or bankruptcy courts to handle cases such as bank bankruptcy. More seriously, both judges and arbitration receivers have been accused of being influenced by powerful creditor groups, producing inconsistent or biased results. There have also been allegations of self-dealing and of financial interests between judges, arbitration receivers, and certain creditors. There is a pronounced need for general enhancement of the quality of the judiciary, including education of judges and structural reform. The system of arbitration receivership is also in need of sweeping change, possibly by replacing the use of individual receivers with the use of a private corporate or a quasi-governmental entity as liquidator. There may be significant hurdles to enabling private corporations (such as "Big 5" accounting firms) to act as liquidators, not the least of which is the need for amendment of the existing law before they can legally act in such a capacity. Their high cost presents another impediment. At present, there are discussions among the Russian authorities about the possibility of creating a governmental or quasi-governmental entity dedicated to bank liquidation. This concept merits further exploration. A public entity such as this would be advantageous in that it would allow for the rapid development of a group of persons trained and competent in bank liquidation. It would also promise greater accountability than the current system of individual arbitration managers.

3. *Amicable settlements.* Despite the fact that amicable settlements are by law prohibited in bank bankruptcy proceedings, they have been a feature of a number of bankruptcies, particularly those

involving large Moscow banks. Rather than a prompt liquidation of the bank, the result is a compromise agreement in which all creditors receive some type of reduced payment. Sometimes this is characterized as a tradeoff for allowing the bank to continue in business, and there are instances in which the CBR has reinstated the license of a bank placed into bankruptcy proceedings. The result for retail depositors (who are first priority creditors) is typically that they receive less than they would have in a straight liquidation. They may receive a partial cash payment immediately, with a balance to be paid over a number of years. This assumes that the bank will have the financial resources to make those payments in the future. Even if a settlement is not ultimately entered into, nevertheless the depositors are stalled in payment, sometimes for over a year, as the parties discuss and consider the possibilities of settlement.

This problem is completely avoidable, requiring only the application of the existing legislation as written. As noted above, the Law on the Insolvency (Bankruptcy) of Credit Organizations provides an explicit procedure for the restructuring of banks in Russia. These procedures have been supplemented and detailed by regulations issued by the CBR. There are sufficient opportunities for restructuring of the bank under the existing restructuring legislation to obviate the need for restructuring negotiations during liquidation proceedings. The need for prompt liquidation of the bank is tied to the need for taking advantage of existing bank assets which can be applied toward depositor claims. This is particularly true now that legislation has been enacted that allows for prompt payment of depositors in bank liquidation from cash held by the bank in its reserve account at the CBR. This payment can be made early in the proceedings, without awaiting the formal process of collecting and then liquidating the bank's assets. Consequently there needs to be improved enforcement of the provisions of the bank bankruptcy law that prohibit these kinds of settlements.

4. *Undue court involvement.* Under the Russian law prior to July 2001, before a bank could be liquidated it had to be found bankrupt by a court. The recent amendments allow, in several instances, for liquidation of a bank based solely upon defaults in regulatory standards. For instance, a bank can now be liquidated, whether technically "bankrupt" or not, for failure to maintain a capital adequacy ratio of 2 percent. A new judicial procedure has

been created that governs the liquidation of banks under these nonbankruptcy circumstances. This represents a significant improvement in the legislation, as it supports the CBR's prerogative as a regulator to determine that a bank is unsound before it reaches the level of insolvency, and thus to preserve an adequate capital cushion for the satisfaction of depositor claims in the event of liquidation. This change in the legislation corrects an undue emphasis on judicial involvement in what should otherwise be an administrative decision made by the CBR as regulator. However, there are a number of other facets of bank liquidation that could benefit from enhanced administrative procedures. One in particular is the role of the court in overseeing the liquidation process. There is no need to have the court continually reviewing the disposition of assets if an equally, if not more, effective administrative oversight system could be put in place. One possibility could be the creation of a public entity designated for bank liquidation. This concept has been endorsed in the joint government/CBR strategy paper. There are a number of other aspects of bank liquidation that might benefit from implementation of administrative, as opposed to judicial, processes. These processes are in evidence in much of international practice, and the possibilities of adapting this international practice to the Russian context should be given greater examination.

While the CBR's role in restructuring is based upon early intervention, ARCO becomes involved in the restructuring of a bank at a later stage, and then only if the bank meets certain additional criteria. The bank must be referred to ARCO by the CBR, and ARCO must evaluate it and accept it for administration. But there are also difficulties associated with ARCO's role in bank restructuring (see Box 1.6).

(Improving bank restructuring and liquidation practices is the subject of Chapter 11 and the involvement of ARCO is discussed in Chapter 12.)

IMPROVING ENTERPRISE FINANCING

To broaden the base for financial intermediation and help create trust in the financial sector, the authorities will need to take measures to improve the access of enterprises to finance. These measures will involve strengthening the foundation for capital market development.

> **Box 1.6 Problem Areas in ARCO's Approach to Bank Restructuring**
>
> The following briefly summarizes problem areas encountered in bank restructuring initiatives undertaken by ARCO in recent years:
>
> - *Timing of intervention:* Because of the application of the dual criteria of illiquidity and capital insolvency, as specified in the Law on Restructuring of Credit Organizations, by the time a bank meets the criteria for ARCO eligibility it will be in a fairly advanced state of financial decay and restructuring will be difficult. Added to this is the fact that the criteria are measured by RAS, rather than IAS, and so the problem of delayed intervention is magnified.
> - *Measurement of restructuring success:* RAS also cause problems inasmuch as they are used in measuring the success of ARCO restructurings (i.e., profitability). The banks that are currently shown by ARCO to be profitable may still be in financial trouble.
> - *Restructuring of banks in bankruptcy:* ARCO's involvement in some instances has come so late that the banks were already involved in bankruptcy proceedings. Restructuring efforts in these cases amounted primarily to compromises of creditor claims in lieu of liquidation, wherein creditors, including depositors, were obliged to take pro rata, reduced payment on their claims rather than receive full cash payment. Though restructuring of debt can be one element in a viable restructuring plan, it is not—alone—sufficient as a total restructuring plan. ARCO is entitled, pursuant to legislation, to employ a number of tools in restructuring a bank, including amicable settlements. However, it is not clear that such settlements were effectively or equitably employed in these cases.
> - *Deposit insurance:* ARCO provides deposit insurance for accounts at some of the banks that it is restructuring and this coverage has been extended to continue for an initial period of 18 months after ARCO has privatized the banks concerned, which may serve as a precedent encouraging other, non-ARCO banks to demand similar deposit insurance. This insurance is being developed in an ad hoc manner and does not take into account regulatory and supervision issues relating to the banking sector as a whole. There is significant potential that initiation of this deposit insurance coverage will set a bad precedent; provision of deposit insurance in Russia should await improvement in the climate of supervision and financial reporting (see the discussion of deposit insurance in Chapter 10).
> - *Bank privatizations:* ARCO undertook the privatization of several banks in 2001, but the procedure used for these privatizations unduly narrowed the range of strategic investors participating in the sales and did not provide for adequate review of purchaser qualifications. As a result there is a risk that privatization will simply return ownership to the types of investor likely to mismanage a bank. The authorities should consider measures designed to strengthen the governance of restructured, potentially viable banks currently administered by ARCO. One possibility might be to create a state trust operated under the governance of respected and independent individuals to assume, for a specified period, stewardship of the remaining (and any future) ARCO banks.

Stimulating Lending to the Private Sector

Due to lack of trust in financial intermediaries and to the small size of the Russian banking and capital markets, Russian enterprises have very little access to financing from the formal financial sector. This problem was even more acute prior to the 1998 financial crisis, when the incentive for banks to lend to unrelated third parties was limited; less risky returns were possible by lending to related parties and by investing in government treasury bills (GKOs) and foreign exchange products. Although the incentive structure for the banks changed following the 1998 crisis, there is still a shortfall in lending by banks and other financial intermediaries, such as leasing companies, to unrelated third parties, and especially to the small and medium-size enterprise (SME) sector. The SME sector is normally the locomotive for broad-based and sustainable growth in transition economies. As illustrated in Box 1.7, a significant contributor to this problem is the lack of a sufficient legal framework for the enforcement of creditor rights.

Thus only a narrow segment of large, usually raw material–producing and exporting enterprises has relatively easy access to formal bank and capital market financing. Many enterprises continue to rely on payment and tax arrears as their predominant source of financing. Veksels also provide some short-term financing for large enterprises and banks. Reliance on these informal financing tools has, however, declined since the late 1990s in response to improved corporate profits resulting from the ruble devaluation and higher prices for raw materials, as well as the imposition of harder budget constraints by producers of public utilities.

Box 1.7 Overcoming Constraints on Lending to the SME Sector

Given the unwillingness of banks to lend to the SME sector and the crucial role of SMEs as the engine of sustainable growth in transition economies, experience with credit lines to support this sector opened by the European Bank for Reconstruction and Development and the World Bank is pertinent. Experience with these credit lines has demonstrated that high collection rates can be maintained, provided that they include tested credit enhancement safeguards as an integral part of their closely monitored administration, including the following:
- Undertaking extended pre-lending due diligence to ensure proposal soundness and explore such factors as the true (rather than nominee) ownership of the borrower, in order to minimize connected- or related-party lending
- Exploring, through careful monitoring of cash flows, the borrower's commitment and ability to repay loans
- Insisting on cash-generating assets as collateral and ensuring that collateral is adequately documented and properly assigned
- Locking in the cash flow of borrowers and their affiliates for debt repayment through the pledges and guarantees of managers and related companies.

Experience shows that such safeguards can provide protection even in an environment in which repossessing and foreclosing on collateral is time-consuming and notoriously unreliable, in part as a result of asset-stripping, and where little reliance can be placed on bankruptcy proceedings to provide fair or expeditious protection of creditor claims. However, while these measures help protect creditors and support credit availability, they reflect underlying lack of trust and weaknesses in the infrastructure for bank lending. The need for such safeguards significantly limits the expansion of credit and increases its cost.

These factors have resulted in greater cash payment for goods and services. If, however, these structural improvements are to be sustained it will be crucial to supplement implementation of the banking reform agenda with measures designed to facilitate the access of enterprises to capital market financing. (Chapter 13 discusses the role of alternative, nonformal financing instruments for the enterprise sector and hindrances to enterprise access to finance.)

Strengthening the Foundations for Capital Market Development

Capital market infrastructure. While the fundamental market infrastructure (including trading systems, security registers and depositories, and several exchanges) is in place and has been strengthened in recent years, the capital markets in Russia are still in their infancy. Stock exchange capitalization and turnover are still very small, even in comparison with other emerging markets.

A number of factors are at play in seriously constraining the development of the capital market. One of the more significant problems relates to corporate governance. Past experience in the Russian investment arena has left many investors wary—the result of poor regard for minority shareholder rights, lack of transparency in company financial dealings and ownership structures, management conflicts of interest, and surreptitious corporate asset shifting by management. The problem is compounded by the lack of a viable judicial forum for enforcement of rights due to inefficiencies in the judicial system, which have been noted in relation to other aspects of the Russian financial system. Investors are reluctant to participate in a system that has historically proven to be a trap for the unwary, and so Russian capital markets are stunted because of the lack of trust reposed in them.

Another area in which trust is key is that of capital markets supervision. A considerable amount of securities legislation and regulation is already in place, although its effectiveness is weakened by the fact that it is spread throughout a number of laws and can consequently suffer from lack of clarity and consistency. This also impedes enforcement efforts as the lines of demarcation between supervisory authorities tends to blur, resulting in poor coordination of supervisory efforts. Enforcement is also hampered by the lack of familiarity of the judiciary with the body of securities legislation, as well as securities and financial principles in general. Capital markets supervisors are hampered by poor reporting on the part of capital market participants; and for the data that they do possess, they are in need of improved systems for its efficient quantitative analysis.

There is also a need for further improvement of analytical, as opposed to formalist, approaches to regulation in general. Added to this is the chronic underfunding of the regulatory agencies.

Another issue related to trust in capital markets is that a well-functioning capital market depends on a well-functioning banking system to act as a sound temporary depository of funds, as a custodian for securities, and as the mechanism for ensuring timely and secure payment for, and settlement of, security transactions. The Russian capital market does not have a well-functioning banking system on which it can rely.

Development of the equity and corporate bond markets in Russia also depends on the development of a well-functioning government debt market. Broader development of capital market instruments and institutions depends on market confidence in the good credit standing of the government. Related to this is the adoption of sound debt management practices by the government. This has consequences not only in terms of the government's absolute and continued commitment to honoring its own obligations in a reliable and timely fashion, but in preventing undue recourse to government-issued debt, the yield of which can be greatly inflated in response to crisis borrowing. Development of a sound government debt market also has the benefit of providing the marketplace with a risk-free benchmark asset against which to measure a spectrum of higher-yielding corporate instruments, thereby assisting in the development of the market for these instruments. A well functioning government securities market is an essential first step toward developing a capital market where investors—be they banks, retail, or institutional investors—can both assume and diversify risks.

Development of institutional investors, such as the insurance industry, mutual funds, and a system of nonstate, mandatory "second-pillar" pension funds, is also critical for the success of a capital market. Their development depends on the existence of a market with a sufficiently large and diversified number of reliable investments in which to place the accumulating funds. Without reform of the enabling environment for capital market activity, premature establishment of such investor institutions would most likely result in either downward pressure on yields, as fund managers pursue a similar, scarce supply of investment instruments, or the assumption of undue risks by fund managers. In addition, to encourage expansion of the institutional investment industry, it is necessary to develop collective investment institutions and the components of a market-based infrastructure, including securities rating agencies. And, again, it is critical that the interests of small minority investors (as administered by pension funds) are protected in a manner that encourages the development of confidence in investing in the capital market. Given the social importance of institutional investors—for example, in securing an income in old age—there is considerable risk that underperformance by the investment fund industry would result in demands for compensation and thus a fiscal liability for the government.

Given the amount of work required to establish a banking system in Russia, much less a capital market, it might be concluded that Russia would be best advised to abandon its attempts to develop a domestic capital market and to rely instead on the efficient and cost-effective provision of capital market services from abroad. This might be seen as particularly feasible in light of the ease with which international financial transactions can be made via the Internet. However, while certain major Russian enterprises already raise capital on the international market, it would not be practical to require all Russian-based capital markets transactions to be carried out abroad. To require enterprises seeking capital market financing to adhere to the legal and regulatory requirements of foreign markets would pose an insurmountable burden for all but the largest Russian enterprises. In addition, if capital market transactions were predominantly foreign-based, all foreign currency controls would need to be dismantled. Additionally, Russian savings—particularly pension savings—for the most part would have to be invested abroad, subjecting Russian savers to additional costs and risks from foreign currency exchange. Clearly, facilitating access to finance and developing domestic investment vehicles must depend on the development of the domestic capital market.

Reforming the government debt market. The importance of a trusted government debt market in providing a benchmark for the pricing and trading of other security market instruments and a safe investment for bank excess liquidity and institutional investors cannot be overemphasized.

Three years after the government's default on its liabilities in 1998, confidence in Russian sovereign debt issues remains low. Although there has been considerable improvement in the Federation's fiscal situation and in reducing reliance on budget funding by debt issuance, very little progress has been made in addressing the structural issues related to the government debt market. Addressing these structural weaknesses is crucial both to support the development of financial markets and to enable Russia to cover its future funding needs at a reasonable cost. Many of the needed measures can be regarded as good housekeeping measures and are under the direct purview of the government; they are essential to efficient

debt management and to the process of re-instilling trust. These measures include the following:
1. Developing and announcing a clear debt management strategy based on consolidated management of the Russian Federation's domestic and external debt
2. Installing risk-management and information systems to facilitate the measurement and management of the consolidated debt, including forecasting and funding related to treasury cash management
3. Identifying and empowering a single unit to manage the consolidated domestic and foreign debt according to guidelines agreed upon periodically with the government
4. Establishing transparent debt issuance policies and communication channels with market participants concerning Russia's debt management policies.

Although the Ministry of Finance has received technical assistance in the area of debt management for a number of years, the government has preserved a shroud of nontransparency in its debt management practices, thus seriously hampering the process of developing Russian financial markets.

The corporate governance agenda. If financial markets are to play any significant role in supporting enterprise financing and sustained growth in Russia, it will be crucial to establish that the rights of majority shareholders and larger creditors do not have preference over the rights of the minority investor. This is as important to the process of instilling trust in the financial system as protecting the primary status of the claims of retail depositors in bank failures. There are signs that this corporate governance problem is being recognized, but much more needs to be done to support the enforcement of improved practices. Important amendments to the Joint Stock Company Law and the Securities Market Law that address a number of corporate governance lapses have been enacted, and various initiatives to improve company governance, such as the introduction of a code of corporate conduct for company directors, are being supported by the Federal Securities Commission.

The priorities related to improving corporate governance—which apply to both enterprises and financial intermediaries such as banks—include the need to ensure transparency in ownership and control structures and to improve the quality of financial information available to company stakeholders, as follows:
1. Information should be regularly recorded in a publicly available registry for all listed companies as regards company charters, lists

of shareholders, company directors, debt issues, and assets used as collateral. Disclosure of both direct and indirect ownership should be mandatory for shareholdings over a minimum size (say, 5 or 10 percent of a company) and the Federal Securities Commission should be empowered to identify entities lying beyond nominee owners and trusts, whether onshore or offshore. The public should be given access to this information and disclosure should be mandated by law.
2. Measures should be taken to improve the quality of financial information. The authorities should make the immediate adoption of International Accounting Standards obligatory for all publicly traded companies and banks, and—as officially announced by the government—obligatory by 2004 for all large and medium-size enterprises.
3. Other measures include strengthening the roles and responsibilities of boards of directors, encouraging the creation of audit committees (within boards of directors), increasing the liability of auditors, and strengthening the ability of the Federal Securities Commission to apply sanctions.

Supervision and enforcement. While future amendments to the Joint Stock Company Law and the Securities Market Law will need to be considered by the Duma, the more pressing concern is the enforcement rather than the amendment of the law. The focus should therefore be on instilling trust in the marketplace by minimizing the abuse of existing laws and ensuring the effective punishment of abuses. Several reform areas require attention:
1. *Judicial reform.* An important measure for improving the enforcement of the law would be the establishment and empowerment of an independent arbitration court to adjudicate capital markets disputes and to strengthen sanctions to ensure the enforcement of court judgments. Any inadequacies in the current legal system with regard to enforcement of the law will need to be identified and addressed.
2. *Coordination among regulatory agencies.* Law enforcement also depends on improved supervision of the market by the regulatory agencies and better coordination among those agencies. The different parts of the Russian capital market are supervised by different government agencies, including the Federal Securities Commission, the Ministry of Finance, the Ministry of Social Protection, the Ministry of Anti-Monopoly Policy, and the Central Bank. Enforcement

actions also require coordination with the courts and the police. Given the weak capacity of the agencies and a history of competition among certain agencies, there is an urgent need to improve cooperation. Where there is overlapping authority or the potential for the fragmentation of authority, one regulator should explicitly be given lead authority.
3. *Public administration reform.* Improved regulation depends on public administration reform. Regulatory agencies need to be provided with a secure funding base, need to be able to pay market-based salaries to retain qualified staff, and must be made accountable for regulatory failures.
4. *Information requirements.* The Federal Securities Commission has embarked on a program of installing new computer systems to improve its market surveillance capacity. While the installation of new information technology (IT) systems will assist the Commission in collecting information and will support the introduction of improved enforcement practices, the successful implementation of new enforcement practices will depend crucially on a shift in the focus of supervision from compliance-based observance of norms to supervision based on the assessment of material risks. This will strengthen the role of supervision in protecting investors and containing systemic risks. The success of the Commission's IT project thus depends on simultaneous reform of its business practices as market supervisor. Prior to the designing of software for the new IT system, a review of current reporting standards should be undertaken to determine the extent to which they provide adequate information or are in need of revision. In addition, generated reports need to be systematized so that they provide automatic alerts and differentiate between material and immaterial abuses.
5. *Redefining the role of capital markets supervision.* In redefining the role of the Federal Securities Commission as securities market supervisor and ensuring that market participants observe best practices, the Federal Commission has embarked on the process of undertaking a self-assessment of observance with the principles promulgated by the International Organization of Securities Commissions (IOSCO). The principles provide guidelines for protecting investors; ensuring fair, efficient, and transparent markets; and reducing systemic risks. They thus provide an excellent benchmark for measuring current capacity and future developmental requirements.

(Further discussion of the issues related to development of the capital market is to be found in Chapter 14.)

CONCLUSION

The task of building trust in the Russian financial system is a difficult and complex one, which involves the interaction of many variables and players in the financial, governmental, and judicial sectors. This chapter has provided an overview of the extent of the problem and identified the general directions in which reform efforts should be made. The ensuing chapters in this book provide in much greater detail a diagnosis of the problems of the financial sector and proposals for measures to address them. Although there are crucial differences in some key areas—such as in the role envisaged for state banks, the measures for consolidating the banking system, and the introduction of deposit insurance—much that has been recommended in this book corresponds to the broad objectives set by the Russian government and the Central Bank of Russia in their joint banking strategy paper, summarized in Box 1.8. It is hoped that this book will be utilized to further develop the strategy for the development of the financial sector, and that the recommendations for implementation of the reform process contained herein will provide guidance for further action.

The sequencing of reform. Financial systems are complex. Hence defining and sequencing the reform process is by nature difficult. Some sequencing and prioritization of the process is nonetheless necessary in order to provide focus for the reform effort and to measure progress. The key function of financial systems in providing services is to process information about third parties, be they payment agents, depositors, lenders, or borrowers. Depending on the sophistication of the financial service being provided, the demands placed on the service provider in processing information will differ. As a rule, shorter-term financial instruments require less sophistication in forecasting financing costs and investment outcomes than do longer-term instruments. This approach is illustrated in Figure 1.1 below.

In the figure, the vertical axis measures the key function of the financial system—i.e., its capacity to intermediate information among borrowers and lenders. Developing this capacity requires commitment by the authorities and market participants over a number of years. As this capacity gradually develops, participants will gain trust in financial markets and be encouraged to develop the technical and institutional knowledge to

Box 1.8 Summary of the Joint Government/CBR Program for the Development of the Russian Banking System

Objectives: Establish a competitive banking system based on international best practices to improve stability and preclude systemic crises, improve the intermediation of savings, strengthen confidence, limit unfair commercial practices, and provide quality services conducive to economic development. The key areas of focus are outlined below.

Time frame: Approximately 5 years.

I. Increase Competition

Issues: Restrictions on, and political interference in, bank activities. Lack of a level playing field between state banks and private banks, and domestic and foreign banks.

Solutions proposed:

Improve supervision and implement without discrimination—Develop legislation in line with international norms. Bring role of external audit in line with international practices. Simplify but strengthen quality of risk assessment, with greater focus on the quality of intrabank management and internal control. Regulatory bodies to be vigilant against political pressure and the influence of large economic entities on banking activities.

Greater transparency—Adoption of international standards of accounting and consolidated reporting requirements. Requirement to publish balance sheets and financial statements on quarterly basis. Develop, assess, and publish macro-prudential indicators.

State participation—Government to divest stakes in banks where it holds less than 25 percent of shares and to raise efficiency in its participation in those lending institutions where it will retain ownership. Activities of specialized state banks, such as the Russian Development Bank and Rosselkhozbank to be constrained to their area of specialization. Enhanced control of Sberbank's activities to carried out by the bank's Supervisory Council. The CBR to initiate divestiture of its share in Vneshtorgbank by end-2002. The government intends to separate Vnesheconombank into a debt-servicing agency and a bank.

Structure of the banking system—Gradually increase the level of required minimum capital (to EU minimum level of 5 million ECU for all banks by 2007). The role of banks with foreign capital to increase following easing of any constraints on access. Issue [limited] licenses for entities attracting and investing only enterprise funds. Create conditions for expanding banking activities to regions.

Deposit insurance—Phased introduction envisaged—voluntary in the first instance and obligatory only after the introduction of IAS in 2004. Sberbank to participate on special terms.

Legislation—Strengthen investor rights. Level playing field between domestic and foreign credit organizations, and bank and nonbank sectors. Clarify foreign exchange regulation and control. Step up implementation of anti-monopoly regulation.

II. Improve Intermediation and Efficiency

Issues: A general lack of confidence in the banking system stemming from high credit risk due to lack of reforms and transparency of enterprises, high liquidity risk due to mismatch of asset–liability structure, weak legislative protection of creditor and lender rights, low capitalization, lack of liquid financial instruments, poor risk management, and high operational costs.

(Box continues on next page)

> **Box 1.8** *(continued)*
>
> **Solutions proposed:**
>
> *Attract deposits*—Introduce deposit insurance. Foster greater transparency about the financial condition and ownership of banks. Improve management and reduce financial crime and criminal activities by approving a law on money laundering.
>
> *Reduce credit risk*—Banks to better manage and control risks by closely tracking financial conditions of borrowers, including through credit bureaus. Develop quasi-banks, with limited licenses, to take corporate deposits and lend to corporations. Improve transparency of enterprises, including through reporting on IAS basis. Protect creditors' rights.
>
> *Reduce liquidity risk*—Enhance bank liquidity management through better monitoring and diversification of risks, wider range of refinancing instruments, ensuring adequate provisions against losses, and legislative changes. Develop domestic capital markets, including the issuance of mortgage securities.
>
> *Reduce costs*—Improve taxation system by allowing exclusion from tax base of all reserves against risks generated by standard legal bank operations and transactions, revaluation gains/losses, costs of mergers/acquisitions, capital expenditures, and so forth.
>
> **III. Strengthen Financial System Stability**
>
> **Issues:** Poor supervision and regulation, poor and inefficient risk management and internal audit practices, a low level of capitalization, nontransparent property structure, and a lack of sophisticated technology.
>
> **Solutions proposed:**
>
> *Strengthen regulation*—Simplify and tighten licensing procedures. Develop fit and proper criteria for managers, large shareholders, and chief accountants of credit organizations. Raise penalties for noncompliance.
>
> *Strengthen liquidation procedures*—Complete restructuring or liquidation of bankrupt banks following an improvement in the procedures for bank restructuring. Reduce scope for asset stripping by making managers and founders more accountable for actions leading to bankruptcy, banning transactions and intensifying monitoring by temporary administrator after licenses revoked.
>
> *Improve payments system*—Expand scope for noncash settlement and ensure effective and reliable service. Introduce a real time gross settlements system for large, urgent, high-priority payments generated by interbank and securities markets.
>
> *Strengthen corporate management*—Strengthen internal control and risk management on both an individual and a consolidated basis. Increase professional skills and level of ethical standards of management, associates, and founders.

process more sophisticated products (as reflected on the horizontal axis). Russia should be regarded as still being in the first phase of developing its financial system. According to this financial development framework, Russia will need to develop sound, deep, and liquid markets for shorter-term instruments before it is able to develop a meaningful and reliable

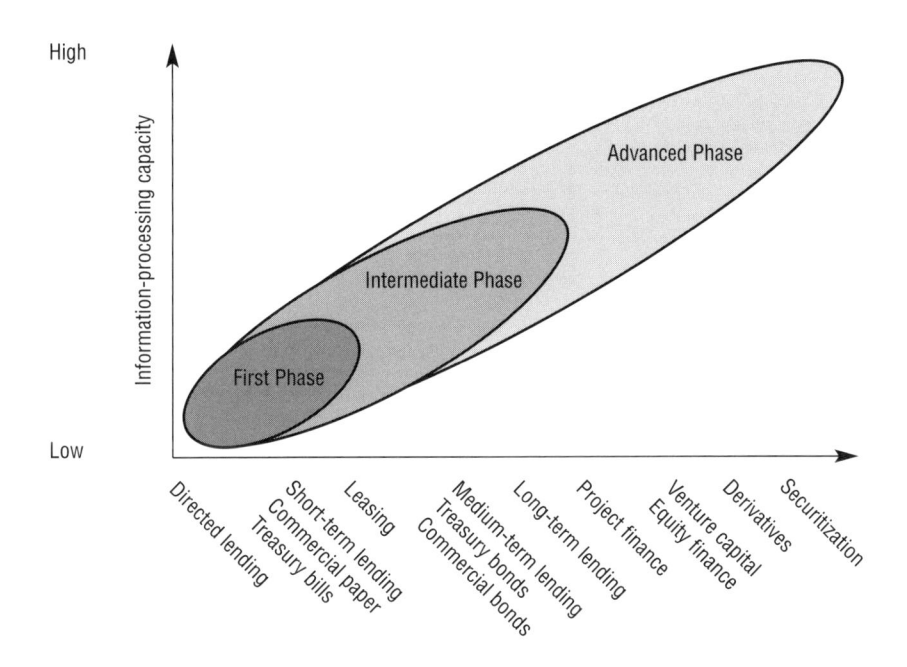

Figure 1.1. Sequencing of Financial Sector Reforms

[Figure: Chart showing three nested elliptical phases (First Phase, Intermediate Phase, Advanced Phase) plotted against Information-processing capacity (Low to High) on the y-axis, and financial instruments on the x-axis: Directed lending, Short-term lending, Commercial paper, Treasury bills, Leasing, Medium-term lending, Treasury bonds, Commercial bonds, Long-term lending, Project finance, Equity finance, Venture capital, Derivatives, Securitization.]

market for more sophisticated financial products with less well-defined income flows. Reform of the Russian banking system is an essential first step in permitting full and effective development of the financial system. The scope of possible reform actions required to deepen and broaden the Russian financial system is quite extensive, as evidenced by those measures described earlier in this chapter (and elaborated further in the subsequent chapters of this book).

Priority measures for financial reform. Many aspects of financial sector reform are for the longer-term, such as improvement of the judicial system. But there is also a substantial existing framework on which to build, and improvement can be realized, provided there is sufficient resolve on the part of the authorities to the agenda outlined in this book.

Though reform of the Russian financial sector will be a sizable task, a number of measures—outlined in Box 1.9—can be made immediately. It is clear that the current state of the Russian financial sector is hampering the advancement of the development of the Russian economy as a whole. The constraint of a weak financial sector will become more and more evident as the real economy tries to revive. In comparison to the development of many other aspects of the Russian economy, the financial sector has seriously lagged behind. Further delay will not only impede the further development of the economy as a whole; it may undermine the progress that has been made since the 1998 crisis.

While enactment of these measures will provide a sound basis for the first phase of reforms and prepare the Russian financial system for the subsequent phases of reform, there are no quick-fixes. Financial sector reform depends on institutional development both within the sector as it

---

Box 1.9 Priority Trust-Building Measures

Legal and Accounting Infrastructures

- Introduce International Accounting and Auditing Standards and enhanced disclosure for banks and enterprises, especially as regards ownership
- Establish enterprise credit reporting system
- Establish centralized registration for movable collateral
- Streamline procedures for foreclosure on movable collateral

Banking System Structure and Performance

- Insist on transparency and improve corporate governance of state/CBR-owned banks
- Complete strategic review of Sberbank
- Limit the expansion of corporate lending by state banks
- Desist from providing new capital support to public banks
- Insist that state-owned banks work toward market-responsive pricing in the provision of services/loans

Regulation and Restructuring of Banks

- Through improved effectiveness of CBR banking supervision, encourage consolidation of the banking system
- Raise minimum capital requirements for banking license
- Replace banking license with finance company license for any institutions not actively soliciting deposits from the public
- Enhance administrative processes in bank liquidation
- Strengthen requirements as to the integrity and accountability of bank management and shareholders/controllers
- Develop on-site supervisory capacity and demonstrate willingness to take timely corrective actions
- Strengthen bank management and financial condition as well as banking supervision as a precondition to the introduction of any general deposit insurance system

Financing Enterprises

- Establish consolidated management of all sovereign debt
- Introduce full and timely public disclosure of government liabilities and planned debt issuance
- Establish public registry of information on all listed enterprises
- Undertake public administration reform designed to support coordination among financial sector supervisors and ensure well-qualified staffing

relates to banks, investment houses, security dealers, and so forth; development of strong government administration in supervision of the sector; and development of a sound legal and judicial system. As pursuit of these institutional goals will take time, success in development of the financial sector will be a measured process and should be assessed against reasonable goals. Establishing trust will depend on learning from and adopting the lessons of experience. One of the greatest threats to this process may prove to be the expectation that development of the financial system can move by leaps and bounds. The danger is that exaggerated expectations may lead to disappointments and postpone the process of building trust.

Part I

Legal and Accounting Infrastructures

Building a financial system depends on providing the institutional infrastructure to support transactions among unrelated third parties. Unless this basic infrastructure is in place, and enforcement has been well-tested and proven to be reliable, there will be no foundation on which to build trust in the financial system. Thus, if the role of financial intermediaries to provide finance to the private sector is to be enhanced, the protection offered creditors will need to be strengthened considerably.

Three areas of critical importance for the development of this institutional infrastructure—the building blocks of financial sector development—are the subject of Part I. They relate to improving creditor rights, strengthening enterprise insolvency practices, and reforming the disclosure and accounting practices for banks and enterprises. Reforms in these areas will provide crucial support for building trust in financial intermediation between unrelated third parties—be it on the part of banks or bond-holders as secured creditors in enterprises, or minority shareholders investing in enterprise equity.

Chapter 2 focuses on the strengthening of creditor rights. The predictable, swift, and inexpensive enforcement of secured creditor claims is important for facilitating lending decisions, instilling market discipline, and thereby reducing borrowing costs. Chapter 2 provides recommendations in the areas of improving the enforcement of creditor claims, strengthening the standing of secured creditors, and introducing registration systems for collateral on movable property and credit-history reporting.

While protection of creditor rights provides a vehicle for resolving disputes between creditors and debtors, insolvency procedures offer a means of collective resolution of claims when enterprise viability is threatened. An effective insolvency process supports the financial restructuring of viable enterprises, the orderly exit of failed enterprises, and the improvement of debt collection mechanisms for creditors. Chapter 3 outlines a number of implementation problems related to current insolvency practices. There is a need to strengthen the qualifications of the judiciary and judicial practices, to increase the involvement of creditors in the insolvency process, and to remove impediments to rehabilitation of enterprises through corporate workouts.

An overarching theme of this book is that building trust in financial transactions among unrelated third parties depends on improving transparency and disclosure. The provision of reliable and timely information on the governance and financial situation of enterprises and banks is crucial to building financial intermediation in market economies. As outlined in Chapter 4, disclosure and transparency would be considerably enhanced by the adoption of International Accounting and Auditing Standards. The adoption of these international standards would, however, require careful planning as well as a concerted effort to ensure their implementation. This implementation involves the support of the regulatory authorities, enterprise and bank stakeholders, and the auditing and accounting professions.

CHAPTER 2

Creditor Rights

INTRODUCTION

On January 1, 1995, with Part I of its new Civil Code in place,[1] the Russian Federation took an important step toward providing the necessary legal foundation for its newly emerging market economy. On March 1, 1996, Part II of the Civil Code took effect. These measures together marked a turning point in the development of Russian civil law. They also represented a significant departure from old Soviet civil law,[2] which had been more concerned with the implementation of state plans rather than with contracts (Vitrianskii 1994, 6:649) and the relationships between state enterprises and other economic units directed by the central economic planning authorities (Vitrianskii 1994, 6:237, fn. 4).

Under the Soviet system, there were only two types of debtors: private citizens and entities participating in the centrally planned economy—mainly state enterprises and collective farms (Vitrianskii 1994, 6:242, fn. 4). Ensuring the performance of obligations and the related provision of priorities in favor of certain creditors over others were matters that were neither necessary nor particularly relevant in the context of a command and control economy. As a result, Russian civil law as it then existed was largely undeveloped.

In a modern market economy, however, the implementation of the rule of law, including honoring the law established between contracting parties pursuant to the terms of the contracts that they freely conclude, is paramount. Equally vital are the means to enforce these contractual arrangements and the ability of creditors to efficiently and predictably execute any collateral security given in support of such arrangements, and to be preferred recipients on the proceeds of realization in accordance with their priority ranking.

The justification is purely economic: the provision of collateral security, combined with an efficient debt enforcement system, reduces credit risk, which in turn leads to more favorable financing conditions (the "price effect") and/or broader or deeper access to credit markets (the "quantity effect") (BIS 2001, 19). The increase in the supply of credit in turn contributes to greater capital investment and increased productivity, and it facilitates nonbank financial intermediation. Reduced dependence on bank credit in turn lessens the potential impact of a banking crisis on the real economy (and thus on overall macroeconomic performance), and enhances the stability of the entire financial system, rendering it better able to withstand external shocks (Working Group on International Financial Crises 1998).[3]

A reduction in credit risk is theoretically achieved as a result of three factors (BIS 2001, 18). First, collateral security reduces the possible loss in the event of debtor default, by an amount equal to the liquidation value of the collateral. Second, collateral security reduces the likelihood of default: the giving of collateral should reduce the possibility that the debtor, despite the ability to do so, will arbitrarily delay or refuse to discharge its obligation ("moral hazard"), and should give the debtor an incentive to incur a lower level of risk than would otherwise be the case (the "incentive effect"). Third, in theory, collateral requirements enable debtors to signal their creditworthiness and therefore overcome problems of asymmetric information that would otherwise result in their access to credit being rationed (the "signaling effect").

In sum, therefore, collateral security, combined with an effective and efficient debt enforcement and insolvency system, instills financial discipline in market participants in the commercial and corporate sectors, resulting in greater trust and greater efficiencies in the market itself.

In addition to legal research concerning creditor rights and collateral security in the Russian Federation and elsewhere, this chapter draws on two weeks of intensive consultations with local and foreign commercial banks, state-owned banks, the Regional Banks Association, local and foreign business lawyers, members of the judiciary, academics, accountants, multilateral development banks, and nongovernmental organizations.

THE FRAMEWORK FOR SECURED TRANSACTIONS

This chapter is generally limited to the treatment under Russian law of creditor rights[4] and collateral security in movable, as opposed to immovable,[5] property. (The consultations in fact established that banks may take immovable property as collateral security for loans.[6])

One of the key objectives of interviewing the many groups and individuals involved with creditor rights and collateral security was to determine the principal constraints in the current legal framework, if any, that prevent or discourage lenders from providing small and medium-size enterprises with access to external financing. In this regard, apart from the high cost of notarial fees—which were the object of frequent complaints as constituting a disincentive to the use of mortgages and enterprise charges, and of concerns expressed over the timing of the passage of the new Land Code—no other material concerns were raised specifically related to the treatment of creditor rights or collateral security in respect to immovable property.

The same cannot be said for movable property. A number of issues common to both movable property and immovable property, particularly related to the enforcement of collateral security, were mentioned time and time again.

In light of these results, and given the widespread attention by policymakers at the international, regional, and national levels and by multilateral development banks and nongovernmental organizations in the area of collateral security over movable property, this chapter and the policy recommendations that it contains focus primarily on issues related to movable property.

The Principal Elements of Reform

Ahead of the other countries of Central and Eastern Europe and the Commonwealth of Independent States, the Russian Federation began its reform of collateral security laws in 1992 with the adoption of Federal Law No. 2872-1 *On Pledge* (Pledge Law). The Pledge Law (as amended)[7] was complemented by the introduction in 1995 of Part I of the Civil Code, more particularly Chapter 23 (articles 329–381) on "Securing Performance of Obligations," which includes articles 334–358 on the contract of pledge.

The adoption in 1998 of Federal Law No. 102-FZ *On Mortgage (Pledge of Immovables)* (Mortgage Law) supplemented the few rules on mortgages contained in the Civil Code and introduced detailed provisions governing the procedure to mortgage immovable property. The provisions of the Mortgage Law prevail over any inconsistent provisions of the Civil Code or the Pledge Law. A recent presidential decree on mortgages (Mortgage Decree) further provides for the establishment of a single state register of proprietary rights and immovable property transactions at the federal level (Zerev 1998, 296).

Types of Collateral Security Available

In addition to addressing pledge and mortgage, the Civil Code sets out in article 329 various means to secure the performance of obligations. These are penalty, suretyship (third person guarantee), earnest money (deposit), the retention of property (withholding), and the bank guaranty,[8] the latter two of which had been introduced with the adoption of the Civil Code. This list is not exhaustive, however, and article 329 CC expressly acknowledges that the fulfillment of obligations may be contractually secured by means other than those contemplated by the Civil Code.[9]

Of the foregoing, only the contract of pledge creates a charge over movable property. Hence, the following analysis will limit itself to the provisions governing pledge. Positive features of pledge under Russian law are summarized in Box 2.1.

Principal Shortcomings of the Framework for Secured Transactions

Given the breadth of the law that the Civil Code covers and the extensiveness of its provisions, the Drafting Committee of the Civil Code achieved a remarkable accomplishment. The committee only began its work in earnest in the spring of 1992; Part I was adopted by the State Duma in October 1994 and Part II just 15 months later. When viewed, for example, through the prism of the International Bank for Reconstruction and Development's (IBRD) *Principles and Guidelines* or the EBRD's Core Principles,[10] however, certain shortcomings of the framework for secured transactions under Russian law become apparent.

The ruble crisis of August 1998 has served to heighten some of the issues that have emerged as a result of these shortcomings, and it has revealed the relative immaturity of the Russian credit culture, both in respect to debtors and to creditors. And yet, perhaps ironically, anecdotal evidence obtained from many of the financial institutions confirms that, in addition to its deleterious effects, the crisis appears to have had a beneficial effect,[11] at least insofar as the credit culture of financial institutions

> **Box 2.1 Positive Features of Pledge under Russian Law**
>
> Positive features of the contract of pledge under Russian law include:
> - *Available collateral.* Virtually any property may be the object of pledge, including movable property, immovable property, property rights (including rights under contracts), and negotiable instruments (including promissory notes or veksels) and shares (art. 336 CC; art. 338 [4] CC). Exceptions and restrictions include certain national assets, licenses (including licenses to explore or extract natural resources), and personal rights.
> - *Available collateral—Goods in circulation (inventory).* While remaining in possession, a pledgor may grant a pledge of its inventory of supplies, raw materials, semifinished goods, and finished goods (art. 357 CC; art. 341 [2] CC; art. 338 [1] CC). The goods become subject to the pledge as soon as they are acquired by the pledgor and cease to be pledged when they are sold to a purchaser (art. 357 [2] CC).
> - *Available collateral—Enterprise.* An enterprise (defined as a property system used for the conduct of entrepreneurial activity—a business, in other words) can be pledged (mortgaged) either as a whole or in part only (art. 132 [2] CC). The enterprise can include land, buildings, equipment, inventory, materials, products, claims, debts, intellectual property, and other exclusive rights, unless otherwise provided by statute or contract (art. 132 [3] CC). Among other advantages (including, particularly, the right of the creditor to sell the enterprise or business as a going concern, subject to arts. 349–350 CC), an enterprise charge allows greater operational flexibility to sell or retire machinery or equipment and place into use new machinery or equipment without requiring a new charge or an amendment to the mortgage documents.
> - *Available collateral—Future acquired property.* Property not yet owned, but that the pledgor will acquire in the future, may be pledged (art. 340 [6] CC; art. 341 [2] CC).
> - *Parties.* Both individuals and legal entities may grant and receive pledges. In addition, both debtors and third parties (e.g., sureties [guarantors]) may secure their obligations using a pledge (art. 335 CC).
> - *Possessory v. nonpossessory.* Both possessory and nonpossessory pledges are recognized under the Civil Code (art. 338 CC; art. 343 [1] CC).
> - *Secured debt.* There does not appear to be any restriction on the type of obligation that can be secured by a pledge (art. 334 [1] CC; art. 4 [1] Pledge Law).
> - *Scope.* Unless the contract otherwise provides, the pledge will extend to the full amount of the claim at the time of satisfaction, including the principal amount of the underlying obligation, interest, damages for delay or nonperformance, and maintenance and enforcement costs and expenses (art. 337 CC).
> - *Proprietary right.* The pledge will remain in effect notwithstanding the sale or other disposition of the pledged property by the pledgor (right in rem: art. 353 [1] CC; also art. 347 [1] CC).
> - *Claim for deficiency.* The creditor will retain a (unsecured) claim against the remaining property of the debtor in the event that the proceeds of realization of the pledged property are insufficient to satisfy the obligations secured under the pledge (art. 350 [5] CC).

operating within the Russian Federation is concerned. Prior to extending a credit, greater emphasis apparently is being placed on a thorough and careful analysis of a debtor's financial condition.[12]

Greater care is also being taken in the preparation of collateral security documentation, and an awareness seems to be taking root that the mere fact of having taken collateral security in respect to a credit can in no way dispense with the need for close monitoring and supervision by a financial institution of the financial health and general business condition of a debtor over the life of a credit that it has provided. While in the short term this may result in a general tightening of the supply of credit, particularly for small and medium-size enterprises (SMEs), which already have had to contend with a dearth of credit to support their operations,[13] in the long term this can only be a positive factor for the Russian economy as a whole.

Small business lending can be conducted successfully in the Russian Federation;[14] however, this has less to do with the framework for creditor rights and collateral security (and the related insolvency system) than it does with the establishment, and the steadfast and methodical implementation, of internal methods and systems. These methods include a considerable up-front investment in training (primarily lending officers and, to a lesser extent, back office staff) and the establishment of a climate of trust between lender and borrower, built on a thorough investigation of a potential borrower's actual (as opposed to official[15]) financial condition and the gradual ramping up of available credit over time.

However, though small business lending can in fact be conducted successfully in Russia, this is in spite of, rather than as a result of, the existing framework for enforcement of creditor rights. The scope of such success will remain limited because the self-protection efforts required of lenders are considerably greater than would be necessary in an environment with a well-functioning regime of creditor rights laws. Lenders are required to make greater—perhaps excessive—scrutiny of their borrowers' circumstances because there is no dependable framework for enforcement of their rights in the event of a borrower default. This situation continues to hamper the development of SME lending in Russia. Although there has been significant reform in the development of the laws themselves, numerous problems exist in the implementation of those laws and in the procedures used for enforcement of creditor rights. These problems are discussed in detail below.

ENFORCEMENT MECHANISMS

In efficient and well-functioning systems of secured transactions, lenders or creditor-sellers can seize and sell collateral rapidly. This is crucial in the case of movable property: many types of inventory perish rapidly, either through spoilage or through becoming obsolete; the collection of accounts receivable becomes increasingly unlikely beyond 30–45 days from the date of their origin; and machinery typically depreciates more rapidly than real estate. All factors potentially can cause a substantial reduction in the liquidation value of the collateral.

Enforcement problems are not only severe (in practice, court procedures are generally too slow, expensive, and uncertain); they also serve as a significant constraint on the supply and availability of credit[16] and they are the single greatest concern of the lenders that were canvassed. There is therefore a pressing need to address this issue in a satisfactory manner if lenders' trust is to be restored in the system of enforcement of collateral security.

Unless otherwise stipulated in a pledge agreement (art. 349 [2] CC), Russian law does not provide pledge creditors with nonjudicial self-help remedies over movable property following a debtor's default. Rather, enforcement of a pledge (levy of execution) must begin with the institution of court or arbitral proceedings. Thereafter, and regardless of whether prior resort to a court or arbitral panel has been effected for purposes of enforcement, the pledged movable property is necessarily[17] realized through sale at public auction (arts. 349–350 and 447–449 CC) conducted by a specialized organization and appointed by a court bailiff.

Anecdotal evidence indicates that these enforcement and realization proceedings are often the object of interlocutory (interim) motions and appeals brought by debtors (frequently, it appears, for dilatory purposes) that result in considerable additional delay to the ultimate disposition of the proceedings,[18] that increase cost and expense, and that add substantial uncertainty to their outcome.[19] As a result, when considering a decision to provide credit, a creditor must generally expect a lengthy and expensive judicial proceeding prior to realizing on the property pledged to secure repayment of the credit.

Lenders' trust in the system of enforcement is also negatively influenced by the following factors:

1. *Postponement of public auction.* Upon application of the pledgor, a court may postpone by up to one year the public auction sale of the pledged property (art. 350 [2] CC). No criteria are established to guide the court in the exercise of its discretion, and these applications are apparently granted systematically. Such delay would be likely to have a material adverse effect on the creditor's ability to obtain market value for the pledged property.
2. *Court establishment of public auction sales price.* The initial bid price at the public auction is determined by the court (art. 350 [3] CC). There is no compelling reason to believe that a court would

be in a better position than a creditor-pledgee to determine the market value for the pledged property at the date of auction. In addition, the setting of the initial bid price is both relevant and material to a creditor as it can influence directly the outcome of the auction process: set too high and the creditor may not receive any bids for the asset, thus frustrating the realization process; set too low and, in the absence of sufficiently interested parties at the auction to bid the price up, the asset may be sold at an undervalue, again negating the utility of the auction process for the creditor.

3. *Treatment of security upon liquidation or bankruptcy.* Although a validly constituted pledge is effective upon the liquidation of the pledgor and in bankruptcy proceedings relating to the pledgor, secured creditors lose their proprietary (in rem) rights against the pledged assets. Instead, they are provided with the priority given by law to creditors whose claims are secured by a pledge. This does not mean that their claims will be satisfied directly from the value of the particular property that had been pledged in their favor. Rather, such pledged property is grouped together with all the other assets of the pledgor, which are sold, and the claims of all the creditors, both secured and unsecured, will be satisfied from the aggregate proceeds of sale, in the order of priority established by law.

If the claims of all the creditors of a particular rank exceed the amount of the proceeds of sale available to satisfy their claims, all their claims will be prorated, regardless of whether any particular creditor had enjoyed collateral security in the pledged property that had been primary or subsequent vis-à-vis other creditors.[20] In sum, therefore, this system results not only in the loss for the secured creditor of its right to exercise its security, but also the loss of its right of first priority (subject to other collateral security) in the pledged property ahead of all other creditors.

In practice, this also means that it is more important for a creditor to ensure that the nature of its claim is one secured by a pledge of the debtor's property—any property—than it is for the creditor to be concerned with the quality, or the leveraged value, of such property; or indeed, whether the pledged property previously had been pledged by the debtor in favor of one or more other creditors (i.e., whether its pledge was first-in-time).[21] While such a system may have the advantage of at least being internally consistent with one that does not require the registration of a nonpossessory pledge of movable property (see below), it certainly runs counter to generally recognized principles of prudent lending and secured lending orthodoxy.

1. *Inconsistent treatment of priority of pledgeholders' claims.* Under Russian law, the precise ranking of the preference that a claim secured by a pledge will enjoy by virtue of article 334 (1) of the Civil Code in the proceeds of realization of the pledged property will depend upon whether the claim is enforced outside of the pledgor's insolvency or bankruptcy, in the context of a liquidation of the pledgor, or in bankruptcy proceedings relating to the pledgor.
    - *If the pledge is enforced in the ordinary course of the pledgor's business*, then such enforcement can only take place if the value of the pledgor's other (unencumbered) property is insufficient to satisfy the full amount of the claim of the pledgee and the claim of any other enforcing creditors.[22] Assuming this is the case, a pledgeholder's claim will rank after the payment in full of the following four prior claims:[23] (1) claims for alimony, and (tort) claims of individuals for loss of life and harm to health; (2) employment-related wage claims, legal costs incurred in connection with wage claims, and royalties for the use of intellectual property; (3) claims related to the payment of pension, social insurance, and unemployment contributions; and (4) all claims of the state budget (i.e., taxes) other than those provided in (3). Only if there are surplus proceeds after the payment of all of these prior claims will the pledgee be able to realize any value from its pledge. If, on the other hand, the surplus is insufficient to discharge all other claims that are enforced at the same time, then all of these claims will be prorated.
    - *If the pledge is enforced in a liquidation of the pledgor*, a pledgeholder's claim will only rank after the payment of the following two claims:[24] (1) (tort) claims of individuals for harm to health or life; and (2) employment and work-related severance and wage claims, as well as claims under publishing contracts. However, the pledgeholder's claim will rank ahead of claims for social contributions and taxes and ahead of the claims of other (unsecured) creditors.
    - *If the pledge is enforced in bankruptcy proceedings relating to the pledgor,* the same order of priority as that applicable in liquidation proceedings will apply, except that a superpriority is added for the repayment of bankruptcy administration-related fees, expenses, and claims.[25]

    The above priority scheme raises several issues. First, from a policy perspective, it seems inconsistent and hard to justify that the claim of a secured creditor should rank after claims for social contributions and taxes if enforcement takes place during the ordinary course of the pledgor's business but not if enforcement occurs in the context of the pledgor's liquidation or bankruptcy. Expressed differently, it is difficult to understand why the Government would be prepared to rank after secured creditors when a pledgor is either in liquidation or bankrupt, but not so during usual circumstances. A consistent approach should be taken in all circumstances, preferably with as few claims as possible ranking ahead of those of secured creditors.

Second, the current approach introduces a significant element of uncertainty into the enforcement process and therefore into the original credit decision-making process, since the position of a secured creditor relative to other claimants (particularly the Government) cannot be known at the outset and will vary as a direct function of the timing of enforcement. In the cases of liquidation and bankruptcy, this may be something over which any particular secured creditor has little or no control.

Third, it is important to note that each of the priorities that rank ahead of a secured creditor is uncapped. This is particularly noteworthy since arrears of taxes and salaries are generally high in Russian companies and there are no means available to creditors to determine quickly and reliably at any time the outstanding amount of any of these prior claims. Also, given the absence of a filing system for security interests in movable property, the Government is not required to file its claim covering unpaid social contributions and taxes following a taxpayer's default, which would at least provide notice of these claims.

Fourth, the superpriority provided for the repayment of bankruptcy administration-related fees and expenses is particularly problematic from a secured creditor's perspective, since the secured creditor is required to submit its claim in the pledgor's bankruptcy proceedings. If a secured creditor could enforce its claims independently of such proceedings, it could avoid these claims, which can be quite substantial.

In the final analysis, secured creditors cannot be certain whether they will be able to rely on their security, and, if they can, to what extent it will reduce their risk of loss in the event of a debtor's default. The result of this priority scheme is that creditors reduce the amount of credit they are prepared to make available, and they require overcollateralization for the credit that they do advance.

2. *Efficiency of court bailiffs.* Several reports called into question the efficacy with which the court bailiff service discharged its responsibilities pursuant to the Enforcement Law to execute judgments. Judgments not uncommonly failed to be executed. Although details are limited, it seems that the situations that were mentioned arose as a result of undue influence, the lack of effective enforcement mechanisms, a lack of experience with enforcement proceedings generally, and inadequate training. Further complicating factors are that court bailiffs are not required to search for a debtor's assets, and that the costs associated with any searches that may be conducted must be met by the creditor.

Possible Solutions

There are several broad options, including the following, that could be considered by the authorities.
1. *Introduce more expeditious procedures for the prompt enforcement of pledge.* The authorities could accelerate the levying of execution by introducing procedures that would not require judicial intervention. Procedures that could be considered include simple repossession, administrative repossession, and receivership. Summary procedures for court-approved seizures would also accelerate enforcement, as would restrictions on the right to file interlocutory motions and appeals, unless it could be established that a judgment was manifestly wrong. The grounds to lodge interlocutory motions and to file appeals should otherwise be narrowed to very limited and specific grounds, and appealing interlocutory decisions should not suspend their execution. Any contract that would purport to waive these provisions would be void as contrary to public policy. The right of a pledgor to seek postponement of a public auction sale should be abolished, or the law should provide clearly defined and narrow grounds upon which a court could exercise its discretion to grant such a request. Suitable amendments could be introduced to the Civil Code or to the Law on Enforcement Procedure.
2. *Allow creditors to control the sale of pledged property.* Generally speaking, Russian law makes no provision for private sale, wherein a creditor, without further recourse to a court, could dispose of the pledged movable property provided by the debtor. All realizations take place by means of court-authorized sale at public auction, which involves substantial costs and delays. To address this,

new rules for creditor-controlled sale of collateral could be contemplated. These rules would apply uniformly to all creditors, and judicial intervention during the process would be minimal. Should judicial issues arise, the law would maximize the value of movable property as collateral by postponing their resolution until after the collateral has been sold and the creditor has been paid. The main revisions to provisions on private sale should ensure that

- The debtor receives the maximum sale price from the sale of the collateral.
- The debtor receives any surplus remaining after the creditor has been paid.
- The law maximizes scope for private action and minimizes court intervention.
- The procedure has broad application to all secured transactions.

A creditor-administered sale lowers the cost of collection to the creditor. This is because the creditor is paid first, without his claim being offset by the other claims on the collateral that usually arise in a court-administered sale. Moreover, the sale can occur when the creditor desires, without expensive delays.

The policy framework for these rules should balance a debtor's rights to due process against the need for expeditious foreclosure. To protect debtors against unfair disposition of the pledged property, a standard of commercial reasonableness should be enacted to which secured creditors would be held. For example, this standard would require a creditor to sell goods in the customary manner for dealers in that type of goods. Delay in the disposition of perishable collateral, or of goods likely to reduce in value rapidly, may constitute failure to act in a commercially reasonable manner, and the creditor would lose any rights to collect a deficiency if the sale did not in such circumstances cover the creditor's claim.

The law would also require creditors to notify debtors and junior secured creditors before any resale of the collateral. The law must always provide the debtor with a redemption period during which the pledged property can be reclaimed following payment of the debt or other discharge of the secured obligation. The law should void any stipulation allowing the debtor to waive its right to redeem the collateral before foreclosure. The debtor should also be allowed to recover damages arising from any wrongful seizure, including cases where the debtor actually did not default or where the creditor in fact did not have a valid pledge of the seized property.

Once the secured creditor recovers the pledged property, the creditor should be allowed to retain it in satisfaction of the secured debt (strict foreclosure). As a policy matter, the law may provide that the parties may not agree to strict foreclosure in advance of a debtor's default and after notice.

3. *Permit a secured creditor to continue to exercise its proprietary (in rem) rights in an insolvency or bankruptcy.* The loss by a creditor of its ability to exercise its security at this time strips the pledge of its value at precisely the time when it is most required by a creditor.
4. *Provide a consistent regime for the priority of claims across all stages of a debtor's business cycle (ordinary course of business; liquidation; bankruptcy).* This would eliminate a significant element of uncertainty in the enforcement process.
5. *Enforce the rank of priority of collateral security and avoid the distribution of proceeds of realization of the pledgor's property without regard to the primacy of the security held by the pledgees.* The pooling of the proceeds of realization of a pledgor's property and their pro rata distribution among unsecured and secured creditors is inconsistent with provisions of the Civil Code that establish the preference of claims secured by pledge.
6. *Consider the merits of introducing a requirement for legal enterprises and entrepreneurs to take out and maintain private third-party liability insurance against (tort) claims of individuals for loss of life and harm to health caused by their activities in lieu of the existing priority for such claims.* A requirement of this nature would be more efficient from an economic point of view than the current system, which effectively shifts the liability for damaging behavior from the party responsible for such damage (the legal enterprise, its officers and shareholders, or the individual entrepreneur) to the creditors of such party. Enterprises and entrepreneurs engaged in risky activities are more likely to cause harm or damage and will correspondingly be required to pay higher insurance premiums. In order to avoid paying these higher premiums, they would have the option to either discontinue these practices or amend them.
7. *Following a careful analysis of the most effective manner to value and resolve all currently outstanding employment and wage-related claims and, once done, settling such claims, also consider the merits of enacting a first-priority ranking enterprise charge equal to unsatisfied employment and wage-related claims of employees and*

workers, up to an agreed maximum (e.g., three months' arrears), subject to the usual perfection and registration requirements of enterprise charges.[26] Employees and occasional workers of failing enterprises who are not paid their due are unwilling creditors. In transition economies in particular, they may have limited alternative employment options to pursue. When wage arrears become significant, they can effectively become economic captives of their employer, as leaving to seek work with another would likely result in their assuming a total loss in terms of their unpaid wages. To compound matters further, employees and occasional workers usually have little, if any, access to information regarding their employer's financial condition or business prospects. As a result, they can unwittingly fall victim to unscrupulous owners and managers.

A registered, first-ranking enterprise charge would protect the legitimate interests of employees and occasional workers. It would also provide the means for prospective secured creditors to assess the impact of unpaid wages on the creditworthiness of the enterprise. Employees' and occasional workers' claims would no longer be a drain on the collateral security system and their trust in the marketplace would be significantly enhanced.

INFORMATION MECHANISMS

The ability for a creditor to have at its ready disposal complete, reliable, and up-to-date information upon which it can rely in order to reach an informed decision whether to provide credit to an individual or to a legal entity in support of a proposed transaction or other economic activity and, if so, on what terms and conditions, is a vital and necessary condition for the prudent and efficient operation of a modern financial system and a modern market economy. Without access to reliable information on the financial condition of a debtor, a creditor is unable to properly assess the credit risk that it would assume in the context of the proposed debtor or transaction.

Armed with the necessary information, however, creditors are able to perform the credit and other analyses that are required in the circumstances. Riskier debtors or transactions may still be able to obtain credit, but generally will obtain less credit, will pay more for the credit that they are offered, and will be required to pay it back sooner; the credit itself will be subject to more stringent conditions. Creditworthy debtors, on the other hand, generally will be rewarded with a greater amount of credit, will pay a correspondingly lower rate of interest, and will be able to pay it back over a longer period; the credit also will be subject to more liberal conditions. In other words, the reduction of informational asymmetry allows the financial system to operate more efficiently.

In the absence of reliable financial information in respect to a debtor, and assuming a creditor is prepared to provide some credit, that creditor is likely to do one or more of the following in order to limit its exposure both to the debtor and to a proposed transaction: (*a*) reduce the amount of the credit (to limit its downside risk); (*b*) increase the rate of interest (to reflect the heightened risk); (*c*) shorten the term of the credit (to increase the rate at which repayments are made and to reduce the time during which the creditor will be exposed); and (*d*) as a percentage of the credit that it is prepared to advance, require an increase in the aggregate value of the collateral property to be provided by the debtor to secure repayment of the credit (to decrease its loss in the event of a default).

Any of these steps, if taken individually, or all of them if applied together, would not only significantly increase the economic impact of the credit upon the debtor, but would also correspondingly either increase the cost or reduce the return of the underlying transaction supported by the credit. That is assuming, of course, that the debtor is able to assume the credit on these terms; i.e., that it can both afford to service such a debt and to provide the greater amount of collateral required by the creditor.

While the Civil Code requires that a pledge of immovable property, the pledge of an agreement which itself must be registered, and the pledge of an enterprise (which by virtue of article 132 CC is deemed to be an immovable) are all to be registered, no such requirement is provided in respect to nonpossessory pledges of movable property.[27]

In most jurisdictions, pledge agreements that stipulate that the debtor will be dispossessed of the pledged property are not required to be registered, since it is felt that the creditor's possession provides sufficient notice; however, the generally prevailing view among jurists and legal commentators is that such mechanisms should not be encouraged, as they prevent the debtor from using the collateral while the credit is outstanding, thus preventing its use for productive purposes.

The only means of publicity that is required for nonpossessory pledges of movable property is their manual entry in a pledge record book, which must be maintained by a pledgor if it is either a company or a natural person registered as an entrepreneur.[28] It is not apparent that any penalties are contemplated if a pledgor fails to keep faithful records in its pledge record book, or if it fails to permit the inspection of the record book by any interested party (a frequent occurrence).

Not surprisingly, the consultations provided repeated examples of manipulation and fraud of the pledge record book system. Such abuse allegedly occurs most commonly at times of a pledgor's financial distress, and typically takes the form either of the addition of creditors not previously known to have provided credit (and, on closer inspection, which are frequently determined not to be at arm's length with the pledgor), or the deletion of prior entries that had been properly made, or both.

Allowing a debtor to have control over the only available means of publicity of collateral security interests in its movable property results in a serious moral hazard, particularly since the current scheme of claim priorities benefits those that have obtained the status of pledge-creditors. This is not a system designed to inspire trust among creditors. This is a crucial flaw in the framework for creditor rights and secured transactions, and together with the resolution of the enforcement-related issues previously discussed should be addressed by the Government as a matter of priority.

The Russian Federation has never had a credit reporting system, whether operated by private companies on a for-profit basis; by financial institutions themselves on a proportional-usage, cost-recovery basis (or some other formula); or otherwise. The collection of and easy access to reliable and transparent credit information on commercial and corporate enterprises[29] are vitally important, as they provide crucial information upon which creditors can, in part, safely base their credit decisions. If Russia were to institute such a credit reporting system, appropriate safeguards would need to be implemented in parallel to protect the legitimate interests of debtors. For example, the functions of credit bureaus and the standards to be applied by them in their operations, debtors' rights to privacy and access to their credit files, issues regarding the accuracy of information and the debtor's right to correct errors, and time limits for keeping information on file would all need to be addressed.

Possible Solutions

The following are some possible solutions to the problems surrounding information mechanisms.

1. *Replace the pledge record book system with a first-in-time priority system based on registration in a public registry and amend the current scheme of claim priorities to provide for priority among secured creditors based on the new system.* The necessary first step in providing for a public registration system involves enacting priority rules that grant a rank of priority to the first to register. Then

and only then is it sensible to invest in modernizing the function of registries. The new provisions should be contained in an amendment to the Civil Code.
2. *Undertake an economic and technical evaluation of and subsequently establish a computerized system for the public registration of collateral security in movable property that would give creditors an easy and inexpensive way to publicly assert the existence of collateral security granted in their favor.* Establishing a public registration system for collateral security in movable property would require an economic and technical evaluation of the many options. Should public or private parties operate the registries? Should multiple registries exist and compete? How should registries structure registration fees? What technical configuration would they need? What is the least information to register that would balance privacy rights, economic usefulness, and public access? What cost-saving designs, if any, should be considered, including, for example, making use of any existing infrastructure established for the registration of other information?[30] These and other related issues should be addressed in separate studies.
3. *Conduct studies for terms of reference, draft rules, and introduce legislation for the establishment and operation of credit bureaus.* A framework for the operation of credit bureaus could be instituted separately from other reforms. Corresponding banking and other financial regulation must proceed in parallel with credit bureau legislation. Regulations must require that banks and other credit providers supply regular credit reports in respect to their account debtors to the entity or entities that will operate the credit bureaus.

OTHER OBSTACLES RELATED TO THE USE OF PLEDGED ASSETS

Pledge of Bank Accounts/Rights

Russian law presents obstacles to the pledge of a debtor's bank accounts—a common form of collateral security taken in international practice. The principal difficulty results from the requirement previously noted under Russian law that pledged property or rights are to be sold at public auction if the pledge is to be enforced. A decision of the Russian Supreme Arbitration Court in 1996 concluded that rubles cannot be sold at auction and, therefore, cannot be pledged. In 1998 there was a further ruling that money in a bank account is not a "res" and cannot be the subject of a pledge. At law, the relationship between a bank and a depositor is one of debtor and creditor, the depositor having a right to claim back from the bank the money it deposited. As Russian law allows the pledge of rights, legal practitioners have begun to use a pledge of the right to claim money deposited in a bank account. The practice has not been tested before the courts, however, and is accordingly uncertain. An alternative approach relies on the assignment of a right to a claim, which is recognized by Russian law, but for reasons previously discussed, an assignment of the bank account may not enjoy the same priority that is afforded to a pledge.

One solution to this problem is to amend the Civil Code to provide for the pledge of rights under a bank account and realization by means of an assignment of the pledged rights by the secured creditor to a third party. Another solution is to amend the priorities established under article 78 (2) Enforcement Procedure Law (for "ordinary" enforcement), article 64 (1) CC (in the event of liquidation), and article 106 (2) Bankruptcy Law (in the context of bankruptcy) to include security by way of assignment.

Notarization Fee

A mortgage of immovable property and a pledge (mortgage) of an enterprise (which is deemed to be an immovable for the purposes of Russian law) require notarization, which attracts a fee of 1.5 percent of the value of the underlying transaction disclosed in the relevant document (which fee is payable to the notary, not to the public purse). This can represent a significant sum of money and serves as a disincentive to the use of these forms of security. Although untested before the courts, as Russian law does not stipulate that such notarization must take place in the Russian Federation or before a duly qualified Russian notary, a practice has developed in some cases to sign and notarize the mortgage agreement abroad.

To solve this problem, the Civil Code could be amended to eliminate the requirement for notarization of mortgages and enterprise charges, and thus render the treatment of these transactions consistent with that for the sale of immovable property.[31]

Approval of Material Transactions

Under Russian law,[32] a transaction involving a sale or other disposal of assets whose value exceeds 25 percent of the value of the company's total assets requires prior approval by the board of directors or at a general meeting of shareholders. There is apparently a fairly widespread practice among companies to intentionally understate the book value of their assets for official purposes in order to reduce tax payables. Since many businesses in the Russian Federation are established as companies, this requirement for approval is frequently applicable. In practice, however, few companies fulfill the requirement, with the result that a great number of transactions are at risk of invalidation at the behest either of the company or of any of its shareholders (participants). Actions to invalidate such transactions are regularly instituted before the courts, particularly when a company is in difficult financial circumstances. In addition, the Supreme Arbitration Court has rendered an opinion[33] subjecting the conclusion of loan agreements to this requirement and, as a matter of practice, courts subsequently have extended this to the granting of collateral security.

While there can be little argument that a substantial sale of a company's assets (presumably outside its normal course of business) warrants Board approval or approval of its shareholders at a general meeting, such requirements essentially address governance issues *internal* to the company, for the protection of its members. However, it should not be open to a company that has, wittingly or otherwise, failed to follow these requirements to raise such failure itself in an attempt to defeat a valid claim of a third party with whom the company has dealt and who has no knowledge of the failure. To provide otherwise legitimizes an inequitable trap for the unwary.

It was precisely to avoid situations such as these that English corporate law over a hundred years ago adopted the so-called "indoor management rule" in order to safeguard the interests of innocent third parties against attempts by owners of companies that a particular transaction was beyond its authority and hence null (the *ultra vires* doctrine).

Under the indoor management rule, unless a company can establish that a person dealing with a company or who has acquired rights from a company had actual knowledge, or by virtue of its position with or relationship to the company ought to have had knowledge, that the company had failed to comply with the terms of its charter documents, the company cannot assert such failure against that person.

The indoor management rule has been enshrined in many corporate statutes around the world and frequently expanded to include protection against other corporate acts or omissions.[34]

To the extent that the Civil Code, the Law on Joint Stock Companies, or the Law on Limited Liability Companies does not already make provisions for analogous safeguards, Russia could consider adopting measures at law similar to the indoor management rule for the protection of third parties.

ANNEX 2.1. CREDITOR RIGHTS: THE INTERNATIONAL EXPERIENCE

International Bank for Reconstruction and Development

The International Bank for Reconstruction and Development (World Bank), as part of its financial sector and private sector development efforts, has conducted economic and sector work and has financed a number of projects to reform secured transactions laws.[35,36] Other such projects are underway or planned in a number of its member countries.

For example, the World Bank published a comprehensive report in December 1994 analyzing the shortcomings of the Bolivian system of collateral security laws and their effect on access to credit in that country, and formulated a number of specific recommendations for reform (World Bank 1994). A similar report was published in June 1997 in respect to Peruvian secured transactions laws (World Bank 1997) (see Box 2.2).

In March 2001, the Board of Executive Directors of the World Bank approved the *Principles and Guidelines for Effective Insolvency and Creditor Rights Systems*,[37] an important milestone in promoting international consensus on a uniform framework to assess the effectiveness of insolvency and creditor rights systems, offering guidance to policymakers on the policy choices needed to strengthen them.

The principles set forth in the *Principles and Guidelines* were developed against the backdrop of earlier and ongoing initiatives to promote cross-border cooperation on multijurisdictional insolvencies, the modernization of national insolvency and secured transactions laws, and the development of principles for out-of-court corporate workouts. The principles draw on common themes and policy choices of those initiatives and on the views of staff, insolvency experts, and participants in regional workshops sponsored by the World Bank and its partner organizations (see Box 2.3).[38]

The consultative process used on the *Principles and Guidelines* is among the most extensive of its kind, involving more than 70 international experts as members of the Bank's Task Force and working groups, and with regional participation by more than 700 public and private sector specialists from approximately 75 mostly developing countries. The

> **Box 2.2 Recommendations for Expanding Access to Credit**
>
> In no particular order, the following were among the legal reform recommendations formulated by the World Bank in these various projects and reports to expand access to credit in the relevant member countries:
> - Allow all tangible and intangible movable property to serve as collateral in possessory and nonpossessory security interests, including fixtures, deposit accounts, and intellectual property; permit security interests to continue automatically in the proceeds of collateral; permit floating security interests by allowing a security agreement to "generally describe" the collateral; and increase the use of accounts receivable as collateral by avoiding notice-and-notarization requirements.
> - Improve the technical functioning of existing registries, through computerization and full public access.
> - Establish a central, computerized public registry for security interests in movable property that permits inexpensive and rapid registration of security interests, as well as information retrieval.
> - Abandon requirements for notarization of documents or the delivery of certificates or other supporting documents.
> - Use standard forms and model contracts for commonly registered documents.
> - Bypass slow procedures for obtaining judgment and permit nonjudicial self-help to repossess collateral upon default in order to provide secured creditors with an expeditious way to enforce collection. Appropriate safeguards should include monetary damages for wrongful repossession, including repossession cases where the debtor actually did not default or where the creditor in fact had no security interest in the repossessed property.
> - Permit creditor-controlled sale of collateral, whether by public sale (for example, an auction arranged by the secured creditor, not by the court) or by private sale, subject to a requirement that the sale take place in a commercially reasonable manner.
> - Following repossession, allow a secured creditor to keep the collateral in satisfaction of the secured debt (strict foreclosure), possibly subject to notice requirements or prohibitions where, prior to default, a debtor has repaid a minimum percentage of the original secured debt.
> - Establish a credit reporting system that pools information about commercial or corporate debtors.

World Bank also included papers and consultative drafts on its website to obtain feedback from the international community.

European Bank for Reconstruction and Development

Recognizing the importance of laws on secured transactions for business development and economic growth and their essential role in achieving successful reform to a market economy, in 1992 the European Bank for Reconstruction and Development established a Secured Transactions Project to encourage and assist the introduction of workable laws on secured transactions in the former socialist countries in central and eastern

> **Box 2.3 Principles and Guidelines for Effective Insolvency and Creditor Rights Systems: Secured Transactions Recommendations (Extract)**
>
> The following are the main recommendations contained in *Principles and Guidelines for Effective Insolvency and Creditor Rights Systems* with regard to secured transactions systems (paragraphs 48–66):
> 1. The legal framework should provide for the creation, recognition, and enforcement of security interests in movable and immovable (real) property, arising by agreement or operation of law.
> 2. The legal regime should recognize security over all types of assets—movable and immovable, tangible and intangible, including inventories, receivables, and proceeds.
> 3. Lenders should be able to take security interests in future property and on a global basis.
> 4. Security should be available for any or all of a debtor's obligations to a creditor, present or future, and between all types of persons.
> 5. The law should permit both possessory and nonpossessory security interests over tangible assets.
> 6. Secured credit systems should encompass all types and uses of property, participants, and transactions.
> 7. Methods of notice should sufficiently publicize the existence of security interests to creditors, purchasers, and the public generally.
> 8. Creation of security interests should be easy and cost-effective.
> 9. A security system should set rules of priority on competing claims or interests in the same assets and minimize the number of priorities that come ahead of secured interests in collateral.
> 10. There should be an efficient and cost-effective means of publicizing secured interests in movable and immovable assets, with registration being the principal and strongly preferred method. Access to the registry should be inexpensive and open to all for both recording and search.
> 11. Enforcement systems should provide efficient, inexpensive, transparent, and predictable methods for enforcing a security interest in property. Enforcement procedures should provide for prompt realization of the rights obtained in secured assets, ensuring the maximum possible recovery of asset values based on market values.

Europe (Simpson and Röver 1994). This was followed by the publication in 1994 of a Model Law on Secured Transactions (MLST).[39] Since the publication of the MLST, the EBRD has supported many projects fostering legal transition in the field of secured credit (Simpson and Menze 2000).

The principal objectives of the MLST were to harmonize the approach to security rights legislation among international investors and lenders and to provide guidance as to the expectations of those investors and lenders (EBRD 1994, App. I, v), with a view to assisting the subject countries in their transition from a planned to a market economy (Simpson and Röver 1994). It was not intended that the MLST be adopted directly into domestic law, but rather that it form a starting point for such legislation.

The MLST sought to produce a text compatible with the concepts of the civil laws that form the roots of the legal systems of many of the countries concerned (Ajani 1995, 97–99),[40] while also drawing on common law legal systems that have developed useful solutions to accommodate modern financing techniques (Ajani 1995, 21, fn. 89).[41] The MLST was prepared by a civil lawyer and a common lawyer assisted by an international advisory board drawn from 15 different jurisdictions.

The MLST creates a single, consensual security right (a "charge") in respect to anything capable of being owned as collateral,[42] including future assets, a changing pool of assets (including inventory), and all the assets of an enterprise ("enterprise charge"). The distinction between various traditional types of security devices, such as pledges of movables, pledges of rights, and mortgages, are merged into one charge. There is a distinction between registered charges, which have to be registered at a charges registry, and possessory charges, for which registration is not required but according to which the secured creditor takes and must retain possession of the collateral. The MLST also provides for charges in favor of an unpaid vendor. A written document is required to create these charges. Priority is mainly determined in accordance with the time at which a charge was created (in the case of a registered charge, the time of registration; in the case of a possessory charge, the later of the time mentioned in the written document or the delivery of possession; and in the case of an unpaid vendor's charge, the time at which title is transferred). Secured creditors are provided with broad self-help enforcement rights, including the right to sell the collateral without judicial intervention, subject to prior notice and damages in the event of wrongful or abusive enforcement. Special provisions are made for the realization of a charge that covers the entirety of an enterprise and that entitles the creditor to sell the enterprise as a going concern.

Drawing on experience gained from its support since the inception of the Secured Transactions Project of secured transactions legal reform, the EBRD has published 10 core principles for a modern secured transactions law (see Box 2.4). The core principles reflect the provisions of the MLST and aim to give, in condensed form, a general formulation of the goals to be pursued and the principles to be applied if secured transactions reform is to foster economic development. They do not seek to impose any particular solution; rather, they seek to indicate the result that should be achieved (Simpson and Menze 2000, 25). The principles thus should aid the assessment of a country's secured transactions laws.

Finally, the EBRD has recently published the results of a regional survey conducted by members of the Secured Transactions Project, the purpose of

> **Box 2.4 EBRD Core Principles for a Modern Secured Transactions Law**
>
> 1. Security should reduce the risk of giving credit, leading to an increased availability of credit on improved terms.
> 2. The law should enable the quick, cheap, and simple creation of a proprietary security right without depriving the person giving the security of the use of his assets.
> 3. If the secured debt is not paid, the holder of security should be able to have the charged assets realized and to have the proceeds applied toward satisfaction of his claim prior to other creditors.
> 4. Enforcement procedures should enable prompt realization at market value of the assets given as security.
> 5. The security right should continue to be effective and enforceable after the bankruptcy or insolvency of the person who has given it.
> 6. The costs of taking, maintaining, and enforcing security should be low.
> 7. Security should be available over all types of assets, to secure all types of debts, and between all types of persons.
> 8. There should be an effective means of publicizing the existence of security rights.
> 9. The law should establish rules governing competing rights of persons holding security and other persons claiming rights in the assets given as security.
> 10. As far as possible the parties should be able to adapt security to the needs of their particular transaction.

which was to monitor and assess the state of collateral laws in the 26 member countries (Fairgrieve and Andenas 2000).

Asian Development Bank

In April 2000, the Office of the General Counsel of the Asian Development Bank (ADB) published the results of a joint session on secured transactions and insolvency law reforms. This session, which included participants from two symposia, was held in October 1999.

In December 2000, the Office of the General Counsel published the results of a survey of the legal framework for secured transactions laws in the People's Republic of China, India, Indonesia, Pakistan, and Thailand (ADB 2000b, 144). Its main conclusion is that the laws and legal processes in each of the five countries largely prevent debtors from using movable property as collateral that is acceptable to creditors. The legal regime for creating security with movable property is costly, complex, lengthy, and uncertain. Problems arise at each stage, from creation to enforcement, in some cases in all countries and in others in a subset of countries (ADB 2000b, xiv, fn. 98). The result is that creditors and debtors pay a huge price in lost opportunities from the inability to use movable property as collateral.

The report sets out a baseline policy model for an economically useful framework favoring secured credit (ADB 2000b, 19, fn. 98).[43] The economic requirements for a regime with the single goal of promoting secured credit are (*a*) creation that is cheap, simple, comprehensive; (*b*) publicity that is public, inexpensive to file, easy to research; (*c*) priority based on a simple and unambiguous rule; and (*d*) enforcement that is fast and cheap.

ENDNOTES

1. Ranking second only to the Constitution of the Russian Federation in terms of hierarchy of statutory instruments, the Civil Code is at times referred to as the "Constitution of the Economy"; *vide* A.L. Makovsky, "Preface to the English Translation of the Civil Code," *The Civil Code of the Russian Federation, Parts I and II*, Moscow, International Centre for Financial and Economic Development, 1997, p. 71.

2. For example, the Basic Provisions of civil law contained in Subdivision 1, Division 1 of the First Part (articles 1–16) "demonstrate the enormous distance between the present Code and its Soviet predecessor. Article 1 stipulates several principles which were explicitly rejected by Soviet law, such as the equality of all who participate in civil law relationships and the freedom of contract." – F.J.M. Feldbrugge, "The New Civil Code of the Russian Federation," 21 *Review of Central and East European Law* 1995 No. 3/4, 237–243 at p. 240.

3. In response to the Asian financial crisis, finance ministers and central bank governors from 22 systemically significant economies met in April 1998 to examine issues related to strengthening the international financial architecture; the Working Group on International Financial Crises was one of three groups formed to study in greater depth certain key areas where it was felt action was needed.

4. As part of their framework of creditor rights, many jurisdictions have adopted legislation for the protection of consumers. Some have also adopted specific legislation for certain economically significant sectors of their economies (e.g., forestry, agriculture). For the purposes of this report, neither have been investigated in or considered for the Russian Federation.

5. For a general survey of the regulation of immovables under Russian law since the introduction of Part I of the Civil Code, see O.M. Kozyr, "The Legal Treatment of Immovables under the Civil Code of the Russian Federation," 44 *McGill Law Journal* 1999, 327.

6. When immovable property is taken as collateral security for a loan made to an enterprise, it is not uncommonly by way of pledge of a residential apartment owned by an individual, majority shareholder of the enterprise (to secure a surety provided by such individual in respect to repayment of the loan). It is not necessarily a pledge of the immovable property of the enterprise itself, although such pledges can be and are also taken.

7. The Pledge Law remains in effect to the extent that its provisions are not inconsistent with those of the Civil Code. In practice, only a few of its provisions continue in effect. However, there is considerable uncertainty among legal practitioners as to precisely which provisions of the Pledge Law continue to apply—a matter that needs to be addressed.

8. Modeled after the rules on demand guarantees established in 1992 by the International Chamber of Commerce, this is somewhat of a misnomer since it is available not only to banks but also to other credit institutions and insurance organizations.

9. As to the principle of freedom of contract generally, see art. 1 CC and art. 421 CC. Nevertheless, and notwithstanding that parties to a contract may establish other security mechanisms since the various provisions that establish the priorities of claims (i.e., art. 78 [2] Enforcement Procedure Law [for enforcement in the "ordinary course of business"]; art. 64 [1] CC [in the event of liquidation]; art. 106 [2] Bankruptcy Law [in the context of bankruptcy]) only refer to security by way of pledge, there remains considerable doubt among local legal practitioners and academics that participated in the consultations whether such mechanisms would be effective under Russian law.

10. See Box 2.4.

11. If experience of credit institutions in developed financial markets can serve as a guide (at least in those markets where there is a degree of competition within the financial sector during "normal" periods), this is unlikely. In the aftermath of a crisis, once an economy has stabilized and some measure of growth and competition has resumed, experience has shown that most institutions develop myopia and short-term memory loss, generally leading to an increase in credit supply and a relaxing of the terms upon which credit is available.

12. This takes place within the considerable constraints imposed on a system that is forced to operate within an environment offering a minimum of financial transparency, due not only to the failure to adopt international accounting standards, but also apparently due to the incentive for enterprises to understate their assets as a result of taxation imposed on, among other things, fixed assets.

13. A fact that can only be attributed in part to the issues raised in this paper; other factors, of course, are at play, including the difficulty for Russian financial institutions themselves to raise capital and, prior to August 1998, their preference to invest in GKOs.

14. See Chapter 13. This conclusion was primarily drawn from interviews with the EBRD's Russia Small Business Fund and KMB Bank concerning their considerable experience in making loans to micro- and small enterprises across the Russian Federation, both pre- and post-August 1998.

15. The consultations confirmed an apparent practice among some borrowers to intentionally understate the fixed assets of their enterprises in order to avoid the payment of certain taxes.

16. The Russian Federation is not alone in this: enforcement emerges as the most intractable problem for the five Asian countries reviewed in the ADB's survey (ADB 2000b, 131). Similarly, in its regional survey of secured transactions laws (Fairgrieve and Andenas 2000, 28–36), EBRD concluded that lawyers and academics familiar with local pledge laws perceive the implementation of collateral laws "as the major impediment in all of the countries surveyed," reinforcing the need, in their opinion, "for governments in the region to give greater priority to ensuring that resources are made available so that modern pledge laws are made effective."

17. In light of art. 28 (2) Pledge Law that contemplates sales other than by public auction, and art. 350 (1) CC that contemplates procedures other than public auction sales if established by statute, there is some doubt as to the mandatory nature of realization through court-authorized public auction sale. However, Resolution No. 7965/95 of February 2, 1996 of the Supreme Arbitration Court has established that parties to an agreement cannot avoid an auction procedure by providing otherwise contractually, a decision which seems at odds with art. 349 (2) CC.

18. Delays of 6 to 18 months are apparently not uncommon.

19. A distinction must be drawn here between the courts of general jurisdiction and the arbitration (commercial) courts. Disputes involving individuals not registered as individual entrepreneurs are resolved in the courts of general jurisdiction, while economic disputes between legal entities are resolved in the arbitration courts. Although quite clearly neither a scientific sampling of users nor a precise examination of results obtained, participants in the consultations expressed general dissatisfaction with the results of proceedings before the former (greater unpredictability of outcome; longer delays), and general satisfaction with the results of proceedings before the latter (greater uniformity among decisions rendered; shorter delays), although regional differences in both court systems were reported, which added to the unpredictability of outcome.

20. Art. 64 (3) CC; art. 114 (3) Federal Law No. 6-FZ of January 8, 1998 *On Insolvency (Bankruptcy)* (Bankruptcy Law).

21. Art. 342 contemplates the possibility of multiple pledges and establishes priority as a function of the time of creation of the pledge.

22. Art. 49 (1) Federal Law No. 119-FZ of July 21, 1997 *On Enforcement Procedure* (Enforcement Law). How a creditor is meant to be in a position to make this assessment is not clear, but the law would seem to require a valuation of the debtor's entire assets, which is not practical.

23. Art. 78 (2) Executive Procedure Law.

24. Art. 64 (1) CC.

25. Art. 106 Bankruptcy Law; including court costs, remuneration of the bankruptcy manager, current utility and operating expenses of the debtor, and the satisfaction of claims incurred after the commencement of the bankruptcy proceedings, which may well exceed the value of the bankrupt's estate.

26. Other than the application of the 1.5 percent notarial fee which, in any event, should be abolished in all circumstances.

27. Exceptions are also provided for pledges of aircraft, sea and river vessels, and other means of transport (art. 40 Pledge Law).

28. Art. 18 Pledge Law.

29. Including, for example, the amount and type of outstanding credit and other liabilities, the identification of the providers of credit, the payment performance record of the debtor, the existence and nature of any collateral security encumbering the assets of the debtor, and whether any collection actions have been brought against the debtor: when, for what amount, and with what result.

30. It would appear that there are systems currently in operation in the Russian Federation for the registration, for example, of cars, weapons, etc.

31. Art. 550 CC.

32. Art. 78 Law on Joint Stock Companies; art. 46 Law on Limited Liability Companies.

33. Information Letter No. 62, dated March 13, 2001.

34. For example, against attempts to assert that a person held out by a company as a director or officer of the company has not been duly appointed or has no authority to exercise the powers and perform the duties that are customary in the business of the company or usual for such director or officer.

35. See generally, United Nations Commission on International Trade Law, Report of the Secretary-General, April 27, 2000 (A/CN.9/475), *Security Interests: Current Activities and Possible Future Work*, Thirty-third session, June 12–July 7, 2000, United Nations, New York, 2000, p. 18.

36. These include Argentina, Bangladesh, Bolivia, Bulgaria, Peru, and Uruguay. See, generally: (1) H. Fleisig, "The Power of Collateral: How Problems in Securing Transactions Limit Private Credit for Movable Property," *World Bank Viewpoint*, Note 43, World Bank, Private Sector Development Department, Washington, D.C., April 1995; and (2) H. Fleisig, "The Right to Borrow: Legal and Regulatory Barriers that Limit Access to Credit by Small Firms and Businesses," *World Bank Viewpoint*, Note 44, World Bank, Private Sector Development Department, Washington, D.C., April 1995. The teams that conducted the research for purposes of the Bolivian and Peruvian reports were led by Dr. Heywood Fleisig, director of research at the Center for the Economic Analysis of Law (CEAL), a nonprofit research institute that provides legal and economic analysis of public policy issues, and also included Prof. Ronald C.C. Cuming, College of Law, University of Saskatchewan (Canada), the chief architect of the Canadian PPSAs; see also: H. Fleisig, "Economic Functions of Security in a Market Economy," *Emerging Financial Markets and Secured Transactions*, J.J. Norton and M. Andenas, editors, London, Kluwer Law International, 1998, chap. 3, pp. 15–38.

37. The paper can be accessed in the "Best Practice" directory on the Global Insolvency Law Database at http://www.worldbank.org/gild.

38. The *Principles and Guidelines* was prepared by World Bank staff in collaboration with the African Development Bank, Asian Development Bank, European Bank for Reconstruction and Development, Inter-American Development Bank, International Finance Corporation, International Monetary Fund, Organization for Economic Cooperation and Development, United Nations Commission on International Trade Law, INSOL International, and International Bar Association (Committee J).

39. The MLST is available at http://www.ebrd.org/english/st.htm.

40. Although the substratum is primarily derived from Roman-Germanic law, the legal cultures of these countries were subject to continental influences (scholarly and statutory) that were sometimes French, sometimes German, sometimes Italian and Austrian.

41. However, the MLST was most influenced by UCC Article 9.

42. It should be noted that article 2 MLST excludes charges by a natural person other than as part of his or her business activity, although the commentary to such article provides that nonbusiness activities could be covered if a jurisdiction has adequate consumer protection legislation.

43. This is based upon criteria set by J.A. Spanogle, *Proposed Polish Charges Act* (1992), cited in ADB 2000b.

REFERENCES

ADB (Asian Development Bank). 2000a. "The Need for an Integrated Approach to Secured Transactions and Insolvency Law Reforms." *Law and Policy Reform at the ADB* Vol. I, 2000 Edition. At http://www.adb.org/Documents/others/Law_ADB/lpr_2000_1.asp?p=lawdevt.

—————. 2000b. "Secured Transactions Law Reform in Asia: Unleashing the Potential of Collateral." *Law and Policy Reform at the ADB* Vol. II, 2000 Edition. At http://www.adb.org/Documents/others/Law_ADB/lpr_2000_2.asp?p=lawdevt.

Ajani, G. 1995. "By Change and Prestige: Legal Transplants in Russia and Eastern Europe." *The American Journal of Comparative Law* 43: 93–117.

BIS (Bank for International Settlements). 2001. *Collateral in Wholesale Financial Markets: Recent Trends, Risk Management and Market Dynamics*, Washington, D.C.

EBRD (European Bank for Reconstruction and Development). 1994. *Model Law on Secured Transactions*. At http://www.ebrd.org/english/st.htm.

Fairgrieve, D., and M. Andenas. 2000. "Securing Progress in Collateral Law Reform: The EBRD's Regional Survey of Secured Transaction Laws." *EBRD, Law in Transition (Autumn 2000), Focus on Secured Transactions*. London: EBRD.

Feldbrugge, F.J.M. 1995. "The New Civil Code of the Russian Federation." *Review of Central and East European Law* 21: 237–243.

Fleisig, H. 1995a. "The Power of Collateral: How Problems in Securing Transactions Limit Private Credit for Movable Property." *World Bank Viewpoint*, Note 43. Washington, D.C.

———. 1995b. "The Right to Borrow: Legal and Regulatory Barriers that Limit Access to Credit by Small Firms and Businesses." *World Bank Viewpoint*, Note 44. Washington, D.C.

———. 1998. "Economic Functions of Security in a Market Economy." In J.J. Norton and M. Andenas, eds., *Emerging Financial Markets and Secured Transactions*. London: Kluwer Law International.

Kozyr, O.M. 1999. "The Legal Treatment of Immovables under the Civil Code of the Russian Federation." *McGill Law Journal*, 44: 327.

Makovsky, A.L. 1997. "Preface to the English Translation of the Civil Code." *The Civil Code of the Russian Federation, Parts 1 and 2*. Moscow: International Centre for Financial and Economic Development.

Simpson, J., and J. Menze. 2000. "Ten Years of Secured Transaction Reform." *EBRD, Law in Transition (Autumn 2000), Focus on Secured Transactions*. London.

Simpson, J.L. and J.-H. M. Röver. 1998. "General Principles of a Modern Secured Transactions Law." In J.J. Norton and M. Andenas, eds., *Emerging Financial Markets and Secured Transactions*. London: Kluwer Law International.

———. 1998. "EBRD Model Law on Secured Transactions. A Response to Comments by John A. Spanogle." (September). Washington, D.C.: World Bank.

U.N. (United Nations). 2000. *Security Interests: Current Activities and Possible Future Work*. United Nations Commission on International Trade Law, Report of the Secretary-General (A/CN.9/475). New York: United Nations.

Vitrianskii, V.V. 1994. "Contract as a Means for Regulating Market Relations: The Draft Civil Code (First Part) of the Russian Federation." 20 *Review of Central and East European Law* 6: 649–656.

Working Group on International Financial Crises. 1998. *Report*. Submitted to Managing Director, IMF. (October 5, 1998). Washington, D.C.

World Bank. 1994. "How Legal Restrictions on Collateral Limit Access to Credit in Bolivia." Report No. 13873-BO. Washington, D.C.

———. 1997. "Peru: How Problems in the Framework for Secured Transactions Limit Access to Credit." Report 15696-PE. Washington, D.C.

———. 2001. *Principles and Guidelines for Effective Insolvency and Creditor Rights Systems*. At http://www.worldbank.org/gild.

Zerev, A. 1998. "Security Issues under Russian Law." In J.J. Norton and M. Andenas, eds., *Emerging Financial Markets and Secured Transactions*. London: Kluwer Law International.

CHAPTER 3

Framework for Corporate Insolvency

THE ROLE AND FUNCTION OF INSOLVENCY SYSTEMS IN MARKET ECONOMIES

Insolvency systems, like general systems for debt recovery and enforcement, stabilize commercial relationships by enabling market participants to more accurately price, manage, and control the risks of default and corporate failure. Where general enforcement systems (creditor rights) provide a vehicle for resolving individual disputes between creditors and debtors, insolvency procedures offer a means for collective resolutions when performance failures raise questions about an enterprise's viability. An insolvency system can therefore play a vital role in supporting commercial and market confidence and stabilizing the financial system, serving as a disciplinary mechanism both for the financial and the corporate sector. An effective insolvency process encourages prudent lending and a sound credit culture by

1. Establishing a mechanism (such as rehabilitation) for the financial restructuring of firms whose going-concern value exceeds their liquidation value, thus preserving both value and employment.
2. Providing an orderly exit mechanism for failed enterprises, ending unproductive uses of business assets and transferring them to more efficient market participants (through liquidation).
3. Providing a final and equitable debt collection mechanism for creditors.
4. Improving the enforcement of creditor rights to expand credit flows.

Insolvency systems stabilize commercial expectations and enable lenders to better manage financial risk. The evaluation of Russia's insolvency systems cannot be separated from the assessment of the treatment of rights of debtors and creditors generally. Insolvency law affects parties and interests at every level of a society, in almost every context and in a variety of ways—some of them subtle and indirect. There are important connections between laws governing debtor–creditor relationships and those regulating insolvency. The efficiency and effectiveness of the procedures for individual enforcement by creditors can have a vital bearing on the approach to insolvency procedures with respect to the creditors' debtors. For example, stringent enforcement of individual debts can be balanced by the availability of insolvency proceedings to assist companies in temporary difficulty. On the other hand, insolvency law should limit adjustments of rights and interests previously established outside insolvency so as to maintain legitimate pre-existing expectations. Prominent among these expectations is the ability of various types of security to remain effective relative to the encumbered assets, despite the commencement of formal insolvency proceedings against a debtor.

The existence or perception of weak creditor rights influences a creditor's approach to all stages of a commercial relationship. Conversely, creditors who perceive that insolvency will reinforce their economic rights will exploit the process to their advantage. An insolvency law that is too difficult for creditors to invoke or that too much favors debtors will tend to reduce the availability of credit and raise its cost, while an insolvency law that is too easy to invoke or too harsh is subject to creditor abuse. The Russian insolvency practice has, to an extent, been vulnerable to both of these problems. The stability of the overall credit culture among financial institutions can likewise be undermined by imbalances in the debtor–creditor relationship.

Effective enforcement and insolvency systems balance incentives and disincentives to encourage responsible corporate behavior. An effective system for enforcing creditor rights and managing business insolvency encourages high standards of corporate governance, including financial discipline. In this way, important social objectives are advanced—including the maintenance of public confidence in the corporate and financial sectors.

Prior to insolvency, the behavior of managers is governed by general corporate law, but this is superseded by insolvency law at the point of insolvency or when insolvency is declared. Under general corporate law, incompetent or negligent managers may be sanctioned or divested of their duties under both nonbankruptcy and bankruptcy procedures, such as through the appointment of a receiver, bankruptcy administrator, or trustee. Under the more exacting provisions of insolvency law, conduct and transactions that occurred before the start of formal insolvency proceedings (in some cases, several years before) can be reexamined in light of what subsequently transpired. Not only may certain transactions be impeachable (even at the expense of disrupting commercial certainty), but managers may be held personally responsible for part of the company's losses. In serious cases, managers may be subject to criminal liability and may be barred from managing companies for a prescribed period. These sanctions—whose elements and operation vary considerably from system to system—supply a necessary backbone to the proposition that the limited liability and greater access to credit enjoyed by companies be balanced by corresponding responsibilities, imposed to maintain public confidence in the credit culture in which companies operate.

Insolvency systems provide an efficient exit mechanism for unprofitable businesses and help rehabilitate viable ones. Insolvency procedures are a way of dealing with the casualties of market competition. When businesses are incapable of competing profitably, the logical move is to provide a means for their voluntary dissolution or exit from the market. Company laws often contain voluntary exit procedures, but such procedures are generally accessible only for solvent companies that can repay their debts from assets liquidated in the windup of the business. These laws should coexist alongside formal insolvency procedures. When an enterprise cannot repay its obligations as they come due, or it cannot raise enough money from asset sales to repay all its obligations, assumptions about enterprise activity, governance, and ownership change; and when a distressed or insolvent enterprise is unable to uphold commercial agreements, market confidence falls. This situation should be resolved through a collective procedure that ensures prompt resolution and maximum recovery by creditors. This procedure must be flexible enough to provide a range of options, including rehabilitation for viable enterprises and liquidation for nonviable enterprises.

Liquidation can occur by selling the business as a going concern, in productive units, or through the more conventional sale of assets. Alternatives to outright liquidation may vary in terms of formality and the degree of involvement of the courts and other official agencies, but they share the common goal of giving the debtor an opportunity to exit from relative (or even absolute) insolvency and to enjoy the prospect of a more balanced existence for the future. For the honest casualties of competition, then, the insolvency process provides a means for enterprise rehabilitation or an exit mechanism to quickly transfer assets and businesses to more efficient market participants. Unlike the insolvency of a bank, where the prospects of rehabilitation are constrained by policies promoting depositor confidence, policies supporting corporate rehabilitation are predicated on preserving jobs and maximizing enterprise value—which is higher if the enterprise is a going concern rather than one in liquidation. Rehabilitation also avoids the broader knock-on effect of insolvency; that is, it minimizes the impact on creditors who rely on the enterprise as a source of business and revenue.

OVERVIEW OF RUSSIAN CORPORATE INSOLVENCY PRACTICE

The 1992 Bankruptcy Law

Russia's first insolvency law following its transition to a market economy—the *Law on Insolvency (Bankruptcy) of Enterprises*—was enacted in 1992 and proved to be completely ineffectual.[1] As in the early stages of transition in most of the other Central and Eastern European countries, early efforts at developing an insolvency system proved ineffective and inefficient, with laws failing to properly take account of capacity and regulatory shortcomings. The 1992 Russian Bankruptcy Law also suffered from a number of defects that distorted incentives and disincentives.[2] The law contained an ineffective trigger for commencing proceedings based on the balance sheet approach (as opposed to a liquidity or cash flow test). According to one authority on Russian insolvency law, commercial players unable to pay their debts were allowed to continue in operation, while other top managers and enterprises able to pay debts were emboldened not to do so, using surplus funds for personal gain. The system invited abuse and bad-faith filings.[3] To make matters worse, courts were obliged to evaluate the debtor's assets and liabilities to determine balance sheet insolvency—a procedure that was extremely time consuming and prone to arbitrary decision-making. Courts often refused to apply a liquidity (or cash flow) test, notwithstanding the failure of the enterprise to pay its debts.[4] Accounting practices that were out of step with international accounting standards and unreliable data and information combined to produce skewed and unpredictable results that could be easily manipulated.

The 1992 Bankruptcy Law also failed to distinguish between the financial status of enterprises (whether no-asset or potentially viable) or between the distinct kinds of legal entities or persons seeking bankruptcy. It instead treated all debtors the same, applying the same complex procedures to each, whether a legal person, an individual entrepreneur, a major enterprise, or an intermediary holding company with no assets, a commercial or peasant (farm) enterprise, or an industrial entity or bank.[5] Gaps in the law were in part the result of drawing on aspects of different legal systems and in part the adoption of many incoherent legal acts. These acts ultimately numbered more than 30 Edicts of the President of the Russian Federation, Resolutions of Government, and departmental regulatory acts, which were often incoherent and at times contradictory.[6]

The 1998 Bankruptcy Law

To rectify the mistakes of the 1992 Bankruptcy Law, work on a new insolvency law began in 1995. This eventually led to Federal Law No 6-FZ of January 8, 1998, *On Insolvency (Bankruptcy)* (called the 1998 Bankruptcy Law), which became effective in March 1999. The new law is also supported by Resolution No. 478 establishing procedures that increase the efficiency of the application process.[7]

The 1998 Bankruptcy Law is a substantial improvement over its predecessor: it simplifies rules and procedures; invests exclusive jurisdiction in the arbitration (*arbitrazh*) courts; encompasses all forms of business entities; allows creditors (including secured creditors) to initiate proceedings; and by permitting such mechanisms as observation proceedings, external management, and amicable settlements, it provides a more flexible and balanced approach to support rehabilitation. Unlike the 1992 law, the 1998 Bankruptcy Law also contains special provisions for dealing with different entities, rather than applying the one-size-fits-all approach. It uses a unitary system, similar to that of the new German insolvency law, allowing for observation and evaluation of a business's prospects before deciding whether to liquidate assets or rehabilitate the enterprise.

The new law adopts a novel but problematic approach to the treatment of claims of secured creditors. The balance struck is intended to protect the payment expectations of secured creditors, and thereby encourage secured lending, while at the same time facilitating enterprise rehabilitation. To do this, assets of secured creditors are now brought within the estate and made subject to the proceedings, and the liens of secured creditors are stripped from the collateral to allow sale of pledged assets without restraint.[8] In exchange, the claims of secured creditors are aggregated in the third category for payment and are satisfied pro rata from the sales proceeds from all assets sold.[9] The approach is novel in that it reduces all secured creditors to the same level, irrespective of the quality of the collateral securing their debt, and then seeks to protect them by affording a higher priority on distribution.

On the surface this approach seems logical, but it raises a number of issues that could inhibit the creation of market confidence in secured lending practices. First, the approach renders meaningless the use of collateral in bankruptcy, increasing the risk to creditors of nonperformance and at the same time making that risk more difficult to measure and manage. For better-secured creditors, bankruptcy is not strategically useful. Such creditors would prefer instead to seek nonbankruptcy foreclosure or seizure of property. For less secured creditors, there is an incentive to use bankruptcy as a threat to other creditors (rather than to the debtor) in an attempt to improve their position, at the expense of such creditors, should bankruptcy subsequently occur.

Second, the approach could potentially undermine the significance of registration systems. Such systems encourage parties to take prompt action to record their security interests or to otherwise face the subordination of their claims to earlier-recorded interests—even though these may have been obtained later in time. The first-in-time, first-in-right concept is a cornerstone of registration systems, but is completely eroded by the treatment of secured creditors under the 1998 Bankruptcy Law. Finally, the approach is not a fair exchange for the bargained-for risk. The right to repayment of a secured creditor is effectively subordinated, and to the extent insufficient assets exist, such creditors must give up their collateral or value to administrative, personal injury, employee, and royalty claims.

The proposed treatment of secured creditors is also potentially prejudicial to unsecured creditors. Some secured creditors undoubtedly will be only partially secured, meaning their collateral is worth less than the amount of their claims. Giving partially secured creditors priority over unsecured creditors, with respect to the unsecured portion of the partially secured creditor's claim, violates a cardinal principle of bankruptcy known as the *pari passu* principle, which holds that similar creditors should be treated the same in bankruptcy. While a secured creditor is clearly not the same as an unsecured creditor, an "undersecured" creditor is a hybrid of both; that is, this creditor is secured to the extent of the value of the collateral or pledged assets and unsecured for any claim or debt that exceeds the collateral's value. To give full payment to a partially secured creditor would be to give funds to that creditor that should rightfully be distributed to the state and unsecured creditors. One problem with this result is that it distorts normal commercial relations and lending practices by rewarding less diligent creditors and penalizing other similarly situated parties. Similarly, it promotes inefficiency in management practices by encouraging management to take on debt well in excess of asset values. Overleveraged or heavily leveraged companies are unable to compete effectively (Altman 1993).[10] And even for unsecured creditors, the result could lead to higher or distorted pricing practices to avoid increased and uncertain repayment risk.

Notwithstanding the significant improvements that the 1998 Bankruptcy Law has introduced to the system, the regulatory void has created a fertile environment for abuse, such as hostile management buyouts or takeovers of otherwise viable enterprises (primarily in the lucrative oil and gas and metals industries).[11] In addition, some commentators maintain that distortions in use among particular industries is the result of improper collusion among companies and local officials, while in other cases management may collude with phantom creditors and external managers to seize control of or to channel assets to third-party insiders or affiliated companies.[12] And while the new system provides a measure of discretion for judges—a mark of a more mature system—some have argued that discretion can be (and likely is being) abused where there is political pressure on judges to avoid liquidation of businesses or where there is an inclination to salvage an enterprise (and jobs) despite the inability of the enterprise to be returned to viability.[13]

Recent Developments

On March 12, 2001, the Constitutional Court of the Russian Federation issued Resolution No. 4-II on the constitutionality of certain sections of the Bankruptcy Law.[14] Various provisions of the Bankruptcy Law were invalidated by this decision, resulting in greater procedural protection of creditors and debtors in the bankruptcy process and the increased accountability of the *arbitrazh* courts.[15] The Constitutional Court made the following findings about the constitutionality of the Bankruptcy Law:
 1. Provisions restricting the possibility of appealing determinations issued by *arbitrazh* courts on disputes between creditors and debtors are invalid. These provisions were deemed to contravene the constitutional right to judicial protection. The effect of this determination is that judicial review of such decisions is immediately allowed until the legislature provides new rules on the subject.
 2. Provisions requiring that a debtor be placed under supervision from the moment a petition for the debtor's bankruptcy is filed with an *arbitrazh* court are also inconsistent with the constitutional right to

judicial protection, and are therefore invalid. These rules allowed the debtor to be placed under supervision solely on the basis of an application of the petitioning creditor, without a court hearing or a summoning of the parties. This meant that courts could not effectively control the bankruptcy procedure and ensure procedural fairness. Now the issue of placing the debtor under supervision may only be decided after the debtor has presented its explanations and objections. Also debtors now have a right to appeal this determination to a higher court.

These findings are a positive step in reducing the power of individual judges over the bankruptcy process. Previously the *arbitrazh* court summarily determined a broad range of matters, including the introduction of supervision, the amount of monetary obligations, creditor and employee complaints about the external manager, and reductions or extensions of the period of external management. Some of these issues are legitimate areas for the *arbitrazh* court to exercise discretion, as they involve issues of a more administrative nature. Conversely, the ability of creditors and parties to exercise rights of appeal invariably will lead to delays in the process. This is an area that should be closely monitored and reviewed to find ways of promoting efficiency without sacrificing or undermining constitutional rights.

Statistical Performance of the Insolvency System

Under the 1992 Bankruptcy Law, although instances of insolvency were systemic, the courts considered only about 100 cases in the first year. This gradually increased over a five-year period to more than 4,300 cases in 1997, for a total of approximately 8,386 cases. Over this period, approximately 46 percent of cases were directed to liquidation (about 3,854 cases), and roughly 16 percent (some 1,398 cases) were external manager proceedings. The ratio of liquidation cases to external management proceedings during 1995–97 was three to one. While this may suggest an increasing trend toward the use of externally managed proceedings, possibly with a view to salvaging the business, there is no indication that these proceedings resulted in effective operational restructurings or led to more efficient use of assets and businesses by market players.

In the three years since the introduction of the 1998 Bankruptcy Law, there has been a steadily increasing trend in the use of the insolvency system, but with proportionately fewer proceedings in which an external manager is appointed. In 1999, only 11 percent of cases were external management proceedings, and in 2000, the number dwindled to 7

Table 3.1 Number of Bankruptcy Cases

Type of proceedings	1993	1994	1995	1996	1997	1998	1999	2000
Claims submitted	n/a	n/a	n/a	n/a	n/a	12,781	15,583	21,034
Proceedings initiated	100±	240	1,108	2,618	4,320	8,337	13,543	18,057
Liquidation ordered	50	n/a	469	1,035	2,200	4,747	10,247	16,601
External mgmt. ordered	n/a	n/a	135	413	850	1,041	1,669	1,544
Total cases completed	n/a	n/a	n/a	n/a	n/a			10,504
Bankruptcy cases								7,460
Returned to solvency								67
Out-of-court settlements								654

percent. Liquidation cases, in contrast, accounted for 60 percent of total cases in 1998 and 76 percent in 1999, reflecting a substantial increase. In 2000, total new cases initiated reached about 18,057, a more than 116 percent increase over 1998. Again, without access to the underlying outcomes for proceedings, it is difficult to say whether the results led to a more efficient use of the insolvency system in transferring assets and businesses to market players or in successfully restructuring businesses. The numbers nonetheless indicate a continuing increase in the use of bankruptcy proceedings and an apparently greater efficiency in handling cases; these facts are no doubt attributable to the better law and procedures adopted in 1998. Table 3.1 contains data for insolvency, including financial sector, from 1993 through 2000.

LEGAL FRAMEWORK FOR CORPORATE INSOLVENCY

Access and Applicability of Bankruptcy Law

The Bankruptcy Law applies broadly to the following entities: (a) commercial entities (except for wholly state-owned enterprises), (b) noncommercial entities (except those that operate in the form of consumer cooperatives, charitable foundations, or funds), (c) citizens (including those registered as individual entrepreneurs), and (d) banks and credit organizations (also regulated separately by the bank insolvency law, as discussed below).[16] The law contains special rules governing the bankruptcy of (a) town-forming organizations, (b) agricultural organizations, (c) insurance organizations, (d) bank and credit organizations, (e) professional participants in the securities market, (f) citizens, (g) individual entrepreneurs, and (h) farm enterprises. Town-forming organizations and banks/credit organizations merit special attention.

Town-forming organizations. Town-forming organizations are defined as legal entities whose employees constitute at least half of a populated locality or that employ more than 5,000 people.[17] Special provisions relating to such organizations include

1. The local government is deemed to be a party to the case, may make a petition for external management, and may extend the period for external management.
2. Various governmental bodies may guarantee the debtor's obligations.
3. Various mandatory conditions of liquidation, such as preservation of jobs, are imposed.
4. The period permitted for restructuring is extended to 10 years.

Banks and other credit organizations. The bankruptcy of banks and other credit organizations is regulated by a separate regime in addition to the general Bankruptcy Law. The other important pieces of legislation here are Federal Law No. 40-FZ, *On Bankruptcy of Credit Organizations,* dated 25 February 1999 (Bank Bankruptcy Law), and Federal Law No. 144-FZ, *On Restructuring of Credit Organizations,* dated July 8, 1999 (Bank Restructuring Law). Below is a brief overview of the processes involved when undergoing bankruptcy and restructuring processes.

Indicia of bankruptcy. Bankruptcy is defined as the inability of a debtor to pay a creditor's monetary claim or to make an obligatory payment in full where such obligation has been outstanding for at least three months after the due date.[18] If the debtor is an individual, it is also necessary that the total amount of his liability should exceed the total value of property owned.[19]

Filing a bankruptcy petition. A bankruptcy petition may be filed with an *arbitrazh* court located in the region or city in which the debtor is located. Petitions can be either voluntary (filed by the debtor) or involuntary (creditor initiated). In voluntary liquidations, the debtor may make an application for the recognition of itself as bankrupt whenever the indicia of bankruptcy are present, and even absent the indicia of bankruptcy where the circumstances indicate that the debtor will be unable to perform monetary obligations or an obligation to make compulsory payments within the established time period.[20] Furthermore, the debtor's executive or an individual entrepreneur is obliged to file a debtor's application within one month of the emergence of one of the following circumstances:

1. The payment of the claim of one or more creditors may result in the company's inability to fulfill its obligations to other creditors.
2. The shareholders or board of directors resolve to liquidate the company.[21]

An entity's executive members personally suffer heavy penalties for failing to meet obligations to creditors. These penalties include:

1. Joint and several liabilities for the debtor's obligations to creditors that arose after the mandatory time for filing
2. Deprivation of the right to occupy management positions or to conduct business activities relating to the management of legal entities
3. Criminal penalties.[22]

The following persons may file a petition to commence an involuntary liquidation, having the debtor declared bankrupt:

1. Creditor or group of creditors (including foreign persons)
2. Tax authorities (or other authorized governmental bodies)
3. The public prosecutor
4. The debtor.[23]

The *arbitrazh* court must accept an application for the recognition of the debtor as bankrupt if the aggregate claims against the debtor amount to at least 500 times the minimum wage rate (equivalent to about US$5,000) if the debtor is a legal entity, or at least 100 times the minimum wage rate (about US$1,000) if the debtor is a citizen.[24]

Preventive measures. The Bankruptcy Law contains provisions aimed at preventing the bankruptcy of organizations. A duty is imposed upon founders or participants of a legal entity debtor and property owners of a debtor that is a unitary enterprise to take timely measures directed toward the financial recovery of the debtor.[25] In addition, criminal and civil penalties are imposed upon debtors and their executive for "fictional" bankruptcy. These penalties apply where the debtor has the ability to satisfy creditors' claims in full but its executives send the firm into bankruptcy anyway, presumably to obtain the firm's assets.[26] While such provisions in theory should be an incentive for good corporate behavior or a disincentive to misconduct, in reality they appear to have little or no impact on corporate behavior, because these provisions are not routinely, if at all, enforced.

Bankruptcy Procedures

In examining a bankruptcy case concerning a legal entity, the following bankruptcy procedures apply:

1. *Observation proceedings.* Following the court's ruling accepting an application of recognition of a debtor as bankrupt, the court will appoint a temporary administrator to supervise the operations of the company.[27] The temporary administrator will notify creditors of the liquidation, supervise the actions of the company's management, analyze the financial condition of the company, determine the amount of creditors' claims, and call the first creditors meeting.[28]

   Proprietary claims against the debtor may be presented only in compliance with procedures established in the Bankruptcy Law, and all proceedings of cases associated with the recovery of monetary resources and other property from the debtor must be suspended. To enforce these measures, the court's ruling accepting an application for the recognition of the debtor as bankrupt shall be sent to banks and other credit organizations with which the debtor has bank account agreements.[29] The debtor is prohibited from executing transactions transferring or disposing of immovable property and adopting various decisions, such as reorganization or payment of dividends, without the consent of the temporary administrator.[30] In addition, the court has the right to remove the debtor's executive if it does not take steps to ensure the conservation of the debtor's property or if it hinders the temporary administrator in the performance of his duties.[31]

   An important role of the temporary administrator is the calling of the first creditors' meeting. Creditors, tax authorities, other authorized bodies whose claims have been established by the *arbitrazh* court, and employee representatives have the right to attend these meetings, but creditors alone have voting rights.[32] The first creditors' meeting elects a creditors' committee and makes a decision as to whether to petition the *arbitrazh* court to institute external management or to commence competitive proceedings. However, the *arbitrazh* court has the right to override any such petition and make its own determination.[33]

2. *External management.* External management may be instituted for no longer than 12 months, with the possibility of being extended to 18 months. The institution of external management proceeds with the following events:
   - The creditors' meeting elects an external manager (although the *arbitrazh* court may override this selection[34]).
   - The debtor's executive is removed and power over management of the debtor's business affairs is assigned to the external manager.

- The powers of the debtor's executive are transferred to the external manager.
- The debtor's property may be seized and other limitations imposed to protect the debtor's assets.
- A moratorium is imposed on the satisfaction of creditor claims.[35]

The external manager has various powers and rights, including the right to

- Take measures to recover debts to the debtor.[36]
- Dispose of the debtor's property.[37]
- Conclude an amicable agreement on behalf of the debtor.[38]
- Refuse to perform contracts of the debtor for a period of three months after the institution of external management.[39]
- In certain circumstances, invalidate transactions executed by the debtor before the institution of external management.[40]

The creditors' meeting and committee remain involved in the process. The creditors' meeting must approve the external management plan[41] as well as any major transactions of the debtor.[42] (The external management plan must provide measures for the restoration of the debtor's solvency, which may include a sale of the enterprise.) The creditors' meeting may also remove the external manager and file a petition with the *arbitrazh* court for recognition of the debtor as bankrupt and commencement of competitive proceedings (liquidation).[43]

3. *Competitive proceedings.* The *arbitrazh* court's adoption of a decision recognizing the debtor as bankrupt entails the commencement of competitive proceedings, the effects of which are the following:
    - All monetary obligations and deferred compulsory payments of the debtor are considered due.
    - All previous seizures of the debtor's property and other restrictions on the disposal of the debtor's property shall be lifted.
    - The management bodies of the debtor are removed from their duties if such removal has not already taken place.
    - The *arbitrazh* court appoints a competitive proceedings manager.
    - A notice of recognition of the debtor as bankrupt and of the commencement of competitive proceedings is published.[44]

The competitive proceedings manager has powers and duties similar to those of the external manager. In addition, the competitive proceedings manager shall conduct an inventory and valuation of the debtor's property and then sell it by open tender. Creditors' claims will then be settled in accordance with the priorities described below.

4. *Amicable agreement.* The debtor and creditors have the right to conclude an amicable agreement at any stage of the *arbitrazh* court's consideration of the case,[45] subject to the approval of the court. However, any such agreement may only be concluded after the claims of first- and second-priority creditors have been settled. The *arbitrazh* court's approval of an amicable agreement is grounds for termination of proceedings on the bankruptcy case and a lifting of the moratorium on the satisfaction of creditors' claims.

5. *Accelerated bankruptcy procedures.* An alternative procedure was introduced by the Decision of the Government of the Russian Federation No. 476 of May 22, 1998, *On Measures to Increase Efficiency of Applying Bankruptcy Procedures.* Pursuant to this decree, the debtor's creditors may consolidate their claims and be represented by the Federal Service of Russia for Insolvency and Financial Rehabilitation, an agency of the Russian government. The service may vote at the creditors' meeting to proceed directly to external management and use accelerated procedures. Under these accelerated procedures the debtor's business is subject to reorganization, including the establishment of a new joint stock company that will acquire the debtor's assets and retain the company's jobs. Stock in the new company is sold, and proceeds from the sale are used to pay the debtor's debts. If proceeds from the sale of stock are insufficient to satisfy all creditors' claims, the arbitration manager files an application with the *arbitrazh* court to terminate the external management, rule the debtor bankrupt, and institute disposal proceedings.

   This accelerated procedure is only useful where the sale of stock in the joint stock company generates sufficient funds to pay off all creditors. This would only happen when the debtor's assets are greater than its liabilities; since for most debtors this is not the case, this procedure has limited application.

6. *Voidable transactions.* Once the *arbitrazh* court accepts a petition to initiate bankruptcy proceedings, the following transactions may be invalidated by the court upon the request of the temporary administrator or creditor:
   - Transactions entered into by the debtor with an interested party, if such transactions would cause losses to other creditors
   - Transactions entered into by the debtor company after, or six months prior to, the initiation of bankruptcy proceedings, if such transactions caused preferential payments to certain creditors to the disadvantage of other creditors

- Transactions involving a return of equity to a shareholder entered into by the debtor after the initiation of bankruptcy proceedings, or in the six months prior to proceedings.[46]
7. *Creditors' claims*. Individual creditors may not directly pursue any of their own remedies. They must act through the creditors' meetings. Creditors' claims may be submitted at any stage of the bankruptcy process by filing a notice with the debtor company and with the *arbitrazh* court. Unless contested by the debtor within seven days, the amount of the filed claim will be entered into the register of creditors' claims. If the debtor contests the creditor's claim, the creditor will need to appeal to the *arbitrazh* court.[47]

 In order to be allowed to participate in the first creditors' meeting, the claims must be submitted within one month of the receipt of notification of the proceedings from the temporary administrator. Also, in order to be included in one of the five established priorities of creditors' claims, a claim must be filed before the date of closure by the temporary administrator of the register of creditors' claims. If a claim is filed after this date it will only be satisfied after all other priority creditors are paid.
8. *Priorities*. Court expenses, the administrator's remuneration, the current utility payments of the debtor, and creditors' claims that arose after the initiation of bankruptcy proceedings take first priority and must be satisfied before other claims can be addressed. All other claims fall into one of five categories. Claims at each level must be satisfied in full before claims at the next level of priority are considered. These categories are
   - Personal injury claims
   - Severance, salary payments, and remunerations under royalty agreements
   - Claims of secured creditors
   - Governmental claims (i.e., tax and social security payments)
   - All other creditors' claims.[48]

 Creditors' claims that are unsatisfied due to the insufficiency of the debtor's property are considered discharged.[49]

IMPLEMENTATION OF THE INSOLVENCY REGIME

A strong institutional and regulatory framework is crucial to an effective insolvency system. The framework encompasses three main elements: (1) the various institutions with responsibility for and jurisdiction over insolvency proceedings; (2) the operational system through which cases and decisions are processed; and (3) the fundamental requirements needed to preserve the integrity of these institutions, recognizing that the integrity of the insolvency system is the linchpin for its success or failure.

Institutional Framework (the *Arbitrazh* Court)

The role, responsibility, organization, and services of the governing judicial institution (in Russia, the *arbitrazh* court) are central to an effective, efficient, and fair insolvency process. A well-functioning and predictable insolvency process provides for the quick disposition of insolvency cases, preserving assets and maximizing their value. Russia has no separate specialized bankruptcy courts. Bankruptcy cases are considered by the *arbitrazh* courts in accordance with the rules established by the *Code of* Arbitrazh *Procedure of the Russian Federation,* dated May 5, 1995 (Code). Bankruptcy cases are not heard by specialized bankruptcy courts but by regional *arbitrazh* courts, whose judges require no special bankruptcy training. The wide discretionary powers given to judges of the *arbitrazh* courts have been criticized as being open to abuse and corrupt influences. In addition, the lack of federal financing of *arbitrazh* courts and the distance—both political and physical—from the federal center make *arbitrazh* courts highly dependent on regional politics.[50] These problems have the potential to undermine the bankruptcy regime.

Russia has endeavored to strengthen its capacity to handle insolvency cases by having specially trained bankruptcy judges. In some countries, judges are specialized and have exclusive responsibility for insolvency proceedings. In others, judges may have wider jurisdictional authority. Given the specialized nature of enterprise insolvency and the issues that arise in bankruptcy proceedings, there is significant value in having independent, specialized commercial and bankruptcy courts (where possible) or judges who have been specially trained in insolvency matters within the commercial courts. The insolvency process is highly complex and demands a specific understanding of and familiarity with financial and business arrangements and with commerce and finance standards and practices. Specialization ensures greater competence and higher-quality decision-making, quickens the pace of proceedings and decision-making, and promotes consistent decision-making on similar issues and in similar situations. In addition, specialization tends to decrease unnecessary litigation by increasing predictability in the outcome of decisions. Where there is little or fragmented insolvency expertise in the judiciary and decisions are inconsistent, parties are often tempted to litigate in the hope of gaining a different or novel decision. The same is also true of appeals courts that have no expertise in insolvency.

Given the numerous allegations of collusion and corruption in the process, procedures should be adopted and measures taken in Russia to ensure that the courts are free of conflicts of interest, bias, and lapses in judicial ethics, objectivity, and impartiality. Clear legal rules should establish remedies to address improprieties, including complaint and investigation procedures. Written standards, guidelines, advisory opinions, complaint and investigation procedures, and tools to redress impropriety should all be vested in an independent and respected judicial or ancillary authority. The court, including judges and court employees, must meet these standards and be perceived as doing so by interested parties and the public alike. Currently, however, Russia has not yet developed and does not enforce such investigative and supervisory procedures.

Regulatory Framework

There are enormous gaps in Russia's regulatory framework, and these threaten to undermine the insolvency process. This is perhaps the single most important area for future capacity building if the system is to mature and play the role envisioned for an insolvency system. An insolvency system should provide firm and public rules and regulations to prevent the corruption and exertion of undue influence that undermine public confidence in the system. Preferably an independent but accountable department, committee, or body should be responsible for establishing, monitoring, and enforcing standards of conduct for judges and other participants. Maintaining ethical and professional standards for judges and, where appropriate, other court employees is also essential for instilling public confidence in the bankruptcy court. Allegations of fraud and other criminal conduct related to bankruptcy should be investigated and redressed promptly, firmly, and uniformly by an authority vested with the power to investigate and take appropriate measures. Misconduct short of criminal conduct also should be addressed promptly by the bankruptcy court or another independent agency invested with the power to investigate and take appropriate measures, including imposing sanctions.

Russian Federation Federal Service on Financial Rehabilitation and Bankruptcy (FSFR). The FSFR serves as the primary regulatory body for the insolvency process. As of 2001, the FSFR comprised a main headquarters in Moscow, 13 interregional territorial agencies, and 2 territorial agencies; it employed more than 900 employees. Ninety percent of its employees are graduates of higher learning institutions; approximately 11 percent have a second higher education degree, and roughly 6 percent hold a Ph.D. The primary duties of the FSFR include the development of pretrial procedures, the analysis of financial and economic conditions of enterprises that are economically and socially vital to the economy, and the initiation of proceedings to collect state debt or rehabilitate/restructure vital enterprises. Additional duties include the training, licensing, and supervision of the activities of arbitration receivers, external managers, and various experts.

Training of arbitration receivers. In 2000, a key objective of the FSFR was to provide the *arbitrazh* courts with an adequate number of licensed receivers, while adopting and implementing stiffer licensing requirements. In 2000, approximately 6,000 arbitration receivers were trained through a crisis managers' training program, as compared to 8,456 receivers in 1999. Two model training programs are used to train receivers for "first-tier" cases involving absent debtors, citizens, business people, and small enterprises, and "second-tier" cases involving citizens, business people, and medium-size enterprises. A new three-tier system has been launched to match categories of arbitration receivers, including those with respect to large enterprises, and a provision for upgrading of skills. To promote more widespread training, FSFR has accredited 74 educational establishments to conduct seminars on FSFR programs, and is now working on the development of a practical manual for receivers under a TACIS-funded technical assistance program.[51]

Licensing and license revocation of arbitration receivers. As of 2001, the FSFR had issued 12,238 arbitration receiver licenses, of which 5,168 were issued in 2000. Tier-one licenses constitute 81 percent of all licenses, with the remaining 19 percent being Tier-two licenses. Some 133 licenses (mainly Tier one) in total have been invalidated for various reasons, including failure to register in the capacity of an individual businessman, expired certificates following passing of exams, lack of requisite six-month minimal experience as a receiver, failure to publish data on bankruptcy proceedings, and violations in the election of the creditors' committee. During 2000, FSFR received 44 applications to revoke the licenses of receivers, which resulted in a revocation of 12 licenses.

Supervision of arbitration receivers. The FSFR is also responsible for supervising the activities of arbitration receivers to ensure compliance with license requirements. In 2000, the FSFR launched a supervisory system over activities of arbitration receivers.[52] Under this program, over 600 complaints against actions by receivers were examined. By 2001, a total of 1,137 complaints had been lodged, of which 614 were accepted for further review. The remainder were found to be without merit. In response to the complaints accepted for review, 232 warnings were issued to arbitration receivers, and 114 receivers had their licenses suspended or revoked. In the remaining cases, no violations were found after further review.

It is worth noting that employees of the FSFR also serve in the capacity of state arbitration receivers and are routinely appointed as receivers in cases. For example, 150 FSFR employees have been appointed as receivers in 808 cases, of which the vast majority concerned absentee debtors, and in 56 of the 112 cases concerning large, economically and socially vital enterprises.

Accreditation of experts. The FSFR has also been tasked with developing criteria for and accrediting various experts, including experts on financial condition and solvency (98), enterprise business plans (61), market value appraisals for enterprise assets (77), and actions of managers and receivers (30).[53] Expert opinions are relied upon as a source of independent information to assist the FSFR in its decision-making. There has been no indication of impropriety in this area, but the fact that the FSFR is a consumer of evaluations prepared by experts who are beholden to the FSFR for their accreditation raises the specter of a conflict of interest that could potentially cast some doubt over the objectivity and integrity of evaluations, i.e., evaluation results could be tailored to meet results perceived to be desired by FSFR. This is especially true given that an accreditation can be revoked. In 2000, expert evaluations were carried out to

- Establish signs of intentional or fictitious bankruptcies (388 cases)
- Identify signs of intentional or fictitious bankruptcies (156 cases)
- Review external receivership plans (456 cases)
- Review measures of bankruptcy proceedings (1,006 cases)
- Assess out-of-court settlements (158 cases).

Role in reviewing vital enterprises. As indicated above, one of the duties of the FSFR is the monitoring of the financial condition of the record-keeping and solvency of large, economically and socially vital enterprises. In 2000, there were 1,714 enterprises included on the list of vital enterprises. During the first three quarters of 2000, the FSFR conducted surveys of 1,529 vital enterprises (employing more than 7.2 million people), of which 242 were fully state-owned, 151 had a greater than 50 percent state ownership, and 217 had state ownership of 25–50 percent. The state held less than a 25 percent interest in the remaining 919 enterprises. Bankruptcy proceedings were instituted against 112 vital enterprises, in which 56 state arbitration receivers (FSFR employees) were appointed.

In some 5,000 other cases, the central and regional interagency balance commissions examined debts owed to the federal budget and state interbudgetary funds, recommending the commencement of bankruptcy proceedings in approximately 700 cases, debt restructuring in roughly 1,300 cases, and financial rehabilitation in about 150 cases. The actions taken resulted in repayments to the budget of approximately 133.5 billion rubles from 1998 to 2000.

ASSESSMENT OF KEY FEATURES OF THE BANKRUPTCY REGIME

At the outset of this section, it was noted that insolvency systems (together with nonbankruptcy enforcement procedures) play a vital role to promote commercial confidence in three significant areas: (1) stabilizing commercial expectations and fostering better financial risk management; (2) balancing incentives and disincentives for responsible corporate behavior; and (3) providing an efficient exit for business failures and a means for salvaging viable enterprises, and with them jobs and other commercial activities and relationships. It is essential to evaluate the implications of Russia's insolvency system in each of these areas.

Stabilizing Commercial Activity

The bankruptcy laws in Russia appear to be comprehensive, and for the most part they comply with international insolvency principles. However, the regime does not in many respects perform as it should, suggesting that there are major problems in its implementation rather than its content. The continuing lack of regulation and the potential for arbitrage in the system have continued to foster distrust of the process. For example, a number of reports have suggested that the system is susceptible to countless forms of manipulation that disenfranchise certain creditors, influence the membership and representation on creditors committees, disallow dividends or distributions to legitimate creditors, and allow fraudulent and illegitimate claims.[54] While the external manager was intended to provide for neutral representation, in fact a high degree of abuse was represented in regions outside Moscow, where incumbent management had prearranged with certain creditors to appoint external managers who would favor them. There have also been some general reports of collusion between judges and external managers. Some degree of abuse is current in all insolvency systems, but it tends to be at its worst in environments with ineffective or lax regulation. In Russia, most lenders still will choose not to use the insolvency system to recover debt, even in cases where the borrower's business is viable.

Inadequate Corporate Governance

There are several ways in which the insolvency system promotes good corporate behavior. First, it may impose liability for the failure of managers to respect the rights of creditors and when they continue to trade the business after insolvency. Laws imposing such liability diverge in the degree to which directors are sanctioned for inappropriate conduct, with the consequences ranging from a mere caution to criminal sanctions. The Russian system imposes personal liability on directors for irresponsible corporate behavior, but its provisions are minimal and ambiguous. For example, directors are obliged to file for bankruptcy when it emerges that the payment of the claim of one or more creditors may result in the company's inability to fulfill its obligations to other creditors. Often it will be unclear whether these circumstances have emerged, but more important, the law appears to have no teeth: there are no reported cases in which directors and officers have been held liable under these provisions of the law, despite the fact that there have been numerous reported accounts of abuse and wrongful trading.

A second way in which the law imposes discipline on management is through its ability to remove management from its place in the business or to displace owners of their control and ownership of the business when it is poorly managed and becomes insolvent. The provisions of the 1998 Bankruptcy Law allow creditors (including secured creditors) to petition for insolvency under reasonable access requirements,[55] with the prospect of removing the owners and former managers in favor of an external manager.

Finally, the bankruptcy trigger has been redefined to provide for a liquidity approach to determining insolvency, in place of the former balance sheet test.

In theory, the combination of these three features should result in an effective tool for disciplining managers. Reports of abuses of the appointment of external managers and of the treatment of creditors have, however, undermined confidence in the system and consequently also undermined the effectiveness of these tools.

A number of companies have taken advantage of low access criteria to effect hostile takeovers of valuable companies at an undervalue. One example involves the takeover of the Russian oil company, Sidanko. A rival company, TNK, acquired the debts of one of Sidanko's more valuable subsidiaries (Chernogorneft) from other creditors, in order to launch bankruptcy proceedings. TNK installed its own external manager, who plundered Chernogorneft, causing a huge increase in its debts despite a boom in oil prices. Chernogorneft, which had an output the previous year of US$1.2 billion, was ultimately auctioned off for only US$176 million (*The Economist* 1999).

In terms of management, there is no choice under the Bankruptcy Law but to remove the debtor's executive during external management procedures. No provision is made in the law for their involvement whatsoever. To get around this, and because of the insufficiency of accredited external managers, judges will often appoint the current manager as external manager, regardless of the law. Creditors' interests are clearly insufficiently protected in this process, with too much power being given to both the *arbitrazh* judge and the external administrator. A judge may override both the decision of creditors to liquidate or restructure the company and the creditors' selection of an external manager. The Sidanko case illustrates this point. In Sidanko, nearly all of the creditors voted to nominate an Arthur Andersen executive as external manager, yet the Moscow *Arbitrazh* judge handling the matter picked another candidate not backed by the creditors.

External managers often just ignore creditors' wishes. The court-appointed manager of the Svyavsky lumber company, for example, refused to follow creditors' instructions to sell the company's assets to investors led by Sweden's IKEA, which was prepared to pay US$7 million; instead, the manager sold the assets to a local company for US$1 million (see Matlack 1999). The new right of creditors to appeal the findings of *arbitrazh* judges should provide greater protection of their interests while the debtor business is under external management. It is nonetheless difficult for creditors to have confidence in the system and unlikely that managers will feel threatened by it as long as there are so many opportunities for abuse, and while self-serving conduct continues to go unpunished.

Efficient Exit Mechanisms and Promotion of Rehabilitation

The rights of creditors to maximum dividends, through maximizing asset values, is again recognized in the law but lacking in practice. Upon the *arbitrazh* court's acceptance of an application for bankruptcy, the operations of the company are supervised by a temporary administrator whose responsibility is to protect the company's assets. Enforcement of all creditors' claims (including those of secured creditors) are stayed upon the initiation of bankruptcy. This is designed to preserve the company's assets so that maximum value can be realized by selling the business as a going concern, and provides for equal treatment among similarly situated creditors. Both of these justifications are strongly recognized principles of best practice. Once external management commences, however, company assets are reportedly often dissipated because creditors have little actual control over or input in the process.

The priorities accorded to the various creditors appear to be fair and in accordance with general principles of international best practice. There are, however, a few exceptions to this observation that pertain to the perverse effect created on market expectations by the treatment of secured creditors. Once a debtor is declared bankrupt, secured creditors lose pledge rights against the specific assets of the debtor, and they rank behind personal injury and wage claimants. As has been suggested above, "secured" creditors are often given an advantage over the body of general unsecured creditors if the debt that they hold is only partially secured, because such debt is given priority in repayment regardless. In practice, however, the loss of previously bargained-for rights in collateral by secured creditors will often lead to reduced recovery, due to the high arrears in wage payments of many companies that must be paid before secured creditors. This situation clearly diminishes predictability in commercial relationships.

Performance indicators suggest a decline in rehabilitation cases. Arguably, this is again attributable to weaknesses in regulation. Most small and medium-size enterprises are unlikely to be capable of rescue, but the prospects are generally better for larger enterprises because of their greater market share and better access to capital and credit, and because they have more options for both operational and financial restructuring. Larger cases are the most susceptible to abuse, however, because of their inherent value. Bankruptcy statistics in Russia reveal that 90 percent of SMEs submitted to investigation are relegated to liquidation, while external management procedures are used mainly in the case of larger businesses. Moreover, in most functional systems, creditors play an important role, acting as a check and balance against potential abuses by the trustee, administrator, or others. In the Russian system, however, creditors are still marginalized and lack sufficient control over the process. Until recently, many of the avenues for appeal were foreclosed. In addition, the provisions relating to town-forming organizations give too much control over the rehabilitation process to local governors by giving them the power to extend the process for up to 10 years. These provisions are particularly problematic given that about 41 percent of industrial production falls within the definition of town-forming organizations. This fact helps explain why larger firms are far more likely than firms with fewer than 5,000 employees to undergo external management rather than liquidation. It also explains the geographical concentration of externally managed companies in regions whose governors are relatively strong.

FRAMEWORK FOR CORPORATE WORKOUTS AND RESTRUCTURINGS

Corporate workouts and restructurings should be supported by an enabling environment that encourages participants to engage in consensual arrangements designed to restore an enterprise to financial viability. An enabling environment includes laws and procedures that require disclosure of or ensure access to timely, reliable, and accurate financial information on the distressed enterprise; encourage lending to, investment in, or recapitalization of viable financially distressed enterprises; support a broad range of restructuring activities, such as debt write-offs, reschedulings, restructurings, and debt-equity conversions; and provide favorable or neutral tax treatment for restructurings. Because informal workouts take place in the shadow of the law, consensual resolution requires reliable fallback systems in the form of legal mechanisms for individual enforcement and debt collection or through collective insolvency procedures. As such, the most conducive environment for informal workouts is having effective insolvency and enforcement regimes, as reflected in the foregoing sections of this chapter.

In addition, the ability to implement a restructuring plan relies on the existence of a legal framework that can accommodate the restructuring plan at a fundamental level; for example, by allowing debt-equity swaps, forgiveness of bank debt, and the taking of collateral. The legal framework must also provide incentives for the parties to accept treatment that will render the restructured business viable (for example, favorable offsetting tax treatment for debt forgiveness). Participants must be provided with sufficient information on a borrower's operations and related financial criteria as well as information about the ultimate judicial or nonjudicial enforcement process. Concerns and issues relevant to informal workouts are often addressed in the context of formal frameworks for rehabilitation procedures, but often are overlooked or ignored in the context of informal arrangements. While there are a variety of different policy choices on the substantive and procedural nature of laws and the allocation of risk among participants, these rules must be clearly specified and consistently applied to encourage consensual workouts.

In Russia, lenders particularly tend to favor the out-of-court workout process where possible. This does not imply that the process is problem-free. Because workouts take place in the shadow of the law, the law itself should be reasonably clear and predictable. It is not. Rather, its weaknesses generally discourage all but a few parties from relying on court-directed insolvency. Where possible, creditors tend to prefer to exercise direct collateral enforcement. In most cases, the tax laws are not conducive to write-downs and restructurings, with the result that the overwhelming share of so-called restructurings are in fact debt reschedulings. In rare instances, debt-equity swaps involving sophisticated enterprises and players, often including foreign stakeholders, have been achieved.

CONCLUSION

The legal framework for corporate insolvency is generally sound, but contains a number of areas that make risk management less predictable and that constrain optimum commercial activity. Following adoption of the 1998 Bankruptcy Law, the legal framework for corporate insolvency law in Russia is fairly well-conceived, relatively comprehensive, and generally consistent with standards of best practice internationally. The 1998 Bankruptcy Law replaced the 1992 legislation, which was poorly designed and contained a mix of different legal systems. The new law corrected many of the mistakes of its predecessor and better aligns with creditor rights created under other laws. In recent years, the increase in cases and the efficiency in handling cases has demonstrated that the system is beginning to mature, with better trained judges and professionals and greater efficiency in the administration of proceedings. Nevertheless, the regime does not perform as it should in a number of respects, and has been criticized for the lack of consistency in its implementation rather than its content. Particular implementation problems pertain to the manipulation of the system to inequitably favor the interests of management or certain creditors to the detriment of creditors in general. A number of abuses have been reported, including

1. "Stacking" of creditor committees
2. Disenfranchisement of certain creditors

3. Wrongful disallowance of claims
4. Allowance of fraudulent claims
5. Wrongful trading and collusion to avoid filing obligations
6. Collusion between external managers, management, and judges
7. Use of bankruptcy proceedings as a form of hostile takeover, utilizing a colluding external manager as a means of gaining control of the bankrupt company's assets
8. Corrupt/irresponsible external managers paying no heed to the demands or interests of creditors.

A recent decision by the Constitutional Court addresses a number of ambiguities in the law and should lead to more uniform interpretation of a number of key issues. The law nonetheless requires improvement in a number of fundamental areas, as follows:

1. Treatment of secured creditors should be properly harmonized with bargained-for secured rights, to promote maximum efficiency in lending and to create proper incentives for adopting risk management practices by lending institutions. Conversely, treatment should similarly promote effective incentives and disincentives for prudent corporate behavior in managing debt levels, to avoid the consequences of insolvency. Three basic amendments are recommended:
   - The provision for lien stripping should be enforced at the point of sale, not before, and only with respect to pledged assets that are essential to a sale of the business as a going concern. Where the business is to be rehabilitated, interests should naturally remain in tact. Likewise, where pledged assets do not advance the liquidation process, secured creditors should be entitled to exercise their legitimate foreclosure rights.
   - The relative priority of interests should be respected. This would encourage holders of collateral to act promptly in registering claims so that all parties are placed on better notice of the debtor's financial condition. This would also penalize those who delay in acting on their rights.
   - Secured creditors should only be entitled to priority for that portion of their claim that is properly secured. This would require partially secured creditors being treated as having a secured claim only to the extent of the value of their collateral, and as having an unsecured claim for the remainder.
2. The criteria for initiating involuntary bankruptcy need to be re-examined to avoid bad faith or fictitious filings by those intent on using the process for self-gain through inappropriate hostile

takeovers or as a safe haven from liability where the enterprise assets have been stripped, tunneled, or fraudulently transferred. Amendments in this area are more complex and require a close examination of the various system weaknesses that invite such activity, and the solutions for rectifying them. Proposed amendments should consider the adoption and enforcement of harsh penalties (potentially even criminal sanctions) for those who abuse the process.
3. Amendments should be made to ensure that genuine creditors are not disenfranchised and have a real voice in the process. This can be done by tightening procedures for assessing disputed claims at the outset of cases, and by promoting stronger involvement and participation by creditors at all critical stages of the proceedings.
4. Priorities of state interests over private claims should be reexamined in the context of the need to promote greater commercial activity. This would shift the burden to the state to adopt stronger debt collection practices outside of bankruptcy and discourage reliance on the insolvency process as a failsafe collection mechanism. Where applicable law establishes a legitimate priority for state claims over private claims, these should be recognized in bankruptcy.

The institutional framework for implementing the insolvency regime remains fragmented and inconsistent with respect to its capacity for handling insolvency cases. Cases are handled by the arbitration courts, which have a wide range of responsibilities, not solely insolvency. In a few jurisdictions where there is generally a higher caseload, such as Moscow, certain judges have been designated as specialized judges to handle bankruptcy proceedings, and are doing so with greater consistency. Most complaints about implementation concern practices outside Moscow, where court capacities and sophistication vary significantly. Moreover, although greater judicial discretion is viewed as a hallmark of a more advanced system, instances of abuse of discretion have been a major criticism and key impediment to implementing an effective and reliable process. Recommendations include the following:
1. Efforts to improve capacity should focus on the criteria for the selection, qualification, and training of judges as specialized insolvency judges, and should include continuing education programs.
2. Emphasis should be placed on achieving greater transparency in the system, specifically with a view to improving creditor access to information. There is also a need to encourage the involvement of genuine creditors, as a necessary counterbalance to the wide discretion of judges and administrators/external receivers.

3. Clear procedures should be established for investigating and addressing allegations of conflicts of interest, abuse, and corruption among judges.

The continuing lack of regulation and potential for arbitrage in the system has continued to foster distrust of the process. The primary regulatory agency is the Federal Service on Financial Rehabilitation and Bankruptcy, which is responsible for training, qualifying, and supervising the activity of external receivers. To date, the FSFR has issued more than 12,000 licenses. This is a major achievement, but it also suggests that licensing standards are low and that there is likely to be a glut of poorly trained and qualified receivers. A simple comparison of the number of licenses awarded with the number of cases filed leads logically to the conclusion that many licensed receivers are inactive in the bankruptcy process. Recommendations include the following:

1. The processes for weeding out and delicensing incompetent receivers and for addressing abuses in the system should be closely monitored and studied for improvement. The FSFR has revoked or suspended relatively few licenses.
2. Criminal procedures and sanctions should be more rigorously enforced. The number of criminal actions to date is inconsistent with the reports of widespread abuse and corruption, suggesting little appetite or ability to enforce criminal measures.
3. In light of the alleged abuses in many areas, the system must be examined to ensure that independence and impartiality are maintained between the courts, administrators, and receivers, and to ensure that conflicts of interest are avoided.
4. The FSFR wears many hats and has many responsibilities, some of which create potential conflicts of interest or a potential threat to the agency's accountability. It is imperative that the FSFR be accountable to an independent body or board to avoid conflicts of interest and self-serving decision-making. The insolvency process will otherwise remain vulnerable to the sort of inappropriate political interference that could tilt the balance in favor of state interests over private commercial interests, which invariably gives rise to unpredictability and distrust.

Russia's current strategy and approach to enterprise rehabilitation does not effectively separate viable companies that can survive in a market economy from those loss-making enterprises that cannot. The new insolvency law is more accommodating to rescue through prebankruptcy measures, amicable settlement, and external receivership procedures than the prior law, but distortions and abuses in the application of the law reveal that the process of rehabilitation is being undermined and abused to keep insolvent businesses out of bankruptcy and to put solvent businesses in, for purposes of conducting hostile takeovers. While the promotion of a more active rescue culture is important, policies need to be properly aligned to ensure that viable businesses are salvaged. In this regard, there is a continuing need for training and capacity development, and other laws will need to be reviewed and reformed to better encourage rehabilitation (an example is tax loss treatment on debt write-off). In addition, the laws must be closely examined with a view to enabling equitable out-of-court workouts that avoid the high costs of the system, and a view to promoting a more efficient credit culture for the management of financial distress.

ENDNOTES

1. RF Law No. 3929-1 of November 19, 1992, On Insolvency (Bankruptcy) of Enterprises (the "1992 Bankruptcy Law").

2. See generally C. Sonin and E. Zhuravskaya, "Bankruptcy in Russia: Away from Creditor Protection and Restructuring," *The European Commission Rev.* 6–12 (2000).

3. See Vitrianskii 1999. The author states: "Such conditions allowed top managers of commercial organizations who had no reason to fear bankruptcy to withhold debt payment and use the available money as their own enterprise funds, ensuring only that the total amount of accounts payable did not exceed the asset value of the enterprise. From this, it is obvious that the legal concept and characteristics of bankruptcy that used to be applied protected bad faith debtors and were thus destroying the principles of commerce."

4. See World Bank. 1999. International preference for a liquidity test in corporate insolvency (as distinguished from a balance sheet test in bank insolvency) is tied to an evolving concept of business. Where a business cannot pay its debts as they come due, the business may not necessarily be balance-sheet insolvent. The effect of being illiquid, however, implies that the business is inefficient and imposes an economic burden on other market players that transact business with the enterprise. If the business is viable and sound, in a normalized market it should be able to obtain financing and/or capitalization from alternative sources. This theory does not necessarily hold in a destabilized market and one where equity and credit markets are insufficiently evolved. On balance, however, the liquidity test is now widely embraced as a better indicator of corporate insolvency or financial distress than the balance sheet test.

5. See Vitrianskii. 1999. at 413.

6. See Vitrianskii. 1999. at 413–14.

7. Resolution of the Russian Federation No. 478 "On Measures to Increase Efficiency of Bankruptcy Procedures Application" (May 22, 1998).

8. For an interesting discussion of the lien-stripping issues and microeconomic policy considerations, see Averch 2000.

9. Claims having priority and paid before secured claims include (1) administrative expenses and claims; (2) personal injury claims (category 1); and (3) severance, back pay, and royalty claims (category 2). Claims paid after secured claims include government or budget claims (e.g., taxes and pension claims), followed by claims of unsecured creditors.

10. This discusses the so-called "zeta" principle on appropriate levels of debt to equity.

11. See Matlack 1999.

12. See, e.g., Lambert-Mogiliansky, Sonin, and Zhuravskaya 2000.

13. See generally World Bank 1999.

14. "On examining the constitutionality of various provisions of the Federal Law on Insolvency (Bankruptcy) relating to the possibility of appealing determinations issued by *arbitrazh* courts in bankruptcy cases and its other provisions, Article 49 of the Federal Law on Insolvency (Bankruptcy) of Credit Organizations, as well as articles 106, 160, 179, and 191 of the code of *Arbitrazh* Procedure of the Russian Federation in connection with the request from the Chelyabinsk Oblast Arbitrazh Court and complaints of citizens and legal entities."

15. Art. 5(1) BL. The *arbitrazh* courts are commercial courts dealing with commercial disputes, including bankruptcy cases. They are neither arbitration nor arbitrage courts in the strict sense. Rather, they are more closely akin to commercial courts.

16. Art. 1, 1998 Bankruptcy Law [hereinafter cited as "Art. __ BL"].

17. Art. 132 BL.

18. Art. 3(2) BL.

19. Art. 3(1) BL.

20. Art. 7(2) BL.

21. Art. 8(1) BL.

22. Art. 9 BL.

23. Art. 6 BL.

24. Art. 5(2) BL.

25. Art. 26(1) BL.

26. Art. 10 BL.

27. Art. 41(3) BL.

28. Art. 61 BL.

29. Art. 57(2) BL.

30. Art. 58(2) BL.

31. Art. 58(3) BL.

32. Art. 12-14 BL.

33. Art. 67 BL.

34. Art. 68(1)-(2) BL.
35. Art. 69 BL.
36. Art. 74(2) BL.
37. Art. 74(1) BL.
38. Art. 74(1) BL.
39. Art. 77 BL.
40. Art. 78 BL.
41. Art. 82 BL.
42. Art. 81 BL.
43. Art. 96 BL.
44. Art. 98 BL.
45. Art. 120 BL.
46. Art. 78 BL.
47. Art. 75 BL.
48. Art. 106(2) BL.
49. Art. 114(5) BL.

50. One commentator and researcher refers to the problem as being one of capture of the courts by the local governments. See *supra* Lambert-Mogiliansky (discussing the distortions on bankruptcy performance and constraints on effectiveness resulting from political interference and external influences on the bankruptcy process).

51. Other facets of the TACIS program have resulted in the development of methodology for analyzing the financial condition and market prospects of insolvent enterprises, and for enterprise restructuring.

52. This was done pursuant to Resolution of the FSFR of Russia No. 23 of August 7, 1999.

53. Numbers in parentheses represent the total number of experts accredited in each of these categories.

54. Creditors have voting rights at the creditors' meeting proportionate to the amount of their debt. Such rights do not take into account the priority of the creditor. Therefore secured creditors are treated like any other creditor when it comes to voting rights. A creditor's right to vote in a creditors' meeting to determine important decisions in the case can be thwarted by the temporary administrator's decision to leave the creditor's claim off of the claims list, or by objecting to its legitimacy. Because the legitimacy is called into question and is subject to resolution through appeals, the case marches on with decisions being made by other creditors. These types of abuses were reported as being intentional and frequent in order to skew the results of voting at the creditors' meetings. It was also reported that some large claims were fabricated to give insiders a voice or control in the process.

55. Debtors and creditors have easy access to the system. A debt of US$5,000 outstanding for three months is all that is required to initiate bankruptcy proceedings against a company. The growing number of bogus bankruptcies indicated in the performance data suggests that the access criteria are in fact too low.

REFERENCES

Altman, Edward. 1993. *Corporate Financial Distress*, 2d ed. New York: Wiley.

Averch, C. 2000. *Lien Stripping under Russian Bankruptcy Law: Is it Fair?* 105 *Comm. Law Journal* 77.

Lambert-Mogiliansky, Ariane, Constantin Sonin, and Ekaterina Zhuravskaya. 2000. "Capture of Bankruptcy: Theory and Evidence from Russia." Center for Economic Policy Research Discussion Paper Series No. 2488: 1–41. United Kingdom.

Matlack, C. 1999. "Russia's Boom in Bogus Bankruptcies." *Business Week*. New York (May 31) 3631: 46.

Sonin, C., and E. Zhuravskaya. 2000. "Bankruptcy in Russia: Away from Creditor Protection and Restructuring." *The European Commission Review* 6–12.

The Economist. 1999. "Rules of War." (December 4) Vol. 353, 8148: 65.

Vitrianskii, V. V. 1999. "Insolvency and Bankruptcy Law Reform in the Russian Federation." *McGill Law Journal*.

World Bank. 1999. "Russian Enterprise Reform: Policies to Further the Transition" 67 World Bank Discussion Paper 400. Washington, D.C.

CHAPTER 4

Disclosure and Transparency

INTRODUCTION

A strong disclosure regime is a key feature of the market-based monitoring of companies, and it is central to the ability of shareholders to exercise their voting rights and investment decisions. Shareholders and potential investors require access to timely, reliable, and comparable information in sufficient detail for them to make informed decisions. A strong disclosure regime is likewise essential for the banking sector, where not only the shareholder of the bank requires full disclosure, but also the depositor who is focused on the security of funds deposited within the bank. Thus, improving disclosure and transparency are essential pre-conditions for increasing the flow of deposits into banks and for increasing the flow of lending to the private sector.

Although it is far from being either perfect or complete, the legal basis does exist for obtaining basic information about a listed or publicly traded company in Russia. The Russian Law on Joint Stock Companies contains a list of documents that a joint stock company is required to disclose. The Securities Market Law establishes additional information disclosure requirements that are supplemented by numerous regulations of the Ministry of Finance (MoF) and the Federal Commission on the Securities Market (FCSM).

The Central Bank of Russia (CBR) directs the reporting requirements for banks and, in the role of regulator and supervisor of the banking sector, details the reporting and disclosure requirements. As regulator the

CBR monitors and evaluates the reports from Russia's almost 1,300 commercial banks. However, the regulatory role played by the CBR provided little warning of the August 1998 financial crisis in Russia, which again caused the public to lose confidence in the financial sector of the economy.

Since 1999, the law *On Protection of the Rights and Legal Interests of Investors* has provided the FCSM with the authority to fine publicly traded companies and their managers for violating information disclosure rules. The FCSM is required to report every penalty it imposes. Important corporate events such as major transactions, changes in the executive and supervisory structure, and board of director decisions must be announced in the regular FCSM newsletter. Moreover, the law explicitly requires the broker to provide shareholders with a complete set of documents that detail the structure, activities, and policies of the company. In 2000, the FCSM imposed a total of 32 million rubles (US$1.2 million) in fines on 1,769 companies that violated the Investor Protection Law; the average fine of 18,090 rubles (US$695) can hardly be considered commensurate with the potential risk of the investor, however.

The disclosure requirements of the FCSM and the CBR are not in themselves sufficient and adequate to protect the investor and depositor. Effective disclosure-based regulation requires a rule-of-law environment, interested and engaged investors and depositors, and strong regulatory institutions. It will take the whole constituency of state regulators, investors, corporate managers, board members, accounting/audit professionals, and public interest groups to change historical notions about transparency and to introduce new corporate objectives of disclosure and transparency.

ACCOUNTING STANDARDS AND DISCLOSURE

Financial statements are the means of communicating financial information about a company or bank. The balance sheet provides a dated snapshot of assets, liabilities, and equity; the statement of operations reports on the period's revenue, expenditures, and profits; and the statement of cash flow provides a summary of the sources and uses of cash for the period. The notes to the financial statements provide additional descriptive information, including information on the accounting policies used by the reporting entity, further details about the assets and liabilities, disclosure of related-party transactions, reporting of material events, and key informational details of the entity and its operations.

Financial statements are prepared in accordance with accounting standards, which provide the framework and underlying foundation to the statements. Historically, the accounting standards in Russia were designed specifically to meet the needs of an economic system in place under a communist regime, and included a detailed and prescriptive chart of accounts, prescribed financial statement formats, and extensive accounting rules. These Russian Accounting Standards (RAS) have been under pressure to change, given the country's transition to a market-based economy. Worldwide, there is a shift toward using International Accounting Standards (IAS), a single set of standards issued by the International Accounting Standards Board (IASB). IAS is gradually becoming the benchmark for accounting standards, as evidenced by its recent endorsement by the International Organization of Securities Commissions (IOSCO), the European Union, the World Bank, and other key stakeholders in the financial sector.[1]

The transition from RAS to IAS has been a continual topic of discussion within Russia. There are two main viewpoints on the issue, favoring either "evolutionary" or "revolutionary" change. The MoF has recently announced that it aims to transfer to IAS by 2004 through the yearly adoption of five or six accounting standards. This approach to rewriting the RAS is considered evolutionary, and is intended to allow for the nuances of the Russian economy to be incorporated into the rewriting of the standards. The second approach, as recently articulated in the minutes of the Foreign Investor Advisory Committee (FIAC), favors the full adoption of IAS with a phased compliance requirement for various categories of enterprises. This approach has been termed revolutionary, as the focus is on full and immediate compliance with IAS.

There are many arguments supporting both sides of the standards transition debate. The evolutionary supporters would argue that it is impossible to move quickly to IAS given the current legal and taxation laws, the training requirements for accountants and auditors, and the lack of supporting guidance and methodology for recordkeeping and accounting tasks. The revolutionary supporters argue that it is too costly to have to prepare financial statements in accordance with two sets of standards; and that there would be continual change and ambiguity with evolving RAS; this would create a problem that would be exacerbated by the fact that IAS is also in the process of continual revision.

A recently completed study by seven major accounting and audit firms highlights the differences between RAS and IAS. (The results of the study can be found in Table 4.1.) It should be noted that many of the differences relate to disclosure of information.

Two of the main obstacles to the transition to IAS are the taxation and legislative requirements. Compliance with tax laws is of highest priority for companies, given the detailed and rigorous compliance and policing reality. The primary focus of tax reporting thus takes precedence over financial reporting. To resolve this impasse there will have to be a legally approved format of reconciling profit, as determined under IAS, with the taxable profit, as detailed under the Tax Code. This reconciliation would adjust for differences in the timing and deductibility of expenditures and other transactions. The legislative requirements, including those related to statistical reporting, and normative acts would need to be amended to facilitate a speedy transition to IAS.

With respect to the banks, it is the CBR that is charged with the responsibility for the development and regulation of accounting standards. These standards, while specific to the banks, cannot under law be in contradiction to those issued by the MoF. On the other hand, the CBR can require banks to report for supervisory purposes on the basis that it chooses. The CBR has recently announced plans to transition to IAS by January 1, 2004, and will be using IAS-based reporting for supervision purposes as well. The banks are faced with a similar dilemma as enterprises with respect to taxation and the need for taxation to be based on IAS versus RAS.

The self-regulating accounting profession in Russia comprises more than 90 different associations and membership organizations. The Institute of Professional Accountants (IPA) is the largest, and has begun a 40-hour IAS training course for members. However, none of the accounting associations has initiated an attestation or certification of members in accordance with the International Federation of Accountants (IFAC) educational guidelines. The issues of IAS training and attestation must be urgently addressed, in order to provide the necessary professional cadre of accountants that will be needed for companies and banks to transition to IAS.

AUDITING STANDARDS AND DISCLOSURE

The external auditor has an important role in providing an opinion on whether or not the financial statements are prepared, in all material respects, in accordance with the identified standards of accounting. The auditor is required to follow a set of standards that provide the fundamental framework for the work and opinion; he or she must also follow a code of ethics with respect to professional conduct. According to the

Russian Securities Law, auditors are appointed at the annual general meeting. Historically, Russian Audit Rules (RAR) were used as the basis for the auditor's work; these have been replaced by Russian Standards on Auditing (RSA). International Standards on Auditing (ISA) are developed and issued on behalf of the International Federation of Accountants (IFAC) by the International Auditing Practices Committee (IAPC). Table 4.4 lists the 39 approved Russian audit standards and provides the ISA equivalent.

The RSA is similar to the ISA, but there is a fundamental difference related to the liability of the auditor with respect to negligence or error. The laws of the Russian Federation allow for a legal claim by the client against the auditor; however, the damages are limited to the amount of the audit fee only. There is therefore limited liability risk for an audit firm and no provision for an outside third party to claim damages against a negligent auditor. While the litigious fervor that has developed in some countries is not desirable in Russia, the audit firm must nonetheless be held accountable to a high professional standard.

The audit profession in Russia is government-regulated through the issuance of audit licenses, with the CBR responsible for the issuance of audit licenses for banks. However, on June 18, 2001, the Duma banking committee recommended that the lower house pass the bill *On Auditing Business* on its second reading. If the Duma approves the bill, the CBR would lose the right to regulate the banking audit market. The bill proposes that a federal body for the state regulation of auditing business control the banking audit market and the other three market segments, namely, the audit of insurance companies, a general audit, and the audit of exchanges, ex-budget funds, and investment institutions. The ministry responsible for this federal body has not been identified, but is thought to be the Ministry of Finance.

The self-regulatory audit profession is in the early stages of development. The Collegium of Auditors became a member of IFAC in 2000; however, it does not have a comprehensive training and certification program based on ISA, and to date does not conduct peer reviews of audit firms. For the audit profession to become credible in the world's marketplace, there must be a concerted training initiative with respect to ISA, coupled with an intensive and professionally recognized examination process. Peer review of audit firms will also be a key step in achieving the desired competency recognition. The recent World Bank review of audit firms in Russia indicates that there is a lack of understanding of the audit process and of the documentation requirements with respect to audit working papers as required under IAS. This may in part be explained by the historical background, where the audit was traditionally focused on a documentation audit rather than on an audit of financial statements.

ENFORCEMENT AND DISCLOSURE

The preparation of financial statements in accordance with ISA, and the engagement of an auditor to express an opinion on the financial statements and conduct the audit in accordance with ISA, are two important steps to disclosure and transparency. In addition to the auditor, there are several other key groups involved in the enforcement of accounting standards.

First, there must be a self-enforcement by the company or bank itself. The management and board of directors are responsible for the financial statements. In Russia this is often misunderstood, because historically the chief accountant had been responsible for the financial statements. There is continual reluctance on the part of management to sign a management representation letter as required under section 580 of ISA—that is, for management to acknowledge its responsibility for the financial statements. Second, the shareholders play a role in the enforcement of disclosure, because the financial statements must be approved at each annual meeting. The preparation of glossy shareholder reports tends to hide the financial statements and mask their importance. Third, the regulators (the FCSM and the CBR) must play a greater role in enforcement. To be effective, the FCSM and the CBR will need a sufficient number of trained personnel to monitor compliance with the disclosed requirements. Also essential are a variety of disciplinary mechanisms to sanction companies and banks whose disclosures contain material misstatements or omissions. Fourth, there must be changes in the various laws, including the Code on Corporate Governance, to articulate the requirements and consequences for noncompliance. Fifth, the public must become engaged in the demand for full disclosure. The use of rating agencies to monitor and report on corporate governance compliance would be an important step toward increasing the amount of information available to the public.

In addition to the disclosure of financial information, recent reform efforts by Russian regulators are an indication that the importance of nonfinancial information is starting to be recognized. In 2000, a MoF regulation set out new rules for disclosing information that is not presented in the financial statements but is necessary to assess the financial position of, performance of, and changes in a company's financial situation. This includes information on accounting policies, changes in equity, details of the number of shares issued, extraordinary events, and affiliated undertakings. There is also an optional provision to include information on environmental policies and material foreseeable risks. It is too early to say if this regulation will be fully complied with, and to what extent companies and banks will consider it necessary to disclose this required information.

With the help of the United States Agency for International Development and the European Union TACIS, two technical assistance projects have gotten underway at the CBR to improve the reporting requirements of the commercial banks. This in turn should improve the off-site supervisory capacity of the CBR. Training of supervisory staff has focused on the shift from merely compliance review to risk assessment and bank performance analysis.

RECOMMENDATIONS

1. There should be a full and immediate adoption of IAS, rather than a gradual transitional rewrite of RAS. The gradual phase-in of companies and banks required to report according to IAS is understood, especially with respect to privately owned or closely held companies.
2. In order to meet the economic demands of investors and depositors, there is an urgent need for all listed companies and all banks to use IAS as the sole basis for the preparation of financial statements. To facilitate a smooth transition process, there will need to be an orderly phased process, beginning with the largest banks and the Tier-one listed companies. The optional use of IAS should be extended to all small and medium-size enterprises.
3. The legal framework of laws and normative acts must be amended quickly to facilitate the move to full IAS.
4. Changes in the tax code are necessary to recognize IAS as the legal basis for taxation, ensuring that taxpayers will not be required to contend with two sets of different requirements.
5. The role of the regulators (the FCSM and the CBR) must be enhanced to ensure full compliance with all reporting requirements. As the primary regulators of the disclosure of financial information, the FCSM and the CBR must focus on training and enforcement and on the exercise of their authority to impose substantial sanctions in the case of noncompliance.

6. The accounting and audit profession must be strengthened through appropriate training, testing, and certification. The self-regulatory nature of the profession means that it must focus on becoming credible in the global forum and must ensure, through their adherence to a code of ethics, that its members are not only technically competent but also professionally responsible.

COMPARISON OF RUSSIAN AND INTERNATIONAL ACCOUNTING AND AUDITING STANDARDS

Russian Accounting Standards can differ from International Accounting Standards because certain areas of business do not have rules or standards in RAS. Table 4.1 lists IAS standards that are not reflected in RAS.

Table 4.1 Rules Missing in RAS and Present in IAS

Standards absent in RAS	Standards present in IAS
The classification of business combinations between acquisitions and pooling of interest	IAS 22
Provisions in the context of business combinations accounted for as acquisitions	IAS 22.31
The restatement of financial statements of a company reporting in the currency of a hyperinflationary economy in terms of the measuring unit current at the balance sheet date	IAS 29.8
The translation of the financial statements of hyperinflationary subsidiaries	IAS 21.36
Impairment of assets	IAS 36
The recognition of operating lease incentives	IAS 17.25; SIC 15
Accounting for defined benefit pension plans and some other types of employee benefits	IAS 19.52
Accounting for deferred tax	IAS 12
Accounting for an issuer's financial instruments	IAS 32.18/23
The treatment of exchange differences resulting from severe devaluation or depreciation of a currency	IAS 21.21; SIC 11
The notion and definition of cash equivalents IAS 7.6–9 and detailed guidance on the preparation of cash flow statements	IAS 7
Consolidation of special purpose entities	SIC 12
Recognition of a decline, other than temporary, in the carrying amount of long-term investments, other than marketable equity securities	IAS 25.23

Table 4.2 Discrepancy between RAS and IAS Disclosure Requirements

Disclosures not required under RAS	Disclosures required under IAS
A primary statement of changes in equity	IAS 1.7
A primary statement of cash flows	IAS 7
The FIFO or current cost of inventories valued on the LIFO basis	IAS 2.36
The fair value of financial assets and liabilities	IAS 32.77
Related parties information except by certain reporting companies with specific legal form (joint stock companies); fellow subsidiaries under common control do not qualify for consideration as related parties	IAS 24.1–4
Discontinuing operations	IAS 35
Certain segment information (e.g., a reconciliation between the information by reportable segment and the aggregated information in financial statements, significant noncash expenses, other than depreciation and amortization, that were included in segment expense and, therefore, deducted in measuring segment result—for each reportable segment).	IAS 14.61/67

Russian standards have different requirements than IAS concerning disclosure. Table 4.2 lists those areas of disclosure required under IAS but absent from RAS.

The inconsistencies between RAS and IAS rules, listed in Table 4.3, have implications for many enterprises.

Russian auditors now use Russian Standards on Auditing (RSA), which replaced Russian Audit Rules. International Standards on Auditing were developed and issued on behalf of the International Federation of Accountants by the International Auditing Practices Committee. Table 4.4 compares the 39 approved Russian audit standards to the ISA equivalent.

Table 4.3 RAS Rules That Differ from IAS

RAS rules	IAS rules
Research costs can be capitalized	IAS 38.42/51
Goodwill is calculated by reference to the book values of acquired net assets	IAS 22.40
Proportionate consolidation may be used for subsidiaries in which the parent has 50 percent or less of the voting power	IAS 27.15
Revaluation of property, plant, and equipment is allowed but gives different results than IAS and need not be kept up-to-date	IAS 16.29
The period of depreciation of property, plant, and equipment is in a number of cases prescribed by the Government and is longer than the period over which an asset is expected to be used	IAS 16.6/41
Finance leases are generally defined in legal terms and capitalization is allowed but not required	IAS 17.3/12.28
Lessors recognize finance lease income differently	IAS 17.30
The completed contract method can be used for the recognition of revenues on construction contracts when the outcome of a construction contract can be estimated reliably	IAS 11.22
Provisions can be established more widely or less widely than under IAS, and there is no requirement for discounting	IAS 37.14/45
Own (treasury) shares are shown as assets	SIC 16
Classification of cash flows between investing and financing activities in the cash flow statement may be different from IAS	IAS 7.6/16/17
Cash flow statements reconcile to cash rather than to cash and cash equivalents	IAS 7.45
The correction of fundamental errors is included in the determination of the net profit or loss for the reporting period, but separate disclosure and pro-forma restated comparative information are not required	IAS 8.34/38
Revenue recognition rules do not differentiate between exchanges of goods of similar nature and value and exchanges of dissimilar goods, and do not discuss adjustment for the amount of cash or cash equivalents transferred in exchange for dissimilar goods	IAS 18.12; IAS 16.21/22
The definition of extraordinary items is broader	IAS 8.6/12
Some parent companies do not prepare consolidated financial statements	IAS 27.7/11
In the definition of control, the ability to govern decision-making is not required to be accompanied by the objective of obtaining benefits from the entity's activities	IAS 27.6
Investments in certain securities held for the short term are not required to be carried at the lower of cost and market value or at market value	IAS 25.19/23
Certain subsidiaries may be excluded from consolidation	IAS 27.13
A subsidiary that is a bank may be excluded from consolidation if it is dissimilar from the rest of the group	IAS 27.14
Certain set-up costs that have been paid by a company's founder can be capitalized	IAS 38.57
The realizable value of inventories can be measured without deduction of costs	IAS 2.6

Table 4.4 The 39 Approved Russian Standards on Auditing and the Equivalent International Standards on Auditing

	RSA	ISA
1	The auditor's report on financial statements[a]	ISA 700
2	Planning[b]	ISA 300
3	Audit engagement letter	ISA 210 Terms of Audit Engagements
4	Audit evidence	ISA 500
5	Using the work of an expert	ISA 620
6	Audit sampling	ISA 530
7	Documentation	ISA 230
8	Fraud and error	ISA 240
9	Evaluation of accounting system and internal control during the audit	ISA 400 Risk Assessments and Internal Control
10	Date of audit report and subsequent events	ISA 560 Subsequent Events
11	Management letter	
12	Glossary of terms	ISA 110
13	Auditing in computer information systems environment[c]	ISA 401
14	Materiality and audit risk	ISA 320 Audit Materiality
15	Analytical procedures	ISA 520
16	Education of the auditor	
17	Going concern assumption[d]	ISA 570
18	Quality control	ISA 220
19	Considerations of laws and regulations in an audit of financial statements	ISA 250
20	Initial engagements—opening balances and comparatives	ISA 510
21	Management representations	ISA 580
22	Related audit services[e]	
23	Related parties	ISA 550
24	Communications with management	ISA 1007
25	Using the work of another auditor[f]	ISA 600
26	Knowledge of business	ISA 310
27	Considering the work of internal auditor	ISA 610
28	Objective and general principles governing an audit of financial statements[g]	ISA 200
29	Other information in documents containing audited financial statements	ISA 720
30	Audit of accounting estimates	ISA 540
31	Examination of prospective financial information	ISA 810
32	Requirements for the internal audit standards of the audit firm[h]	
33	Rights and obligations of the auditor and the client	
34	Procedures for preparation of audit contracts	
35	The auditor's report on special-purpose audit engagements	ISA 800

(Table continues on next page)

Table 4.4 *(continued)*

RSA	ISA
36 Risk assessment and internal control—CIS characteristics and considerations[i]	ISA 1008
37 Computer-assisted audit techniques	1009
38 Tax audit and other related tax services; communications with tax authorities	
39 Particular considerations in the audit of small business	

a. RSA 1 Approved by PCAA 02/09/96 Protocol 1.
b. RSA 2-12 Approved by PCAA 12/25/96 Protocol 6.
c. RSA 13-16 Approved by PCAA 01/22/98 Protocol 2.
d. RSA 17-21 Approved by PCAA 07/15/98 Protocol 4.
e. RSA 22-24 Approved by PCAA 03/18/99 Protocol 2.
f. RSA 25-27 Approved by PCAA 04/27/99 Protocol 3.
g. RSA 28-31 Approved by PCAA 08/20/99 Protocol 5.
h. RSA 32-35 Approved by PCAA 10/20/99 Protocol 6.
i. RSA 36-39 Approved by PCAA 07/11/00 Protocol 1.

ENDNOTE

1. For an introduction to the principles and terminology of IAS, see van Greuning and Marius Koen (1999) and (2001); the first edition was published in English and Russian, the second edition in English only.

REFERENCES

van Greuning, Hennie, and Marius Koen. 1999. *International Accounting Standards: A Practical Guide*. Washington, D.C.: World Bank.

——————. 2001. *International Accounting Standards: A Practical Guide*, 2nd ed. Washington, D.C.: World Bank.

Part II

The Banking System: Structure and Performance

International experience reveals that the financial sector has an important role to play in economic development. After identifying the key contributions that the financial sector can make to stimulate broad-based economic development, Chapter 5 focuses on the development of the Russian banking sector. Development of the banking system is critical for broader-based financial sector development. For example, it is difficult to conceive how investors will gain confidence in securities markets when banks are not trusted to deliver reliable payment, custodial, and settlement services. Thus, the development of a well-functioning banking sector will need to precede the development of other parts of the financial system. While a banking system may be able to function efficiently without a capital market, it is impossible to conceive that a capital market could function efficiently without the services of a well-developed banking system.

The subsequent chapters in Part II focus on specific features of the reform program that relate to the banking system. Chapter 6 analyzes the performance of several subgroups of Russian banks since the financial crisis in 1998, and it outlines a number of banking practices related to the financial reporting undertaken by Russian banks. This analysis draws attention to several weaknesses that need to be addressed because they defray trust in the sector. Improving banking regulation would mend these weaknesses, thereby enhancing trust in the sector.

Based on international experience with state banks, Chapter 7 addresses the issue of reforming the state banks in Russia. Experience from a number of other countries reveals that state banks have been the source of often sizeable fiscal liability. Given their growing dominance in the Russian financial sector since the 1998 crisis, state banks could threaten the stability of the sector. Reforming these banks is thus crucial to building trust in the Russian financial system.

Chapter 8 addresses the issue of entry by foreign banks, basing its conclusions on a survey of the foreign banks currently operating in Russia. International experience reveals that entry by foreign banks can be beneficial, even crucial, to building trust in financial intermediation. The results of this survey reveal that, rather than being constrained by restrictions of a supervisory nature, foreign banks are restrained in their efforts to expand in the Russian market by weaknesses in implementation of the law—especially as it applies to creditor rights. Thus implementation of the legal and accounting infrastructures may hold the key to the development of a sound and trusted banking system.

Chapter 5

The Role of the Financial System

THE IMPORTANCE OF THE FINANCIAL SECTOR FOR ECONOMIC DEVELOPMENT

Russia would likely have grown faster over the last decade if it had had a better-developed financial system. Financial intermediary development has a causal impact on economic growth (see Levine, Loayza, and Beck 2000).[1] While a sound, efficient financial sector is not sufficient to guarantee long-term growth, long-term growth is difficult to achieve without a sound financial sector. Based on international experience, this chapter outlines the major benefits that a well-functioning financial system can have for economic development.

A well-developed financial system would allow Russia to transform more easily into a market economy and to restructure its industrial base. Cross-country comparisons show that countries with a more developed financial system allocate their resources more efficiently and enjoy faster productivity growth.[2] On the other hand, there is no significant relationship between financial intermediary development and private savings rates, and the causal link between finance and capital stock growth is tenuous at best (see Beck, Levine, and Loayza 2000).[3] Rather than filling an investment gap, a well-developed financial sector supports the efficient allocation of resources. Countries with more developed financial systems invest more in growing industries and decrease their investment in declining industries (see Wurgler 2000). Sectoral investment is thus more responsive to sectoral output growth in those economies that are more financially developed.

A well-developed financial system channels resources to the sectors that need them to enhance firm growth. It also fosters, disproportionately, the growth of industries that rely heavily on external financing (see Rajan and Zingales 1996). Financial development thus alleviates the constraints imposed by market frictions on industries that depend on outside finance. Furthermore, financial development helps firms grow beyond the limits imposed by internal cash flow and short-term lending (see Demirgüç-Kunt and Maksimovic 1998). Countries with higher levels of financial development have more firms that grow faster than those that are supported by internal cash flows and short-term debt. Financial development thus would enable Russian enterprises to grow beyond the constraints imposed by internal resources and would benefit the industries that are most dependent on external finance. A developed financial system would also have lowered the recent growth volatility of the Russian economy, and helped Russia move away from a natural resource–based economy. Recent research has shown that countries with better-developed financial systems experience less volatility in their GDP per capita growth rates, and that such a financial system can help dampen the impact of terms-of-trade shocks on economic growth (see Easterly, Islam, and Stiglitz 2000; and Beck, Lundberg, and Majnoni 2001). This is especially important for a resource-based economy such as Russia. While the recent oil price surge has helped Russia's fiscal situation and economic growth, a price slump would have the same degree of impact, albeit negative. A better-developed financial system can help diversify the industrial base, dampen the effect of price shocks on consumers and producers, and help Russia's growth rate become less dependent on commodity price swings. Also, cross-country studies have shown that economies with better-developed financial systems have higher export shares and trade balances in manufactured goods, and that a well-developed financial sector helps countries increase the share of manufacturers in overall exports (see Beck 2001).

A well-developed financial sector is also important for poverty alleviation. While there is limited statistical evidence demonstrating the direct effect of financial development on poverty alleviation, there is substantial anecdotal evidence and a strong argument for an indirect impact. First, recent cross-country studies suggest that growth in real per capita GDP raises almost one-for-one the income of the poor (see Dollar and Kraay 2001). Second, as mentioned above, financial systems help economies absorb shocks better; a more efficient financial system that offers large parts of the population a safe outlet for its savings and better access to credit helps households and small entrepreneurs protect themselves against shocks. Third, financial crises entail large fiscal costs that crowd out social spending; while the small size of Russia's financial system reduced the impact of the financial crisis in 1998 on the real sector and thus on economic growth, the costs of the private banks' losses were to some extent borne by the Central Bank and the Government. These losses and further hidden losses in the banking sector constitute a contingent fiscal liability that will have a negative impact on social spending by the Russian government.

Over the last two years, Russia has shown a strong growth performance despite the lack of a significant contribution from the financial sector. Sustainable growth and a successful transition to a market economy are not feasible, however, without a sound and efficient financial sector. Without a financial sector, the Russian economy will remain concentrated on natural resources and will be susceptible to commodity price swings. Furthermore, the recent real appreciation due to commodity price increases subjects other sectors of the economy to the "Dutch disease," whereby high commodity prices lead to appreciation of the currency and thus reduce the competitiveness of nonresource-based exporters placing them at a disadvantage internationally. While some improvement in productivity has been achieved over the last two years, a better-developed financial sector would help the economy improve resource allocation and increase productivity growth. Box 5.1 summarizes the main functions of a well-functioning financial system (for more information, see Levine 1997).

THE KEY ROLE OF BANKING SYSTEM REFORM

Financial sector reform takes time and therefore needs to be carefully sequenced. Part I of this book outlined a number of legal, judicial, and accounting reforms that are the building blocks for lending by banks to unrelated third parties. Not until these reforms are implemented will the environment be conducive for lending by banks. Banks perform a number of other functions that are crucial to any well-functioning financial system, such as providing efficient payment services, ensuring the liquidity of accumulated savings (especially for small savers), and undertaking custodial and settlement functions for security market transactions.

Development of the financial system also entails developing new nonbank financing mechanisms, such as leasing and factoring, and the development of the capital market. The Russian authorities started establishing the basis for a capital market in the early 1990s, but these endeavors were initiated mostly to provide a mechanism for transferring property

> **Box 5.1 The Main Functions of the Financial Sector**
>
> *Payment services:* Financial institutions facilitate the exchange of goods and services by providing efficient payment services. A monetized economy with a readily accepted means of exchange eliminates the need for double coincidence of wants, economizes on transaction costs, and thus enables greater specialization than does an economy based on barter. Financial institutions can lower the costs of transactions further by offering a trusted, timely, and efficient payment system that reduces the geographic and time barriers to monetary exchange. By offering trusted, timely, and efficient payment services, financial institutions can increase the public's confidence, attract funds, and thus increase inside money; that is, the resources that are intermediated through the financial system. An economy based on a monetary means of exchange also facilitates the formation of prices and thus efficient resource allocation. Compared to a barter economy, a monetized economy offers greater transparency, efficiency, and fairness in price setting.
>
> *Mobilizing savings:* Financial institutions mobilize and pool savings. By aggregating small savings from individuals, financial institutions can make possible large-scale investments and the adoption of better technologies. The capacity of the financial sector to attract savings, however, depends on the trust and confidence that savers have in their financial institutions.
>
> *Risk diversification:* Financial institutions facilitate risk amelioration. Specifically, they help decrease the liquidity risk stemming from investment in long-term illiquid projects. By transforming callable deposits into long-term loans, banks can offer liquid assets to savers, and long-term financing to investors.* Liquid capital markets allow savers to hold assets that they can easily and quickly sell, and at the same time they offer long-term resources to firms. Financial markets also help diversify the risks facing individual firms, industries, regions, or countries, and thus foster innovation and technical change.
>
> *Resources allocation:* Financial institutions facilitate the acquisition of information about potential investment projects and thus resource allocation. A major role of the banking industry is to develop expertise in the process of collecting and analyzing the collection of information about investment opportunities and thus more efficiently identify the most promising entrepreneurs and the projects most deserving of investment. This function is especially important in a transition economy that needs to redefine its industrial structure in order to transform to a market economy and integrate with the global economy.
>
> *Corporate control:* Financial intermediaries can exert corporate control over inside owners and managers. This serves not only to protect the capital provided by outside investors but also to ensure efficient resource allocation. Again, this function is especially important in a transition economy that is in need of industrial restructuring.
>
> *"Long-term" in this context does not refer to a specific maturity, but rather to all loans that, unlike deposits, cannot be easily recalled overnight.

from the control of the state to private parties. Only recently have the authorities turned their attention to laying the key building blocks for the capital market, such as ensuring corporate governance and thereby encouraging the domestic mobilization of savings.

While capital market development is an integral part of the process of developing the financial system, it is difficult to conceive how the capital market would develop without the foundation of a solid and trusted banking system. The use of capital market instruments generally involves commitment on the part of creditors and debtors to more complex, longer-term payment profiles—as would be the case with investment in enterprise equity—while bank deposits and loans have shorter maturities and relatively simple payment profiles. It would not be possible for capital markets to function efficiently as long as banks are unable to deliver their services efficiently, and trust in banks remains weak. Banking system development (further covered in Part III of this book) lays the foundation for the broader agenda of financial sector development. The remainder of this chapter provides a brief overview of the size, structure, and functions of the Russian banking system.

SIZE AND STRUCTURE OF THE RUSSIAN BANKING SECTOR

The Russian banking sector[4] at the end of 2001 had approximately US$104 billion total assets, which represents 34 percent of GDP. Prior to the 1998 crisis, the sector's total assets were 27 percent of GDP, indicating real growth in the banking sector post-crisis.

At the end of 2001, Russian domestic credit was 24.3 percent of GDP, or US$76.0 billion, and the deposit base was 17.0 percent of GDP, or US$52.9 billion. Credit to the private sector was 15.4 percent of GDP (see Table 5.1).

As illustrated in Table 5.2, the Russian banking system is small by regional standards and underdeveloped compared with countries with similar per capita income.

Declining Numbers of Banks and Increasing Bank Capitalization Levels

Table 5.3 summarizes the trend in the number of banks and their capitalization. Rather than being accentuated by the 1998 crisis, the rationalization in the number of banks has actually slowed in recent years and even risen slightly in 2001 (see Figure 5.1). Based on their submissions to the CBR—developed under Russian Accounting Standards—at end-2001, only 230 Russian banks have paid-in capital of more than 150 million rubles, which is slightly below the ruble equivalent of the EU minimum capital requirement of 5 million euros (RUR 170 million at end-2001 exchange rates). If the EU standard were to be applied in Russia today,

Table 5.1 Monetary Survey Data on the Russian Banking System
(percent of GDP)

Monetary survey	1997	1998	1999	2000	2001
Bank deposits	13.0	16.1	15.5	15.9	17.0
Money and quasi-money (M2)	18.4	23.3	21.7	22.0	23.5
Domestic credit	26.5	41.1	32.7	23.9	24.3
of which:					
Claims on general Government (net)	15.4	26.8	19.9	10.4	7.8
Claims on nonfinancial public enterprises	1.3	1.2	1.0	1.0	0.9
Claims on private sector	9.5	12.8	11.5	12.3	15.4
Claims on other financial institutions	0.3	0.3	0.3	0.2	0.2
Nominal GDP, US$billion	428.5	277.8	184.6	251.1	311.0

Source: CBR, and International Financial Statistics (IMF).

Table 5.2 International Comparison of the Banking System Depth
(percent of GDP)

	1997 Private credit	1997 Deposits	2000 Private credit	2000 Deposits
Russia	**10**	**13**	**12**	**16**
Eastern Europe average	18	24	21	30
Czech Republic	67	63	50	65
Hungary	24	35	26	39
Poland	17	31	26	38
Ukraine	2	7	11	11
Lower-middle-income countries	50	33	54	38
OECD countries	123	55	128	56

Source: International Financial Statistics (IMF), and World Development Indicators (World Bank).

Table 5.3 Number of Credit Organizations by Paid-in Capital

Credit institution	1997	1998	1999	2000	2001
Under RUR 3 mln (US$0.1 mln)	806	817	230	174	128
RUR 3–30 mln (US$0.1–1 mln)	685	453	678	595	535
RUR 30–60 mln (US$1–2 mln)	206	201	253	256	255
RUR 60–150 mln (US$2–5 mln)	n/a	n/a	93	126	171
RUR 150–300 mln (US$5–10 mln)	n/a	n/a	43	69	97
Over RUR 300 mln (US$10 mln)	n/a	n/a	52	91	133
Total number	1697	1471	1349	1311	1319

n/a = not available.
Source: CBR Internet site: Monthly Bulletin of Banking Statistics.

Box 5.2 The Post-1998 Crisis Period: A Missed Opportunity for Consolidating the Banking System?

Following the 1998 crisis, the authorities succeeded in stabilizing the Russian banking system, but they failed to use the opportunity of widespread distress in the sector to consolidate the number of banks. The number of banks remains almost unchanged in the years following the crisis (see Figure 5.1). While the situation of the banks has improved since 1998, weak banking practices and inadequate supervision continue to conceal serious banking system fragility (for further discussion, see Chapters 6 and 9).

In countries with deep financial systems, financial crises can be seriously disruptive and financially very costly. However, in shallow financial systems—such as in Russia—the disruption and attendant costs caused by financial crises are likely to remain quite small. Under these circumstances financial crises may actually be beneficial, especially if such practices as the provision by banks of subsidized loans to politically "favored" customers are discontinued as a result of the crisis. In addition, in those countries where noncash payments and barter are tolerated as alternative sources of short-term working capital finance, the effects on the enterprise sector of interrupting financial intermediation through official channels will be muted. Thus, in transition economies financial crises provide an opportunity for systemic change designed to increase the efficiency of the financial system and increase its depth.

Several stages of the *financial deepening process* in the transition economies of Eastern Europe and the former Soviet Union have been identified (Peachey and Roe 2001). According to this analysis the ability of the financial system to achieve genuine stability depends on

- *Reducing tolerance for noncash payments:* Nonpayments—often representing tax privileges—allow inefficient enterprises to survive and provide alternatives to more conventional payment and credit arrangements. Noncash payments became much more prevalent in Russia immediately following the 1998 financial crisis, but they have declined significantly in recent years (see the discussion in Chapter 13). In part the decline in nonpayments reflects improved enterprise payment capacity (stemming from rising raw material prices) and the 1998 devaluation rather than structural changes. Thus, it is not certain that the greater use of official payment mechanisms will be maintained in less conducive economic circumstances.
- *The willingness of the authorities to consolidate the banking system:* Consolidation can only take place if the authorities are willing to drop protection of weak, nonviable banks. In achieving genuine stability there are sizeable gains to be made from consolidating the domestic banking system to concentrate on the better-managed, lower-cost banks, thus improving the overall efficiency of intermediation. As the failure to consolidate raises the cost of intermediation, there is a risk that without the closure of nonviable banks, the real preservation of domestic savings that has been achieved in Russia since 1998 may be undermined. The real cost of borrowing is unlikely to fall to credible levels until the intermediated financial savings of the economy are consolidated around a smaller number of banks with a significantly reduced cost base.

Thus, while the Russian authorities have managed to maintain the stability of the banking system in the post-1998 crisis period, they did not address the necessary process of system consolidation. Going forward, the consolidation process will depend on the adoption of increasingly low supervisory tolerance of high operating costs and low earning-to-asset ratios that characterizes many banks—both private and state-owned—and the adoption of explicit supervisory policies to accelerate bank consolidation and concentrate a bigger percentage of banking business in lower-cost banks. This will include a lower degree of supervisory tolerance of marginal performance by smaller banks as well as explicit efforts to broker mergers.

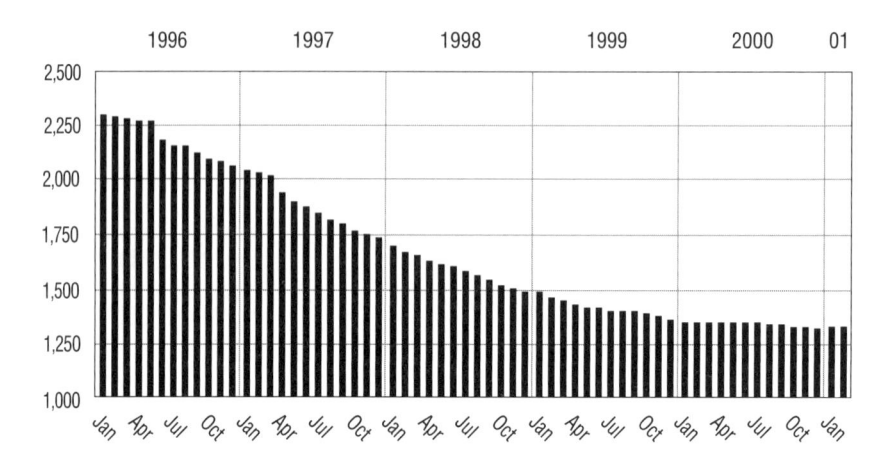

Figure 5.1 Number of Operating Banks

Source: CBR Internet site: Monthly Bulletin of Banking Statistics.

about 1,100 banks would thus require merger or recapitalization. At the beginning of 2001 only 76 banks had assets in excess of US$100 million, with the largest bank (Sberbank) dominant with assets of US$20 billion, or around five times the value of the assets held by the second-largest bank, Vneshtorgbank at US$4 billion (CBR 2001).

The small size of Russian banks means that they cannot take advantage of economies of scale, and are consequently inefficient. Banks in Russia today are caught in a vicious cycle: they need to grow to increase their retained earnings but lack the retained earnings that would enable them to grow. For most of the smaller banks, long-term survival will depend inevitably on their ability to raise capital or merge with other banks.

DOMINATION BY STATE BANKS

While the concentration of the Russian banking system is not unusual internationally, the dominance of state banks in Russia is high and has been increasing since the financial crisis in 1998.

As of January 1, 2001, the top 30 Russian banks, including nonstate banks, controlled around 67 percent of total bank assets and accounted for more than 53 percent of paid-in capital (CBR 2001).[5] The top 50 banks, including Sberbank, hold 76 percent of total assets, 89 percent of retail deposits, and 78 percent of loans within the system. Sberbank alone holds around 75 percent of the household deposits in the system. The larger state-owned banks control around 32 percent of banking sector assets.[6] If the banks that are majority-owned by regional governments are included in this calculation, the proportion of banking sector assets controlled by the state rises to at least 40 percent. Since the demise of the government securities market in 1998, state banks have emerged as important providers of loans for Russia's largest corporations.

ROLES AND OWNERSHIP STRUCTURE OF THE BANKING SECTOR

While Russian banks have not been particularly effective as financial intermediaries, they have learned to rely on alternative sources of earnings, such as the following.

1. *Providing financial services to specific enterprise-owners.* A large number of banks have served as the financial arm of a large enterprise or group of enterprises rather than providing banking services to unrelated third parties. Many banks perform such functions as settling payments for shareholders and the client enterprise; providing banking services to the enterprise's managers and employees; and engaging in investment activities on behalf of the enterprise. One factor supporting the development of such "clearing center" banks is the tax treatment of interest payments. According to the Russian Civil Code, interest payments on intercompany lending, including trade credit, are not tax-deductible. It therefore serves the interests of business groups, in the event of one or more companies within the group generating excess liquidity, to transfer that liquidity to another part of the same group through a bank. This has led to a number of groups and companies setting up their own banks to handle their interenterprise trading and intercompany liquidity management.

2. *Facilitating quasi-money operations.* Many Russian banks are engaged in managing or supporting Russia's quasi-money and/or nonmonetary system, issuing veksels for tax and/or regulation-evasion purposes or structuring and brokering transactions to help companies and government agencies manage the intricate operations of barter and receivable offsets. Some banks that are owned by regional governments or municipalities are active in these transactions.

3. *Acting as lender to federal and local government.* Prior to the 1998 crisis some banks held as much as 70 percent of their assets in government paper. With the demise of the government securities market and lack of trust in the interbank market, many banks now hold large clearing balances with the CBR.
4. *Performing treasury functions for federal and local government.* A major source of earnings coveted by Russian banks is the provision of treasury functions for federal and local governments—that is, banks acting as repositories and/or transfer agents for government funds, including budget subsidies; salary, wage, and pension payments; tax payments; various budgetary funds; and customs revenues.
5. *Provision of short-term financing.* Banks provide short-term working capital loans (up to three months on average) for import and export finance. However, the role of nonformal finance, such as tax arrears and barter transactions is still considerable. Other financing vehicles, such as factoring and leasing, are only beginning to emerge (for a further discussion see Chapter 13).
6. *Facilitating capital flight.* An attractive source of earnings for banks is the capacity to facilitate capital flight through foreign and offshore accounts and subsidiaries, particularly those based in Cyprus.

As a result of the limited role of the banking system, very little intermediation is provided to the benefit of unrelated third parties. Russian enterprises finance themselves mostly with retained earnings and budget arrears. Although the economy has a serious need for finance to support investment and restructuring, capital continues to flow to safer, more trusted havens abroad. One important result of the financial sector reform agenda outlined in this book would be the reversal of this drain on economic wealth.

As a result of Russian banks' unwillingness to expose themselves to lending to unrelated third parties, financing is allocated within financial industrial groups (FIGs) rather than through the financial system. This allocation within financial groups is usually not optimal, because (*a*) a clear measure of the opportunity cost of capital remains unidentified; (*b*) there is no internal market discipline within such groups to mirror the obligation to compete, which would exist on an external market; and (*c*) powerful business groups often create barriers to entry and thus prevent competition. Particularly in economies with weak legal and institutional environments—such as in Russia—these financial groups often serve the purpose of facilitating asset stripping, working to preserve current enterprise structures, and maintaining subsidies and privileges. The consolidation of the number of banks should lead to the dismantling of such structures and thereby diminish these economic costs. The joint Government/CBR strategy agreed upon in December 2001 does address the consolidation of the number of banks. However, although certain steps to raise minimum capital levels have already been taken, the strategy postpones for several years the implementation of key measures related to consolidation of the banking system (see Box 5.3).

CONCLUSION

The August 1998 crisis did not result in a consolidation of the Russian banking sector; instead the authorities chose not to manage the resolution of many of the failed banks. In many cases the principals of the major failed banks simply transferred the assets of those banks to other so-called "bridge" banks, leaving an empty shell to honor the bank's outstanding liabilities. Given ten years of high inflation and devaluation, the

---

Box 5.3 Consolidation of the Banking Sector: The Government/CBR Joint Strategy

In the joint Government/ CBR "Strategy for the Development of the Banking Sector" (finalized in December 2001) the authorities recognized that there remains a need to consolidate the sector. A step was taken in this direction in the fall of 2001 when the minimum capital level for newly licensed banks was raised to 5 million Euros (the minimum capital level applied within the European Union). The joint strategy recognizes the need to establish "nonbanking lending institutions," thereby allowing the authorities to limit the licenses of certain banks so that they can no longer solicit deposits from the general public. Nonetheless, the joint strategy in effect *further delays* the implementation of actions for the existing 1,300 banks. The following measures were proposed in the joint strategy:
- As of 2005 a rule will be applied whereby the licenses of banks below 5 million Euros are automatically revoked if their capital adequacy falls below 10 percent. Currently, similar action can be applied to all banks, but only if their capital adequacy is below 2 percent (see Chapter 9).
- In 2007 a minimum capital requirement of 5 million Euros will be applied to all banks irrespective of the size of their capital, which in effect removes any "grandfathering" of current lower capital requirements for existing banks.

The joint strategy states clearly that any reorganization of banks—including any merger with other banks—must be *"based on the principle of voluntary participation."* In this respect the strategy reflected continued hesitancy on the part of the authorities to use the powers already at their disposal to consolidate the banking system. These powers include stricter accounting and reporting requirements, more effective use of supervisory powers, and full implementation of the recently tightened legal framework for bank liquidation.

failure of the authorities to actively manage the crisis only confirmed the population's general distrust of the banking sector.

As outlined in this chapter, many institutions holding banking licenses in Russia today exist mostly to fulfill the internal, treasury-related needs of their associated companies, rather than to actively solicit deposits from the public. One course of action, which would contribute significantly to building trust in the Russian banking system, would be to review the principal business of each bank to see whether the bank requires a public deposit-taking license. If rapid action were taken to reduce the number of marginally viable or less efficient institutions holding full banking licenses, gains could be made by (*a*) reducing the costs of intermediation, (*b*) restricting the privilege of holding a banking license to only those institutions interested in soliciting deposits from the public, and (*c*) focusing the efforts of banking supervisors on effectively upgrading the remaining reduced universe of banks.

Given the growth in the relative importance of the state-owned banks, steps will need to be taken concurrently to limit the expansion of the loan portfolios of these banks, and to lay the groundwork for their reform into fully commercial institutions (further discussed in Chapter 7). Issues related to applying supervisory actions and implementing bank restructuring and liquidation are discussed further in Chapters 9 and 11.

ENDNOTES

1. This study controls both for other determinants of economic growth and for reverse causality and the simultaneous determination of growth and financial development.

2. Productivity growth is measured as the residual of real growth per capita minus 0.3* capital per capita growth, where 0.3 is the estimated share of capital in the production function. Taking into account human capital as an additional production factor does not change the conclusions.

3. This implies that while there is a correlation between capital accumulation and financial development, this does not necessarily imply causality flowing from financial development to faster capital accumulation.

4. This description of the state of the Russian banking sector is largely based on RAS statistics. As further discussed in Chapter 6, these statistics have significant flaws, including somewhat overoptimistic assets valuation and thus overestimated capital bases, and a "form over substance" approach to the classification of certain categories of balance sheet and income statement data, which leads to inadequate reflection of banking risks, and so forth.

5. Statutory capital per Russian regulations. The paid-in capital can be in cash, up to 25 percent real estate and up to 25 percent in pre-1998 government paper. The paid-in capital in foreign currency is recognized and maintained in foreign currency.

6. The CBR owns 58 percent of Sberbank; 99.99 percent of Vneshtorgbank; the Government owns 100 percent of Vneshekonombank, the Russian Development Bank, the Bank for Agricultural Development, and Roseximbank.

REFERENCES

Beck, Thorsten. 2001. "Financial Development and International Trade: Is There a Link?" Policy Research Working Paper 2609. World Bank, Policy Research Department. Washington, D.C.: World Bank.

Beck, Thorsten, Ross Levine, and Norman Loayza. 2000. "Finance and the Sources of Growth." *Journal of Financial Economics* 58: 261–300.

Beck, Thorsten, Mattias Lundberg, and Giovanni Majnoni. 2001. "Financial Development and Economic Volatility: Does Finance Dampen or Magnify Shocks?" Policy Research Working Paper 2707. World Bank, Policy Research Department. Washington, D.C.: World Bank.

CBR (Central Bank of Russia). 2001. Monthly Bulletin of Banking Statistics at website: http://www.cbr.ru

Demirgüç-Kunt, A., and V. Maksimovic. 1998. "Law, Finance, and Firm Growth." *Journal of Finance* 53: 2107–2137.

Dollar, David, and Art Kraay. 2001. "Growth is Good for the Poor." Policy Research Working Paper 2587. World Bank, Policy Research Department. Washington, D.C.: World Bank.

Easterly, William, Roumeen Islam, and Joseph Stiglitz. 2000. "Shaken and Stirred: Explaining Growth Volatility." Presented at the ABCDE conference, World Bank. http://orion.forumone.com/ABCDE/files.fcgi/154_easterly.pdf

Levine, Ross. 1997. "Financial Development and Economic Growth: Views and Agenda." *Journal of Economic Literature* 35(2): 688–726.

Levine, Ross, Norman Loayza, and Thorsten Beck. 2000. "Financial Intermediation and Growth: Causality and Causes." *Journal of Monetary Economics* 46(1): 31–77.

Peachey, Stephen, and Alan R. Roe. 2001. "Financial Deepening and the Role of Financial Crisis." In Lajos Bokros, Alexander Fleming, and Cari Votava, eds., *Financial Transition in Europe and Central Asia*. Washington, D.C.: World Bank.

Rajan, Raghuram G., and Luigi Zingales. 1996. "Financial Dependence and Growth." Working Paper Series 5758. Boston: National Bureau of Economic Research.

Wurgler, Jeffrey. 2000. "Financial Markets and the Allocation of Capital." *Journal of Financial Economics* 58: 187–214.

CHAPTER 6

Analysis of Banking Practices

INTRODUCTION

For the purpose of analyzing the Russian banking sector, a sample of 35 larger banks was reviewed. The banks were divided into three subsets as follows:
1. *Subset 1: Larger banks owned by the Government and local/regional governments.* This subset is composed of the two largest state banks, Sberbank and Vneshtorgbank (VTB), plus Bank of Moscow, Bashcredit, and Eurofinance. All these banks are in the Central Bank of Russia's (CBR's) list of top 30 banks.
2. *Subset 2: Large, domestic, privately owned banks.* This subset includes a number of banks from the CBR top 30 list.
3. *Subset 3: Private, domestic banks living up to more stringent reporting requirements.* This subset includes some banks that are in the CBR list of top 30 banks as well as a number of smaller banks.[1]

The review sample includes most of the domestic banks in the CBR's list of top 30 banks, plus a few others that have worked with the Financial Institutions Development Project (FIDP). These banks account for roughly half of the total assets of the banking system as measured by the Russian Accounting Standards.

Data for four years were retrieved, starting with 1997 RAS numbers. Compilation of a four-year time series is intended to provide some idea of the trends characteristic of the entire reviewed sample.[2] To make the trends analysis more meaningful, the numbers were translated into U.S.

dollars.[3] An attempt was also made to do some peer group analysis, despite the fact that the peer group subdivision was quite superficial and was used with the sole purpose of checking for any features or trends that might be unique to a particular subset of banks. Subsets 2 and 3 were combined to compare major trends in privately owned banks against government and quasi-government banks. It was not easy to decide to which subset of banks Gazprombank should belong for analysis purposes, because it is majority-owned by an entity that is perceived to be government-owned or -controlled. Because it has a business profile that is reminiscent of a financial industrial group structure, the bank was ultimately included in subset 2.

It should be noted that the 2000 data on some of the banks became available very late—toward the end of April 2001. Audited IAS financial statements are generally released even later than RAS numbers. Past experience shows that most of the banks that commission such audited accounts make them publicly available toward the end of the second quarter or even into the third quarter.[4] Since many of the operations of Russian banks continue to be conducted on a short-term basis, these delays limit the usefulness of such audited financial statements. However, audited IAS accounts, largely because of the more conservative IAS approach to loan valuation, can in some cases give an earlier warning of potential problems facing the reporting entity. For example, the low level of Sberbank's capital, which became public knowledge toward the end of 2000, was exposed much earlier by the bank's IAS audited accounts than by its RAS accounts.

Systemwide comparisons are not possible based on IAS accounts, because IAS data on the whole banking sector do not exist. Moreover, comparison of RAS and IAS data on those banks that do publish their audited IAS accounts is not possible for the end of fiscal 2000, because of the application of IAS 29 (hyperinflationary accounting). Furthermore, application of IAS 29 has rendered trend analysis very difficult, because IAS 29–adjusted numbers for most banks exist only for two years. Peer group analysis is also complicated, because some of the international audit firms chose to issue IAS accounts not adjusted for IAS 29. Finally, any further trend and/or peer group analysis based on IAS accounts is bound to be even more difficult because as of mid-2001 some banks began to introduce IAS 39 (fair value accounting). This standard has caused significant international debate and raised serious supervisory concerns.

While trend analysis of the reviewed sample is difficult using IAS data, RAS data are characterized by significant distortions. These include overoptimistic assets valuation and thus overestimated capital bases, and a "form over substance" approach to the classification of certain categories of balance sheet and income statement data, which leads to inadequate reflection of banking risks. More detailed comments on distortions under RAS can be found in the following sections of this chapter. Thus, although a large quantity of financial information on the reviewed banks was processed in order to substantiate the observations presented in this chapter, these observations are inevitably only general in nature. More in-depth analysis would require on-site verification and adjustment of the banks' numbers to ensure that they provide a more accurate reflection of the banks' risk profiles. Obviously the scope of this exercise does not include such verification for the whole reviewed sample, although many of the bank weaknesses described below have been noted during on-site reviews carried out under FIDP.

ASSET STRUCTURE AND QUALITY

By the end of year 2000, the banking sector had recovered approximately 70 percent of its pre-1998 crisis asset value, as measured in U.S. dollars.

Key statistics on the asset composition of the sample banks are presented in Table 6.1. Between 1997 and 2000, the banks of subset 1 suffered a decline in asset values of approximately 25 percent. The recovery of the banking system as a whole toward its pre-crisis levels appears to be accelerating with year-on-year growth reaching 43 percent in 2000, compared with 17 percent in 1999.

Highest Asset Growth in Bridge Banks

The highest pace of asset growth in 2000 among the 35 banks of the review group was recorded by the private banks of subsets 2 and 3, which saw their assets increase by more than 60 percent. Subset 2 demonstrated growth of almost 40 percent from pre-crisis levels, primarily through the contribution of the so-called "bridge banks." Assets were transferred to these banks by banks formerly associated with FIGs after they defaulted on their creditors in the aftermath of the 1998 crisis. The audited IAS accounts of such banks are not publicly available, but there is cause for concern that these bridge banks may adopt the same poor banking practices that caused their predecessors to fail.

Table 6.1 Key Statistics on the Asset Composition of the Russian Banks
(millions of U.S. dollars)

	1997	1998	Percent change in 1998	1999	Percent change in 1999	2000	Percent change in 2000	Percent change in 1998 to 2000
Total assets of the banking system	114,581	50,270	−56	58,653	17	83,710	43	−27
Total assets of the sample reviewed	51,576	23,431	−55	30,923	32	46,913	52	−9
Subset 1 (including Sberbank)	35,115	14,948	−57	18,673	25	26,541	42	−24
Sberbank alone	29,764	11,427	−62	13,963	22	19,668	41	−34
Subset 2	9,615	5,712	−41	7,922	39	13,339	68	39
Subset 3	6,846	2,771	−60	4,328	56	7,033	63	3
Gov. debt securities of the banking system	26,180	8,765	−67	7,915	−10	11,032	39	−58
Gov. debt securities of the sample reviewed	19,144	6,828	−64	6,799	0	9,428	39	−51
Subset 1 (including Sberbank)	17,087	6,516	−62	6,415	−2	8,249	29	−52
Sberbank alone	15,982	6,236	−61	5,429	−13	6,239	15	−61
Subset 2	1,379	148	−89	226	53	857	279	−38
Subset 3	678	164	−76	158	−4	322	104	−53
Total loans of the banking system	49,693	24,079	−52	25,668	7	38,380	50	−23
Gross loans of the sample reviewed	19,962	11,466	−43	16,356	43	25,862	58	30
Subset 1 (including Sberbank)	9,812	5,221	−47	8,650	66	13,399	55	37
Sberbank alone	6,870	2,711	−61	6,282	132	9,980	59	45
Subset 2	5,988	4,259	−29	5,272	24	7,937	51	33
Subset 3	4,162	1,986	−52	2,434	23	4,526	86	9

Source: CBR website, individual bank reports.

State Banks Expanding Their Lending Portfolios

The asset structure of the reviewed banks has changed quite dramatically, with loans to customers accounting for 50 percent of total assets at end-2000, compared with 36 percent in 1997. This trend is most visible among the government banks, which increased their loan-to-assets ratios from 25 percent in 1997 to 46 percent in 2000. The volume of lending also rose: aggregate gross loans to customers of the total review sample increased by US$5,900 million over the review period. Government and quasi-government banks accounted for 61 percent of this increase, with Sberbank alone accounting for 53 percent.

In 2000 Sberbank increased its loan portfolio by US$3,698 million, or by 60 percent. Given the time it takes to acquire credit risk assessment skills, this increase in loan volume is cause for concern, especially given the concentration of credit risk in Sberbank's loan portfolio and the bank's weak capital base. As of January 1, 2001, Sberbank accounted for almost 30 percent of aggregate loans extended by the banking sector. Some of Sberbank's larger loans, which from time to time receive a certain amount of publicity, have been extended to companies that have experienced difficulty in honoring their financial obligations on time and in full. It is worth noting also that the failure of certain corporations to service their debt was the most significant element in the demise of the largest banks in 1998–99. Particular attention needs to be paid to influences beyond the borrower's control, such as the movements of commodity prices and changes in local tariffs.

Significant Concentration in the Banks' Loan Portfolios

At the end of 2000, government and quasi-government banks accounted for 35 percent of aggregate loans of the Russian banking sector. Audited IAS accounts of two subset 1 banks show their loan concentrations to be badly unbalanced. According to audited IAS financial statements, as of December 31, 2000, Sberbank had 16 borrowers with aggregate loans above RUR 2.2 bln (US$78 million). The aggregate value of these loans was RUR 89.7 bln (US$3,185 million) or 32.6 percent of the loan portfolio. Loans to the two largest borrowers amounted to RUR 43 bln (US$1,527 million) or 15.7 percent of the loan portfolio. Vneshtorgbank had 15 borrowers with aggregate loans above US$15 million. The aggregate amount of these loans was US$732 million or 62 percent of the bank's loan portfolio. The two largest borrowers had outstanding loans totaling US$272 million or 23 percent of the total loan portfolio. Audited accounts of other banks in the subset are not publicly available, but it seems unlikely that the concentration of loan portfolios held by these banks would be much different. This concentration of loans by government banks is a significant contingent fiscal liability, and an indicator of the highly skewed distribution of enterprise financing.

There is even less information available in the public domain on the loan portfolio mix of the banks in subset 2. It is entirely possible that the loan portfolios of banks such as Rosbank, DIB, and Menatep St. Petersburg are as concentrated as those of their failed predecessors. Many of the loans of these banks may also be to related parties. The loan portfolios of subset 3 are similarly highly concentrated. It is not unusual for fewer than 10 borrowers to account for 50 percent of the loan books held by these banks.

Use of Schemes to Avoid Official Loan Concentration Limits

Loan concentrations are often established in violation of CBR concentration limits. Banks also often circumvent CBR rules by creating sophisticated schemes that may involve "friendly" counterpart banks. One common scheme involves one bank placing significant balances on its correspondent account with another bank. The second bank then conveys these funds to the designated borrower. This scheme has the effect of both disguising the liquidity positions of the participating banks and distorting the aggregate data on the liquidity of the system. A second common scheme involves the purchase of veksels of a number of shell enterprises, which in turn transfer the funds gained to the borrower. It should be noted that veksels are a particularly convenient instrument for schemes. As they approach a CBR reporting date, some of the banks that have high concentrations of veksels from a single issuer will execute fake sales of the veksels for deferred consideration, and will subsequently nullify these deals, once the reporting date has passed. Banks can, of course, be seen on both sides of such schemes: one bank extends loans against the matching deposit of another bank. In this case the first bank artificially inflates its balance sheet and the second bank avoids proper recognition of concentration of its loan book.

The spreading of risk that such schemes entail might be interpreted favorably and as similar to the syndication of large risks seen in developed market environments. However, these schemes are dangerous because of (*a*) the relatively small size of the banks involved, (*b*) the fact that the counterparty banks are often little more than shells, (*c*) the relative size of this type of business compared with the banks' other lending, and (*d*) the concentration of lending to relatively few borrowers. The development of a credit bureau covering the borrowings of large corporations and obligations in the form of veksels could provide an important contribution toward a solution of this problem.

Underprovisioning for Loan Losses, Especially under RAS

Official statistics demonstrate improvements in the quality of loans across the banking sector after the 1998 crisis, based on the level of

Table 6.2 Loan-loss Provisions as Percentage of Gross Loan Books
(percent)

	1997	1998	1999	2000
Loan-loss provisions/gross loans of the sample reviewed	7	10	9	7
Subset 1 (including Sberbank)	10	14	9	9
Sberbank alone	11	15	8	6
Subset 2	3	6	7	4
Subset 3	4	10	14	8

Source: CBR website, individual bank reports.

loan-loss provisions (LLPs) (see Table 6.2). While there may have been some improvement, the low level of provisioning shown by many banks under RAS would not appear to fully reflect the poor quality of credit. In this respect VTB is a unique and interesting case. As of end-2000 VTB's recorded LLPs equaled 25 percent of its gross loan book (in 1999 it was 20 percent). This level of provisions is probably a more accurate reflection of the true credit risk of the bank's loan portfolio than of other banks in the sample, or indeed in the sector at large, especially because VTB has many of the bigger and more successful companies among its borrowers. Applied to the total sample, a 25 percent provisioning rate would be equivalent to almost five times the profits recorded by the banks.

Many banks have had to recognize larger provisions under IAS than under RAS. For example, in their 2000 IAS accounts the LLPs of subset 3 banks accounted for 11 percent of their gross loan books (in 1999 it was 18 percent), while their RAS provisions accounted for only 8 percent (in 1999 it was 14 percent). RAS/IAS discrepancies are also evident among state-owned banks. For example, under 2000 IAS, Sberbank's LLPs were approximately 12 percent of gross loans (in 1999 it was 18 percent), while under RAS they accounted for some 6 percent of gross loans (in 1999 it was 8 percent).

This situation is further aggravated by the large share of nonearning assets in the balance sheets of the reviewed banks. As of January 1, 2001, these accounted for almost one-fifth of total assets—a figure similar to the end-1997 level (see Table 6.3).

Table 6.3 Share of Nonearning Assets in Total Assets
(percent)

	1997	1998	1999	2000
Nonearning assets/total assets of the sample reviewed	22	17	17	18
Subset 1 (including Sberbank)	24	19	18	20
Sberbank alone	25	21	18	20
Subset 2	12	11	15	16
Subset 3	26	19	18	19

Source: CBR website, individual bank reports.

THE STRUCTURE OF BANK LIABILITIES

During 2000 the total liabilities of the reviewed sample increased by US$13,662 million, or 53 percent. The fastest growth, 80 percent, was recorded by the subset 2 banks. Over the four-year period of the review, the subset 2 banks recorded total growth of almost 40 percent, or roughly US$3,045 million, in their liabilities. This rapid growth may be largely attributed to customers (many of which might be related parties) transferring their accounts from failed banks into "bridge" bank entities. Despite this growth, the liabilities of the entire review sample, as measured in U.S. dollar terms, have not yet returned to pre-crisis levels, in large part due to a 30 percent decrease from the pre-crisis level of Sberbank's liabilities (see Table 6.4).

Issued debt securities is one liability item that has been growing in all three subsets and across all banks of the sample. During 2000, issued debt securities (including veksels) of the entire reviewed sample increased by US$1,786 million, with year-on-year growth of almost 70 percent. Overall, since 1997, debt securities issued by the sample banks grew by US$2,106 million, or more than 90 percent.

There is a widespread perception that issued veksels are a good tool for liquidity management, since they are, in theory, fixed-term instruments that cannot be exchanged for cash before maturity. As of January 1, 2001, however, on-demand veksels accounted for approximately one-quarter of all issued bank veksels, with on-demand veksels issued by Sberbank accounting for roughly one-half of all on-demand veksels in circulation.

Table 6.4 Key Statistics on the Composition of Liabilities
(millions of U.S. dollars)

	1997	1998	Percent change in 1998	1999	Percent change in 1999	2000	Percent change in 2000	Percent change 1998 to 2000
Total liabilities of the sample reviewed	43,688	20,318	−53	25,637	26	39,299	53	−10
Subset 1 (including Sberbank)	30,273	13,475	−55	16,317	21	23,091	42	−24
Sberbank alone	26,386	10,289	−61	12,746	24	18,153	42	−31
Subset 2	7,726	4,441	−43	5,934	34	10,711	81	39
Subset 3	5,689	2,402	−58	3,386	41	5,497	62	−3
Interbank deposits of the sample reviewed	5,026	3,240	−36	3,533	9	4,219	19	−16
Subset 1 (including Sberbank)	1,792	1,557	−13	1,337	−14	1,108	−17	−38
Sberbank alone	620	179	−71	283	58	176	−38	−72
Subset 2	2,236	1,062	−53	1,365	29	1,957	43	−12
Subset 3	998	621	−38	831	34	1,154	39	16
Customer deposits of the banking system	48,293	20,113	−58	23,192	15	34,337	48	−29
Sample reviewed	33,417	14,635	−56	18,506	26	28,806	56	−14
Subset 1 (including Sberbank)	25,756	10,749	−58	13,178	23	19,337	47	−25
Sberbank alone	23,671	9,198	−61	11,278	23	16,432	46	−31
Subset 2	4,213	2,506	−41	3,366	34	6,365	89	51
Subset 3	3,448	1,380	−60	1,962	42	3,104	58	−10
Household accounts included in customer deposits of the banking system	28,253	9,724	−66	11,128	14	16,094	45	−43
Sample reviewed	n/a	n/a	n/a	9,293	n/a	13,559	46	n/a
Subset 1 (including Sberbank)	n/a	n/a	n/a	8,583	n/a	12,371	44	n/a
Sberbank alone	n/a	n/a	n/a	8,392	n/a	12,103	44	n/a
Subset 2	n/a	188	n/a	368	96	610	66	n/a
Subset 3	n/a	244	n/a	342	40	578	69	n/a
Issued securities of the banking system	7,037	2,177	−69	4,316	98	7,130	65	1
Sample reviewed	2,267	988	−56	2,587	162	4,373	69	93
Subset 1 (including Sberbank)	806	457	−43	1,419	211	2,140	51	166
Sberbank alone	627	378	−40	954	152	1,243	30	98
Subset 2	845	378	−55	733	94	1,329	81	57
Subset 3	616	153	−75	435	184	904	108	47

Source: CBR website, individual bank reports.

SCHEMES THAT DISTORT THE STRUCTURE OF LIABILITIES

In four years, customer deposits of the sample, as measured in U.S. dollar terms, have dropped by US$4,611 million, or 14 percent, with Sberbank alone losing customer deposits equivalent to US$7,239 million. Although this decrease in customer deposits is largely attributable to the movement of the ruble/U.S. dollar exchange rate, another contributing factor would appear to be the widespread practice of circumventing the CBR mandatory reserve requirements by using schemes with friendly, usually off-shore, banks. The purpose of these schemes was to turn customer deposits into interbank funds, to which mandatory reserve requirements were not applied. The information on household deposits is significantly distorted by a variety of salary schemes. The substitution of veksels for deposits may also account in part for the movement in the banks' deposit base. All in all the widespread use of schemes allows banks to manipulate their funding base and makes it almost impossible to analyze the level, trends, and structure of the banks' liabilities. The fact that the bulk of bank liabilities are still of a very short maturity suggests a continued low level of depositor trust.

Maturity Mismatch between Banks' Liabilities and Assets

The mismatch between short-term liabilities and long-term assets is recognized by many parties, including the CBR, as one of the main problems facing the banking sector. In certain banks, the liquidity gap in the time band of 0 to 30 days is cause for concern. One of the worst liquidity gaps is reported by Sberbank. While it can be argued that Sberbank has a core of individual depositors that are loyal to the bank, the considerable negative mismatch of the bank's liabilities is of serious concern, especially against the background of an underdeveloped interbank market and an overall lack of trust in the system. If public confidence in the banking system were to fall further, the liquidity situation might become unmanageable. Under such circumstances, undue pressure could develop on the lender of last resort.

Mechanisms for Window-Dressing Banks' Liquidity Positions

There are several banks in the reviewed sample whose maturity mismatches appear to be less of a problem. It is common practice, however, for banks to achieve a balanced liquidity position through artifice. Bank X, for example, might do this by maintaining a large NOSTRO balance (a foreign exchange balance held offshore by a commercial bank), usually with a second-tier bank that in turn invests the incoming funds in loans or securities of parties designated by Bank X. This provides apparent liquidity, but not genuine unencumbered liquidity that would be readily available for depositor payouts. In other examples, banks will report, under RAS, significant NOSTRO balances with offshore banks, but the balances will disappear in IAS consolidation. Such schemes achieve the objective of disguising a bank's true liquidity position. These are the most common examples, but probably not the only ones, of devices aimed at misleading the general public and even statistical analysts.

Another problem facing some of the banks under review is that of concentration of corporate deposits. Such concentrations are normally not easily traceable in RAS accounts. They are usually only revealed in audited IAS statements, which may or may not be publicly available. IAS audits often show that as few as 10 or 15 depositors or creditors account for the bulk of the deposit base. In some cases, concentration of the deposit base is disguised by yet another common scheme, which involves the bank persuading some customers to make their deposits with a subsidiary or a friendly bank; the deposit will then show up in the first bank's books as an interbank account.

ASSESSING BANK CAPITAL

As a result of the above observations it follows that capital can be one of the most illusory quantities in the Russian banking environment. There are many ways in which banks can manipulate their capital positions, and many of them take advantage of the available opportunities. Until 1999, IAS financial statements tended to give a more conservative assessment of the bank capital than RAS, but the introduction of IAS 29 as of end-2000 has reversed this situation in many banks. As past experience shows, the viability of a bank ultimately depends on the intentions of its beneficial owners and/or controllers in choosing whether to keep their bank alive or to transfer any good assets the bank might have to another "bridge" institution and start anew.

PROFITABILITY

Profitability is one area that is showing signs of improvement (see Table 6.5). In 2000 there was a significant increase in the share of net interest income in the overall income stream recorded by many of the banks in the reviewed sample. This represents a significant change over previous years, when the bulk of the profits was derived from securities trading (1997) or from foreign exchange trading and translation gains (1998 and 1999). However, the increase of net interest income is clearly the result of growth in lending volumes, which in turn entails significant credit risks. As many of the banks are underprovisioned in relation to the risks they are taking, it is to be expected that the positive trends in profitability will eventually be compromised by the need to increase provisions. Without incurring undue risks, banks probably also have little room for improving their net interest margins. Due to the on-demand nature of their deposit base, bank interest expenses are already low.

Detracting from profitability are the high operating costs of many banks. These numbers obviously vary from bank to bank, but the most

Table 6.5 Key Statistics on the Profitability of the Reviewed Banks
(millions of U.S. dollars)

	1997	1998	Percent change in 1998	1999	Percent change in 1999	2000	Percent change in 2000	Percent change 1998 to 2000
Net profit of the sample reviewed	990	70	–93	404	477	985	144	–1
Subset 1 (including Sberbank)	742	147	–80	326	122	652	100	–12
Sberbank alone	492	318	–35	310	–3	451	45	–8
Subset 2	203	–53	–126	166	–413	311	87	53
Subset 3	45	–24	–153	–88	267	22	–125	–51
Return on assets of the sample reviewed	1.9%	0.2%		1.5%		2.5%		
Subset 1 (including Sberbank)	2.1%	0.6%		1.9%		2.9%		
Sberbank alone	1.7%	1.5%		2.4%		2.7%		
Subset 2	2.1%	–0.7%		2.4%		2.9%		
Subset 3	0.7%	–0.5%		–2.5%		0.4%		
Net interest income/ pre-tax profit before provisions of the sample reviewed	–8.7%	–15.2%		25.5%		85.5%		
Subset 1 (including Sberbank)	–34.9%	–30.7%		37.6%		97.2%		
Sberbank alone	–64.2%	–33.2%		27.9%		131.8%		
Subset 2	44.8%	26.5%		10.9%		63.4%		
Subset 3	70.2%	23.6%		–2.3%		41.6%		

Source: CBR website, individual bank reports.

extreme examples report cost-income ratios in excess of 80 percent. It must also be noted that the use of a variety of salary schemes means that the actual level of overheads is in many cases disguised under RAS. Overall, the return on assets has improved between 1999 and 2000 and has basically exceeded the pre-crisis level.

Finally, it should be noted that profitability has always been an area where there are quite significant variations between RAS and IAS. In part this reflects generally higher provisioning expenses under IAS. In addition, IAS auditors tend to reclassify some income and expense items to reflect their economic function rather than their legal form. While comparisons of RAS and IAS numbers in this area have previously proved to be quite revealing, since the introduction of inflation-adjusted IAS audits for financial year 2000, such comparisons are no longer possible.

CONCLUSION

The following conclusions can be drawn from the off-site review of RAS data and audited IAS accounts of some of the major banks, supplemented with information from on-site reviews of some banks under FIDP:

1. Banks continue to be inadequately capitalized for the risks they are taking.
2. Sustainable profitability remains elusive.
3. Most of the banks still either fail to recognize or tend to conceal the risks inherent in their loan portfolios, and thus remain significantly underprovisioned. Thus the contribution to earnings provided by improvements in banks' net interest margins may eventually be compromised by the need to set up more provisions.
4. Excessive concentrations in the loan portfolios continue to be a major problem for most banks. This asset concentration is often mirrored by large concentrations of deposits on the liability side.
5. On the surface, there is ample liquidity in the sector, but the banks' core business still does not provide them with an adequate inflow of cash. Under these circumstances banks will continue to suffer from periodic liquidity crunches.
6. Most banks claim that they maintain covered foreign exchange positions and thus are not vulnerable to currency risks. However, currency risk is often passed on to bank customers (or the Government, in the case of large holdings of foreign-denominated government debt), and this makes the banks vulnerable to any adverse movement of the currency.

7. Internal controls and management information systems remain inadequate. Risk management systems still fail to send proper warning signals to bank managers, especially regarding large concentrations.
8. Banks persist in schemes to circumvent CBR regulations—for example, on concentration limits, mandatory reserve requirements, and limits on open currency positions—and to optimize their taxes.
9. Disproportionate foreign borrowing and large positions in derivatives—two of the major contributing factors behind the 1998 crisis—may have all but disappeared, but this is a consequence of the crisis itself rather than a calculated decision by banks. Some banks are once again starting to tap foreign markets. However, access to these markets is very limited as indicated by the amounts, terms and conditions, and dubious counterparties' names related to these borrowings.

Concerns Related to Bank Corporate Governance

By far the biggest problem related to Russian banks is weak corporate governance. Opaque ownership structures are a characteristic feature of Russian banks. Bank ownership structures typically contain a number of shell entities with unclear business profiles and ownership. Moreover, ownership lists are constructed in such a way that the disclosure of most names is optional, because in many banks none of the owners has an ownership stake exceeding the threshold set for mandatory legal disclosure. The degree of influence of each of the shareholders or shareholder groups is also unclear, because affiliations between shareholders are not disclosed, and information on related-party transactions is incomplete. Corporate governance is weak even in those banks that are majority-owned and/or controlled by the authorities (as further discussed in Chapter 7).

Standards regarding financial disclosure and transparency are also far from adequate. Even where audited IAS financial statements are prepared, they are rarely publicly disclosed. The scope of the auditors' role is sometimes unclear, making it difficult to assess their independence. Annual reports of many banks often lack sufficient information on risk management systems and controls.

There is also a need to develop proper policies and procedures in the banking industry. The role of bank managers in relation to the bank's owners and/or controllers often remains unclear or undefined. Proper policies and procedures in key risk management areas are either nonexistent or can be overruled by stakeholders. This situation persists, although many bank failures in 1998–99 were the direct responsibility of bank owners. The owners, when faced with a choice of which part of their empires to save, stood behind their industrial interests at the expense of their bank's creditors and depositors. Under such circumstances the purpose of the analysis of bank financial statements is drawn into question for much more fundamental reasons than whether they represent a true and fair picture of the bank's financial situation.

Despite these caveats it appears that the authorities—primarily bank regulators—have managed to preserve a certain degree of stability within the sector following the crisis in 1998. Now the major challenges are to create an environment that would support those banks that are prepared to address the above weaknesses, and to continue to rid the system of those institutions that are not willing to work toward achieving the necessary improvement.

ENDNOTES

1. This subset includes those banks that regularly report to the World Bank's Financial Institutions Development Project.

2. Although the end-2000 numbers do not always reflect the most recent developments (e.g., further growth of loan portfolios), the next set of comparable annual data would not be publicly available until April/May 2002.

3. Translation into U.S. dollars was done at CBR's official exchange rates as of reporting dates, as follows: January 1, 1998—RUR 5.96 = US$1; January 1, 1999—RUR 20.65 = US$1; January 1, 2000—RUR 27 = US$1; October 1, 2000—RUR 27.75 = US$1; January 1, 2001—RUR 28.16 = US$1.

4. According to estimates by international auditors, international audits of IAS accounts are commissioned by some 130 banks, or approximately 10 percent of credit institutions operating in Russia.

CHAPTER 7

Reforming the Role of State Banks

When developing financial systems in transition economies, it is important to identify the appropriate role of state banks in providing financial services. The purpose of this chapter is to examine options for reforming the Russian state banks against the backdrop of experience in other countries with extensive state banking.

International experience has shown that state-owned banks are not efficient in providing financial services and, although government ownership of banks is common internationally, their numbers are declining over time. A study by La Porta, Lopez de Silanes, and Schleifer (2000) sampled the ten largest commercial and development banks in 92 countries and found that up to 42 percent of banking assets were in publicly owned banks as of 1995.[1] In 1970 the average had been 59 percent; the average is much higher in the former socialist countries (62 percent) (see Table 7.1). While comprehensive data are not available, the decline of state banks since 1995 has been quite sharp in many parts of the world. The sharpest decline has been in the former socialist economies, but a decline is also evident in other countries.

Many claims have been made about the benefits and advantages of state banks; these are balanced by reports of costs and damages made by state banks. Two recent studies have used a broad cross section of countries to evaluate the accomplishments and drawbacks of state banks.

Table 7.1 Government Ownership Stake in the 10 Largest Banks
(percent)

	1970	1995
Total sample of 92 countries		
Mean	58.9	41.6
Median	57.1	33.4
Nonsocialist countries		
Mean	52.7	38.5
Median	53.0	30.0
Former socialist countries		
Mean	100	61.8
Median	100	60.0
Median for all 92 countries	70.4	35.8

Source: La Porta, Lopez de Silanes, and Schleifer 2000.

INFLUENCE OF STATE-OWNED BANKS ON PERFORMANCE AND GROWTH

La Porta, Lopez de Silanes, and Schleifer (2000) investigated the claims that state banks can foster growth in a financial system and economy, especially in low-income countries. The study also addressed the claim that state banks reach a broader clientele than private banks. Economic costs from public ownership of banks have been high and the benefits less than expected. The authors found that countries with high state ownership of banks in 1970 had less financial sector development, lower growth, and lower productivity in subsequent years than those countries with private banks.[2] The channel from state ownership to lower growth is through productivity; state banks generally do not allocate capital to its highest use. State banks do not have a positive impact on capital accumulation, and countries with large state ownership of the banking sector do not have a widespread distribution of credit. Credit allocation was more concentrated in those countries with state-owned banks; typically the largest 20 firms, which often included inefficient state enterprises, received more credit the greater the degree of state ownership.

The negative effects of state banks were greater in low-income countries where there was less financial sector development and weaker property rights protection. Conversely, high state ownership of banks caused fewer problems in economies with high incomes, greater financial sector development, and strong protection of property rights.

Another cross-country study, by Barth, Caprio, and Levine (2000), found similar (negative) results for state banks. Systems with greater state ownership of banks tend to have higher interest rate spreads, less private credit, and more concentrated credit, with a higher proportion going to the largest 20 firms. The countries with high state ownership also had slower financial sector development with less activity on the stock exchange and less nonbank credit. In the systems where state ownership is greater, more applications for bank licenses are rejected, and there are fewer foreign banks. These results held after taking account of real GDP per capita, corruption, expropriation risk, bureaucratic efficiency, and the law and order tradition of the country; all of these variables can influence financial development. The Barth, Caprio, and Levine study also suggested that greater state ownership is associated with financial instability.

Barth, Caprio, and Levine (2000) found that state banks contribute to instability, and that monitoring by the market tends to be significantly weaker with higher state ownership. Monitoring by official supervisors is expected to be weaker because governments are exposed to incentive conflicts when one part of the Government is charged with monitoring another.

THE TREND AWAY FROM STATE BANKS

Designing and implementing a plan to reform state banks by introducing trusted private sector governance is an integral part of a viable strategy to develop the financial system. Consistent with international evidence that state ownership of banks is not a desirable strategy over time—because it slows development of the financial system and the economy—countries are moving away from state banking. However, a quick exit from state banking may not be feasible. International experience has also shown that poorly executed or premature bank privatization programs create additional problems. Chile in the late 1970s and Mexico in the early 1990s both sold state banks into weak regulatory environments. In both cases the banks were sold to industrial groups. This led to the next generation of problems, which is related to lending within the groups, or "connected lending," a problem that Russia is familiar with in their current structure of banking.

Given the potential problems with inappropriate and premature privatization, it may be prudent to adopt an approach to privatization that is moderate and spans several years. The strategy should carefully prepare banks for privatization, address weaknesses in the overall incentive environment, allow new entry by credible safe banks (including foreign private banks), improve financial infrastructure, and importantly, control the damage done by state banks to the competitive environment (e.g., in preserving quasi-monopoly rents and accumulating contingent fiscal liabilities). Additional material regarding international experience in reforming state banks is provided in the annex to this chapter.

STATE BANKS IN THE RUSSIAN FEDERATION

Although a government working group set up in early 2001 by President Putin and chaired by Prime Minister Kasyanov concluded that the state, at both the federal and regional levels, holds equity in up to 400 Russian banks, most of these holdings are minority shareholdings. At the time the state held more than 50 percent of shares in only 19 banks, 15 of which were under the supervision of the Agency for Restructuring Credit Organizations (ARCO).[3] The remaining substantial government holdings were in a handful of banks. CBR holds majority stakes in Sberbank and the Bank for Foreign Trade (Vneshtorgbank), while the Federal Property Fund has stakes in RoseximBank, the Russian Development Bank, and Rosselkhozbank. In 1991, following the collapse of the former Soviet Union, the foreign trade–related banking operations of Vnesheconombank (VEB) were transferred to VTB, which at the time was a new entity established by the CBR. VEB continued to manage the sovereign liabilities of the former Soviet Union remaining under government ownership. However, in the ensuing years VEB also built significant banking operations in its own name. In addition, some banks are owned by either regional or municipal authorities. As of end-2001, the two largest banks, Sberbank and VTB, together accounted for almost 30 percent of total system assets. Overall, approximately 39 percent of banking system assets were on the balance sheets of state banks (see Table 7.2).

As a result of the Government's preferential treatment of state banks, as well as the decline in the private banking sector, the relative importance of state banks in Russia expanded in the aftermath of the 1998 crisis. State banks received many privileges, including more favorable treatment in government debt restructuring, and (until recently), lower reserve requirements. Both Sberbank and VTB enjoyed major recapitalizations in the aftermath of the 1998 crisis.[4] VTB had major capital injections during 1999 and 2000. Sberbank's capital injection took the form of shares predominantly sold to the CBR. Amendments to Sberbank's charter approved by the AGM in the summer of 2001, authorize the bank to issue

Table 7.2 Data on Various Segments of the Banking Market
(percent)

	Market share of assets	Market share of capital	Interest spread	RoA (RAS)	RoE (RAS)
State banks	38.7	40.6	7.2	2.2	15.2
Foreign banks	4.9	5.7	12.1	6.9	54.4
Large banks	41.1	41.1	9.6	1.7	11.3
Medium banks	9.2	6.9	12.4	2.5	12.4
Small banks	5.8	5.7	9.0	0.2	1.1

RoA Return on assets.
RoE Return on equity.
Source: Troika Dialogue 2000.
Notes: The calculations are based on RAS accounts as of July 2000.
Large banks are the top 100 commercial banks in terms of assets (excluding state and foreign banks). Medium banks are banks rated 100 to 200. Small banks are the remaining 1,000 banks. The large bank category includes the banks in ARCO. Annualized profitability is for the first half of year 2000 (based on pre-tax profits). Interest spreads are calculated for interest-bearing assets and liabilities and therefore include securities. The numbers for RoE and RoA may be overestimated where equity is overestimated. This reflects under-provisioning under RAS.

yet more shares, and the CBR will probably have to participate in further subscriptions, if for no other reason than to keep its stake above the minimum 50 percent level prescribed by the law. Also new specialized banks for agriculture and development have been established. Discussions are under way on the future role of VEB. If it is granted a full banking license, then yet another fully fledged state-owned banking institution will be exploiting a market niche, in which it already has certain competitive advantages. Thus despite the avowed intention of the authorities—as stated in the joint CBR/government strategy for the Development of the Banking System—that the state intends to reduce its presence in the banking sector, the current trend runs contrary to those intentions.

As to smaller banks, the joint CBR/government strategy states that the Government plans to disengage from minority shareholdings. This strategy builds on the findings of the working group set up by the Government in early 2001. The working group concluded that it would be advisable to reduce state ownership in the form of minority stakes in about 400 state banks, and to focus on relatively few banks in which the Government would continue to own at least 25 percent of the banks' share capital. Consistent with this strategy, the state is already in the process of withdrawing from the capital of banks under ARCO management.

Thus, even though the Government seems to be poised to divest some of its holdings in smaller banks, Russia will almost inevitably face many of the same issues as other countries in the region when they reduce the dominance of state banks. These issues include the detrimental impact of state bank dominance on economic growth and financial development both in the near term and the long term (see the annex to this chapter). In this respect the following key issues will need to be addressed:

1. What to do about the market dominance of Sberbank? Should Sberbank be allowed to continue expanding into a full-service commercial bank?
2. When and how to privatize VTB?
3. Should VEB become a bank, an export credit agency, or a debt management agency without a banking license?
4. Is there a role and a justification for institutions such as the Russian Development Bank and Rosselkhozbank (the Russian Agricultural Development Bank)?

THE ROLE OF SBERBANK

The Central Bank of Russia holds a 62 percent stake of Sberbank's voting stock. Sberbank dominates financial markets in many business lines. Especially in the corporate loan business, its market share has grown considerably since the 1998 crisis.[5] Sberbank continues to control approximately 75 percent of total retail deposits and 23 percent of banking system assets. Sberbank has several advantages: a large branch network with broad geographic distribution, a perceived state guarantee on deposits, a strong internal payment system, and a key role in distributing state pension payments. Sberbank also has a monopoly on the processing of settlements on certain municipal services and the receivables/payables of the state pension fund. As of end-2000, Sberbank had 21,778 outlets: 17 territorial banks, 1,511 branches, and 20,250 internal structural subdivisions. Sberbank has considerable market power, accounting for up to 75 percent of commercial lending in some regions.

Until mid-1998, Sberbank had the bulk of its assets invested in government securities. Prior to the financial crisis, gross loans to companies were only 20 percent of total assets, while government securities were 54 percent. Despite the reduced share of Sberbank's assets placed in government securities after the crisis, Sberbank is still the largest holder of government securities.[6]

Since the crisis, Sberbank has aggressively expanded lending to the corporate sector. Although in dollar-adjusted terms there appears to be a reduction of the size of the loan portfolio as of end-1999 compared with end-1997, the share of lending in total assets increased from 20 percent (1997) to more than 40 percent (1999). Measured in dollar terms, there also appears to be dramatic growth of the loan portfolio in 2000—almost 60 percent. As of end-2000, the gross loan portfolio was equivalent to almost US$10 billion, accounting for almost 50 percent of total assets. Almost all of this loan growth is in the form of lending to the corporate sector. Loans to individuals represent less than 4 percent of the loan portfolio[7] and inter-bank lending is not a major activity. Sberbank accounts for almost 30 percent of aggregate loans of the banking sector (see Table 7.3). A large part of the Sberbank's credit portfolio is in lending to the gas, oil, and chemical industries, construction, trade enterprises, and state and municipal bodies and institutions.[8] Sberbank is poorly capitalized for the expansion in its activities, especially against the background of the concentrated nature of its loan portfolio. Before the new capital injection in 2001, Sberbank struggled to meet the CBR's capital adequacy requirement of 10 percent. Under RAS the capital-to-asset ratio was 7.7 percent as of end-1999 and 8.72 percent as of end-2000. Although the bank came into compliance with capital adequacy requirement after the capital injection in 2001,[9] it was still in violation of the CBR's large lending limits. Thus, while benefiting from the forbearance of the supervisory authorities, Sberbank continues to be engaged in an aggressive expansion plan, which will result in further capitalization needs.

In the past, regional governments have politicized credit allocation undertaken by Sberbank's territorial banks. In Dagestan, for example, 90 percent of the credits extended by the regional Sberbank were said to be overdue in late 2000 (Oxford Analytica Brief 2000). During 2000, the system of territorial bank offices was consolidated from 71 to 17. This may lessen the problem of local government influence on Sberbank, but this political influence will most likely remain an important factor even after the restructuring and amalgamation of territorial banks.

THE GOVERNMENT'S MANAGEMENT OF SBERBANK

While it is probably too strong a statement to say that the population "trusts" Sberbank, it may well be trusted more than other Russian banks, and does therefore play a significant role in savings mobilization.

Factors benefiting Sberbank are its internal payment system, which eases inter-regional payments and thereby facilitates internal trade and the processing of state pension payments—these account for a considerable part of Sberbank's deposit base. However, these benefits come with certain costs, including the moral hazard of a bank that is state-owned and considered too big to fail; the conflicts of interest inherent in CBR ownership; the detrimental impact on competition of market dominance by a state bank that gets preferential treatment from CBR; and the risks associated with its aggressive business strategy, etc. The rapid growth and recapitalization of the bank, largely with public funds, has taken place while major public policy issues are still unaddressed. While the Government has been planning to undertake a strategic review of Sberbank for some time, it still appears to be uncommitted to the value of this process.

The following issues would need to be resolved on the basis of that strategic review:

1. *Balance between risk and reward.* While the events of 1998 proved that holding government securities was not a riskless activity, the Government restructured its debt so as to reduce the impact of the government default on Sberbank. Both corporate and consumer lending are higher risk activities than the previous strategy of holding public securities. As Sberbank has focused predominantly on expansion of its corporate lending since the 1998 crisis—a period of relatively good economic performance—any estimates of credit risk will have to take into account more representative estimates of borrower performance in terms of corporate debt and not just the experience of the recent past. A broader evaluation of alternative business strategies should be undertaken before Sberbank continues to expand its corporate lending and, as a result, increase its capital base. Because corporate lending is one of the riskiest business areas in banking—particularly in the Russian environment—extreme caution would seem advisable when expanding a portfolio of concentrated corporate loans, especially for a bank that is supported by a full government guarantee on its deposits.

    In the course of deciding on a business strategy, the authorities and/or Sberbank will face a variety of trade-offs—for example, between risk and profitability of corporate lending and government securities. They will also need to consider the trade-off between providing public services and increasing efficiency and lowering costs. Maintaining a large branch network is an important public service, but the current structure is unlikely to be cost efficient.

Sberbank also undertakes public service activities that are not commercially oriented, such as issuing low-interest mortgages and educational loans. Sberbank may want to spin off some activities/branches/services, and downsize some branches to agencies, but this can only be decided when a more thorough, overall strategic analysis has been undertaken.

Sberbank's business strategy should be decided in the context of the longer-term reform strategy for the bank. This reform strategy should involve improving the governance of the bank, which would be best achieved by privatizing the bank to reputable, strategic investors. While privatization may be a medium-term objective (taking up to five years as suggested in the joint CBR/government strategy paper), the privatization strategy should be decided as soon as possible to guide the efficient use of resources and to improve the prospects for successful privatization over the medium term.

2. *Lack of competition in the banking sector.* Sberbank far outstrips other banks in many business lines, most dramatically in the market for individuals' (households') deposits (see Table 7.3). Sberbank's market dominance appears to rest on the government guarantee of its deposits, the bank's quasi-monopoly in paying pensions, and the bank's extensive branch network. Sberbank does not appear to have a competitive advantage in working with enterprises, in which quality of service is important. Sberbank is perceived as being extremely slow with loan approval (taking 6–9 months), so its market dominance is obviously not based on quality of lending services.

Table 7.3 Sberbank Share of the Russian Banking System (according to RAS)
(percent)

	1997	1998	1999	2000
Gross loans (banks, enterprises, individuals)	14	11	24	26
Government debt securities	61	71	69	57
Total assets	26	23	24	23
Deposits of individuals	n/a	n/a	75	75
Issued securities	9	17	22	17

Source: CBR.

Clearly this type of market dominance will slow the development of the private banking sector. The following suggestions are offered to reduce the preferential treatment that Sberbank enjoys:
- Identify and quantify the value of preferential treatment by and subsidies from the Government and implement a program for removing unjustified subsidies.
- Compensate Sberbank for the costs related to undertaking quasi-fiscal activities, such as paying pensions (or acting as a payment agent for the MoF).
- Introduction of a generalized deposit insurance scheme might encourage competition, but would impose a potentially high fiscal cost. As discussed further in Chapter 10, deposit insurance is not feasible at this time in Russia due to the lack of credible banking reforms. Introduction of a generalized deposit insurance scheme would not be advisable prior to a strengthening of the disclosure, accounting, and supervision applied to Russian banks. Another prerequisite for a deposit insurance scheme is the effective enforcement of fit and proper requirements as applied to bank owners/controllers and executive management. Finally, a necessary precursor for instituting a deposit insurance scheme in Russia would be to develop a strategy for Sberbank. As an interim step and as a means to encourage the leveling of the playing field, consideration will need to be given to whether Sberbank should function as a "narrow" bank, which would invest in "safe" assets such as government securities, or whether it should operate as a fully fledged commercial bank (see further discussion below).

Sberbank's large deposit base gives the bank a significant advantage in lending. As the only bank able to lend large amounts within the large exposure limit, Sberbank may be in a position to exercise undue control over the distribution of credit to large firms. Also, as mentioned above, because many banks only operate in Moscow, Sberbank has considerable power over the corporate sector in some regions.

Other banks complain of unfair competition from Sberbank on lending rates.[10] Many loans are reportedly priced below market value. There appears to be an increasing tendency to perceive Sberbank's massive deposit base as a source of cheap funding to support "strategically important" industries. Sberbank's lower lending rate may reflect lower funding costs or less pressure to generate returns, implying that Sberbank is treating its capital base like a free resource. The bank's funding costs are low because it handles state pensions and has implicit deposit insurance. Also, in the past, the reserve requirement for Sberbank was lower than for other commercial banks (5 percent vs. 7 percent), but the requirement has been equalized at 10 percent recently. The low lending rates set by Sberbank may be forcing competitors to moderate rates so that they can hold onto clients. Given its privileged position, Sberbank should not be allowed to undercut market lending rates if that forces other banks to charge rates below what is needed to adequately cover risks.

Undercutting market lending rates and paying deposit rates above the rates offered by competitors would be consistent with a strategy for sacrificing returns in order to build market share. Currently the interest rates paid on "social deposits" is higher in Sberbank than in other banks, which would hardly appear to reflect the bank's cost base, because providing depository facilities through an extensive network of outlets is a high-cost activity for Sberbank. Deposit rates should be lowered to enable a fuller cost recovery, while simultaneously supporting the competitive position of other banks and giving Sberbank an extra margin to compensate the owner—the Government—with a return on capital and/or for the benefits provided by deposit insurance. Establishing a more rational pricing policy should be a high priority for Sberbank, regarding both the bank's assets and the bank's liabilities.

3. *CBR ownership results in serious conflicts of interest, but further privatization should be undertaken with caution.* The Central Bank Law and the charter of Sberbank currently mandate that at least 50 percent of Sberbank's shares must be held by CBR. Following the issue of new shares in 2001, the CBR now holds 62 percent of Sberbank's shares. The remainder of the shares are held by a wide range of enterprises and private investors, including a number of other banks. More than 25 percent of shares are in private hands.[11,12] An important part of any medium-term strategy for the reform of Sberbank will be to improve the governance of the bank and hence the market participants' trust in the bank; it is also crucial that any further privatization of the bank takes place to reputable, private investors. However, it cannot be stressed enough that privatization of Sberbank is not a short-term objective. Prior to privatization Sberbank needs to be restructured into

a viable commercial entity. Any privatization to insiders or entities controlled, for example, by financial industrial groups will only cement the opaqueness of the bank's governance and further defray trust in the financial sector.

There are clearly some potential conflicts of interest with the CBR being both owner of Sberbank and responsible for monetary and liquidity policy as well as the regulation and supervision of Sberbank. If there were another appropriate agency in the Government with sufficient political independence and financial expertise to exercise ownership role, then the Government should consider transferring the responsibility for exercising the ownership role. The most likely candidate is the Ministry of Finance. Regardless of which government agency exercises the ownership role, the operations and management of Sberbank should be made more transparent. As discussed in further detail below, given the potentially seriously compromised role of the CBR, disclosure requirements should go considerably beyond the current practice of just posting the bank's financial statements on the website.

The question of ownership was pushed to the forefront in 2001 by the issuance of five million new shares for US$140 million that had been authorized in 1996. This new issue will allow Sberbank to further expand its lending operations and still maintain a capital adequacy level just above the minimum level of 10 percent. Although Sberbank did not violate Russian law, the new share issue was structured inappropriately according to international practice: existing private shareholders should have been given right of first refusal for the new shares. The open subscription disposal of the shares could have resulted in a new domestic shareholder emerging with 19 percent of the shares, thus diluting the position of current shareholders. There are, however, more fundamental problems with share issues of this kind, and there have been recent proposals to issue another 10 million shares (expanding the share issue base by another 53 percent). Additional shares should not be issued until fundamental decisions are made regarding the reform of the bank, including decisions on implementing a business strategy for Sberbank that is consistent with establishing a more level playing field in the banking sector. Such decisions will affect the amount of capital the bank will need to have and the timeframe and strategy for privatization. In the meantime, it would seem appropriate that Sberbank should adjust the asset side of its business to raise the capital-to-asset ratio or, if need be, improve its capitalization by issuing subordinated debt.

THE STRATEGIC REVIEW OF SBERBANK

Taking into account the dominant position of Sberbank in the Russian banking sector, the Government should restrict Sberbank's further growth or its taking on new risks until the following issues are satisfactorily addressed within the framework of the envisaged strategic review.

Business Strategy

The Government needs to decide what type of business strategy Sberbank is allowed to pursue in the medium term. The following options should be considered:
1. Limit Sberbank's activities to those of a state savings bank. This means transforming public savings (in the form of banking deposits) into a specific range of investments (first of all, government securities), which will limit operations on the asset side of the balance sheet. The bank would focus on providing savings and payments products to its (predominantly individual) clients.
2. Let Sberbank maintain its present business mix, which is weighted toward lending to large corporations resulting in a highly concentrated loan portfolio.
3. Increase further Sberbank's range of operations as a fully fledged commercial banking operation in line with international practice, in both wholesale and retail markets, with a full range of clients.
4. Break up the bank into viable (maybe regional) autonomous units, thus reducing the dominance of the bank and preserving the social functions associated with the bank's large number of local outlets.

There needs to be clear *identification of the risks* in each of the above strategies. For example, there may be certain risks related to funneling Sberbank's deposits into financing the Government through the purchase of government debt instruments. Were Sberbank obliged to undertake sizeable new purchases of government securities, this strategy would need to be carefully coordinated with the upgrading of the Government's debt management capacity. If conducted in a coordinated fashion, this path would incur suitably low levels of risk for an institution whose liabilities are believed to be guaranteed by the state. On the other hand, were Sberbank to continue to pursue its preferred option of expanding its corporate lending, a thorough assessment would need to be made as to whether the bank has the effective management ability and autonomy as well as institutional capacity to continue along this route without accumulating sizeable contingent fiscal liabilities for the Government.

The *time dimension* associated with implementation of these various strategies also needs to be considered very carefully. The first proposal—preserving Sberbank as a "narrow" savings bank—may be expedient in the short term while other reform measures related to improving the governance and viability of the bank as well as reforms related to the enabling environment (e.g., the legal and judicial framework) are implemented; this option is likely to be an appropriate transitory measure rather than a medium-term strategic choice.

Interest Groups

Consideration of the above options needs to be based on the analysis of how the various scenarios affect the following interest groups:
1. *Federal Government.* Sberbank is the dominant savings institution with deposits, which are perceived to be guaranteed by the state. Thus the GoR has to recognize the contingent fiscal liability arising from any course of development adopted by Sberbank.
2. *Regional governments.* Consideration needs to be given to the extent of the influence of regional governments on the activities of Sberbank.
3. *The CBR as shareholder, regulator, supervisor, and provider of lender of last resort liquidity facilities.* There is a serious potential conflict of interest between the CBR's influence on the policy of Sberbank and the CBR's roles as banking regulator and supervisor, majority shareholder in Sberbank, and the CBR's responsibility for liquidity support (lender of last resort) to preserve the stability of the banking system.
4. *Private minority shareholders.* The ability of private minority shareholders to consolidate and coordinate the actions as a blocking shareholder. Private shareholders may gain the ability to siphon funding to their own industrial interests as well as to receive gains from their investments guaranteed by the state.
5. *Management and the Board of Directors.* An analysis will need to be undertaken of the forms of direct interests of bank management and the Board of Directors in developing the bank, including the influence/patronage exercised by management on local industrial development. Consideration also needs to be given to any link between the financial results of Sberbank and the amount of the management remuneration (including the possibility of share options).
6. *Customers.* An assessment will need to be undertaken of the service requirements placed on Sberbank by the large number of individual customers, of the ability of larger customers to exert influence on

the bank to receive easy credits, and of the consequences of any development strategy to be adopted by the bank on its ability to service its large retail depositor client base.

Ownership

Assessment of and decisions regarding the Government's strategy on the future development of Sberbank require careful consideration of a number of possible ownership structures. Each ownership structure will need to be considered objectively in terms of the advantages and disadvantages for each of the different interest groups outlined above. There should be no rush to privatize the bank; it will be crucial to coordinate the timing/sequencing of any change in ownership structure with implementation of the operational restructuring of Sberbank:
1. Maintain the status quo; that is, preserve the current ownership structure with CBR being a major stakeholder.
2. Return to full state control.
3. Privatize, and decide whether to continue deposit insurance.
4. Consider other options for future ownership structure, such as management contracts, based on international experience.

Competitive Position

An assessment of the current and future competitive position of the bank and analysis of how this affects the (potential) viability of Sberbank will contribute to answering the following questions:
1. Does the bank need the government guarantee of its deposits to continue its activity?
2. Is it possible to attribute any monetary value to this guarantee?
3. What other competitive advantages does the bank have?

As part of the process of evaluating different strategy options, Sberbank will need to undertake a due diligence review including the following:
1. A full portfolio review, adjusting for losses, to evaluate the returns on different types of assets and activities
2. A comprehensive evaluation of the cost and returns on different lines of business, including the cost effectiveness of the branch network, the bank's automation systems, the management structure, and so on.

Although a financial assessment was undertaken in 2000, in the form of a financial review of the bank performed by its international auditors, this assessment is now largely outdated. Such a review needs to be repeated at regular intervals. In any event the review performed in 2000 failed to address a number of fundamental questions, including the following:

General Management

1. What are the actions recommended by Sberbank management to improve the general operations, performance, and financial structure of the organization?
2. What was the substance of the advice of the auditors as possibly contained in the Management Letters which they submitted to Sberbank's management, and how did management view this advice?

Bank Operating Cost and Risk Structures

3. A description of the earnings potential and operational cost structure of Sberbank: How does the bank generate its cash flow/net income to support its headquarters group and extensive branch network? What are the staffing and cost implications thereof?
4. Have Sberbank's retail deposit volumes increased or decreased because of market/currency fluctuations or interest accruals? Is the bank's cash flow relatively stable or does it fluctuate positive/negative on an annual basis?
5. Does Sberbank have to subsidize the cost of its branch network from earnings on government securities and loans, currency trading, etc.?
6. Does management have an appropriate internal loan review function, which regularly conducts a comprehensive review of Sberbank's assets portfolio and the majority of outstanding loans, in accordance with BIS/IAS guidelines?

Potential Operating Advantages/Burdens

7. Has there been a thorough review of Sberbank's liabilities and a comparison with the marketplace? Has there been an analysis of influence of a lower reserve requirement relative to other banks resulting from possible tolerance on part of the CBR (in particular, at the regional level) for delays in compliance?
8. Is Sberbank affected by implicit positive or negative subsidies, for example, as sole distributor of pension payments and low-cost government deposits? Are there specific areas where Sberbank operations and/or profitability benefits are penalized by special circumstances, such as post-crisis funding and/or government securities

provided to the bank, informal encouragement to entities to work with Sberbank, etc.?
9. Are there special areas where Sberbank's character and/or position regarding the rest of Russia's banking sector give it a comparative advantage or pose a threat to its sustainability/profitability/competitive posture?

Developing materials that answer these fundamental questions will provide the backbone for in-depth strategic work, thereby allowing the authorities to adopt a development strategy for Sberbank that both preserves the bank's valuable features and contributes to leveling the playing field between Sberbank and privately owned banks.

RESTRUCTURING SBERBANK

While privatization of Sberbank should remain a medium-term goal, it will take time to prepare and consider strategic options. In the meantime, interim measures urgently need to be taken to minimize the damage that Sberbank's operations could inflict on the economy and the financial system. These measures are essential to setting in motion the self-reinforcing process of building trust:

1. *Perform a full ongoing assessment of Sberbank's financial situation.* Meaningful assessment of strategic options cannot be undertaken without further analysis of Sberbank's operations and financial situation. In particular there is a need to conduct a full portfolio review, adjusting for losses, to evaluate the return on different types of assets and liabilities. Given Sberbank's expansion of its lending to the corporate sector combined with recent, relatively good macroeconomic performance, it will be particularly important to scrutinize Sberbank's lending risks. A comprehensive evaluation is needed of the costs, returns, and risks within various business functions, including the cost-effectiveness of the branch network, the automation systems employed by the bank, and the bank's management structure. As outlined above, the financial review undertaken in 2000 is in need of being updated, and it failed to address a number of Sberbank's potential weaknesses, including issues related to the bank's management structure, the bank's operating costs and risk structures, the benefits associated with operating privileges enjoyed by the bank, and the cost of servicing obligations imposed on the bank.
2. *Improve governance.* The operations and management of the bank should be made much more transparent. In addition to

releasing timely annual external audit material, the bank should publish a full annual loan portfolio review; provide notification of all decisions affecting the bank's business strategy; undertake rigorous due diligence regarding the suitability of the bank's private owners; and provide full disclosure on decisions related to new share issuances, which should include providing pre-emptive rights to minority shareholders. Given the conflicted role of the CBR as majority owner, regulator, supervisor, and provider of liquidity/capital support to Sberbank, the importance of these immediate measures cannot be overemphasized. These would be the first steps toward improving the governance of the bank; these steps are essential for the strategic restructuring of the bank.

3. *Limit emphasis on corporate lending.* As Sberbank benefits from capital infusions and availability of a stable funding base, at least as an interim measure, some form of constraint (i.e., moderation and/or independent oversight) needs to be applied to the rapid expansion of Sberbank's corporate lending. Given the risks inherent in this rapid expansion—for example, the political pressures potentially placed on the bank in making lending decisions—quantitative limits should be placed on Sberbank's corporate lending function.

4. *Take measures designed to establish a more commercial framework for Sberbank's operations.* This might involve establishing arrangements to compensate Sberbank for quasi-fiscal activities such as processing the payment of pension services.

It is important that these safeguards are put in place immediately, to contain unsound business practices and to provide time for a thorough evaluation of the bank's future business development plans. In the short-term, the appropriate emphasis should be on strengthening the governance of Sberbank and ensuring that the bank is run according to commercial principles. This new focus would allow more emphasis to be placed on the return on capital and it would gradually reduce the need to monitor such factors as the bank's lending growth and interest rates. At the same time, however, plans for the medium-term reform of Sberbank need to be agreed upon and carefully designed. These plans need to include time-bound measures to ensure their staged implementation.

VNESHTORGBANK

At the time of its creation in 1991, Vneshtorgbank took over the foreign trade operations of Vnesheconombank, the old Soviet foreign trade bank. It is 99 percent owned by the Central Bank of Russia.[13] Although it is the second largest bank in Russia in terms of capital, it is considerably smaller than Sberbank. VTB accounted for about 5 percent of the banking system assets and 5 percent of total banking system loans as of end-1999, but it is expanding rapidly. Largely through capital injections undertaken by the CBR, the RAS capital increased from US$199 million at end-1998 to US$1,643 million by end-2000, making VTB one of the best capitalized Russian banks (IAS capital of minus US$514 million at end-1998, plus US$821 million as of June 30, 2000). Unlike Sberbank it does not have a large network of branches in the country, but the network of its subsidiary banks is still quite extensive. VTB is in the process of taking over the overseas banks owned by CBR.[14] In early 2002 VTB confirmed its intention to expand its corporate banking services and the size of its branch network, but it is still not yet clear whether VTB will become a business competitor for Sberbank.

According to audited IAS accounts as of year-end 2000, over 30 percent of the VTB portfolio was in securities. As of the same date, net loans were about 20 percent of assets. VTB's lending is primarily to the energy and manufacturing sectors (51 percent of total loans) with the trade and commerce sector accounting for 16 percent of total loans. The loan portfolio is highly concentrated with two-thirds of the loans to the bank's 15 largest borrowers, and with just two of these loans accounting for 23 percent of the total loan portfolio.

In the joint CBR/government strategy paper of December 2001, the authorities announced their intention to divest the CBR of its ownership stake in VTB by January 1, 2003;[15] the intention of the Government is to ensure its presence in influencing the bank's policies by assuming part-ownership of the bank; that consideration will be given to privatizing a portion of the bank. There would appear to be a strong case for privatizing VTB to a strong international bank as strategic buyer to bring in new skills, international quality technology, and introduce more competition into the market. However, the significant capital increases of 1999 and 2000 will make it more difficult to find an appropriate buyer, at least until the bank's surplus capitalization is absorbed in the form of sound, high-yielding assets. Also, recent history in Russia has shown that poorly executed privatization strategies entail large risks. For example, the loan for shares deal for the corporate sector led to the emergence of oligarch structures in the enterprise and financial sectors that have serious adverse repercussions.

The Government has announced that it is considering a proposal by EBRD to purchase an equity stake in VTB. Any such investment by EBRD would most likely entail a time-bound commitment by the Government to further privatization of VTB to strategic investors. While the first steps toward privatization involving the EBRD may take time to finalize, and the Government's commitment with regard to further privatization may be of a medium-term nature, a strategy regarding restructuring and further privatization of VTB needs to be agreed upon by the Government and announced as soon as possible. Only if the restructuring and privatization of VTB is based on a comprehensive strategy will it be possible for potential strategic investors to evaluate the bank's potential. For example, it is now unclear how the recent acquisitions of the CBR's foreign subsidiaries will contribute to the bank's viability and the prospects for its successful privatization. Setting the strategy would help to provide a framework for evaluating the influence of market developments on the bank's future viability and therefore the prospective benefits available to potential strategic investors.

VNESHECONOMBANK

Vnesheconombank, the former Soviet foreign trade bank, is owned by the Government. Its main activity is managing the Russian foreign debt incurred during the Soviet period. VEB does not have a banking license, but it is performing some banking functions. VEB is now violating the banking law by taking deposits, and this situation needs to be resolved. There are several options for resolving the question of VEB's business strategy and structure:
1. VEB could function as a debt management agency, paying market-based salaries, which would not be possible were this function to be performed by a department of the MoF.
2. VEB could become an export credit agency. The debt management services now performed by VEB could be put into other banks on a fee basis.
3. VEB could get a commercial banking license, and make an agency agreement to manage the foreign debt for a fee.
4. VEB could be merged with VTB and manage debt for a fee.
5. VEB's commercial banking functions could be merged with Roseximbank with the establishment of a separate debt management function.

Once the process of separating VEB's debt management business and other government-related transactions has been completed, the key issues that still need to be assessed are (*a*) whether VEB should continue as a government agency providing export/import guarantee support to Russian enterprises, and whether it should receive a banking license; and (*b*) whether the stand-alone commercial activities of VEB provide the foundation for a viable business operation. A case might be made for supporting foreign trade through partial guarantees provided by a government agency, but as illustrated in Box 7.1, this business does not require the agency to have a banking license. Given that there has already been considerable expansion of the role of state banks in Russia in recent years, and that there is a need for a more level playing field, any step toward expanding VEB's role as a banking institution should be taken with caution and be preceded by thorough analysis and justification. The weak performance of state banks in other countries suggests that using significant budget resources for capitalization of yet another large state bank would not be beneficial to the development of the Russian banking system.

NEW DEVELOPMENT BANKS

Two new state-owned banks, an agricultural bank and a development bank, were formed on the basis of the assets and branch network of the banks closed in the aftermath of the 1998 crisis. However, neither has fully developed its operations yet.

Experience with national development banks has on the whole been negative. Examples of good development banks are hard to find.[16] Moral hazard problems almost always swamp such banks within a few years. Development or policy banks are normally funded from the budget or from borrowing, usually from the commercial banks under some type of government guarantee. With no bottom line and with guaranteed funding, it is almost impossible to mandate reasonable performance. The problems do not end with the losses generated by development banks. International experience also clearly shows that government intervention to guarantee credit or subsidize interest rates will inhibit the functioning of financial markets. Other instruments for government intervention, such as direct government subsidies, should be considered rather than intervention through financial markets.

Many national development banks were closed in the 1980s. Those that survived usually drifted off into commercial banking activities to try to improve their earning capacity.

Given poor international performance that has led to widespread questioning of the development bank model, it must be asked whether it is a good use of resources for Russia to try and develop such banks. Direct government lending might be more efficient because it keeps the

Box 7.1 State Export Credit Agencies

The first state Export Credit Guarantee Department (ECGD) was formed in the United Kingdom in 1919. Similar export credit insurance and/or guarantee programs were founded in France, Italy, Spain, and in the United States in the 1930s, and in Germany in the early 1950s. The International Union of Credit and Investment Insurers, or the "Berne Union," was established in 1934 to facilitate cooperation in the development of underwriting techniques and to exchange information on payment practices. The following table summarizes the programs offered by some of the large developed country export credit agencies.

Types of Government-Supported, Export Financing Assistance

Country	Provider	Export Credit Insurance	Export Loan Guarantee	Direct Loans	Interest Rate Subsidies
U.S.	Eximbank	yes	yes	yes	no
France	Coface	yes	yes	no	no
Germany	Hermes	yes	yes	no	no
	KfW	no	no	yes	no
Italy	SACE	yes	yes	no	no
Netherlands	NCM	yes	yes	no	no
U.K.	ECGD	yes	yes	no	yes

Over the years many state export credit agencies have been privatized, and many private insurers have entered the export credit insurance market. The Berne Union has 45 state and private members and 3 observers from 40 countries. The members of the Berne Union provided coverage for US$397 billion of exports in 1998, nearly as high as the private credit insurance provided worldwide. The Berne Union members include almost all state export agency businesses, some surety and direct lending businesses. The main services provided by the Berne Union members are:

Investment insurance—normally covering only political risks.

Limited recourse finance—also known as project finance, limited recourse finance is a technique for the export credit agencies to finance or insure major projects on the basis of the economic viability of the project and its cash flow, rather than on the basis of the financial strength of the buyer and/or the seller. The earnings of the project thus provide the security for the lender and the insurer.

Until the 1990s the state export credit agencies faced little or no competition because they were the only providers of export credit in their respective countries. Increasing competition from the private sector and the privatization of some of the large export credit agencies (ECGD most notably) raise some questions about the future of the state-owned export credit agencies. Governments expect state export credit agencies to provide insurance to exporters not insured by the private sector, and also to remain financially solvent. How the state export credit agencies will be able to cope with these challenges remains to be seen.

Source: Sigma No.7 2000 and the national export credit agencies.

budgetary impact transparent. Furthermore, as development banks represent re-adoption of government-directed lending, it is highly questionable whether such banks can efficiently address the issues associated with the dearth of enterprise-financing, the so-called investment gap. As described in Part I of this book, these issues relate more to the poor enabling environment than to the supply of finance per se.

The Russian Development Bank (RDB) was established in early 1999, but its business strategy and mandate have not yet been clarified. The initial capitalization was RUR 660 million subsequently increased to RUR 4 billion (equivalent to US$160 million at that time). The bank is 100 percent owned by the Russian Federal Property Fund, with representation of the Government, Ministry of Finance, CBR, Ministry of Economic Development, and other government agencies on its supervisory board. There is a strong likelihood that the RDB will merely duplicate functions that could just as well be undertaken by the Economics Ministry directly; that is, redistributing budget and foreign assistance to industry.

The Russian Agricultural Bank (Rosselkhozbank) was established by ARCO to assist in the process of restructuring SBS-Agro. Although the business strategy of this bank is not completely transparent, it appears to be based on directing subsidies made available through the agricultural support fund. The fund is an on-lending facility for government funds to agricultural producers through selected commercial bank(s) (e.g., through SBS-Agro, prior to the crisis). However, it appears unclear whether the fund will survive, which makes the future of the bank even more uncertain. It is not clear that the fund should survive. Cross-country evidence suggests that the economic benefits of loan programs to the agricultural, heavy-industry, or other sectors of the economy have proven dubious and may just lead to an expansion of the role of state banks and future fiscal liabilities.

CONCLUSION

International experience shows that dependence on state banks slows economic growth and financial sector development. As described with references to a number of country cases in the annex to this chapter, it is hard to find examples of countries that have done well for long periods with state banks. China is one country cited as having had impressive economic growth with state banks. However, now that the process of cleaning out the state banks has started, it is clear that the losses are large and the operation of those banks unsustainable. Furthermore, the policy initiatives to make the banks commercial or to encourage the growth of competitors are proving difficult to implement.

In Russia, in the near term, there appears to be an argument for maintaining the safe depository facilities provided by Sberbank. It appears that the public mistrust of state banks is less than that of private banks. But while there may be an argument for keeping a state savings bank as a transitional institution, there is not a strong argument for aggressively expanding the role of that or other state banks.

In order to keep Sberbank as a state bank until the private banking system is reformed and deserves more public confidence, and to minimize the potential damage to the development of the financial system (the unlevel playing field) and the economy (inter alia in the form of contingent fiscal liabilities), the following issues will need to be resolved:

1. It should be a top priority to make the operations, business strategy, and share issue decisions of the banks transparent. An annual audit should be required, and it should include a full portfolio review to BIS/IAS standards. Publishing the financial statements is not enough. Given weaknesses in their governance structures, state banks need to live up to high disclosure requirements.

2. The preferential treatment of state banks should be discontinued. The Government should, as far as possible, remove noncompetitive features in order to level the playing field. Sberbank should pay a lower interest rate on deposits that are guaranteed by the state, and compensate the Government for the value of the insurance. The public perception that Sberbank is a safer bank rests on other types of preferential treatment, not just deposit insurance. While a medium-term strategy for the reform of Sberbank is developed and implementation measures are agreed upon, interim measures should be taken to contain the contingent fiscal liability associated with the bank's current status. Sberbank should increase its holdings of safe assets, such as public securities. Lending to corporates, even the largest corporates in the economy, is a high-risk activity when compared with investing in government securities.

3. Sberbank should pay for the benefits it enjoys, but the Government should also remunerate Sberbank for services that it provides, such as the payment of pensions. It would be premature in the near term to allow other banks to bid on undertaking payment services for the Government. Devolving responsibility for

such services to the private sector should await the upgrade of banking supervision as described in Chapter 9 of this book.
4. International experience has shown that banking supervision is less effective when applied to state banks because it is asking one arm of Government to supervise another arm. This problem becomes even more acute when the state bank is considered "too big to fail." This is an argument for limiting corporate lending by Sberbank in the short term and adopting a strategy for the medium term that reduces the bank's market dominance.
5. Even though Sberbank may not be privatized for several years, and should probably be the last state bank to be privatized, the strategy for the future development of Sberbank should be developed now. That strategy would provide a framework for evaluating Sberbank's business development. It would also help in providing guidelines for the bank's business plans, such as whether to dilute state ownership through new share issuance. Private ownership of Sberbank shares should be subject to rigorous fit and proper tests supervised by the CBR.
6. There is no argument for keeping VTB as a state bank. It should be privatized to a reputable international bank that can offer a strong brand name, new skills, and new technology.
7. VEB should not be conducting banking business without a banking license. The role and organization of the bank should be resolved as soon as a feasibility study can be done. Experience with state banks in other banking markets would speak against establishing a new, large state-owned bank in Russia.

ANNEX 7.1
REFORMING STATE BANKS

Countries have used a variety of monitoring, supervisory, and incentive packages to try to control the damage done by state banks. Unfortunately, there are more examples of failures than successes. The severity of the problems with government oversight, prudential supervision, competition, protection of depositors, and potential for fiscal losses depends to a large measure on the business strategy pursued by the bank and the role it plays in the market.

Business Strategy for State Banks

Traditionally, public banks have been savings banks, development banks, or commercial banks. Recently some countries, like China, have established policy banks. Many savings banks were originally considered "narrow banks," thus limiting the potential fiscal losses. Postal savings banks in most countries and savings banks in the United Kingdom and France were required to invest all deposit funds in government debt. In other countries, such as Germany, Italy, the Netherlands, Sweden, Switzerland, and the United States, savings banks are also allowed to lend to firms and households, although in the United States regulations differ from state to state (Vittas 1995). The problems of adverse impact on competitive conditions in the market, conflicts of interest between the role of owner and supervisor, potential fiscal losses, etc., are easier to deal with, the more narrow the range of services available through the bank.

In recent years, the tradition of public savings banks that invested in safe securities is giving way to commercial and universal banks; savings banks are losing their distinct identity. In many countries the need to change has been accelerated by the development of insurance plans and mutual funds that pulled much of the business from savings banks. Now globalization of banking services is adding another layer of competition for deposits. In many higher income countries, savings banks are being absorbed by larger universal groups and are no longer publicly owned. The speed of change varies considerably between countries. The Trustee Savings Bank in England is now part of Lloyds-TSB Bank. Many of the building societies, especially the larger ones, have become banks and now play a key part as retail banks (Halifax, Abbey National). Similar trends exist in Holland (Rabobank, for rural savings banks, and ING, for the postal bank), and in Nordic countries as well as Australia. Even the savings and cooperative banks in Germany, which long maintained a separate identity but with broad commercial lending powers, have been merging and gradually mutating toward the universal bank model. In the Czech Republic, the large savings bank has been taken over by First Erste Bank of Austria, which itself is a mutation of the traditional savings bank. In Switzerland some regional and cantonal banks, which replicate the functions of the German savings banks, have been taken over—actually rescued—by larger commercial banks. The question in Russia is whether it is premature for Sberbank to move away from the role as a traditional savings bank.

Many development banks were closed during the 1980s and early 1990s as the model failed to produce the expected benefits, and most development banks had accumulated significant losses. Dozens were closed in Latin America, Africa, and Asia. The development banks that remain, like savings banks, are migrating to become commercial or even universal banks.[17] Others are shifting to become bankers for households offering depository facilities and small loans, like BRI in Indonesia. These bankers for households are now more like the traditional savings banks than the ambitious development banks of the 1970s and 1980s, which were trying to support infrastructure and industry, or the specialized banks that focused on sectors that were difficult to serve, such as agriculture.

As state banks have expanded their role (most are now commercial), difficult issues regarding supervision and government oversight are being raised, and the potential for severe fiscal losses is recognized. The combination of politicized lending and weak management, which operated under greater regulatory forbearance, have led to cases of spectacular fiscal losses in recent years. Two well-known examples occurred in France and Brazil: Credit Lyonnais, the French bank nationalized in 1945 and privatized in 1999; and the Brazilian bank, Banespa, owned by the state of Sao Paolo before it was purchased by the Spanish bank, BSCH. In 2000 each ran up losses estimated in the range of $22–28 billion under government ownership. There are, of course, cases of expensive private bank failures, and the costs frequently fall on the public sector, but in the private bank failures there is at least some private capital to help absorb losses, and regulatory forbearance is usually not as generous. In many countries the losses in state banks continue to grow. For example, in China the expenditures on the four state banks are already up to about 20 percent of GDP, and may go as high as 40–50 percent of GDP as the cleanup continues. In addition to the explicit costs, state banks frequently receive implicit or explicit subsidies to prevent financial problems from becoming public. This increases the fiscal drain, distorts financial markets, and may prevent the growth of viable competitors. The full extent of the vulnerability of state banks to financial problems, and the cost of implicit subsidies are rarely made public.

Oversight, Prudential Supervision, and Competition

The business strategy of public banks will influence the options and severity of supervision and the responsibility for losses. For example, the problems of credit quality and potential for fiscal losses are clearly worse for development or commercial banks than for "narrow" savings banks. Similarly, the problems of establishing a level playing field to encourage safe competition is likely to be more important for a public commercial bank than for a development bank that targets only very large long-term infrastructure projects. Some of the issues to be addressed, in light of the business strategy chosen, are listed below.

Issues related to monitoring and supervision would include the need to
1. Clearly assign and exercise an ownership role.
2. Make explicit and minimize the conflict of interests between the roles of regulator/supervisor (avoid regulatory forbearance) and owner (safeguard equity).
3. Make explicit and rationalize the conflict of interests between the public sector provider of services and its effort to minimize fiscal costs. Remove taxes or other implicit benefits to show true fiscal costs.

Issues related to corporate governance would include the need to
1. Separate the government agency functions from traditional commercial banking.
2. Corporatize specialized state banks.

Issues related to establishing the framework for safe competition in banking would include the need to
1. Level the playing field by removing competitive advantages, subsidies, or other unfair advantages for the state banks.
2. Liberalize trade in financial services if it is consistent with other macroeconomic strategy. Agree on a business plan that is consistent with government objectives and eventual privatization plans.
3. Encourage the entry and growth of safe private banks.
4. Consider limitations on Government's ability to absorb risk and to inject additional capital to cover potential losses.
5. Formulate and approve the privatization strategy.
6. Set objectives for improvement in governance, competitiveness, and profitability. (Performance agreements with state banks tend to work when reputation matters and the system is transparent; they do not work as well when the system is not transparent.)
7. Monitor efficiency.
8. Enforce strong disclosure rules with transparent accounts.

9. Set the incentives needed to motivate management and staff; for example, in Poland the compensation for senior managers was linked to the future privatization value of the bank through stock options (Caprio and Honohan 2001).

Country Experience

In order to review some of the key issues related to public banks identified above, the following sections draw on the experiences of Brazil, China, and Germany. These country cases were chosen to highlight different business strategies in state commercial banks. The public banks in Brazil, at both the federal and state levels, have played the role of development, as well as commercial, banks. The distribution of credit has been highly politicized. In the decade since their inception, the state commercial banks in China have lent to public enterprises, and have been slow to move away from their traditional clients. The banks have been asked to provide commercial and project finance and even to take the kinds of risks that would have been funded in equity markets in a more advanced financial system. The public banking system in Germany is decentralized under local control and primarily lends to local markets. Germany also has an efficient contract enforcement system, and creditor rights are strong. These factors help explain why Germany has not had as many problems with their public banks as have the other European countries like France and Italy. The case studies show the important differences in the business strategies in these banks and the costs and problems with attempted reforms during the 1990s.

Public Banks in Brazil

Brazil has had public banks since the 1890s. Public banks owned by both the federal and state governments have been assigned quasi-fiscal, political, redistributive, and development functions. The system of federal banks includes the Bank of Brazil (the largest Brazilian bank, heavily involved in agriculture and export credit); the National Economic and Social Development Bank, which provides project finance to both the private and public sectors; the Federal Savings Bank (Caixa Economica Federal), which lends for housing and local government infrastructure; and regional banks in the Northeast and Amazon, which have both commercial and development functions. By the 1970s, there were also 24 commercial banks controlled by the state governments, so each state had at least one development bank, and several states had financial complexes with several banks. Most state banks have had private participation in their capital, and shares of 20 of the 23 state banks were traded on the Brazilian stock exchanges. In the federal system, the Bank of Brazil, Bank of the Northeast, and the Bank of the Amazon have private shareholders, and their shares are traded on the stock exchanges.

After the 1970s, public banks made up about half of the Brazilian system. During the 1980s and early 1990s, banks rapidly expanded their balance sheets using the "float" of high inflation[18] and low-cost liabilities, such as tax receipts and government deposits (see Figure 7.1). The high inflationary environment made savers unwilling to hold term deposits, and the public banks stepped in to fill this investment gap, making term loans to both the public and private sectors.

High inflation and bad accounting helped hide the losses that came from highly politicized lending, including the use of state-level banks to support employment-generating projects and to fund large infrastructure projects. Inflationary revenues accounted for over a third of revenue in the early 1990s. While losses were usually disguised, financial problems periodically bubbled to the surface. During the 1980s and 1990s, the Central Bank was forced to intervene on behalf of almost all public banks, as the several generations of programs put the state banks temporarily under Central Bank control. The banks were audited and restructured, and sometimes Central Bank debt was removed.

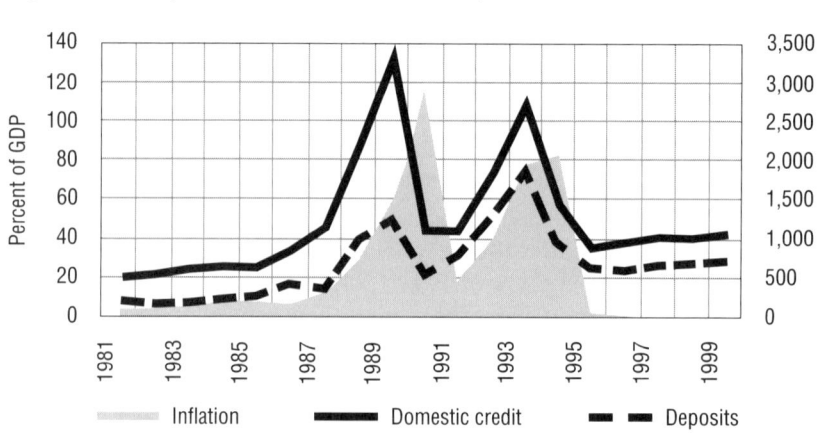

Figure 7.1 Development of the Brazilian Financial System

Source: International Financial Statistics (IMF).

As of end-1993—the beginning of the "real" stabilization program—public banks had a 55 percent market share of lending while private banks had a 45 percent share. Almost all term loans were in public banks. The difference in loan performance was marked. In the public banks, 45 percent of loans were nonperforming loans (NPLs), while in private banks, the figure was only 2 percent (Ness 2000). With the exception of the state bank, Banespa, lending to state government was not the main cause of NPLs per se. The problems were more fundamental; there were bad incentives for public banks, weak credit analysis for both public and private projects, high operating costs from excessive branching and overstaffing, etc. Almost all state banks were insolvent. Having private shareholders in the state banks did not control their poor performance. Private banks were more stable because they had more money invested in securities. Private banks had 25 percent of assets in securities, while public banks had only 15 percent. The public banks were dependent on low-cost public sector funding; that is, public deposits and movement of public funds through the accounts (Ness 2000).

The public banks deteriorated noticeably after the currency was stabilized in 1995. Even with bad accounting standards, over 60 percent of the public banks lost money each year in the 1995–98 period after inflation slowed and the "float" disappeared from the system (Ness 2000). All public banks had periods of substantial losses, with the exception of the Bank of the Northeast, which had very low returns. An examination of 12 state banks for which data are available reveals losses in excess of Rub 1 billion (US$1.089 billion) in the period 1994–95, and NPLs to the public sector accounted for 5 percent of total loans. The four federal banks lost close to Rub 5 billion (US$5.45 billion) in 1995 as loan-loss provisions for the private sector loans increased from 8.6 percent in 1995 to about 14 percent in 1996 (IMF 1997, cited in Baer 2000).

But the explicit costs understate the burden of the public banks on the economy. There were numerous effective subsidies by federal and state governments in the placement of loans and deposits, low returns on public deposits, etc.

After 1995 economic liberalization and stabilization made the burden of the public banks more apparent and unsustainable. With the deterioration of the state banks, the need to restructure state government debt to the federal Government,[19] and the need for the federal Government to reduce the recurrent fiscal drain from public banks became crucial. Political support for state banks weakened. In 1996 a more aggressive program was introduced to allow the federal Government to step into financial institutions at the state level to privatize them or to convert them into nonbank development agencies. Only occasionally was the decision made to restructure the state banks. If the state government wanted to recapitalize the state banks for continued operation, this had to be done with state funds. Federal assistance was available only if the state banks were to be privatized or turned into development agencies.

The process of resolving the state banks was interwoven with the process of restructuring the state governments' debt to the federal Government. Federal debt replaced state debt on the balance sheets of the state banks. Also, the state banks were no longer to fund state governments. The Federal Savings Bank took over the task of lending to state governments, and the federal Bank of Brazil held an increasing share of state government securities.

While an attempt was made to deal with the state banks over the period from 1997 to 2000, the federal banks continue to operate, and they will be even more difficult and expensive to resolve. Given the history of accounting irregularities, regulatory forbearance, and political use, making up the missing capital in these banks is going to be extraordinarily costly.

The remaining public banks still have substantial market share in various commercial banking activities, and they continue to distort the competitive banking landscape. The public banks control over 49 percent of the core funding and 40 percent of managed assets in the system. As of March 2000, public banks had 57 percent of lending, but only 31 percent of the earnings in the system. The intrinsic inefficiency and poor asset quality of the public banks impairs profitability and capital (Moody's Investor Service 2000).

State Banks in China

China established four large state banks in the late 1980s: the Bank of China, the Industrial and Commercial Bank of China, China Construction Bank, and the Agriculture Bank of China. The state banks (SoCB) have been the core of the financial system, which has grown rapidly since the two-tier system was reestablished. Domestic credit grew from 67 percent of GDP in 1985 to 141 percent in 2000 (see Figure 7.2). Over the same period, total deposits grew from 40 percent of GDP to 132 percent. Even though other financial institutions have been licensed, the four large state banks continue to dominate the banking system. As of end-2000, these four banks accounted for about 70 percent of both loans and deposits. They employ nearly 2 million people in about 103,000 branches across China. But while the Chinese state banks are large, they are not strong.

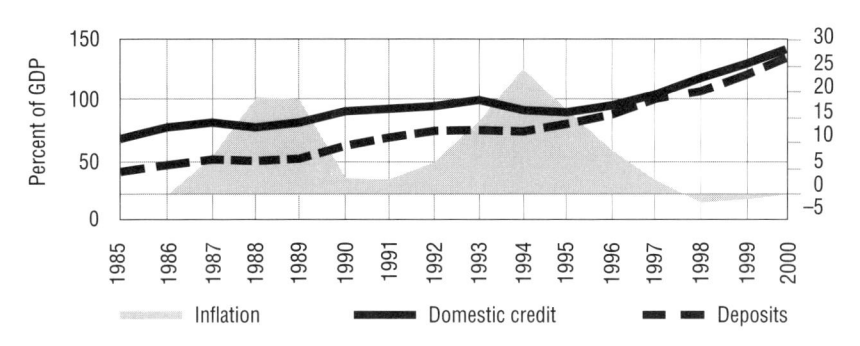

Figure 7.2 Development of the Chinese Financial System

———— Inflation ———— Domestic credit — — Deposits

Source: International Financial Statistics (IMF).

Source of savings. China has one of the highest household savings rates in the world, thanks to the economic reforms in the 1970s and 1980s, which shifted the flow of surplus income from enterprises to households. Much of that surplus has been channeled into financial savings in the public banks. The deposit base is US$1.6 trillion. The local-currency deposit base is $1.5 trillion, with more than half the money from households. In addition, on-shore U.S. dollar deposits total $130 billion, of which $75 billion is owned by individuals. There are several factors that have helped the domestic banks attract deposits. There are few alternatives available for holding savings: access to securities markets has been limited and capital controls are still enforced and are fairly effective at holding savings in the country. Until last year interest on deposits was not taxed, and the population could place money in no-name accounts without revealing their identity.[20] Interest rate policy has been generous during certain periods, including an indexing provision during periods of high inflation. While China does not have explicit deposit insurance, the Government has provided implicit deposit insurance, and the population perceives greater safety in the big state banks. Unfortunately much of the deposit base has been lost through inefficient politicized lending.

Portfolio problems. In the mid-1990s the Government tried to make the state banks into commercial banks, or at least to make them more commercial. The state set up three policy banks in 1994 to take pressure for policy lending off the four SoCB, but the strategy was not successful. The policy banks were too small to take over the insatiable demand for policy lending, and in some cases bad loans from the policy banks were transferred back into the state banks. The law was changed in 1995 to make the SoCB responsible for lending on commercial principles. However the SoCB—frequently with official encouragement—continued to direct credit to state and public enterprises.[21] This led to the accumulation of bad assets on the banks' books through the 1980s and 1990s. As the growth rate slowed and the state sector continued to decline under reforms, many firms were unable to service debts, owing to general inefficiencies, difficult markets, and increased competition. While loans to state-owned enterprises (SoEs) were a major part of the problem, it has not been the only problem. In general the lending policies of the SoCB reflected the perception that they were too big to fail, and they did not face hard budget constraints. Credit analysis had been perfunctory. The SoCB took on excessive risk and, for example, lent heavily into the real estate bubble in the mid-1990s. The SoCB stepped in to lend to high-risk ventures that would have been funded by venture capital or equity in better-developed financial markets. Also, regional and local governments encouraged local branches of the SoCB to lend to "favored" local public enterprises.[22] While the magnitude of the portfolio problems has never been revealed, and may never be known with any accuracy because of weak loan classification practices, it is understood that several of the large banks have significant losses, and three of them would probably be insolvent under international accounting practices.

Pressure to reform. Internal and external pressure to reform the banks intensified in the late 1990s and continue without any assurance of success. Economic growth slowed and the state banks did a poor job of serving the growing parts of the economy in the private sector. A disproportionate share of credit continues to flow to large enterprises that are stagnant or declining. While some businesses in the new private sector may be better credit risks, those businesses are less likely to have audited accounts and do not yet have years of financial records, so the SoCB ends up concentrating credit in declining industries. Also with moral hazard, the Government has been seen as more likely to cover the losses of lending to SoEs. This perception is accurate and will be almost impossible to dispel as long as both banks and enterprises are state-owned.

As the prospect that China could join the World Trade Organization (WTO) increased during the 1990s, pressure was added to clean up the banks to prepare for international competition. China agreed with the United States and the European Union that within five years of accession, the domestic banking sector would be opened substantially to direct foreign competition. This would allow foreign banks access to local currency business and expose the still rudimentary domestic institutions to competition from the sophisticated marketing and risk-assessment skills of international banks. On entry, foreign banks would be allowed to set up joint ventures with Chinese partners, and wholly owned foreign banks would be able to operate after five years. These agreements add urgency to the reform process.

Fiscal burden. The cost of cleaning up the state banks has already been high, and it will definitely go higher. In 1998 the Government injected capital of US$32 billion into the four state banks. In 1999 four asset management companies (AMCs) were set up and charged with acquiring—and, if possible, disposing of—nonperforming loans. To improve the balance sheets of the banks, the assets were transferred to the AMCs at face (not market) value. In 1999 and 2000, the AMCs bought assets worth US$170 billion, and 580 SOEs had agreed to swap a further US$41 billion for equity. The assets transferred to the AMCs accounted for about 20 percent of the combined loans of the SoCB. The amount spent in the 1998 recapitalization and the move to the AMC was about 20 percent of 1999 GDP.

The process of cleaning up the balance sheets is not yet finished; only loans made before 1995 have been transferred to the AMCs. All loans after that date, even those to the same companies, are still in the banks. The full extent of the remaining problems is not publicly known, but it is clear that the losses are large, and that the fiscal implications will be significant. One estimate suggests that there is an additional US$150 billion in bad loans that must still be written off.[23] The cost of cleaning the state banks may total as high as 40 percent of GDP before it is finished. Furthermore, there are other losses in the system. The three policy banks have not been cleaned up yet. Also many of the smaller financial institutions are owned by local or provincial governments that can not cover the losses in those institutions; the central Government is being forced to cover the losses when those institutions fail. In general, banking supervision allows insolvent financial institutions to continue operating because many public owners are unwilling or unable to cover the losses.

Continuing market dominance. Government efforts to introduce credible competition into the financial system and to lower the dependence on the four state banks have not succeeded. The Government started licensing other financial institutions in 1986. Since that time, the Government has established ten national joint stock commercial banks,[24] approximately 90 city-based commercial banks, about 3,000 urban and 42,000 rural credit cooperatives, and some finance companies.[25] While these financial institutions are not owned directly by the central Government or the Central Bank, the stockholders are, almost without exception, state-owned or public sector entities. There is only one private bank, Minsheng Bank, which was founded in 1996 with about 85 percent of the shares held outside the public sector.

The strategy for shrinking the market share of the four big banks through competition has not worked (see Table 7.4). The other financial institutions have not offered enough competition to discipline the state banks. Especially in the late 1990s, after the failure of a development bank, the population continued to depend on the big banks for depository facilities. It is clear that the four state-owned banks have implicit guarantees from the Government, because they are regarded as too big to fail. Even though the Government has covered all depositors in other banks and credit cooperatives that did fail, the population perceives that the big banks are safer. This perception has made depositors less willing to place their savings in the smaller banks. During the 1990s, the state banks continued to hold approximately 70 percent of all deposits.[26]

Especially disappointing was the continuing modest market share of the joint stock commercial banks. Most of the inroads of these commercial banks have been in urban areas along the eastern seaboard. Their combined share of total deposits and lending is growing, albeit from a very low base. At the end of 2000, their combined share of total lending amounted to 7.9 percent, while their share of deposits stood at 8.6 percent. Most of the increase in deposits has been in the four big banks (see Figure 7.3).

Table 7.4 Market Share within the Chinese Banking System
(percent)

Market share	Deposits 1993	Deposits 2000	Change	Domestic credit 1996	Domestic credit 2000	Change
State commercial banks	67.9	68.8	0.9	77.5	68.2	−9.3
Other commercial banks	5.6	8.6	3.0	3.7	7.9	4.2
RCCs	15.5	13.1	−2.4	9.5	9.9	0.4
UCCs	4.8	5.9	1.0	2.6	4.6	2.1
Finance companies	0.4	1.5	1.1	0.5	1.3	0.8
TICs and policy banks	5.7	2.1	−3.6	6.2	8.0	1.8

Note: RCCs are rural credit cooperatives; UCCs are urban credit cooperatives; TICs are trust and investment companies.

As accounting is nontransparent and disclosure weak, it is difficult to evaluate the financial position or performance of the joint stock commercial banks. Analysis of the available data by Moody's Investor Services suggests that the joint stock banks are comparatively healthy in the Chinese context; the return on assets amounted to 0.6 percent in 1999, compared with just 0.1 percent for the state commercial banks. The joint stock banks have lower cost bases because they have fewer employees and branches than the SoCB. With less policy-based lending to the state sector, the ratio of nonperforming loans is probably smaller. However, the repercussions of the ongoing process of industrial state-owned-enterprise restructuring have also exposed these banks to rising nonperforming loans. The few joint stock banks that disclose data on asset quality have reported a deterioration in the loan portfolio since 1997.

Many of the rural credit cooperatives are in desperate financial trouble and only survive because of political pressure on the Government to keep any credit cooperatives from failing. The 90 city commercial banks were formed by merging weak, often insolvent, urban credit cooperatives—often to avoid failures. Many of banks will not be viable and the losses must be recognized. Thus, while the best hope for competition for the big state banks are the joint stock banks, their ability to attract market share has been disappointing.

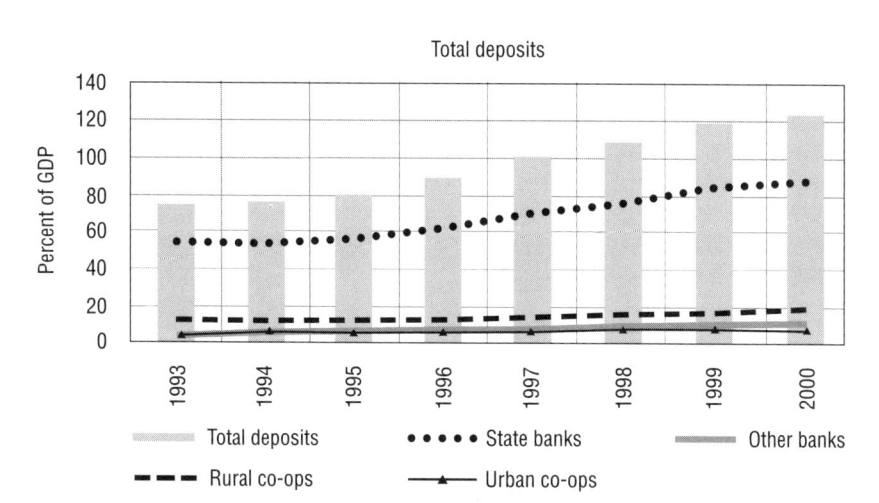

Figure 7.3 Total Deposits of Sectors within the Chinese Banking System

IMF (internal material).

Negative Impact on Economic Development

The Government now faces some difficult options. Accurate and transparent bank financial records are needed to hold the banks accountable for their performance, but a move to reliable accounting would reveal the depth of losses, and probably insolvency. This might shake the confidence of the population in the safety of depository facilities. While banking supervision has been strengthened, it is far from effective, largely because the big state banks are more politically powerful than the supervisory authority.

In the last year or two, the big SoCBs have started competing among themselves for the largest and most lucrative accounts. However, the majority of enterprises are too weak to switch banks and are therefore captive clients. The quality of service is low with very little credible competition from the joint stock banks to stimulate greater efficiency. This imposes heavy costs on the economy from bad banking services.

Public Banking in Germany

In most of Europe state banking is declining rapidly. It is in particular decline in Germany, falling from 52 percent of assets in 1970 to 36 percent in 1995 (La Porta, Lopez de Silanes, and Schleifer 2000), but that market share is still high compared with the rest of Europe (see Table 7.5). The gradual deepening of the German financial system is reflected in Figure 7.4.

Germany is frequently cited as a country where state banks have been less problematic than the norm. Some structural characteristics of the economy, as well as the business strategies and corporate governance of the public banks have been important in keeping those banks viable. The cross-country studies cited above (La Porta, Lopez de Silanes, and Schleifer

Table 7.5 Comparison of Market Share of Assets in Public Banks, 1995
(percent)

	Market share of public banks
Germany	36
European Union	25
OECD	28

Note: The share of public banks is defined as the percentage of the ten largest banks in each country owned by the Government divided by the total assets of these banks in 1995 (cited in Beck 2001).
Source: La Porta, Lopez de Silanes, and Schleifer (2000).

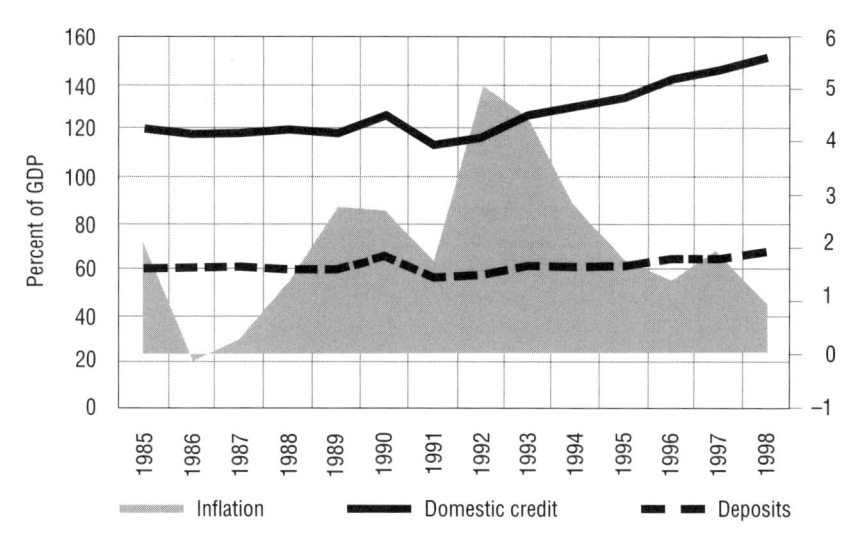

Figure 7.4 Development of the German Financial System

––––––– Inflation ––––––– Domestic credit – – – Deposits

Source: International Financial Statistics (IMF).

2000) found that state banks tend to be less problematic in higher income countries with better-developed financial markets. Other authors have suggested that countries with a strong institutional environment and a dispersed political process may have more success in controlling state banks (Caprio and Honohan 2001). There are strong enforceable creditor rights and little state ownership in the enterprise sector, so there is not the usual problem of state banks lending to state enterprises. Also the public banking system in Germany, like Austria, is decentralized and built on local rather than nationwide banks.[27]

Most public banks, both savings and cooperative banks, were started at the city or county level, and almost all continue to be owned by local municipalities and serve a specified geographic area. Now these local banks are connected through the state savings banks, which serve as clearinghouses for the local savings banks, as well as banker to the state. There is also a central savings bank, which serves as the central clearing bank to the savings bank system and holds the liquidity reserves. Of the three types of banks, savings, cooperative, and commercial, the savings bank system has the largest market share of assets and deposits (see Table 7.6). The dominant funding source for local savings banks is household deposits. While savings banks are now universal, the asset policies of the savings banks have been conservative, holding government paper and lending against

Table 7.6 Market Share of Different Bank Groups in Germany, 1999
(percent)

	Total assets	Total deposits
Savings banks	36.1	39.4
Cooperative banks	13.0	18.7
Commercial banks	25.2	24.6
Of which: largest four	14.4	12.8
Other banks	25.7	17.2

Source: Deutsche Bundesbank 2000.

real estate. About half of assets are in long-term loans to households, municipalities, and some nonbank firms. Local savings banks have had only limited exposure to industry and large commercial ventures, but the regional organizations may have some exposure to medium and large firms. The cooperative banking system is organized in tiers like the savings bank system. Cooperative banks are important for providing services to small and medium-size businesses in their localities. Restrictions limiting lending to members have been relaxed. In recent years, the differences among the savings, cooperative, and commercial banks have narrowed. The long-preserved separate identity of the savings and cooperative banks are gradually moving toward a broad commercial bank model.

Local ownership and control make the banks more transparent and have contained the fiscal losses. But it should be noted that the importance of state banks in Germany, with their implicit guarantee, may have hurt competition in the markets. Germany has a lower level of foreign penetration than most European countries, which may bear out the generalization that economies dominated by state banks tend to attract and admit fewer international banks.[28]

Summary

The banking system in Brazil has been mixed, with private banks competing with the public ones. The public banks are known to be weak, and the fiscal costs of restructuring have already been substantial. The Government started to privatize the state-level banks in the second half of the 1990s, but the public federal banks remain, and they are going to be very expensive to resolve.

China is cited as a country that has achieved strong financial growth with dominant state banks. The reality is that the Chinese banks are in bad financial condition. Reform efforts since the mid-1990s have been very expensive and have not yet succeeded in cleaning up the banks. The strong financial growth probably had more to do with the high savings rate in the economy than the banks.

The public banking system in Germany is decentralized under local control and its primarily lending is in local markets. Germany also has an efficient contract enforcement system and creditor rights are strong, thus limiting any possible accumulation of contingent fiscal liabilities.

Tables 7.7 and 7.8 summarize the structural characteristics of the economies and public banking sectors in the country cases reviewed in this Annex.

Based on these country cases and on the international studies cited in the introduction to this chapter, there is a significant risk that the expansion of state-owned banking in Russia since the 1998 financial crisis will result in increased financial fragility and the accumulation of fiscal liabilities. In building a sound and trusted banking system in Russia, the reform of state banks is therefore of the highest priority.

Table 7.7 Comparison of Banking System Structures

	China[a]	Brazil	Germany[b]	Russia
Per capita income	US$750	US$4,630	US$26,570	US$2,260
Quasi-liquid liabilities	124.3	29.7		20.2
Interest rate spreads	2.6%		6.1%	12.3%
Gross domestic savings / GDP	42.6%	16.6%	22.8%	21.2%
Credit to private sector / GDP	112.8%	34.6%	119.1%	12.9%
Creditor rights[c]		2		
Contract enforceability[d]		2.02		
Assets in public banks,1970[e]	100.0%	70.1%	51.9%	100.0%
Assets in public banks,1995[f]	99.5%	31.7%	36.4%	33.0%

a. Four "big" state banks have about 70 percent of both loans and deposits. Joint stock banks have 9 percent of deposits and 8 percent of loans.
b. Public banks have controlled about half of the system for several decades.
c. Creditor rights: Index of secured creditor rights, with values between 0 (worst) and 4 (best) (La Porta, Lopez de Silanes, Schleifer, and Vishny 1997).
d. Contract enforceability: Indicator of the degree to which contracts are honored, with values between 1 (worst) and 4 (best) Source: Business International Corporation.
e. La Porta, Lopez de Silanes, and Schleifer 2000.
f. La Porta, Lopez de Silanes, and Schleifer 2000.

Table 7.8 Comparison of Public Bank Structures

	China state commercial banks	China joint stock banks	Brazil federal commercial, savings, and development banks	Brazil state banks	German savings/ cooperative banks
Ownership role	MoF	Provincial/local Government or public entities. Possible to have some private shareholders, but almost all owners are public	Federal Government. Several have private shareholders, and shares are traded on the stock sector.	State Governments. Most have private shareholders, and shares are traded on the stock exchange.	Local Governments
Traditional business strategy	Lending to public entities. The SoCB have all of the large clients.	Lending to public entities. May be able to provide better service to attract better clients, but not large enough to serve the largest clients.	Commercial and specialized	Commercial and development. Public banks had access to low-cost public sector liabilities.	Depository facilities for households/ local businesses and lending to local enterprise.
Responsibility for losses	Central Government	Local Government owners are nominally responsible, but implicit deposit insurance means that central Government frequently has to pick up some or all of losses.	Federal Government	Losses repeatedly passed to the Central Bank and federal Government.	Separate deposit insurance for savings and cooperative banks, independent scheme for commercial banks.
Restructuring	Partial recapitalization in 1998. 20% of loan portfolio passed to AMCs in 1999/2000. Cost so far US$202 bln (20% of GDP). Remaining losses estimated at additional 20% of GDP.	Regulatory forbearance of losses.	Has not started yet.	1997–2000 state banks privatized or converted into development agencies.	
Restructured business strategy	1995 banking law mandated commercial lending but client base is still many SoEs.	Smaller SoEs and some private businesses.			Moving toward broader range of services.

ENDNOTES

1. In almost all countries, the top ten banks, which include development banks, capture about 75 percent of total banking claims on the private sector.

2. This result held after controlling for differences in the initial levels of per capita GDP, different measures of financial development, inflation, the black market premium, an index of government intervention, taxes and subsidies, and a variety of variables.

3. Several ARCO banks were privatized during 2001; see further discussions in Chapter 12.

4. While the exact extent of government and/or CBR support to these banks in the aftermath of the 1998 crisis is not public knowledge, it is perceived that recapitalizations (apart from outright capital injections) took place in the form of liquidity support, assistance in settlement of foreign exchange forwards with nonresidents at off-market rates, and so on.

5. CBR used Sberbank as a safe haven for deposits in the aftermath of the 1998 crisis. CBR encouraged the transfer of household deposits from a number of failing Moscow-based and regional banks to Sberbank on a voluntary basis while explicitly announcing the deposit guarantee for this bank. Some RUR 10 bln (representing around 70 percent of local currency and 30 percent of foreign currency deposits of the largest commercial banks in Russia) were transferred out of the commercial banks through this scheme. In addition to the household deposits, many enterprises also shifted their accounts from other banks to Sberbank during 1998–99. Sberbank emerged from the crisis with 85 percent of local currency and 46 percent of hard currency deposits. Many of those deposits have since been moved, so the advantage for Sberbank was to some extent temporary.

6. As of end-2000, three state banks, Sberbank, VTB, and VEB, held over 70 percent of government securities placed with banks. Sberbank held about 56 percent of government securities placed in Russian banks and about 32 percent of Sberbank assets were in government securities.

7. While this is a small percent of Sberbank assets, and because this type of lending is rarely done by Russian banks, Sberbank controls up to 20 percent of total credit to households. Sberbank is the largest intermediary for the EBRD small business lending. The management has indicated that they have provided loans to 6,000 SME and micro-borrowers utilizing EBRD funds, and to another 40,000 small enterprises through their own funds that utilize crediting methodology learned from the EBRD project.

8. Some noted transactions in 2000 were lending US$300 million to Tyumen Oil Company in March; a loan for the equivalent of US$200 million to UES (Unified Energy System of Russia) to finance its arrears to Gazprom and tax authorities in June; a planned loan for US$80 million to Vympelkom and one for US$50 million to Severstal.

9. If the Basel methodology for risk-weighting were to be applied, Sberbank's capital adequacy would be much lower, even despite recent capital injection.

10. The Minister of Antimonopoly Policy (MAP) launched an investigation of the interest rate policies of Sberbank in November 2000.

11. "The recent abolition of the 5 percent limit on foreign holdings of Sberbank shares (which had, in any case, been breached via various 'grey' schemes) may provide a further line of defense against any pressure to break up the bank." Although officially nonresidents hold only 0.11 percent of Sberbank shares, at least 15 percent is held by Russian companies that are 100 percent foreign-owned. Still more Sberbank shares are held by entities that are substantially foreign-controlled. Sberbank's management believes that further foreign investment would increase the bank's capital and provide further protection from any restructuring efforts (both by increasing the range of interests opposing change and raising the costs of restructuring). The CBR has indicated that the CBR may sell some of its stake, possibly to nonresidents (Oxford Analytica Brief 2000).

12. Any sale of Sberbank's shares should be subject to a stringent "fit and proper" test.

13. Following capital increases in June and September 1999, the majority stake of the Central Bank of the Russian Federation in Vneshtorgbank increased from 97 percent to 99.9 percent of the shares.

14. At the breakup of the U.S.S.R, the CBR inherited five banks abroad: Eurobank (Paris), Moscow Narodny Bank (London), Ost-West Handelsbank (Frankfurt-am-Main), Donau Bank (Vienna), and East-West United Bank (Luxembourg). The consolidated assets of these banks were about $3 billion.

15. These intentions have been reconfirmed in a series of press statements by Prime Minister Kasyanov in January 2002.

16. Reportedly the Caribbean Development Bank has been adequate. Another development bank that performed reasonably for a while was TSKB, the Turkish Industrial Development Bank, which was owned by the commercial banks. Over time, performance deteriorated, reportedly because of corruption. Now the bank has diversified into investment banking.

17. Universal in the sense of offering a broader range of services, not necessarily taking equity in enterprises.

18. Inflation averaged 17 percent in the 1950s, 45 percent in the 1960s, 34 percent in the 1970s, over 350 percent in the 1980s, and 1660 percent in the first half of the 1990s, falling to 7.7 percent over the period 1996-99.

19. Two states banks, Sao Paulo and Banespa, were responsible for much of the state debt.

20. This policy has now ended, partially because of concern over corruption.

21. Chinese economic reforms decentralized economic power, but kept it in the public sector. The Government allowed provincial and local governments and cooperatives to start public enterprises.

22. This problem was eased but not eliminated by the 1997–98 reforms, which reorganized the SoCBs so that their business service areas did not correspond with political boundaries and limited lending authority at the local level.

23. Sye Ping, director of the People's Bank of China's Policy Research Bureau, estimate reported by Zhou Jamila. "Mainland has to write off RMB 2.5 trillion in bad debts."

24. Some of these banks, including Bank of Communications, CITIC Industrial Bank, and China Everbright Bank, are national in scope, while others—such as the Guangdong, Pudong, and Shenzhen development banks—have a regional focus.

25. A range of nonbank financial institutions were also allowed after the mid-1980s, including trust and investment companies. Some 160 foreign banks have branches or representative offices, but their activities are currently restricted and their share of the market is tiny.

26. The market share of the state banks in lending fell slightly from 78 percent in 1993 to 68 percent in 2000, primarily because the state banks were under pressure to cut high-risk lending.

27. This can be contrasted with France and Belgium, who had centralized state institutions.

28. The German markets may not attract foreign banks because British banks earn a return on equity of about 19 percent, while the return for German banks is in the single digits.

REFERENCES

Baer, Werner. 2000. "Privatization and Restructuring of Banks in Brazil." *Quarterly Review of Economics and Finance* 40(1): 3.

Barth, James, Gerard Caprio, and Ross Levine. 2000. "Banking Systems around the Globe: Do Regulation and Ownership Affect Performance and Stability?" World Bank. Processed. Washington, D.C.

Beck, Thorsten. 2001. "Deposit Insurance as Private Club: Is Germany a Model?" Working Paper 2559. World Bank Policy Research Department, Washington, D.C.

Caprio, Gerard, and Patrick Honohan. 2001. *Finance for Growth: Policy Choices in a Volatile World.* Washington, D.C.: World Bank.

CBR (Central Bank of Russia). *Monthly Bulletin of Statistics.* Website: http://www.cbr.ru.

Deutsche Bundesbank. 2000. *Monthly Report* (February): 24–25.

IMF (International Monetary Fund). 1997. World Economic and Financial Surveys: International Capital Markets Development, Prospects and Key Policy. Washington, D.C.

La Porta, Rafael, Florencio Lopez de Silanes, and Andrei Schleifer. 2000. "Government Ownership of Banks." Harvard University. Cambridge, Mass. Processed.

La Porta, R., F. Lopez de Silanes, A. Schleifer, and R.W. Vishny. 1997. "Legal Determinants of External Finance." *Journal of Finance* 52: 1131–1150.

Moody's Investor Service. 2000. "Brazil: Banking System Outlook."

Ness, Walter L., Jr. 2000. "Reducing Government Bank Presence in the Brazilian Financial System: Why and How." *Quarterly Review of Economics and Finance* 40(1): 71.

Oxford Analytica Brief. 2000. Website: http://www.oxan.com.

Sigma No. 7. 2000. "Trade Credit Insurance: Globalization and e-Business Are the Key Opportunities." Zurich: Swiss Reinsurance Company. Website: http://www.swissre.com.

Troika Dialogue. 2000. "Russian Banking Reform." Website: http://www.troika.ru.

Vittas, Dimitri. 1995. "Thrift Deposit Institutions in Europe and the United States." Policy Research Working Paper 1540. World Bank, Policy Research Department, Washington, D.C.

CHAPTER 8

Encouraging Foreign Entry to the Banking Sector

INTRODUCTION

An informal survey among foreign banks, a list of the regulations regarding foreign bank entry, and a review of operations in the Russian Federation have revealed that foreign bank subsidiaries face no major explicit barriers to entry or operations in Russia. However, there is concern that future regulatory action may limit the share of foreign capital in banking relative to the total banking sector capital.

The perceived high Russian sovereign risk and the nontransparent and uncertain banking environment in Russia are the reasons cited that foreign banks have not increased their activities in Russia. Only a few foreign banks have applied for banking licenses. Foreign bank subsidiaries at present hold about 10 percent of the total banking sector capital and assets.

The Russian authorities should encourage the entry of foreign banks by removing limits on the share of foreign capital in the banking sector, and also by seeking foreign strategic bank shareholders for the state banks to be privatized. Increased foreign bank presence, however, would require collaboration with home country supervisors to minimize the risks of contagion from crises and bank failures.

Recent studies have confirmed the economic benefits from admitting foreign-owned banks (Caprio and Honohan 2001). Introduction of foreign banks can provide a powerful means of stimulating both operational efficiency and competition and eventually stabilizing the financial sector. The entry of foreign banks has generally been associated with improvements in the quality of both regulation and transparency, particularly if the entry of foreign banks is accompanied by the introduction of international standards of accounting and auditing. The pressure of competition from foreign banks may encourage less than reputable local banks to take higher risks, thereby weakening the banking sector. This emphasizes the urgency in strengthening prudential regulation of the banking sector.[1]

THE PRESENCE OF FOREIGN INVESTMENT AND FOREIGN BANKS IN RUSSIA

By end-2000, 22 banks in Russia had 100 percent foreign[2] ownership, while 31 banks reported over 50 percent foreign ownership. In addition, more than 150 Russian resident banks had reported some percentage of foreign capital.

Precise figures for the share of foreign capital in the Russian banking sector is not available. However, Tables 8.1 and 8.2 show the status of the major foreign banks in Russia as of October 2000 and January 2001, respectively. Accordingly, the 31 banks with more than 50 percent foreign ownership (Table 8.1) hold approximately US$6.7 billion in assets and US$0.7 billion in equity. As of end-2000, these banks had approximately 10 percent market share in total capital and assets of the Russian banking sector.

Some of these Russian banks with majority foreign ownership rank among the top 20 Russian banks. Table 8.2 shows relative ranking by assets of the top 20 Russian banks as well as the rankings of the largest foreign banks in Russia. Accordingly, four banks with more than 50 percent foreign ownership rank among the top 20 banks, and most of the major foreign banks are in the top 50 Russian banks by asset and capital size.

Relative to many developed and transition countries, the penetration of foreign banks into Russia ranks lower than many, but about the same level or higher than some of the industrialized countries (see Box 8.1).

Table 8.1 Foreign Banks Operating in Russia, as of October 2000

Bank	Foreign Shareholder	Type of Entity	Total Assets (bln. RUR)	Total Capital (bln. RUR)	Profit/Loss (bln. RUR)
International Moscow Bank	Merita Bank, Hypovereinsbank	Joint venture	60.4	0.98	-0.149
Citibank LTD.	Citigroup	Subsidiary	22.1	3.00	0.839
Eurofinans	BCEN-Eurobank	Subsidiary	13.2	1.99	0.290
BNP-Dresdner	BNP, Dresdner Bank	Subsidiary	12.5	0.05	-0.141
Raiffeisen Bank Austria	Raiffeisen Zentralbank Oesterreich	Subsidiary	11.5	0.65	0.047
ABN-AMRO Bank	ABN-AMRO Bank	Subsidiary	9.9	1.05	0.161
ING Bank (Eurasia)	ING Bank	Subsidiary	8.6	1.44	0.534
Deutsche Bank	Deutsche Bank	Subsidiary	7.7	2.41	0.646
Bank Austria Kreditenstaldt	Bank Austria	Subsidiary	6.6	1.29	0.029
Credit Lyonnais Rusbank	Credit Lyonnais	Subsidiary	5.6	0.45	0.069
Credit Suisse FB	CSFB	Subsidiary	5.6	1.55	0.765
Westdeutsche Landesbank Vostok	Westdeutsche Girozentrale	Subsidiary	3.0	0.59	0.119
Societe Generale Vostok	Societe Generale	Subsidiary	2.5	0.14	-0.075
Commerzbank (Eurasia)	Commerzbank	Subsidiary	2.4	0.21	-0.044
Chase Manhattan Bank Ltd.	Chase Manhattan Bank	Subsidiary	2.2	0.74	0.044
Mosnarbank	Moscow Narodny Bank	Subsidiary	2.1	0.74	-0.029
Garanti Bank-Moscow	Turkiye Garanti Bankasi	Subsidiary	1.7	0.47	0.041
RN Bank of New York	Bank of New York	Resident office	1.3	0.37	0.043
Yapi Kredi Moskva	Yapi ve Kredi Bankasi	Subsidiary	1.1	0.34	0.142
HSBC Bank	HSBC (from B of America)	Subsidiary	1.3	0.43	n.a.
Finansbank Moscow	Finansbank	Subsidiary	0.9	0.08	0.005
Bank of China (Elos)	Bank of China	Subsidiary	0.9	0.157	0.011
KMB Bank	EBRD, Soros Fund	Joint venture	1.5	0.049	n.a.
AIG Investment Bank	AIG Russia/NIS Financial Services	Joint venture			
Iktisat Moskva	Iktisat Bankasi	Subsidiary	0.1	0.042	
Western Union DP Vostok	Western Union				
First Czech Russian Bank	Investicni a Postovni Banka	Subsidiary	0.8	0.221	
JP Morgan	Morgan Guaranty Int.		0.9	0.466	
Investment Bank of Kuban	EBRD, Soros Fund				
Michinoku Bank	Michinoku	Subsidiary	0.4	0.3	
Cuban Investment Bank			0.09	0.07	
TOTAL			**186.89**	**20.275**	
		In USD	**6.7 BLN**	**0.7 BLN**	

n.a. Not available.

207

THE REGULATORY ENVIRONMENT FOR FOREIGN INVESTMENT IN BANKING

Currently CBR's regulations and some parts of the Law of Foreign Investment define the regulatory framework for the entry and operation of foreign investment in Russian banking.[3] The CBR's written instructions indicate that:

1. Foreign banks cannot directly open branches but need to be incorporated as a foreign-owned subsidiary of the parent company for domestic operations in Russia.
2. Foreign banks that want to establish subsidiaries in Russia need prior approval/protocol. CBR has the right to refuse if there are conflicting customs or tax issues with the home country, or CBR may request reciprocity from the home country of the bank.
3. CBR has the right to limit the volume of foreign capital relative to the total bank capital in Russia.[4]
4. The licensing process after the protocol for a majority foreign-owned bank or a Russian-owned bank are the same, except that foreign bank subsidiaries have to put in 10 times more charter/paid-in capital than Russian banks.[5]
5. The composition of the paid-in capital (cash, up to 25 percent federal loan bonds, up to 20 percent real estate) is treated similarly for foreign and domestic banks.
6. Both foreign and local banks need the prior permission and licensing of the regional CBR authorities in order to open branches.[6]
7. Both foreign and local banks are precluded from collecting household deposits before the lapse of two consecutive years of profitable operations.
8. Any resident Russian bank that wants to sell up to 1 percent of its paid-in capital to a nonresident bank has to get the approval of its regional CBR prior to the capital issue. If the nonresident participation in the bank capital is going to exceed 1 percent, the bank has to get the permission of the CBR Head Office.[7]
9. A minimum of 75 percent of the employees and at least 50 percent of the Board of the foreign subsidiaries must be Russian citizens.
10. The profit remittance of foreign bank subsidiaries are treated in the same way for all foreign direct investment in Russia under the relevant legislation.

Table 8.2 The Size of Some of the Foreign Banks in Russia
(billions of rubles)

Bank		Total Assets	Total Capital	Profit/Loss
1	Sberbank	553.9	42.7	16.5
2	Vneshtorgbank	111.6	46.3	0.6
3	Gazprombank	83.4	18.6	0.6
4	Alfa-Bank	71.3	22.3	0.0
5	Meshdunarodny Promshelenny Bank	74.0	29.6	0.5
6	**Meshdunarodny Moskovsky Bank**	**71.8**	**2.24**	**–0.0**
7	SBS-AGRO (ARCO)	22.6	–35.6	–8.6
8	Surgutneftebank	53.9	0.7	0.0
9	Doveritilny i Investitsiony Bank	48.8	2.9	1.0
10	Bank Moskovy	43.0	2.4	0.3
11	Rosbank	46.9	7.5	3.2
12	**Citibank**	**27.8**	**2.8**	**2.1**
13	Rossisky Credit (ARCO)	13.2	–21.4	–14.0
15	MDM	25.3	4.3	0.3
17	Menatep-St. Petersburg	22.4	1.6	0.6
18	Globeks	16.2	5.7	0.0
19	**Raiffeisen Austria**	**15.1**	**1.1**	**0.1**
29	**ABN AMRO Bank**	**12.3**	**1.2**	**0.4**
33	**Credit Lyonnais Rusbank**	**8.2**	**1.3**	**0.1**
34	**ING Bank**	**8.1**	**1.5**	**0.6**
35	**Deutsche Bank**	**6.6**	**2.5**	**0.8**
36	**Westdeutsche Landesbank**	**2.5**	**0.6**	**0.1**
40	**Credit Suisse First Boston**	**6.7**	**1.6**	**0.9**
43	**Bank Austria Kreditanstalt**	**8.5**	**1.3**	**0.0**
70	**Commerzbank**	**2.7**	**0.3**	**0.0**

Note: All figures as of January 1, 2001. Foreign banks are shown in bold text. Numbers on left reflect CBR ranking in banking system according to asset size.
Source: Central Bank of Russia.

Box 8.1 Where Is Russia in Foreign Bank Presence?

A study on the role of foreign banks in domestic banking systems was conducted based on the scale of foreign bank operations in 80 countries, including all OECD countries, as well as many developing and transition countries (Claessens and Jansen 2000)* Data from about 7,900 individual commercial banks from these countries were gathered according to the BankScope database provided by IBCA during 1988–1995. The data summarize the scale of foreign bank operations in the table below.

(Box continues on next page)

Box 8.1 *(continued)*

The study views the percentage of a number of foreign banks (with more than 50 percent foreign ownership) among the total, as well as the percentage of assets held by foreign banks to total banking assets as measures of banking sector penetration and control. Russia's figures are added for comparative purposes for end-2000.

	Number of Foreign Banks as Percent of Total	Foreign Bank Assets as Percent of Total
Africa	0.31	0.27
Asia	0.28	0.30
Latin America	0.25	0.28
Middle East and North Africa	0.26	0.19
Transition economies	0.54	0.52
Industrial economies	0.25	0.15
Russia	**0.02**	**0.10**

A comparison using the same methodology and time periods for selected economies in terms of shares of more than 50 percent foreign ownership to total banking sector assets is given below:

Country	Share of Foreign Bank Assets to Total 1988–95 Average
France	8.0
Netherlands	10.0
Spain	31.0
United Kingdom	19.0
United States	3.0
Italy	1.0
Russia (2000)	**10.0**
Japan	21.0
Canada	7.0

Economy	Share of Foreign Bank Assets to Total 1988–95 Average
Brazil	30.0
Malaysia	11.5
Chile	25.0
Argentina (as of 1999)	48.6
Mexico (as of 1999)	33.4
Taiwan, China	9.0
Poland (as of 1999)	52.8
Indonesia	16.0
India	1.0
Democratic People's Republic of Korea	4.3
Thailand	5.6

*See article "How Does Foreign Entry Affect the Domestic Banking Market?" by S. Claessens, et al.

THE SURVEY AND OPINIONS OF THE FOREIGN BANK SUBSIDIARIES IN RUSSIA

An informal verbal survey was conducted with 11 Russian subsidiaries of the foreign banks based in Moscow from February 15 to March 2, 2001. The purpose of the informal survey was to determine if the foreign banks in Russia found the present environment suitable to expanding their investment in Russia, and also whether the foreign banks felt that there were major gaps in the regulatory framework that discriminated and discouraged foreign bank entry to Russia. A summary of survey responses is given below.

Entry

All of the foreign subsidiaries indicated that the minimum amount of entry capital, although higher than for local banks, was not a deterrent to their entry into Russia. There are few banks with less than the minimum amount. Except for some of the Turkish banks (Iktisat, Finans) where there is uncertainty as to whether the banks are direct branches or subsidiaries of the parent banks, the rest of the banks interviewed indicated that they are in the process of registering additional capital to meet the minimum capital requirement either because of losses from the 1998 crisis or because they are in the process of entry.

All of the interviewed banks indicated that they had prior approval from the CBR, and some have expressed an awareness of reciprocity agreements between their home countries' supervisory authorities and the Russian CBR. All have emphasized long delays (1 to 1.5 years on average) for getting the final license for operations after the pre-approval period—this period is far shorter for the local banks. The paperwork for the licensing process was reportedly just as detailed as in some other countries. Poland was frequently cited as a case in point.

All the banks interviewed indicated that the decision of their parent banks to enter into Russia as a subsidiary was part of their corporate strategy. Several banks already had representative offices dating back to the U.S.S.R. Contrary to the perception that foreign banks follow their home country clients, all of the subsidiaries stated that the parent banks' decision to enter Russia was based on (*a*) the desire to be close to their Russian client-banks and corporations, and (*b*) the need to tap into the perceived potential of Russian business.

As for branching, the answers were different depending on the corporate strategy of the subsidiaries. Those that want to go into retail banking did complain about the long and sometimes restricting approach of the CBR (especially in the regions) and that of the regional authorities to open branches outside of Moscow. Few mentioned a limit of two branches per subsidiary, but it was not clear whether this was a restriction for banks within Moscow or for banks all over Russia because no written instruction was found about this issue. There also appeared to be no restrictions from CBR on the limit of ATMs or cash-service branches.

Those that have a strategy to go into retail banking indicated that the licensing restriction for a minimum two years' operation prior to accepting household deposits and a written instruction from CBR limiting the total size of household deposits to the capital of the bank was noncompetitive. However, the same restrictions or noncompetitive attitude apply to Russian banks as well.

Operations

All eleven interviewed banks indicated that CBR's supervision process is not discriminatory. They all intimated that the quantitative and rules-oriented approach of CBR is time- and labor-intensive and sometimes uncoordinated within the CBR. However, they all try to comply with the prudential requirements because of their culture of compliance. All are unhappy about the noncompliant culture of the Russian banks for which CBR does not take proactive correction. This is a matter that they find noncompetitive for their operations.

Table 8.3 shows the main balance sheet structure of some of the major foreign subsidiaries. Commercial lending is a major activity for the overwhelming majority of them. Prior to the 1998 crisis, foreign subsidiaries in Russia were active in the government securities markets. However, since the crisis—where all banks lost considerable sums of money and capital—corporate lending has been increasing. Some of the subsidiaries have a policy of doing business with only the multinationals and large Russian export corporations. There were two subsidiaries interviewed that have indicated they have no plans to go into large scale lending in the near term unless compelled. Those who are in the lending business all indicated that they find the Russian corporate risk better than the Russian sovereign risk; that is, they have never experienced a default from a Russian corporation. However, lending subsidiaries have all expressed a preference for lending to the top 100–200 and reputable Russian corporations. Three banks also stated that they eventually want to go down-market to lend to small and medium-size Russian enterprises.

Table 8.3 Major Assets and Liabilities of Some of the Foreign-owned Banks in Russia, as of December 2000
(thousands of rubles)

Bank Name	Assets	Capital	Clients' Accounts Total	Share in Total Liabilities	Household Deposits	Commercial Loans Total	Share in Earning Assets	Securities Portfolio Total	Share in Earning Assets
Citibank T/O	25,019,243	2,648,269	10,423,636	41.7%	377,512	14,294,614	64.2%	4,971,439	22.3%
Raiffeisenbank Austria	14,582,198	966,152	8,960,668	61.4%	1,472,992	7,447,685	60.8%	595,306	4.9%
ABN Amro Bank A.O.	13,824,684	1,117,917	9,360,048	67.7%	426,850	4,463,569	36.5%	289,950	2.4%
BNP-Dresdner Bank	11,352,301	376,689	3,976,582	35.0%	268,239	1,359,054	13.6%	552,473	5.5%
Bank CSFB A.O.	9,544,537	1,623,054	3,253,431	34.1%	543,292	947,744	13.8%	91,697	1.3%
Austria Kreditanstalt (Russia)	8,205,621	1,333,988	4,364,033	53.2%	1,646,282	1,378,554	19.1%	805,167	11.1%
ING Bank (Eurasia)	8,154,297	1,566,708	2,777,797	34.1%	288,906	4,574,475	69.9%	492,895	7.5%
Deutsche Bank	7,439,741	3,450,517	1,617,545	21.7%	0	814,989	13.2%	0	0.0%
Credit Lyonnais Rusbank	6,611,235	1,048,005	3,449,584	52.2%	37,433	3,258,930	58.7%	526,349	9.5%
Chase Manhattan Bank International	3,458,254	983,141	1,163,555	33.6%	16,398	1,858	0.1%	19,441	0.8%
Garanti Bank—Moskva	3,397,418	434,783	239,703	7.1%	69,504	347,235	11.1%	2,027,814	64.9%
Westdeutsche Landesbank Vostok	2,720,404	661,851	557,863	20.5%	6,560	858,849	37.0%	66,064	2.8%
Banque Societe Generale Vostok	2,344,888	346,125	1,242,586	53.0%	84,076	1,138,330	60.9%	0	0.0%
Kommerzbank (Eurasia)	2,185,918	261,930	691,559	31.6%	0	962,572	49.3%	0	0.0%
KMB—Bank	1,477,235	49,808	123,109	8.3%	9,973	1,259,893	90.8%	0	0.0%
HSBC Bank (RR)	1,290,370	432,806	86,365	6.7%	0	69,263	5.9%	973,189	82.2%
Financebank (Moskva)	1,085,119	81,516	629,062	58.0%	126,984	335,797	43.2%	64,761	8.3%
Bank of China (Elos)	966,042	132,722	712,299	73.7%	461,328	62,074	13.1%	187,869	39.7%
J. P. Morgan Bank	895,563	466,640	0	0.0%	0	0	0.0%	169,443	22.2%
First Czech-Russian Bank	809,354	221,512	96,751	12.0%	6,343	234,277	35.8%	111,522	17.0%
Michinoku Bank (Moskva)	411,809	313,824	34,454	8.4%	0	2,900	0.8%	136,103	35.2%
Iktisat Bank (Moskva)	117,638	42,840	31,771	27.0%	0	0	0.0%	0	0.0%
Cuban Investment Bank	85,856	71,359	0	0.0%	0	61,772	76.0%	0	0.0%

Source: Izvestiya 2001.

All the lending banks indicated that pre-lending decision-making is the critical step in the credit process. In other words, nonfinancial and qualitative information (like the true ownership of the enterprise and the commitment of the borrower) were more important than the financials submitted to them. The majority of the large Russian corporations, which are the borrowers of many of the subsidiaries, present IAS financials. Most of the lending is short-term (less than one year) and some subsidiaries engage only in pre-export finance, whereas others also provide working capital loans.

Apparently CBR does not recognize variable rate lending and revolving credit lines as products. Trade finance processing is limited to specially licensed banks—foreign or local—due to the foreign exchange regulations in place. All of these create additional costs to doing business in Russia but are not discriminatory because Russian banks face the same difficulties. One authority that has been implicitly discriminating against foreign subsidiaries for accepting customs guarantees is the Customs Authority. Some of the banks also indicated that Russian enterprises (state or private, although mostly state enterprises or those engaged in doing business with the state) are either not allowed to work or are directly discouraged from working with foreign banks. State entities are apparently prohibited from opening accounts with foreign subsidiaries.

Given this background, foreign banks have not made further efforts to introduce other new products and services. One main reason is that CBR neither encourages nor discourages the introduction of additional or better services and products to the banking sector. In terms of being able to seize collateral and to resolve disputes through the courts, all the interviewed banks implied that, provided they have the correct documentation and good Russian legal support, the processes are not discriminatory and can be settled even though they may be time-consuming. Doing business in Russia requires an in-depth understanding of the legal and regulatory intricacies and the necessity of taking preventive measures to avoid pitfalls. This level of scrutiny is a time-consuming and costly process.

The multi-branch banks explained that the fixed costs of operating a branch are very high. Operating costs to income ratio for those interviewed were around 65 percent, which some banks stated are much higher in Russia than in other large transition or developing countries. None of the foreign banks interviewed considered Sberbank's monopoly position with explicit state guarantees on deposits a competitive factor for their activities. As for lending, the complaint against Sberbank was not because of its volume—since there is no capital in the Russian banking sector to satisfy the borrowing needs of some of Sberbank's borrowers like UES, Gazprom—but rather because Sberbank was offering lower interest rates.

The subsidiaries that have been inspected by their parent offices and/or supervisors have indicated that CBR did not block access to relevant data. All interviewees suggested that there is a psychological resistance to foreign bank entry and expansion in Russia at all levels of regulatory and administrative branches; this resistance is a reflection of public opinion.

FUTURE PLANS

All the subsidiaries preferred to call themselves "Russian Banks with foreign ownership" meaning they are here to stay for the long term and that they look at the Russian domestic market for future growth. There has been one exit—Bank of America—since the crisis, but that was due to the internal global strategy of this bank, not the Russian market's dynamics. There are four new entrants among the banks listed in Table 8.1, and license applications for three more banks are pending. All banks that have suffered during the 1998 crisis have recapitalized or are in the process of increasing capital. Most of the recapitalization funding came from internally generated earnings when the parent contribution has varied.

All the subsidiary banks interviewed indicated that their parent banks would rather have a controlling share of a Russian Bank than to buy, merge with, or form a joint venture with a Russian Bank. However, at the current time foreign banks are hesitant to invest in Russian banks.

The majority of the banks interviewed indicated that there is limited potential for corporate banking business growth in Russia. This is due to (*a*) the competitive lending and servicing of multinational corporations; (*b*) the capability of large Russian enterprises to tap either international credit lines/bond markets, etc., or to have their own banks; (*c*) the limited number of creditworthy or transparent Russian corporations; and (*d*) the slow growth in the real sector except in specific industries.

The foreign subsidiaries indicated that the present Russian corporate banking system consisted primarily of a few state-owned banks and themselves. Private Russian banks are too small either in capital or operations to suit their shareholder needs, and thus are not competitive with them. Growth potential in retail banking or SME lending is limited not because of the banking sector constraints but because the average Russian does not yet trust the ruble after repeated crises during the 1990s.

All the interviewed banks indicated that their parent banks see long-term potential for banking business in Russia. However, the Russian sovereign risk is considered to be high and thus none have near-term plans to commit substantial amounts of additional capital to their subsidiaries.

CONCLUSION

Russian regulatory authorities have allowed direct or indirect foreign capital entry to the Russian banking sector since the early 1990s. Despite implicit resistance to foreign bank entry and fears that the Russian banking sector would be dominated by foreigners, no major explicit discrimination or discouragement of foreign capital entry exists. The fears of foreign banks leaving Russia in a crisis have proven wrong; all of the foreign banks that suffered major losses during the 1998 crisis have recapitalized their operations. In fact, the foreign bank subsidiaries hold around 10 percent of the assets and the equity of the banking sector in Russia. This figure may be higher if one adds to it minority shares held by foreign investors in the banking sector in Russia.[8]

Historically, the foreign banking presence had followed the trade finance business, where banks that have global trading customers and/or that represent the global trading interest of their home countries, would open branches or establish subsidiaries in selected countries. There has also been the traditional banking left over from the colonial days in many developing countries (e.g., British and French banks in African countries and the Middle East, Italian banks in Libya, Dutch banks in Indonesia, Australian banks in Papua New Guinea and the Pacific Islands, U.S. bank branches in China and Japan). Some U.S. and European banks decided to expand internationally during the 1970s and 1980s partly to service the petrodollars, partly to diversify their domestic risk, and partly to become global banks.

The 1990s also saw an emergence of internationalization of financial services, in which foreign banks and foreign strategic investors were keen to invest in the equity of emerging and transitional country banks as well as to increase their domestic presence through branches or subsidiaries in many countries. The increased interest and investment of foreign banks in these countries has been both supply- and demand-driven. On the supply side, the globalization and the liberalization of financial services under GATT/WTO, NAFTA, EU, etc., have encouraged foreign banks to penetrate the new markets. On the demand side, many large developing countries that were restricting foreign presence in their domestic markets have liberalized the entry of foreign banks. Box 8.2 summarizes experiences of some countries from Southeast Asia, Latin America, and Central Europe that opened up their domestic banking sectors to foreign strategic investors during the 1990s either after a major currency and banking crisis (as part of their banking sector restructuring strategy; i.e., Latin

---

Box 8.2 Large Foreign Bank Entry during the 1990s: Some Case Studies

The 1990s have seen large increases in the foreign bank ownership and control of total banking sector assets in the major countries of Central Europe, Latin America, and southeastern Asia. Central European countries opened up their banking markets to foreign investors through the privatization efforts of the state banking sector inherited from the 1980s. The South American and Southeast Asian countries encouraged foreign bank entry after the major systemic crises in the banking sector in their respective countries.

Country	Share of Foreign Banks'* Assets in Total, 1994	Share of Foreign Banks' Assets in Total, 1999
Hungary	26.8	56.6
Poland	39.4	52.8
Argentina	17.9	48.6
Brazil	8.4	16.8
Mexico	1.0	18.8
Republic of Korea	0.8	4.3
Malaysia	6.8	11.5
Thailand	0.5	5.6

*A foreign bank is defined as 50 percent or more foreign ownership.
Source: IMF 2000.

Central Europe

Poland—Initially the foreign investors were only allowed to purchase minority stakes in large Polish ex-state banks. The Polish authorities also favored consortia of investors rather than single strategic investors. Direct foreign bank entry through branches is not permitted. Some foreign banks entered the Polish banking market through establishing their own locally incorporated subsidiaries. Gradually, foreign investors increased their stakes as state ownership in the banks was divested and decreased through public offerings or stock market sales. As of end-2000, 71 percent of the banking system was foreign.

Hungary—The Government decided to allow foreign strategic investors who are "fit and proper" to have unlimited access to the purchase of existing banks in 1995. The foreign bank entry came through the outright purchase of bank shares. Foreign banks are also permitted to directly enter the market through establishing branches. By end-2000, more than 90 percent of the Hungarian banking sector was foreign.

Both Hungary and Poland are also committed to fully opening their financial markets to EU country origin financial institutions as part of EU accession.

(Box continues on next page)

Box 8.2 *(continued)*

South America

Argentina—Foreign bank entry was not restricted by the type or the amount of capital, and foreign banks have always had a strong presence in Argentina as reflected in the high 1994 figures above. Foreign bank entry, primarily Spanish banks, accelerated during 1997–98 as these institutions started buying out the family-owned large domestic banks. The existing foreign banks also increased their presence through purchases benefiting from low stock valuations of the banks during 1998–99.

Brazil—No visible or explicit barriers to entry were in place, but Brazil always had several large well-capitalized and well-managed private Brazilian banks that had control over the market. Nevertheless, foreign bank entry in the form of subsidiaries increased since 1995 in the context of two bank restructuring programs. The sale of the Banespa shares to Banco Bilbao Vizcaya Argentina (BBVA) in 2000 has increased the foreign bank ownership in total assets to 25 percent.

Mexico—By law, foreign banks were restricted to owning no more than 20 percent of local banks. Foreign bank branch operations were allowed selectively. Subsequent to the 1994 devaluation, the authorities allowed the acquisition of local banks up to 51 percent—the full control limit, with the approval of the Ministry of Finance. In December 1998, the Mexican Congress lifted the historical restriction of buying up the local banks, and by end-2000, the share of foreign ownership had increased to 40 percent.

Southeast Asia

Thailand—Foreign bank participation in Thailand was restricted to 25 percent of total sector equity and only one branch for foreign banks. By tradition, local banks have been closed to foreign banks because large and important families owned and ran the local banks. The 1997 crisis changed that situation. Ownership restrictions were lifted, and the five intervened banks were offered to foreign banks for sale. The existing family-owned local banks started seeking international strategic partners and/or investors. Some of these banks raised Tier-two capital in foreign markets. Four banks (one private, three intervened) were sold to foreign banks during 1998–99. The waning interest by foreign buyers and/or investors in Thailand resulted in the government transfer of ownership of the other two intervened banks to the Thai Pension Fund in 2001.

Malaysia—After a very liberal period up to 1971 when foreign banks controlled up to 90 percent of the banking market, Malaysia implemented a series of prohibitions of foreign bank expansion—30 percent shareholding limit, prohibition to open new branches, ATMs allowed only on existing branch premises, etc. As a result, foreign banks now control about 23 percent of the total assets and concentrate primarily on corporate banking. However, Malaysia has a commitment under the General Agreement on Tariffs and Trade (GATT) to liberalize its financial services.

Democratic People's Republic of Korea—DPR Korea had allowed only foreign bank branch entry on a selective basis since 1967. In September 1987, there were 52 foreign bank branches with a total market share of 2 percent of banking sector assets. Foreign bank participation in the DPR Korean banks has been allowed since the 1997 crisis where one large intervened bank was sold and two others had negotiations terminated during 1998–99. Some other DPR Korean banks have used Global Depository Receipt programs or raised Tier-two capital in the international subordinated debt markets. The foreign involvement as a strategic shareholder has stayed as minority shareholder investments in general.

Sources: IMF 2000, and Caprio and Honohan (2001).

America and southeastern Asia) or during a transition to a market economy and EU accession (Central Europe).

Arguments in favor of increasing foreign ownership in the domestic banking sectors can be grouped into three broad areas. First, foreign bank presence is argued to increase the amount of funding available to domestic projects because foreign banks not only bring in capital but can also act as conduits for additional international capital flows. Foreign bank presence may also increase the stability of available domestic lending by diversifying the sources. Second, foreign banks are said to improve the quality, pricing, and availability of financial services both directly as players in the domestic markets and indirectly through increasing domestic bank competition. Third, foreign bank presence is argued to improve financial system infrastructure, including accounting and transparency, supervisory practices, and risk management.

The recommendations to the developing countries to increasingly open up their domestic banking sectors to international banks gained new momentum during 1998–2001, after the Asian, Russian, and Turkish crises. The emergence of global banking capability, in all geographic regions of the world (directly or through internet connections) and the interrelated capital flows in all financial sector activities (through mergers and acquisitions in the banking and nonbanking financial industries) also encouraged this pattern. The need to develop international standards for best practices and compliance to these standards will be supported by the international regulatory and financial institutions (BIS, OECD, IMF, and the World Bank under the Global Stability Forum) so that future crises can be avoided. These institutions also support the idea that more foreign banking presence would introduce best practices or good examples to the developing banking markets.

There are three arguments against increasing foreign ownership in domestic markets. First, foreign bank presence is said to decrease financial stability of domestic credit by providing additional sources of capital flight or by rapidly withdrawing from the market during times of crisis. Second, foreign bank entry is argued to increase the risk of the domestic banks, since the foreign banks choose the best customers and leave less competitive distributors to move to more risky areas of business. Third, some argue that financial services are a strategic industry and should therefore be controlled by domestic interests.[9]

Empirical research on the benefits of increased foreign bank presence in the developing countries has recently started, given the fact that increased foreign bank entry into developing markets is a new trend. The research results all support the benefits of foreign bank entry: they show that the competitive pressures created by increased foreign bank ownership lead to improvements in banking sector efficiency; the local banks are generally not left at a competitive disadvantage in lending, and the funding base for the real sector is increased and diversified. Some country-specific empirical research has also shown that increased foreign bank presence increases the technology, human skills, and product diversification in the domestic banking markets (Goldberg, Dages, and Kinney 2000; IMF 2000; Claessens and Jansen 2000[10]). However, there is not yet enough empirical evidence to show whether increased foreign bank presence provides a more volatile or a less volatile supply of credit, and whether greater foreign bank presence increases the stability of the domestic financial system.

Given the low level of capital and the size of the Russian banking sector, the authorities may consider encouraging further foreign bank entry in all forms—directly through branch openings, and indirectly by removing all explicit and implicit restrictions for foreign bank ownership—where foreign banks can be the controlling shareholders of Russian banks, including the state banks that will be privatized. In addition to technology, human resource skills, and competition, the entry of foreign banks might be another source of much needed investment and lending capacity to the real sector in Russia. In short, increased foreign bank presence could be viewed as a complement to the domestic banking sector rather than a competitor.

The following are major policy issues that would face the supervisory and the regulatory bodies due to increased foreign bank presence:
1. The need to develop effective prudential supervisory capability and arrangements, especially for large complex banking institutions and their products and instruments
2. The need to get proper assurance for the degree of parental support that would be required in support of local establishments in cases of own or systemic failures
3. The need to take proper precautions that increased foreign bank entry does not increase systemic risk in the banking system from contagion effects
4. The need to decide on the coverage of official and explicit safety nets.

Supervision

All foreign bank entities in a host country are expected to comply with the prudential requirements of the host country's supervisory authorities in addition to their home country requirements. However, increased foreign bank presence brings with it more responsibility to the host country supervisors to oversee not only the local foreign entities but also their parent institutions. Box 8.3 summarizes the accepted division of supervisory responsibility between the host and home country supervisors for

---

Box 8.3 The Generally Accepted Guidelines for the Supervision of Foreign Banks

The activities of the representative offices of foreign banks in the host countries have not been an issue for cross-border banking supervision since these offices are considered to be marketing units for the parent banks overseas. Accordingly, any business generated by the representative office is booked by the head office falling under the supervision of the home country supervisors of the parent. The consolidated supervisory responsibility for the overseas affiliates of the banking group or banks falls under the responsibility of the home country of the bank/group.

As for the subsidiaries, equal ownership joint ventures and branches, the initial Basel "Concordat" in 1975 states that the host supervisory authority would have the primary responsibility for the solvency of the foreign subsidiary and the joint ventures, whereas the home supervisor would be responsible for the branches. In 1983, the Concordat was revised to introduce the principle of consolidated supervision and to make the solvency of foreign subsidiaries the joint responsibility of the host and home countries.

Following the failure of BCCI, the Basel Committee on Banking Supervision issued four minimum standards for the supervision of cross-border banking in 1992:
1. All international banking groups and banks should be supervised by a home country authority that capably performs consolidated supervision.
2. The creation of cross-border banking establishments should receive the prior consent of the host and home country supervisory authorities.
3. Home country supervisory authorities should possess the right to gather information from the cross-border banking establishments of the banks for which they are the home country supervisor.
4. If a host country authority determines that any one of the foregoing minimum standards is not met to its satisfaction, that authority could impose restrictive measures necessary to satisfy its prudential concerns consistent with these minimum standards, including the prohibition of the creation of banking establishments.

Further recommendations were issued to supplement the above four minimum standards in 1996. These standards and recommendations have led to a set of practices for the effective supervision of cross-border banking activities. The most important of these are
1. The licensing of cross-border banks should require the informed and explicit consent of both the host and home country authorities. Moreover, the host country authority should evaluate the level of support that the parent is capable of providing to the proposed establishment.
2. The home country supervisory authority has the responsibility for the consolidated supervision of the bank or banking group on a global basis. Host countries are primarily responsible for the liquidity of a foreign bank. Moreover, the host country is responsible for the solvency and supervision of foreign subsidiaries. Despite the division of responsibilities, the host and home country supervisors need to be in close contact and cooperate effectively.

(Box continues on next page)

> **Box 8.3** *(continued)*
>
> 3. The flow of information between the home and host country supervision authorities should be of both quantitative and qualitative natures. Together with data, the host country should permit home country on-site inspections.
> 4. If the host country is not convinced that the home country supervisory standards are sufficient to maintain the above standards, it has the right to prevent the creation in its jurisdiction of any cross-border establishments by banks or banking groups from that home country.
>
> The above guidelines specifically cover the cross-border banking establishments where banks based and supervised in a home country are the majority or sole or equal partner in host country banking establishments. Special problems can be posed by so-called shell-banks—licensed or registered in one center but effectively controlled or managed from another jurisdiction—or parallel-owned banks, where a bank in one jurisdiction is under the same nonbank ownership as a bank in another jurisdiction.
>
> It is generally understood that host country supervisors have the full responsibility for the proper supervision of the subsidiary banks and/or joint ventures banks established with nonbank foreign ownership.
>
> The supervision of foreign bank branches is left to the home country under the assumption that a branch has no independent legal personality distinct from its parent, and the claims on the branch constitute claims on the parent. Historically however, some foreign banks have not been able to honor deposits in their overseas branches due to the imposition of capital controls or expropriation (i.e., China, Cuba, Vietnam).
>
> Recent episodes of "ringfencing" of the obligations of the local branches of some major international banks in Asia for derivatives and foreign exchange obligations also raised questions about the commitment of the parent banks to their branch obligations in times of crisis or difficulty. Despite the home country supervision principle, many host countries continue to supervise the activities of the host country branches separately.
>
> *Source:* IMF 2000.

different types of foreign bank presence. Accordingly, the Russian supervisory authorities have to increase cooperation with the home country supervisory authorities as more complex forms of foreign banks or bank holding companies increase their presence in Russia. Given all the weaknesses in Russian banking supervision, foreign entry would likely bring renewed trust to the Russian banking system because of the home country supervision principle.

Parental Support

Legally the parent institution is expected to be fully responsible for the commitments of its branches, because a branch does not have a distinct legal personality. The parent bank is expected to stand behind its branches in times of difficulty so that its reputation can be maintained. However, the recent episodes of "ringfencing" and historical precedents (see Box 8.3) have proven that, under certain circumstances, the parent may not fully stand behind its branches.

Most of the host country authorities allow bank branch entry when the parent is obligated to allocate a minimum specified amount of locally paid-in capital for the operations of the branch. This capital limit is generally used to limit the lending size of the branch, which will protect domestic banks and give the assurance that this capital is the minimum parental support for the local branch.

As for the subsidiaries and the joint ventures with foreign bank shareholding, the parent bank's commitment is legally limited to the amount of capital it has subscribed to the entity since these entities are legally independent and locally incorporated entities. Many host country regulators would insist on a letter of comfort and/or an explicit guarantee that the parent bank would support the subsidiary in case of insolvency or major losses.

Information-sharing with the home country supervisory bodies would also ensure timely recognition of the parental capability to continue supporting its subsidiary in the host country.

Systemic Risk

The systemic crisis or large-scale failures in the home country banking systems may have a contagious effect on the host country if the parent bank resorts to the funds of its subsidiary to support its position, and if that subsidiary has a dominant position in the host country banking sector. This is particularly true for small countries with a limited number of banks.

There does not seem to be a major parent bank that holds a large market share in the Russian banking market today that would cause a concern for the contagion of systemic risk from a home country. However, the authorities might carefully monitor the overseas exposures of the foreign and domestic Russian banks to minimize any risks in the asset quality deteriorations of these banks should a crisis occur in those countries (see Box 8.3).

In general, the subsidiaries are expected to be under the deposit insurance coverage of the host country, and should contribute accordingly. Branches have the option to pick either the home or the host country deposit insurance coverage. For example, in order to minimize regulatory arbitration, EU countries are expected to have the same deposit insurance coverage at a minimum. EU accession will imply "single license" where the foreign banks will have the choice to enter not only as subsidiaries but also directly as branches.

Host country regulatory bodies would have to decide on the treatment of foreign bank deposit insurance coverage as well as the costs and benefits associated with it. The Central European countries that have opened up their domestic markets to foreign banks have opted to align their deposit insurance programs to meet the minimum EU requirements until accession. Most of the other non-EU countries in Europe are also taking this route.

All of the countries that have opened up their domestic banking sector to foreign capital assume that the lender-of-last-resort facilities are available to all of the banks that operate in that market. The foreign banks in a host country face the same risks of systemic failures as the rest of the sector.

ENDNOTES

1. See article "How Does Foreign Entry Affect the Domestic Banking Market?" by S. Claessens, et al.

2. Excluding those banks owned 100 percent by Russian banks domiciled overseas: Eurofinans, Mosnarbank.

3. The following CBR instructions have direct implications for foreign investment in banking in Russia: Instruction No. 02-195 of April 1997; No. 75 of July 1998; No. 559-Y of May 5, 1999; No. 586-Y of June 24, 1999; No. 589-Y of June 28, 1999; No. 829-Y of August 28, 2000; No. 895-U of January 3, 2001. In addition, all of the banks in Russia, regardless of ownership, are obliged to comply with all CBR regulations.

4. There was an assumption in the market that this was 12 percent. However, it was never implemented since (a) it is not clear whether this would imply direct and indirect foreign capital and (b) the share of more than 50 percent foreign banking capital had never exceeded this ratio in the past. There is a mention of another 25 percent limit in the CBR Policy Paper with unclear definition.

5. According to the January 2001 Decree, the minimum paid-in capital for a foreign bank subsidiary is 261.5 million RUR (10 mm Euro) versus 2.6 million RUR for a Russian bank (1 mm Euro).

6. Although some foreign banks mentioned a limit of two branches per foreign subsidiary, no such limit is expressly written.

7. Again there is a verbal argument that the foreign ownership in a nonforeign subsidiary Russian bank cannot exceed 46 percent; i.e., foreign investors cannot own majority or controlling shares in Russian banks. That was not implemented for EBRD's and International Finance Corporation's (IFC's) equity investments

in Russia—nor for the AIG Russia and nonresident Russian banks that have controlling ownership in Russian banks (see Table 8.1).

8. If the Russian banking statistics were presented under IAS, the share of foreign capital would also increase substantially.

9. Some also cite the "infant industry" argument to protect the small domestic banking sectors from foreign competition.

10. See the following articles: "How Does Foreign Entry Affect the Domestic Banking Market?" by S. Claessens, et al.; "Lessons from European Banking Liberalization and Integration" by X. Vives et al.; "The Opening of the Spanish Banking System: 1985/98" by J.M. Pastor et al.; "On the Kindness of Strangers? The Impact of Foreign Entry on Domestic Banks in Argentina" by G. Clarke et al.; "Foreign Entry in Turkey's Banking Sector, 1980/1997" by C. Denizier; "Foreign Direct Investment in the Banking Sector: A Transitional Economy Perspective" by L. Papi et al.

REFERENCES

Caprio, Gerard, and Patrick Honohan. 2001. *Finance for Growth: Policy Choices in a Volatile World*. Policy Research Report. World Bank, Policy Research Department, Washington, D.C.

Claessens, Stijn, and Marion Jansen. 2000. "The Internationalization of Financial Services: Issues and Lessons for Developing Countries." A joint publication by WTO and World Bank. Boston, Mass.: Kluwer Academic Publishers.

Goldberg, Linda, B. Gerard Dages, and Daniel Kinney. 2000. "Foreign and Domestic Bank Participation in Emerging Markets: Lessons from Mexico and Argentina." Working Paper 7714. NBER Working Paper Series, National Bureau of Economic Research, Cambridge, Mass. Website: http://www.nber.org/papers/w7714.

IMF (International Monetary Fund). 2000. *International Capital Markets*. Washington, D.C. September 11, 2000.

Izvestiya. 2001. Website: http://www.izvestiya.ru.

Part III

Regulation and the Restructuring of Banks

Having outlined the building blocks of financial sector reform as it relates to the legal and accounting infrastructure (Part I), and identified the restructuring needs of the banking sector (Part II), Part III focuses on the implementation of legal and regulatory measures to support bank restructuring.

Building trust in the financial system depends on developing banking supervision with the primary goal of protecting the financial standing of the weakest participants in the financial system, the retail depositors. As outlined in Chapter 9, the CBR has made considerable progress in establishing a banking supervision function, but a number of measures still need to be made to improve the effectiveness of banking supervision. Crucial to improving trust in banks will be a switch in emphasis by bank supervisors away from exhaustive and bureaucratic verification of compliance with technical norms, to a more forward-looking assessment of the financial condition of banks, the integrity of their operations, and their capacity to manage risks.

While the motivation for introducing deposit insurance may be to increase trust in the financial system by formally protecting smaller depositors and also creating a more level playing field between state and private banks, the question raised in Chapter 10 is whether deposit insurance is an effective means of achieving these laudable goals. There are significant risks associated with introducing deposit insurance—not least in the form of encouraging risk-taking activities by banks and the accumulation of contingent fiscal liabilities by the Government—and controlling these risks requires a sufficient regulatory and supervisory infrastructure, which is still in its development phase in Russia.

Building trust in the Russian financial system will depend on establishing a reliable framework for bank restructuring and liquidation. Chapter 11 reviews measures to improve this framework, and Chapter 12 provides an assessment of the application of bank restructuring measures by the Agency for Restructuring Credit Organizations (ARCO). The key problem of bank restructuring in Russia is that trust is defrayed due to the less than full satisfaction of depositor claims. This results from delayed bank restructuring actions that are often based on unreliable or unrealistic assessments of bank viability. Improvements are also recommended in the liquidation process, including reducing judicial delays, doing away with the use of amicable settlements, improving the expertise of those responsible for bank liquidation, and reducing court involvement by creating a public entity responsible for bank liquidation.

CHAPTER 9

Building Trust through Effective Banking Supervision

A banking license provides bank owners and managers with the privilege of soliciting deposits from households. However, small, retail savers cannot have the capacity or knowledge to understand the condition of the banks where they place their deposits. In addition, troubled banks are often able to maintain their liquidity (by generating new deposits) for some time after they have eroded the cushion of security provided by their capital base. Thus, creating trust in the financial system depends crucially on developing a banking supervision function with the primary goal of protecting the financial standing of the weakest participant in the financial system, the retail depositor.

The Central Bank of Russia has made significant progress in establishing a bank supervision role, particularly considering that the principle of bank supervision has been introduced to Russia only within the last decade. All the key functions of banking supervision are in place, and they are supported by a comprehensive set of laws, regulations, and internal rules, which provide the supervisors with broad powers of enforcement. The bank supervision staff have had to learn how to apply new laws, regulations, and procedures. Furthermore, although the CBR's reputation for supervision was savaged by the 1998 banking crisis, it has survived the experience, and all the key staff will have gained tremendously valuable practical experience from it. These are formidable strengths on which to build. Moreover, improvement in the overall economic environment has helped the banking sector to improve its viability somewhat, which should make dealing with weak banks and toughening the supervisory system easier. Continuing low usage of banks (lack of depth in the financial system by international standards) should make it easier for the authorities to make difficult decisions in dealing with problem banks. Bank restructuring and/or liquidation should result in relatively small consequences for the economy as a whole. However, despite the strengths and opportunities, as well as the significant effort that has gone into upgrading the banking regulation and supervision framework, banking supervision still has quite a number of weaknesses that need to be addressed for banking supervision to fulfill its primary goal of protecting individual depositors and equally ranking creditors, and thus contribute to reforming the banking system into a viable, legitimate system capable of supporting economic growth. This is especially important if a deposit guarantee system is to be introduced as planned by the authorities. A guarantee system could provide reasonable protection for depositors without accumulating disproportionate contingent fiscal liability, but only if it is underpinned by effective supervision capable and willing to keep unsound banks out of the system.

The CBR appreciates that it still has some way to go to achieve this goal, and the Joint CBR/GoR program for development of the banking system has put together a comprehensive program for improvement of the bank supervision function, which includes the following main areas:

1. Improvement of the licensing process, including tightened requirements for financial strength and fit and proper characteristics for bank owners
2. Continued introduction and implementation of Basel Core principles of effective bank supervision, focusing on assessment of risk management systems and internal controls in banks rather than on compliance checks
3. Development of proactive approaches to bank supervision and improvement of early warning systems
4. Tightening of prudential requirements with a view to better reflection of risk profiles
5. Strengthening definition and the role of capital adequacy
6. Strengthening oversight of banking groups on a consolidated basis
7. Increasing the emphasis on on-site supervision (inspections), focusing inspection efforts on problem banks, banks involved in high risk-taking, and/or those with inadequate risk management systems and weak internal controls
8. Improving the bank supervision process through the transition to International Accounting Standards and the adjustment and streamlining of bank reporting. (As discussed further below,

transition to IAS will require amendments to the Federal Law on Accounting as well as the adjustment of laws regulating taxation
9. Reorganization of the bank supervision function, in order to find an optimal balance between centralization and decentralization of the supervision process
10. Enhancing bank rehabilitation and liquidation procedures
11. Improvement of corporate governance in banks, including enhancing the role of bank external auditors in line with best international practice.

Recognition by the CBR of the need to improve banking supervision along these lines is a very important step forward. These plans are in line with the recommendations that the World Bank and the International Monetary Fund have previously proposed to the Russian authorities. The high-level assessment of the effectiveness and efficiency of the CBR supervision function, which was carried out by the World Bank at the request of the CBR in autumn 2000, may have contributed to the development of such plans by the CBR, especially the consolidation of off-site monitoring and on-site inspection functions into one department, which could streamline the supervision process.

At the same time, development and implementation of bank supervision principles based on international approaches is fraught with significant risks. Such approaches have been developed for less volatile banking environments, and assume far more deep and liquid markets for assets than those available in Russia. They provide wafer-thin margins of safety for a typical Russian bank, requiring constant on-site supervisory reappraisal.

Now is the time for the CBR to implement its plans, which will require a lot of support, both external and internal, to be successful.

IMPROVING THE ENABLING ENVIRONMENT

In the final analysis, everything rests upon the willingness of the major market players (both state and private banks) to conduct their business in a prudent and trustworthy manner. They must be willing to submit to rigorous supervision in the interests of the market as a whole. Even when a comprehensive legal framework and a well-developed supervisory function exist, the mechanisms for banking reform and oversight will not be effective if the enabling environment does not support that reform and oversight. The government and supervisory authorities must have the political will to enact change, for example, as demonstrated in part in the economic role that they set for the banking sector and the role that they set for banking supervision.

The political will to uphold and enforce the tenets of a properly functioning market economy is at the root of reform and of building a safe and sound financial system. The surrounding legal framework and political system must have market and commercial rules that recognize criminal and noncommercial activities as a threat to the country's overall economic well-being—and that explicitly define, enforce, and penalize such activities. The roles of both the banking sector and of banking supervision must be well established, and a certain level of economic health and viability must exist to provide the balance of risk and reward that can motivate healthy investment and banking activities.

In Russia, the enabling environment has yet to be developed to the point where it can support a strong banking sector and effective bank supervision. In fact, it remains extremely weak, and efforts to reform the banking system into a viable, legitimate system have in consequence been largely unsuccessful. The infrastructure is not complete, and it is implicitly designed and operated to accommodate vested interests that have noncommercial and nonmarket motivations. Likewise, reform of the political and economic climate, which is severely constraining the ability of banking supervision and regulation to reform the financial system, appears difficult.

POLITICAL WILL

The various constituents of the system—the Duma, CBR, court system, large corporations, and especially the banks themselves—have demonstrated little inclination to address the root problems of the banking sector. While political will is difficult to quantify, the byproducts or the symptoms of its absence can be easily described. They include:

1. *Lack of transparency.* The financial condition of banks and enterprises, in part due to their use of Russian Accounting Standards, is difficult to ascertain. Financial disclosure requirements are weak, and in many cases the ownership structure of the banking system is ambiguous. Given the absence of reliable information, the activities and economic health of the system are not easily determined. Rapid implementation of selected aspects of IAS would be a major step forward, but full transparency will require more than the application of minimum levels of disclosure and rote compliance with new standards.

2. *Unreliability of bank reporting to the CBR.* Although the CBR rigorously enforces the technical accuracy of reporting (including the imposition of fines, although these are often only nominal amounts), the more serious problem is when banks engage in deliberate actions to conceal the economic nature and risk structure of their transactions. As a result, the CBR does not possess adequate information to detect and act in the case of deteriorating bank and systemic conditions.
3. *CBR reticence to apply the full extent and spirit of the law.* Some improvements are needed, but Russia's banking laws and regulations generally are adequate. The compliance and enforcement environment, in contrast, is so weak that it renders the legal framework ineffective by its lack of application.
4. *Bank linkages with big business and government.* A large portion of the banking sector is connected to the government or to government-owned enterprises. The legal requirement that corporate business transactions, such as intracompany cashflow and transfer pricing, must occur through a bank-like institution means that many other banks are directly connected to financial industrial groups. Until there is some separation of interests and motivations, until market-driven incentives are permitted to stimulate banking and economic activity, and until banking supervision is permitted to occur objectively and independently, the banking sector will remain unreformed.
5. *Responsibility and accountability for prudent banking behavior.* Bank managers and shareholders have not been forced to answer for their misdeeds and for the losses incurred by the system and by depositors and creditors. Many of the managers and shareholders of banks that failed in the 1998 crisis continue their involvement in the sector by way of bridge banks and newly chartered banks. Until the system can be freed of the influence of the individuals and corporations whose conduct led in large measure to that crisis, there will always be a fundamental instability of, and lack of confidence in, the banking system.
6. *Suspicious and criminal activity.* The practice of asset stripping and misallocation of funds goes on unabated, and is even publicly acknowledged by its perpetrators. The lack of coordinated, concerted, preventive, and punitive action by the authorities—or even of adverse comment—suggests a tacit approval of this activity.
7. *Lack of a coordinated, concerted effort to reform and restructure the banking sector.* Many banks on the brink of bankruptcy are

left to negotiate their own, inequitable creditor workouts. There is no attempt to rationalize the number of banks or to withdraw deposit-taking abilities or licenses, even from those institutions that have no intention of using depositors' funds for any purpose other than to support their shareholders' activities.

8. *Government participation in the banking sector and conflicts of interest.* A large portion of the banking sector is owned by the Government, rendering governance and accountability issues even more complex. The ability of supervision to objectively and independently assess state-owned banks and to mandate remedial action is clouded and ambiguous.

9. *Personal benefit.* Politicians and legislators have implied through their actions that they would rather focus on the short-term benefits of holding office than make the decisions that would challenge powerful vested interests and that are necessary to promote long-term reform actions.

The best way for Russia's banks to promote depositor confidence would be to demonstrate a genuine commitment to the honest and prudent conduct of their business. However, both the banks and the authorities alike seem more focused on developing detailed normatives, standards, and structures that would create the appearance of systemic normality to outside parties. All parties, it seems, should be reminded that integrity and prudent banking practice are not the automatic products of a set of accounting standards or of legislation. Individual institutions must also be seen to act in a manner appropriate to their position and responsibilities.

ROLE OF THE BANKING SECTOR

The banking system to date has existed largely for the benefit of large corporations and powerful business interests. The vast majority of banks are associated with Government, Government-owned entities, and/or large corporate groups for which they facilitate corporate cash flows, payments, transfer pricing, and credit access. Banks in Russia do not effectively perform the traditional role of intermediation. The retail deposit base is miniscule, lending to small and medium-size enterprises is seriously underdeveloped, and the overall size of the system is extremely small when compared internationally. Without a sound enabling environment and legitimate profit incentives to encourage banks to provide the necessary financial services and to support economic growth, the role and existence of banking institutions will continue to be ambiguous, thereby contributing to the delay in establishing a true market economy. Economic growth, equitably distributed throughout the country and population, will continue to be stifled.

Since the role of the banking system remains inconsistent with other typical market economies, and since the sector does not engender the confidence of a well-developed retail deposit base and creditor participation, the role of supervision is likewise problematic. In Russia, the banking system does not significantly perform the traditional role of public deposit taker and intermediator of funds in the economy at large, but is instead founded on relatively self-contained entities with limited focus, vested interests, and goals that do not extend beyond those of immediate personal benefit. Under such circumstances, when the banks do not play a significant role in the larger public/national economy, the role of the supervisor to regulate activities to protect the public trust and promote stability is undefined. Since the banks have little interface with public interests, the regulator's role is marginalized and becomes increasingly difficult to fulfill. Since the infrastructure of the enabling environment is flawed, the expectations of the authorities, the public, and international constituents that bank supervision should lead and ignite banking sector reform and restructuring are misplaced.

Any evaluation of banking supervision in Russia or of any developmental program must be considered in light of the marketplace and environment in which the function must operate. Notwithstanding these challenges, the review that follows focuses on selected key elements that, if further enhanced, could potentially add value to the needed banking sector reform.

ESTABLISHING THE ROLE OF BANKING SUPERVISION

For bank supervision to fulfill its responsibilities and duties, the supervisor must first understand and explicitly acknowledge its proper role in financial sector oversight. This role must also be understood and generally accepted by the Government and be promulgated throughout the banking industry. Ultimately the banks must accept the supervisor as an equitable arbiter of law and good practice, who acts in the interests of the system as a whole and not in a capricious or authoritarian way. The supervisor must possess the freedom to act without undue influence from Government, bank owners, or other special interests. He/she must assume a leadership role in restructuring the financial sector and in maintaining the sector's safety and soundness. He/she must also possess the tools to address any activity that threatens this safety and soundness. The supervisor must have the ability to interpret legislation as it applies to individual bank cases and as the sector evolves and introduces new risk configurations. And the supervisor must be prepared, when required to do so, to exercise his/her authority to the fullest extent of the law. Anything less, and the supervisor is not fulfilling his/her responsibility to protect the public trust, depositors, and ultimately the general public.

In Russia, the role of bank supervision is not fully understood by the range of vested interests within the financial system, including the public and government authorities. The role of protecting depositors and ensuring the safety and soundness of the banking system does not appear to be the motivating factor in much of the supervisory practice or philosophy. This view is supported by the strict, legalistic manner in which supervision is conducted; the large amounts of time expended in identifying the need rather than requiring swift bank corrective actions; and the apparent continuing abusive banking practices conducted by banks, their owners, and various vested interests. It is further demonstrated by the lack of responsibility and accountability charged to owners, directors, and managers for lack of management of their institutions, and by the supervisors' reluctance to consistently apply the full force of the existing legal framework. These factors, together with the lack of a well-defined role for the banking sector in Russia's economic landscape, further complicate and cloud the focus and mission of bank supervision.

The role and objectives of supervision must be established and serve as the focal point for all supervisory policy, procedures, and activity if the function is to guide the banking system through the reform process. Establishing the role of the supervisory function and ensuring that the requirements of the new role are truly fulfilled will require that the existing culture and management process in bank supervision fundamentally change. The motivations and focus of supervision will have to shift to make banks the first line of defense for legal compliance, for monitoring, and for responding to existing and changing risk profiles; to focus supervision on the proactive identification of banking problems; and to ensure that responsibility and accountability are properly assigned to bank owners, management, and boards. In short, the supervisory culture of the CBR and the banks themselves must change in order to meet the performance expectations a market economy places on bank supervision.

One of the first steps necessary to more clearly focus supervisory objectives and to clarify the supervisors' role within the CBR, Government, banking sector, and public is to establish the protection of depositors as the primary objective of banking supervision; without this objective, supervision cannot ensure systemic stability. The supervisor must have the power to interpret the substance of transactions—rather than just the form—and to enforce supervisory norms and guidelines on that basis.

A set of operational-level principles and objectives could rapidly be prepared that emphasize the most critical issues or actions to be taken for the supervisor to accomplish that mission. This set should include guidance on the compliance culture that needs to be inculcated in the banking system and on the manner in which the supervisor should interpret key aspects of regulations and laws. Although there are exceptions, most Russian banks seem to have internal systems and policies to address their day-to-day activities. Such systems are used to ensure that the banks fulfill the objectives of their controllers; they are not necessarily constructed in accordance with sound banking principles. The guidance to supervisors might therefore include the need to ensure

1. the commitment of bank owners, controllers, and managers to the spirit (rather than the letter) of supervisory requirements
2. responsible ownership by bank shareholders, which defines and prohibits conflicts of interest and abusive practices and requires business practices and behavior that allow the institution to conduct legitimate banking activities in a safe and sound manner, thereby helping to build a sense of confidence in the banking system
3. core risk management and control processes
4. requirements to establish strong legal, regulatory, and internal policy compliance systems
5. prompt corrective actions by the supervisor in cases of bank abuse (including fictitious or inaccurate reporting), financial deterioration, capital insolvency, or legal infractions. Triggers for action should be based on substance rather than on formal, technical compliance with normatives, particularly in the areas of large exposure reporting, related-party exposure concealment, capital creation schemes, and loan-loss provisions.

Although the compilation of a set of operational objectives should help the supervisors to measure their performance internally, a similar statement of principles should be published and made available to the banking community. Ultimately the supervisor should issue public reports detailing his/her performance against the stated objectives. This would add an increased level of accountability to the statements made by the CBR in its annual report.

The difficulty of accomplishing such a cultural shift in the Russian financial system should not be underestimated, but failure to achieve this shift would undermine and invalidate all other proposed reforms. A start should be made, in the shortest possible time, on the process of advising banks that their conduct, if not actually illegal, is generally unacceptable. Attempts should be made to bring as many cases of abuse as possible into the public domain, preferably by actions leading to the withdrawal of licenses and therefore the authority to take public deposits. Nothing would boost public confidence as much as seeing appropriate action taken, particularly against high-profile banks. The CBR must accept and not be deterred by the fact that its actions may result in court cases.

It is essential that the matter of addressing the abuses being perpetrated by banks be brought into the public domain. If this can be done, public opinion may begin to make the shift required for Russia to take its place in the global economy.

IMPROVING SUPERVISORY EFFECTIVENESS

Establishing a new role for supervision necessarily implies that bank supervision must substantially improve its effectiveness. To achieve this, the organizational arrangement of supervision should be evaluated to ensure that it is aligned to deliver the highest and best use of its resources. Given the overall condition of the sector and the predisposition of bank managers and shareholders to circumvent the laws and rules, the nature of the supervisory practice must shift. Staff and management can no longer be permitted to merely assess strict technical compliance with rules and ratios, but must proactively and aggressively assess the operating condition and integrity of the banks in the system.

Improving the effectiveness of bank supervision requires change at all levels, from the supervisory management level to the regional staff level; in policies and procedures; and in the supervisory actions ultimately taken with banks. Effective and successful supervision cannot be achieved without a sustained shift in the attitudes and working culture of the function, repeatedly confirmed and demonstrated by executive and senior CBR management, nor can it be achieved without a commitment to continued training. The effectiveness of supervision depends to a much greater extent on its content than on its organization. The first priority in improving effectiveness is to ensure that the purpose of supervision is clear to all, and that it is reinforced by every component of the structure, policies, procedures, and management of the process. The ultimate aim is to ensure that bank depositors and lenders have confidence in the banking system and in its supervision, such that the failure of one bank does not significantly diminish the confidence of depositors in other banks.

For example, at the licensing stage most attention is given to merely ensuring that minimum requirements are met. Little attention is given to evaluating the proposed bank's business strategy, internal controls and risk management plans, and safety margins of capital and liquidity—that is, the factors that determine whether or not depositors will be able to withdraw their money in full and on time. Ongoing supervision appears to focus more on compliance with required accounting procedures, regulatory ratios, and other procedural requirements than on the proactive evaluation of safety and soundness of the institution and therefore also on depositors' ability to withdraw their deposits as contracted. History further demonstrates that the rehabilitation process is highly procedural, involving considerable delays and allowing even very distressed institutions to continue operations in the marketplace. The initiative to restructure or rehabilitate a bank is virtually passed back to the bank while the CBR awaits remedial plans and management action.

The necessary steps to strengthen and improve the effectiveness of bank supervision are many and detailed, and span the need for cultural change at the highest levels of CBR management to the need for change at the furthest outreach of the supervisory process. The thrust of supervision must become more proactive, using more qualitative analysis, judgment, and decision-making. For example, the CBR should be empowered to make licensing decisions based on qualitative fit and proper testing for bank owners, directors, and management.

The on-site examination process, off-site monitoring, and early warning analysis should be focused on a qualitative assessment of the safety and soundness of institutions and of the potential threats to their operational status. Qualitative assessment and judgment should form the basis of the CBR's supervisory response—that is, whether to monitor, rehabilitate, or close the institution. While a number of strengthening steps are evident, certain of them are key to shifting the culture and focus of the function.

The supervisor needs to become accustomed to exercising judgment, but judgment reached following a structured assessment of the institution. Banks should not face serious supervisory sanctions simply on the basis of the opinion of one official. Clear guidelines for the delegation of the exercise of judgment should be developed, giving appropriate powers to appropriate levels. Ultimate authority over issues such as licensing, delicensing, and findings of improper conduct in banks should probably be left to a committee, but to a committee that includes an element of real debate and an assessment of the proposals of individual officials, rather than to one that simply endorses a previously prepared resolution.

Clear supervisory responsibility for each bank in the system must be delegated to an individual official, who will coordinate and oversee all aspects of a bank's operations, including licensing, on-site and off-site supervision, disciplinary action, and delicensing. The examiner or supervisor in charge should be supported by the various supervisory functions that bear on the subject institution. The official should also be protected from political and other pressure, external and internal to the CBR, in order that he or she might execute the responsibility of the position in a fair and objective manner.

For the CBR to shift from reactive responses to bank and system distress to a proactive, anticipatory oversight function, the true economic health of each bank must be known. Acquiring this knowledge must be the primary aim of supervisory monitoring as it must form the basis for the supervisory decision-making that follows. Full knowledge of each banks' condition allows the supervisor to anticipate events and their impact; to make informed and early supervisory decisions to protect the depositors and the system; and, above all, to avoid surprises. This, in and of itself, is one of the best ways to promote confidence in the system.

Regulatory Reporting: Importance of Accurate Information

On the most basic level, financial and regulatory information reported by the banks, their management, directors, and owners must be truthful and reliable. However, in Russia the truthfulness of bank reporting continues to be suspect. It is widely acknowledged that a large majority of the reporting to the CBR is deliberately structured to avoid regulation. Even if reports are prepared reliably and according to instructions, the chance that meaningful economic information is conveyed is relatively low. This is in part due to the fact that the markets for banking assets in Russia are rarely liquid or deep, and that reported values in terms of asset classification, loan-loss provisions, liquidity, and capital therefore have only limited relevance. The lack of adequate information constrains the CBR's ability to proactively monitor banks and the system at large, with the result that corrective action by the CBR comes late and banks operate while distressed—at the expense of depositors and creditors.

Transparent, full, and accurate information regarding shareholders, particularly beneficial owners and/or controllers, is at best difficult to obtain. The lack of reliable information has recently facilitated the movement of unsuitable owners through the system as additional banks have been activated or changed the terms of their licenses to accommodate the needs of those seeking shelter from the 1998 crisis. In the worst cases, it has even permitted such people to seek licenses for new banks. It is important therefore that the CBR enforce and expand the requirements for truthful regulatory reporting at all levels.

Given that the integrity of financial information reported to the CBR is questionable, and given the need for an effective supervisory process to produce a comprehensive picture of the economic value and financial standing of the banks in the system, proper emphasis on the on-site examination process is critical. There is no substitute for on-site inspection by well-trained inspectors who can rigorously judge the realizable value of bank assets in the current marketplace.

Strengthen the On-Site Inspection Process and Priority

The CBR, similar to the central banks of other countries, uses a mix of both on- and off-site monitoring. The weight afforded to each form of monitoring varies from country to country, but for developing and transition economies the value and importance of the on-site examination process cannot be overemphasized. In Russia, given that the integrity and accuracy of bank reporting is known to be deficient, the use of the on-site examination process is key to effective bank supervision and ultimately, therefore, to protecting the safety of the deposits. Exercised in a risk-prioritized manner, the process can be used to (*a*) verify information and asset values, (*b*) assess the overall operating condition of the subject institution, and (*c*) provide certain key supervisory decision-making input on the depth and level of distress and on any needed rehabilitation measures.

The implementation in Russia of a rigorous on-site examination process will require that (*a*) adequate numbers of suitably trained inspectors are available to conduct the inspections, (*b*) banks are placed on a risk-prioritized schedule, and (*c*) the schedule is flexible enough to accommodate change as risk indicators shift.

The on-site process and the inspectors should be the focal point of the supervisory process. This requirement raises important issues concerning the delegation of the supervisory process; it raises the role of the inspector in the decision-making process for actions taken with a bank; it requires sufficient expert resources; and it requires an overall quality control process to ensure the integrity of the reports and procedural consistency. Coordination between the findings of inspectors and the other elements of supervision is vital, and appropriate delegation, as previously discussed, is also essential.

Banking Regulation

Good laws, regulations, rules, and procedures alone will not create an effective supervision process; good executive judgment and application of those rules are also needed. Russia's existing regulations appear generally comprehensive, and are set to be enhanced by the enactment of certain amendments to the banking laws that have recently passed third reading in the Duma. Bankruptcy, liquidation, and accounting legislation are also in the process of being amended.

Some areas of regulation nonetheless still require strengthening. In particular, the rules addressing licensing, bank exit procedures, capital adequacy, corporate governance, corrective action and enforcement procedures, asset classification, ownership thresholds, and approval authorities must be improved, specifically for licensing, "fit and proper" standards of ownership and control, acquisition and control, etc.

Licensing. Given that the system is burdened with an abundance of unsafe and unsound banks, more supervisory attention should be given to preventing the entry of problematic banks and their shareholders. The management and shareholders of failed banks additionally have rarely been called upon to take responsibility and account for their actions, with many of those responsible for distressed institutions continuing to circulate in the banking sector, post-1998 crisis. The phenomenon of the bridge bank provides perhaps the most striking evidence of this problem. The bridge banks allowed managers and shareholders of distressed banks to continue in business using new or changed banking licenses, thus effectively aiding the stripping of assets from failed institutions. It is imperative that the CBR escalate its efforts to purge the system of problematic banks, to hold their management and shareholders accountable for their actions, and to prohibit them from reentering the banking sector in the future. If such steps cannot be effectively ensured, those and similar banks will continue to be a source of ongoing system instability.

"Fit and proper" standards of ownership and control. The "fit and proper" requirements made of bank managers, shareholders, and controllers are among the most important safeguards of the safety and soundness of a bank or banking system. They allow regulators to block participation in the banking system by those whose past actions have demonstrated a proclivity for mismanagement, fraud, and inappropriate self-dealing. This is particularly germane in the Russian context, in which the owners and managers of numerous failed banks have almost

immediately established new banks using the assets of the old. The result is a continuation of the same substandard business practices in the new bank, and the cause of the failure of the old bank is likely to be repeated in the new. "Fit and proper" standards are not based on a generalized desire for respectability in the banking profession. They are designed to prevent recurring bank failures resulting from the malfeasance of those who have historically proven their inability or unwillingness to soundly manage their businesses.

In Russia, guidance on fit and proper tests and requirements is disseminated through selected laws and instructions. Limited requirements for managers include evidence of legal or economic education and/or experience as a bank manager and possession of a "business reputation"; rejection can be made based on the prior commission of certain offenses, on unsatisfactory job performance, or on submission of incorrect information. Previous bank managers determined by a court to have been responsible for bringing a bank into bankruptcy are precluded from holding any other bank managerial positions for a period of five years. Requirements placed on shareholders are less restrictive and include satisfactory financial standing, compliance with antimonopoly rules, fulfillment of tax obligations, notification to the CBR of a 5 percent purchase, and approval from the CBR for a 20 percent purchase. Persons who previously owned shares in a failed bank and are determined by a court to have contributed to that bank's failure are precluded for 10 years from owning more than 5 percent of the shares of any other bank.

The gap between the scope of requirements for controlling shareholders (i.e., any holdings over 5 percent) and that for management should be addressed. It is not clear how the CBR currently could act against unsuitable indirect shareholders, how it could exercise an effective licensing policy if a court judgment were needed to keep former owners of bankrupt banks from obtaining approval to own large blocks of shares, or how managers that have been convicted of crimes can be prevented from returning to the system (legally, all they need to do is wait for a year to pass after conviction). Management abuses rarely lead to court convictions.

To assess an individual in terms of his or her probity, competence, soundness of judgment, diligence, and potential danger to depositors, while critical, is counter to the culture of Russia and Russian banking. Worse, the establishment of norms of what is fit and proper—for example, for the percentage of equity that a shareholder should control before becoming subject to testing—risks raising the already high levels of concealment of ownership. Full implementation of the fit and proper test will clearly be difficult for Russia, but it is a part of the real key to progress—the exercise of judgment in the supervisory process—and must be pursued.

Acquisition and control. The approval requirements for share acquisition do not capture indirect shareholders, despite the potential of such shareholders to form a controlling interest. The law governing the Central Bank and the Law on Banks and Banking should be amended to define "control" more broadly and subjectively; specifically, to capture those entities or groups that alone or collectively can influence a bank's decision-making activity or that may act to control the bank with less than a 20 percent ownership. Banking legislation should also require CBR approval on shareholders, direct or indirect, acquiring 5 percent or more of a banking institution (the current threshold is 20 percent); and should require the periodic disclosure of all beneficial shareholders, direct and indirect, to the CBR. Steps should be taken to improve the overall transparency of bank ownership throughout the system.

Streamlining the licensing process. Currently, a plethora of licensing requirements exists for the array of activities conducted by banks. Such activities include those by which a bank constitutes a de facto corporate treasury for associated companies or FIGs. Steps should be taken, both through law and in practice, to streamline the licensing requirements, and these should be complemented by more rigorous supervisory requirements to ensure that banks establish strong and effective internal risk management systems to monitor and approve new activities and new products.

There should also be a sharper distinction between those institutions that request a license in order to take public deposits and those that require a license in order to fulfill the internal (treasury-related) needs of their associated companies. In other words, the principal business of each bank should be reviewed to see if it requires a public deposit–taking license. Rapid and urgent action should be taken to reduce the number of institutions that hold a full banking license. The reform of banking supervision should then concentrate on those banks that remain, rather than on the present universe of 1,300 "banks." This would radically improve the chances of success in the development of effective supervision. To further improve the possibility of increasing public confidence, there should be obvious indication in the name of financial institutions of their status. Although the best alternative would be to restrict the use of the word "bank" to those institutions allowed to take public deposits, there are presumably other options.

Capital Adequacy

Definitions of capital and capital insolvency. Information on the availability of true capital—that is, funds readily available to absorb and cushion loss—is confused in Russia by the generous definition of qualifying capital, by the well-developed concealment of capital inflation schemes and valuation rules, and by an ineffectively enforced provision against using borrowed funds as capital. Also, under current law a bank's insolvency is measured in terms of its liquidity position rather than its capital adequacy. This has the effect of allowing a bank, which may technically be capital-insolvent, to continue to operate in the marketplace, tapping various sources of funding, potentially depleting all forms of asset liquidity, and stripping the bank of its remaining value for depositor and creditor compensation. To allow such institutions to continue to operate escalates the costs to depositors and creditors, undercuts confidence in the system, and perpetuates the present environment of mistrust.

Supervisors are currently unable to take action against banks that have for all intents and purposes experienced capital insolvency and failed. Basing the measure of solvency on capital adequacy would refocus the supervisor and the marketplace on a more proactive measure of bank soundness. It is critical that this be done to enable more proactive risk detection and prompt corrective action.

Amendments to the Law on Banks and Banking that have passed third reading in the Duma would introduce a minimum capital adequacy ratio of 2 percent as the threshold for license revocation. Pursuant to the provisions of these amendments, if a bank's capital adequacy ratio falls below 2 percent, the CBR is required to revoke the bank's license and to commence liquidation proceedings. However, the measurement of this 2 percent threshold remains an issue.

The level of capital sufficient to operate in a financial environment such as the one in Russia should be continually reviewed. The recommended 8 percent level suggested by international standards is intended for banks operating in a viable economic setting that possesses relative operating health. An argument easily can be made for requiring a higher absolute level of capital to cushion against systemic shock in Russia's less stable environment. The authorities should work to establish a higher level of required capital based on the historical experience of the banking sector and the relative instability of the current environment.

Capital write-down. Under the recent amendments Russian banks are now required to write down or decrease authorized capital to the actual level of equity capital, and the supervisor is now empowered to charge down equity capital to real value based on the results of a fair and objective on-site inspection. These requirements and powers will allow the true economic picture of an institution to be conveyed, and will enhance the ability of the supervisor to ascertain a true and accurate picture of the safety and soundness of the institution and of the need for remedial actions. The adoption of IAS would provide a starting point for supervisors in their efforts to make accurate assessments of an institution's capital strength. But because very few banks could pass a rigorous test of the amount and quality of their capital, the further write-downs necessary could initially be made only in supervisory calculations, with remedial action instituted. Full publication could follow at a later date. A near-term date should be set to ensure that banks do not continue to postpone full compliance.

Corporate Governance

The ability of the CBR to hold owners, directors, and management directly responsible, accountable, and liable for mismanagement and/or abuse of their subject institutions continues to be weak. Many of the existing corrective and enforcement actions address the bank itself but not the individuals responsible for unsafe and unsound business activity.

The supervisor must have the full capacity to address the key parties who are responsible for and determine how the business of banking is conducted. Since the banking business involves the public trust and responsibility to manage the public's money in a prudent manner, the responsibilities and accountability of such persons must be clearly defined. Furthermore, the supervisor must be provided with and must use the remedial tools to address activity that threatens this trust. A review of the legal provisions in this area should be undertaken, and the necessary amendments introduced.

Suspicious or Criminal Activity

Neither the framework nor the mechanisms are in place adequately to define what constitutes misappropriation of funds, personal benefit, and other illegal actions in the financial sector. Furthermore, the supervisory and financial police do not have the capacity or, as demonstrated by the significant asset stripping and abuse of the system, the will to hold responsible parties accountable and liable for desecration of the system. Consequently, criminal statutes need strengthening. They should be reviewed and changed to ensure that the scope of prosecutable crimes is broad enough to be effective in the current environment and that rigorous enforcement actions are provided and sufficiently linked to banking law and laws addressing corporate governance. Ideally, operating procedure should allow the supervisor to be informed of the disposition of any criminal referrals passed to the police, but it may be some time before such practice is possible in Russia.

A comprehensive definition of "imprudent activities," which have the potential for prompt, significant enforcement action, should be provided within the context of the banking law. For example, this might include inaccurate statements to the supervisor, lack of rigorous "know your customer" (real name) procedures, misstatement of the financial condition, and subsequent inaccurate or untruthful public disclosure.

Consolidated Supervision and Associated Powers

The legislative framework should be expanded to address and empower the supervisor to oversee banks in consolidated groups. Provisions creating the notion of "banking groups" and "bank holdings" in amendments to the Law on Banks and Banking have passed third reading in the Duma but have not yet been enacted into law. However, this is only one part of the process and just one of the possible options to approaching consolidated supervision.

There is one major problem that should be borne in mind in the implementation of consolidated supervision: the plethora of institutions associated with FIGs. The potential risks and ownership ramifications to banks in these groups can be many. Although these FIG banks act essentially as corporate treasuries, their use of a banking license means that their actions are liable to influence the trust of the public, depositors, and creditors in the banking system as a whole. The supervisor must have the authority to assess all potential risks facing a bank in a consolidated group. However, it would be wrong to consolidate industrial companies with financial ones for overall supervision, particularly if the industrial balance sheets tend to improve the financial standing of the whole group. Consolidated supervision implies the collation and consideration of all risks to a bank, and should not permit the capital weakness of a deposit-taking institution to be concealed.

Exit and Consolidation

Depositors and the public will gain confidence from witnessing the supervisor taking timely and necessary corrective steps with a deteriorating institution. In Russia, remedial action has been slow at best, and a number of highly distressed institutions continue to operate in the system. Challenges by vested interests to the CBR's attempts to revoke a license abound in the court system, and when a license is revoked the liquidation process is frequently lengthy and slow, further reducing the opportunity of depositors and creditors to recoup any remuneration. The scope and nature of these problems are discussed in detail in Chapter 11.

While the CBR acknowledges that much must be done to clean the system of the existing distressed and insolvent banks, it is hampered by a weak enabling environment and by the momentum and focus of the supervisory process itself. A shift of focus to obtaining and analyzing more timely and accurate financial information would significantly improve the CBR's ability to deploy prompt corrective action. However, the CBR should also continue its efforts to strengthen the remedial process; to place greater emphasis on the core problems of bank distress, including mismanagement; to encourage consolidation of the system; and to seek out economically viable banks for rehabilitation.

CHAPTER 10

Does the Russian Federation Need Deposit Insurance?

INTRODUCTION

Recent cross-country comparisons of explicit deposit insurance schemes have exposed the risks inherent in such schemes, especially when they are deployed within a deficient regulatory and supervisory environment. Although deposit insurance schemes have come into increasing use in recent years, poorly designed schemes can reduce the market discipline exerted by bank depositors, increase the likelihood of banking crises, and impede financial development. These effects are strongest in countries that fail to enforce adequate regulations, to thoroughly supervise their banking system, and to intervene promptly when banks fail.

Given the deficient regulatory and supervisory framework in Russia, the lack of possibilities and incentives for depositors to exert market discipline in banks, and the bailouts of well-connected bank owners after the 1998 crisis, the introduction of a deposit insurance scheme seems a premature undertaking that might increase financial fragility and impede further financial development. Improvements in these various areas—resulting inter alia in the consolidation of the sector—as well as reform of the state banks should be seen as pre-conditions for the successful implementation of deposit insurance.

Cross-country comparisons have shown that the design of a deposit insurance scheme can affect financial development and fragility. A scheme that offers limited coverage and that is privately managed and funded would have lower moral hazard risks and would align incentives between the owners and managers of the scheme. As described in Box

10.1 below, the proposed Russian scheme does envision limited coverage —although, given the recent history of select creditor bailouts (such as the use of amicable settlements in the context of ARCO's restructuring), this might not be very credible. On the other hand, the insurance fund is to be managed by the Government, which opens the door for political capture. And while funding through premiums levied on banks is planned for the future, the initial capital would come from the Government, raising concerns of potential abuse by banks. Furthermore, the limited power of the deposit insurer in relation to its member banks restricts its ability to minimize potential insurance losses.

Box 10.1 The Design of the Proposed Russian Deposit Insurance Scheme

The major aspects of the design of the proposed Russian deposit insurance scheme refer to:

Limiting the coverage of the insurance: The proposed coverage limit of RUR 143,600 and the coinsurance of 10 percent for deposits between RUR 2,000 and 20,000 and of 50 percent for deposits between RUR 20,000 and 143,600 produces a maximum reimbursement of RUR 80,000, a sum that is one and two times GDP per capita and thus around the international average. Only household accounts would be covered, while it seems unclear whether insider accounts would be excluded*—although the lack of transparency of the ownership structure of banks would make enforcement of such exclusion difficult. Furthermore, the precedence of previous bailouts of bank owners and creditors by the CBR after the 1998 crisis makes the limitation of the coverage to household deposits not very credible, especially given that a significant share of the initial capital of the scheme will come from the Government. Overall, while the suggested coverage seems incentive-compatible, transparency and credibility of the authorities are needed to make it effective in fostering market discipline.

Insuring incentive-compatible governance: The proposed governance structure of the Russian deposit insurance system increases the risks of political and regulatory capture and poses significant moral hazard risks. The proposed law calls for public management of the deposit insurance scheme, which bears the risk of political capture of the deposit insurer. According to international experience, it would be preferable to have the scheme managed by representatives of the banks, who have the strongest incentives to avoid losses through failing banks, if they are the main financing source.

Private versus state funding: Given the currently weak institutional environment and the lack of markets for bank debt, the introduction of risk-based premiums would seem premature. However, the option should be kept open for the future. The current arrangement of premiums based on insurable deposits seems therefore appropriate.

While funding of the scheme by banks is envisioned as the long-term goal for the scheme, the Government will provide the initial funds. The ex ante funding of up to five percent of insured deposits by the government—an arbitrarily chosen number†—eliminates the incentives for the participating banks to minimize the loss rate stemming from bank failures. Rather, it amounts to a state guarantee of the insured deposits. Instead of providing liquid assets to the deposit insurer, the authorities should insist on exclusive funding by member banks and provide the deposit insurer with the capacity to access a contingent line of credit through the CBR. This would make the member banks liable for any losses incurred even after a bank failure and

(Box continues on next page)

> **Box 10.1** *(continued)*
>
> thus give them better incentives to monitor each other. Further, the provisions to raise additional contributions in the event of a shortfall of resources should be extended to ensure the financial viability of the fund except for a systemic crisis.[‡] The investment strategy spelled out in the proposed law seems sufficient to guarantee the liquidity and safety of the investment funds.
>
> *The regulatory and supervisory authority of the insurer:* The proposed law does not give the insurer any regulatory or supervisory rights beyond information-sharing with the CBR. On the contrary, the deposit insurer would have to accept any bank licensed by the CBR to collect household deposits without being able to check its financial viability. While recent proposals call for a substantially higher screening and monitoring of licensed banks, this should be implemented before proceeding with deposit insurance. According to the proposed law, no actions could be imposed on banks to prevent them from aggressive risk taking, and member banks could not be excluded should they jeopardize the financial position of the bank, and thus the insurer, through reckless lending. While not duplicating CBR's supervisory and regulatory work, the deposit insurer should have a role in both the licensing and the supervisory process. It should be given the option to (1) reject any new applicant if the decision is based on objective criteria, (2) order (via subcontracting) extraordinary audits of banks it perceives to be unsound, and (3) be allowed to threaten expulsion (and therefore de-licensing) of banks that are recklessly managed. These rights do not require the build-up of a substantial supervisory department within the deposit insurer, but are important, since the deposit insurer (if financed by its member banks) has the largest incentives to minimize insurance losses and thus monitor and discipline banks. Giving the deposit insurer a role in the regulatory and supervisory process does in no way reduce the urgent need for an improvement in supervision by CBR; it rather reinforces it, since the deposit insurer's decisions might be based on information obtained from the CBR.
>
> *Inclusion of state banks:* Finally, it is recommended that Sberbank and other state-owned banks not be included in a deposit insurance scheme in their current form. Including them would not limit their competitive advantage unless they are subject to an effective hard budget constraint. Thus, the decision to introduce a deposit insurance scheme encompassing the state banks would have to be linked to strategic decisions regarding the reform of these banks (as discussed in Chapter 7).
>
> [*] In the most recent version of the draft law, there is only reference to "deposits on favorable terms." This should be spelled out in detail.
> [†] A much more thorough analysis of the size distribution of deposits and failure rates would be necessary to determine a reasonable target rate.
> [‡] Deposit insurance schemes are typically not designed to cover systemic crises, but rather individual bank failures. In the event of a systemic crisis, government involvement might be necessary. However, it might be best to make this event unpredictable in order not to raise market expectations.

While the introduction of a deposit insurance scheme seems currently an inadequate instrument to increase trust in the banking system, the institutional framework and enabling environment should be a priority for Russian policy-makers. Among other measures, a sound regulatory and supervisory framework should be put in place, and private agents should be given the means and incentives to monitor banks. This would lead to the development of efficient and sound financial intermediation and could eventually allow the introduction of a deposit insurance scheme.

DEPOSIT INSURANCE IN OTHER COUNTRIES

The last two decades have seen a rise in explicit deposit insurance schemes around the world, as part of the overall financial safety network. Most OECD countries and an increasing number of developing countries have adopted some form of an explicit deposit insurance scheme, and in 1994, the European Union adopted a mandate to introduce deposit insurance schemes in all member countries. Many of the transition economies have introduced schemes, and while Russia has never had an industrywide explicit deposit insurance scheme, there are now plans to establish one. ARCO, the bank-restructuring agency, has already created a deposit insurance scheme for five of the banks in its portfolio.

Depositors will often perceive the implicit existence of deposit insurance even where there is no formal provision for it. Except for countries such as New Zealand, where the state is legally prohibited from providing funds to depositors and creditors of failing banks, depositors and other creditors will often assume an implicit deposit guarantee extended by the Government. This assumption is supported by the fact that, in times of crisis, many countries have chosen to extend an unlimited deposit guarantee for the whole banking sector in an attempt to prevent a systemic bank run. The assumption is particularly strong in the case of state-owned banks.

Those who advocate deposit insurance give the establishment of trust and the creation of a level playing field as the main objectives behind the proposed introduction of a Russian deposit insurance scheme. By introducing such a scheme, Russia would hope to increase trust in the financial system, attract more deposits into the formal banking system, reverse capital flight, develop financial intermediation, and thus foster economic development. It is also believed that the extension of deposit insurance to all banks could reduce the competitive advantage that the state-owned banks hold over private banks.

THE BENEFITS AND RISKS OF DEPOSIT INSURANCE

Deposit insurance aims to protect small depositors and foster banking sector stability. By guaranteeing the savings of small depositors, deposit insurance encourages small savers to entrust their savings to banks and discourages them from bank runs in times of crisis. Thus a deposit guarantee not only protects small savers, but could also foster banking stability and the long-run development of financial intermediation. These benefits have often been stressed when introducing deposit insurance.

To understand the risks of deposit insurance, one has to consider the incentive structure of bankers. Even in the absence of deposit insurance, bank owners, particularly those working with low levels of capital, can face strong incentives to lend aggressively, ignoring risk management. The lower their capital base, the less they have to lose and the more they can gain through aggressive lending. Market discipline exerted by creditors and regulatory discipline from the authorities aim to reduce this form of aggressive risk-taking. Bank creditors can withdraw funds or demand a risk premium if observing a decline in banks' liquidity and solvency. Large creditors and depositors, such as other banks or nonfinancial enterprises, have the capacity to follow closely the banks in which they entrust their deposits. Since small creditors, such as retail depositors, do not have the ability or incentives to monitor banks carefully, they are reliant on a strong supervisory authority that is willing to take prompt action against weak banks. This is important since banks usually turn insolvent long before they become illiquid.

There are several risks inherent in deposit insurance schemes. By encouraging the confidence of depositors in the safety of their deposits, they can make depositors complacent and decrease their interest in monitoring banks. Especially the large depositors that are the most likely and most able to monitor banks might reduce their efforts if they perceive the introduction of a deposit insurance scheme for small depositors as a signal that the coverage will be extended to them in times of crisis. The existence of a deposit insurance scheme and the resulting reduced market discipline can also change the incentive structure for bank owners and managers. In the presence of insured deposits, negative shocks to a bank's capital base reduce the downside of risk even more, and when hit by a negative shock a bank is therefore more likely to take large aggressive risks. Generous deposit insurance has the effect of subsidizing this aggressive risk-taking.

Deposit insurance thus has the potential to induce greater risk-taking by banks, especially in a weak supervisory and regulatory environment. Since deposit insurance decreases the incentives of bank creditors to monitor and discipline banks, the regulatory and supervisory authorities take on greater responsibilities. This, however, requires transparency (i.e., the ability of supervisors to detect when banks take on aggressive risk), and deterrence (i.e., the ability to convince bankers that rules will be enforced). Deterrence in turn depends on the accountability of both deposit insurance officials and regulatory and supervisory authorities regarding the taxpayer, who often has to pick up the bill for bank failures. Other components of the financial safety net, such as lender-of-last-resort facilities and bank failure resolution are also important for the success of a deposit insurance scheme. The absence of an effective lender-of-last-resort that can provide immediate liquidity to sound banks undermines the safety net's function of preventing bank runs. The lack of prompt action in the case of failing institutions, of a quick-exit strategy, and of clear and transparent resolution procedures encourages owners and managers of insolvent banks to take additional risks, thus increasing bank fragility and the strains that are put on the deposit insurance scheme. The success of deposit insurance thus crucially depends on the other elements of the financial safety net—prudential regulation and supervision, lender-of-last-resort facilities, and bank failure resolution.

Recent cross-country comparisons have shown the risks of adopting explicit deposit insurance schemes. International comparisons have shown that the likelihood of a banking crisis tends to increase in the presence of a poorly designed deposit insurance scheme (see Demirgüç-Kunt and Detriagache 2000). This likelihood is even greater in countries with deregulated interest rates and an institutional environment that lacks transparency. The U.S. savings and loan crisis of the 1980s has been widely explained by the coexistence of a generous deposit insurance scheme, financial liberalization, and the failure of regulators to intervene promptly in failing institutions.

Deposit insurance can undermine market discipline exerted by depositors. Evidence supports the existence of banking market discipline exerted by depositors and other creditors in many countries, both developed and developing (see Demirgüç-Kunt and Kane [2001] for a literature overview). Cross-country comparisons, however, have shown that such market discipline is weaker in countries with explicit deposit insurance and lower levels of institutional development (see Demirgüç-Kunt and Huizinga 1999).

The introduction of deposit insurance is not a panacea for financial sector development; on the contrary, it has substantial risks. The introduction of a poorly designed deposit insurance scheme in a weak institutional environment would not only increase the probability of a banking crisis by diminishing market discipline, but would also hurt financial development (see Cull, Senbet, and Sorge 2001). Cross-country studies have shown that in weak institutional environments more generous deposit insurance schemes are related to greater subsequent financial sector volatility and to lower subsequent growth in financial development. Furthermore, while an explicit deposit insurance scheme might encourage savers to entrust more of their savings to banks, these additional resources are typically not intermediated effectively.

INTRODUCING DEPOSIT INSURANCE IN RUSSIA

The potential introduction of a deposit insurance scheme should be preceded by an "audit" of the institutional framework and environment of the country. Do depositors have the means and incentives to monitor and discipline banks? Do bank supervisors have the ability to detect aggressive risk-taking by banks and enforce the rules to prevent them from doing so? Can the authorities make the credible commitment to limit the deposit insurance in the event of a bank failure to insured deposits? Are the other elements of the financial safety net in place?

In Russia there are both limited capacity and few incentives for bank creditors to monitor and exert market discipline. Even if depositors had the incentives to impose market discipline on the banks, they have only limited means to do so. The financial information provided by banks is of notoriously low quality, in part because of the use of Russian Accounting Standards that tend to overestimate assets and thus profitability; and in part because of the lack of enforcement of truthful reporting by the Central Bank. Bank directors, moreover, are not legally liable for erroneous or misleading information.

The regulatory and supervisory environment in Russia does not discourage banks from aggressive risk-taking. The CBR, as regulatory and supervisory body, takes a passive rather than a proactive attitude to protecting depositor interests. There is an emphasis on form over substance—it is compliance with rules that is checked rather than the viability of bank activities that is considered—and supervision is not sufficiently based on on-site inspection. Furthermore, the CBR does not use its powers to intervene early in troubled banks. The decision to intervene or not often seems to be based more on political considerations than on the financial situation of the bank. The discretionary and selective provision of liquidity support during the 1998 crisis, which was done without disclosure of the criteria on which the receiving banks were chosen, and regulatory forbearance have set a bad precedent that might encourage banks—especially politically connected ones—to bet on another bailout should the need arise.

Given the extremely weak supervisory and regulatory framework and deficiencies in the other elements of the financial safety net, the introduction of a deposit insurance scheme at this stage seems premature. Given the substantial and undefined banking risks in Russia, it would be difficult to contain the risks to be borne by the insurer of such a system. Establishing a deposit insurance scheme for Russia's nontransparent and fragile banking sector could create a large contingent liability, and one that might go beyond even the Government's resources. Defaulting on this contingent liability in the case of a crisis would again destroy what little trust remains in the banking sector. The lack of serious supervision and prompt supervisory action additionally means that such a scheme would pose a high risk of moral hazard to the system. In the absence of the necessary market and regulatory discipline, the increased ability that an insurance scheme would give to private banks to attract additional resources would likely encourage those banks to lend aggressively and imprudently. Given current regulatory and supervisory weaknesses, it is of serious concern that ARCO has embarked on providing deposit insurance to some of the banks that it owns and is even extending this insurance for a period of 18 months after these banks have been privatized (discussed further in Chapter 12). Because the scheme launched by the ARCO is very similar to that outlined in the 1999 draft law, which was eventually rejected by the Federation Council, ARCO would appear to be trying to introduce deposit insurance for selected banks "by the back door."

This does not imply that Russia should not consider the establishment of a deposit insurance scheme. It implies rather that in order to fulfill its promise of providing stability and enhancing trust, savings, and financial intermediation, a number of pre-conditions have to be fulfilled. First, the transparency of banks should be ensured so that both bank creditors and bank supervisors have the ability to detect aggressive risk-taking by banks. Second, the supervisory authorities have to enforce the already existing regulatory rules. This not only implies a much more thorough supervisory process, including both off- and on-site inspections, but also prompt action when detecting violations of the rules, including intervening and closing insolvent and nonviable banks. Both measures would most likely result in consolidation and strengthening of the banking system, a prerequisite for a successful deposit insurance scheme.

It has been proposed that the deposit insurance scheme be used as a tool in the process of leveling the playing field and consolidating the banking sector. By restricting entry into the scheme to well-capitalized and viable banks, a large number of undercapitalized and unviable banks would be de-licensed. By forcing government-owned banks into the scheme and into contributing to the fund, the deposit insurance scheme would impose a payment on state banks for the privilege of accessing deposit insurance, thus creating a more level playing field between government-owned and private banks. However, restricting membership to well-capitalized and viable banks requires a well-developed supervisory and regulatory framework. As mentioned above, such a framework seems currently not to be in place in Russia. Further, historic experience suggests that politically well-connected bankers can easily abuse such a process. Finally, the effect of the deposit insurance scheme on the relative competitive position of government-owned compared with private banks depends on a hard budget constraint being imposed on the government-owned banks, so that they price risk correctly and function according to fully commercial terms. Rather than using the deposit insurance scheme as a tool in this process, such a process should precede the introduction of a deposit insurance scheme.

THE DESIGN OF DEPOSIT INSURANCE SCHEMES

The design of deposit insurance is important for its impact on banking sector stability. Recent cross-country comparisons have shown that well-designed deposit insurance, applied in an efficient regulatory and supervisory environment, can reduce the moral hazard of banks taking aggressive risks (Demirgüç-Kunt and Detriagache 2000; Demirgüç-Kunt and Huizinga 1999).

It is important for the impact on banking sector stability and financial development that a deposit insurance scheme provide limited coverage; it is important to assign a margin of loss to private parties to force them to monitor banks, and thereby to increase market discipline. The objective is to identify the group that is best able and most likely to exert market discipline when forced to do so. A limit to the coverage makes the insurance incomplete, and forces large depositors to monitor banks. Coinsurance might force depositors to bear a share of any losses, if reimbursed for less than 100 percent of their deposits. Excluding interbank deposits from the insurance forces banks to monitor each other, and thereby also fosters market discipline. Excluding insider accounts—that is, the deposits of management and influential owners—reduces moral hazard by making owners and managers participate personally in the downside risk of the bank business.

It is important that the management and funding of the scheme be designed in an incentive-compatible way. Making the scheme compulsory can decrease adverse selection. If voluntary, strong banks might have incentives to leave the scheme in order to avoid cross-subsidizing weak banks. Funding and management by the participating banks gives them the necessary incentives to monitor each other carefully and thus decrease the insurance risks they are paying for. Industry-based management and funding, however, can only work effectively if accompanied by certain regulatory and supervisory powers of the deposit insurer in relation to member banks.

The design of premiums can be important to limit aggressive risk-taking by banks. Risk-based premiums offer several advantages over flat premiums. They contribute to better risk-pricing by banks and help avoid underpricing the deposit insurance. They raise awareness about the variation in the risks banks are taking and strengthen incentives for member banks to monitor each other more carefully. However, the calculation and application of risk-based premiums pose practical problems. If based on the regulators' judgment and disclosed to the market, risk-based premiums can compromise supervisory independence and might even give rise to legal problems for the supervisory agency if a highly rated bank fails. Using market prices to measure risk requires the existence of deep markets for bank stock or for bank uninsured liabilities, or very capable rating agencies. Using formula-based approaches has advantages: if formulas are objective and nondiscretionary, they can be easily disclosed and understood by the market. But they also have significant limitations: accuracy in ratings cannot be guaranteed by mechanical application of numeric ratios,[1] and the choice of quantitative indicators and weights always has elements of arbitrariness. Finally, the issue of whether and when to disclose risk ratings is important in terms of maintaining confidence in the banking system.

LEVELING THE PLAYING FIELD?

Deposit insurance is not a suitable tool for leveling the playing field between public and private banks. On the contrary, a deposit insurance scheme should be restricted to private banks, for several reasons:
1. Public banks are perceived as already enjoying the full backing of their owner—the Government. As a result, and as long as the Government's solvency is not in doubt, the depositors and other creditors tend to behave as if their claims on public banks do not face default risk. There is, thus, no obvious need for a deposit insurance to help prevent runs on public banks.
2. Including public banks in the deposit insurance scheme does not automatically level the playing field, as is often assumed. Only if the hard budget constraint is enforced on public banks will the lending risk and the insurance premium be priced into the lending and deposit interest rates, respectively.

3. Even then, public banks would be at a competitive advantage since, given the state ownership, all deposits are insured, not just small or a fractional part of household deposits.
4. The above-recommended industry-based management of the scheme is made more difficult since the management of public banks is generally subject to different incentive constraints.

Finally, ex post funding combined with easy access to contingent funds might be preferable to ex ante funding. On the one hand, ex ante funding increases the confidence of the insured depositors to be reimbursed rapidly in the event of a bank failure. On the other hand, accumulating a large fund of liquid assets by a deposit insurance scheme carries the risk of abuse and looting if the institutional environment is weak. Ex post funding has the advantage of creating incentives for member banks to monitor and discipline each other since they have to share the insurance loss.[2] In the case of a scheme that is at least partially funded ex ante, the assets should be invested in safe and liquid assets. Furthermore, the value of the assets should be preserved even in the midst of domestic financial turbulence. This would point toward investing any resources in international reserves. (The design features of the deposit insurance scheme being considered by the Russian authorities are outlined in Box 10.1.)

CREATING TRUST THROUGH INCENTIVES

Instead of attracting depositors with the promise of a deposit insurance scheme, the authorities can create trust by creating a conducive incentive structure: (*a*) enforce rules and regulations effectively, (*b*) allow only sound and viable financial institutions to operate, (*c*) offer depositors a safe outlet for their savings (one option would be to turn Sberbank into a narrow bank, while at the same time actively encouraging foreign bank entry), and (*d*) give private agents the ability and the incentives to monitor banks and exert market discipline.

Regulation and supervision of the banking sector must be made more efficient, and this can in part be achieved by limiting banking licenses to real financial intermediaries. This does not necessarily imply the liquidation of the "pocket" banks, but the license to collect deposits should be strictly limited to banks that serve as financial intermediaries.[3] These institutions should be thoroughly supervised, not just on form but also on substance. Intervention in troubled banks should be fast, and should occur before they become insolvent. Imposing regulatory discipline on banks and thus avoiding excessive risk-taking would have a greater positive effect on depositor confidence than the promise of deposit insurance.

It would especially protect smaller, retail depositors by allowing them—as the first in order of priority—to recover their savings during the liquidation process.

The possibilities and incentives for the monitoring of the banking sector by private agents should be created. There is a long list of financial and other relevant information, such as off-balance sheet items and risk management procedures, that should be disclosed to the public. The disclosure of correct financial information and transparency of ownership structure should be enforced, and the role of external auditors has to be strengthened. Furthermore, directors and major shareholders have to be made liable for erroneous and misleading financial information. Finally, by sending clear signals that bank creditors will not be bailed out, the necessary incentives to carefully monitor and exert market discipline should be created.

To provide a safe outlet for retail savings, the activities of government banks may need to be restricted in an interim period while reform plans are prepared and implemented. In the case of Sberbank this would entail increasing the bank's investment in government bonds and other low risk assets, thereby curtailing the rapid expansion in the bank's corporate lending (see further discussion in Chapter 7). The outlined agenda is challenging, but promises to set the stage for the development of a sound financial sector that contributes to the long-run economic development of Russia. The developed economies in Western Europe have achieved high levels of financial development without an explicit deposit insurance scheme. The introduction of such a scheme came at the end of the process, not at the beginning. Similarly, Russia should focus on creating a sound incentive framework before introducing deposit insurance.

CONCLUSION

On the one hand, it seems doubtful whether Russia would be able to gain any real benefit from introducing deposit insurance at this stage. On the other hand, there does not seem to be any cost associated with delaying the adoption of a deposit insurance scheme. The premature introduction of such a scheme, however, would seem to be a risky undertaking if the adequate regulatory and supervisory framework is not in place. Only after the other elements of the financial safety network are able to efficiently fulfill their functions should the introduction of a deposit insurance scheme be considered. Instead of using the deposit insurance scheme as an instrument to level the playing field and consolidate the banking sector, these actions should be first priority and pre-conditions to establishing a deposit insurance scheme. In this connection the precedent set by ARCO in introducing deposit insurance for a number of the ARCO-owned banks—which it intends to extend for a period of 18 months after the banks are privatized—is of particular concern (see Chapter 12).

In the event that Russia nevertheless were to decide to introduce deposit insurance, the Russian Federation should carefully consider the structure of such a scheme. Apart from the proposed limited coverage, insider accounts should be excluded. Bankers should play a larger role in both the financing and the management of the scheme. Most importantly, the scheme should be given a supervisory and regulatory role in relation to its members. While not duplicating the work of the CBR, it should have a decisive voice in the decision to accept and expel member banks and in imposing prompt action against banks that do not comply with regulatory norms and thus increase the risk for the scheme. When establishing deposit insurance, the Russian Federation should consider different models that are used around the world. One possible model might be a scheme managed and financed completely by the banking industry.[4] Most importantly, the deposit insurance scheme has to be designed in a way that maximizes market and regulatory discipline and minimizes the potential abuse. It has to be part of a financial safety net that is designed to foster banking stability and financial development.

ENDNOTES

1. Furthermore, bank-specific, CAMEL-type indicators (i.e., capital, assets, management, earnings, and liquidity) alone would be insufficient. Any rating should also take into account macroeconomic and sectoral indicators.

2. Ex post funding might have the shortcoming that banks are not capable of contributing after a crisis. However, deposit insurance schemes are typically not designed to handle systemic crises.

3. This certainly does not imply that nonbank financial institutions, such as finance companies, are left without supervision. The experience of the East Asian crisis has shown the risk of such an approach.

4. In the United States, before the creation of the Federal Deposit Insurance Corporation, the primary source of assistance against a depositor run was other banks. That assistance, however, was not guaranteed, but rather depended on the willingness of those other banks to help out (see Calomiris 1997 and the literature he quotes). Germany provides an example of a private deposit insurance scheme that has worked relatively successfully over the last 25 years (see Beck 2001).

REFERENCES

Beck, Thorsten. 2001. "Deposit Insurance as Private Club: Is Germany a Model?" Working Paper 2559. World Bank Policy Research Department, Washington, D.C.

Calomiris, Charles W. 1997. "The Postmodern Bank Safety Net. Lessons from Developed and Developing Economies." American Enterprise Institute, Washington, D.C.

Cull, Robert, Lemma W. Senbet, and Marco Sorge. 2001. "Deposit Insurance and Financial Development." Financial Sector Policy Department. World Bank, Washington, D.C. Processed.

Demirgüç-Kunt, Aslı, and Enrica Detriagache. 2000. "Does Deposit Insurance Increase Banking System Stability?" IMF Working Paper. Washington, D.C.

Demirgüç-Kunt, Aslı, and Harry Huizinga. 1999. "Market Discipline and Financial Safety Net Design." Working Paper 2183. World Bank Policy Research Department, Washington, D.C.

Demirgüç-Kunt, Aslı, and Edward J. Kane. 2001. "Deposit Insurance: Lessons on Design and Implementation." Financial Sector Policy Department. World Bank, Washington, D.C. Processed.

CHAPTER 11

Bank Restructuring and Liquidation

LEGAL PROTECTION OF DEPOSITOR INTERESTS

One of the fundamental objectives of banking regulation is to maintain depositor confidence in the banking system. This is supported by ensuring that banks generally operate in a well-run and sound manner. However, in the event that a bank becomes troubled or fails, the need for protecting depositor interests in the course of resolving the bank's problems becomes critical if depositor confidence is to be maintained. Two areas are of primary importance: first, it is necessary to ensure that banks maintain an adequate reserve of capital for payment of depositor claims in the event of liquidation. Second, it is imperative that bank failure be resolved in a way that preserves the continuity of depositors' access to their funds; the result otherwise can be panic and a run on the bank, which can spread to other banks in the system.

In addition to maintaining confidence in the banking system generally, capital reserves and continuity of access are important because there are social dimensions to the protection of depositor interests in these circumstances; many of the deposits may represent life savings and their loss would mean extremely dire consequences for the account holders. In Russia, confidence in the banking system was undermined after the August 1998 crisis, due in part to the outcome suffered by depositors in failed or failing banks. In many cases depositors lost their savings because the failed bank had inadequate assets for payment during liquidation. In others, even in cases where funds were adequate for full payment of deposit claims, payment was delayed for years, was made in installments, or was otherwise compromised.

Had it existed, a system of deposit guarantee, such as state guarantee or deposit insurance, may or may not have ameliorated this situation. There are some arguments for creating wider deposit guarantee coverage than existed at the time of the 1998 crisis or that exists now (a broad-based deposit insurance scheme rather than Sberbank's exclusive government guarantee), but there are also many arguments against it (these issues are treated in Chapter 10). The focus of this chapter is on the possibility of providing full compensation for depositors from existing bank assets in accordance with existing Russian legislation. Adequately implemented, the regulatory and legal framework should provide a capital reserve that can be readily utilized for satisfaction of depositor claims in the event of bank closure and liquidation. A corollary issue is the adequacy of the regulatory/accounting standards that are used for measuring this capital reserve. The objective of this chapter is to identify how the legislation might be better implemented or refined to ensure the equitable treatment of depositors in the context of troubled banks.

DEPOSITOR PREFERENCE

Russian legislation and the Civil Code reflect a preference toward depositor interests in the event of a bank's liquidation. Pursuant to Article 49 of the Law on Insolvency (Bankruptcy) of Credit Organizations (hereinafter "bank bankruptcy law"):

> The claims of individuals who are creditors of the lending organization under bank-deposit and bank-account agreements concluded with them, the claims of individuals to whom the lending organization is liable for harm caused to life or limb, and the claims of the Federal Mandatory Deposit Insurance Fund shall be the first to be satisfied from the lending organization's property that constitutes the bankruptcy assets.
>
> [Note: When the legislation was drafted it was expected that creation of a deposit insurance fund would follow. To date, no such fund has been created.]

Article 64 of the Civil Code similarly states that the claims of citizens who are creditors of the bank shall be given priority in satisfaction. (This is generalized, but would apply to individual depositors.)

This preference toward depositors pertains explicitly only to payment of depositor claims in bank liquidation, but it would be fair to infer an underlying public policy in favor of depositor interests generally. It is important to note that this preference relates only to natural persons and not to commercial depositors, who are treated in the event of a bank liquidation as general, unsecured creditors of the fifth priority ranking. This is not to minimize commercial depositors' importance as creditors, but affording them a preference in payment is not needed like it is with individual depositors. Commercial depositors have greater sophistication in their dealings with banks and a greater ability to assess the soundness of a bank. Commercial customers of Russian banks tend to have close working relationships with bank ownership, and in some cases may themselves be the owners. Where this is true, they would clearly have early warning of financial trouble and, unlike retail customers, would therefore be able to protect themselves. Also unlike retail depositors, the greater size of their financial dealings means that commercial depositors are able to spread their risk across several banks.

It should be noted that the same logic would apply to deposits of bank insiders; due to their knowledge of bank operations, they are better placed to protect themselves from any potential bank failures. Added to this is the fact that preferential payment of insider depositors could contribute to moral hazard in their operation of the bank. However, on the face of the statute, such insider depositors are not excluded from first priority payment. It would be useful to consider revisions to the statute to specifically exclude priority payment to insider depositors—either through a definition of what constitutes an "insider," or through limits of priority payment per account, such as found in deposit insurance proposals, which are designed to match the afforded protection with the targeted group (small retail depositors). Included with such amendments would be exclusions of accounts held by related parties to insiders, used fraudulently to increase protection of insider accounts.

The fact that retail depositors are paid as first-priority creditors means that it should be possible even in the absence of a deposit guarantee system to fully satisfy their claims in a bank liquidation. This is contingent, however, on the existence of a reserve of capital adequate for payment of their claims. If the reserve is too low, steps should be taken to rehabilitate the bank to a viable business condition that would allow it to maintain this reserve. If the reserve reaches a low enough point, or if the bank's business viability is such that it cannot maintain an adequate reserve, the bank should be liquidated.

Distortions produced by Russian accounting standards mean that it is difficult, however, to realistically monitor bank capital levels. Such distortions will hamper restructuring and liquidation efforts, which should be triggered and guided by a realistic evaluation of a bank's capital level. (This topic is addressed in more detail in Chapter 4.) Although Russian bank restructuring and liquidation legislation and regulations are basically adequate, their effectiveness can be significantly diminished because they are premised on flawed economic evaluations.

EFFECTIVE RESOLUTION OF TROUBLED BANKS

Resolution of a troubled bank entails either a restructuring/rehabilitation of the bank or the bank's liquidation. Early intervention in a troubled bank by the bank regulator is essential if the bank is to have any chance of a successful turnaround. Early intervention also minimizes the dissipation of assets if the bank shows no promise of rehabilitation, thereby ensuring adequate funds for payment of depositors in a liquidation. Another important principle of bank restructuring is that license revocation and liquidation of the bank have certain consequences for lack of cooperation by the bank owners. The success of restructuring is additionally tied to the manner in which liquidation is undertaken: if liquidation is equivocal or compromised in its execution, there is little incentive for bank owners to try to rehabilitate the bank. If the owners believe that liquidation proceedings will result in, at worst, a delay in the termination of their business and, at best, a settlement and reinstatement of the license, clearly they will have little interest in undertaking early restructuring efforts.

The Russian legislation that deals with bank restructuring is basically sufficient in responding to these principles, and the legislation with regard to liquidation is adequate, in light of certain recently enacted amendments. But implementation of these bank resolution laws has been unsatisfactory with respect to depositors' interests. In both restructurings and bankruptcies, depositors have often come away with reduced and deferred payment—despite this being financially avoidable and in some cases contradictory to statutory requirements.

Effective bank restructuring can prevent the crisis-mode resolution of bank problems and can promote the uninterrupted operation of a bank's business with minimal hardships imposed on creditors. Most important, it can enable the bank's deposit business to continue and can afford depositors unimpeded and undiminished access to their funds. A potential problem of restructuring, however, is that it may prolong the operation of a bank beyond the limit of its commercial viability, thereby worsening the ultimate situation of depositors and creditors. The objective of restructuring should therefore be the rehabilitation of the bank to a commercially viable position. This necessitates the continuance of the deposit business throughout the restructuring period, as any interruption or compromise of this business would effectively undermine the validity of the bank as a going concern, hence undermining depositor confidence.

Nonbank commercial enterprises are often restructured during the course of bankruptcy proceedings. This is typically not the case for banks, since they operate in a highly regulated environment, and the concern for adequate coverage for depositor claims requires more active efforts to ensure preservation of assets. These factors require the use of early, preemptive efforts to restructure the bank, directed not by a court but by an administrative entity such as the regulator.

The Bank Restructuring Mandates of the CBR and ARCO

According to Russian legislation, there are two possible ways for a bank to be restructured: one is directed by the Central Bank of Russia pursuant to the provisions of the "measures to avert bankruptcy" of the bank bankruptcy law (Articles 3, 4, and 7 through 15); the other is through the Agency for Restructuring of Credit Organizations, pursuant to the provisions of the Law on the Restructuring of Credit Organizations. The mandate of ARCO, which deals only with a selected portion of banks in need of restructuring, is more specialized than that of the CBR and is addressed in detail in Chapter 12.

One significant difference between ARCO and CBR restructuring is the earlier intervention of the CBR in the affairs of a troubled bank. Under its mandate, the CBR can enforce measures to avert bankruptcy when (a) a bank is unable for three days to make payments, (b) when the level of a bank's own funds falls 20 percent in one year while the bank also violates one of the required regulatory ratios, (c) when a bank violates the regulatory capital adequacy ratio (currently 10 percent), or (d) when a bank has violated the regulatory liquidity ratio by more than 10 percent (Article 4). ARCO is not able to begin restructuring a bank until significantly later, namely, when a bank's capital adequacy ratio is less than 2 percent, and the bank fails for seven days to make payments.

Measures to Avert Bankruptcy

The "measures for averting bankruptcy" contained in the bank bankruptcy law provide a fairly detailed list of measures that a bank may employ when trying to restructure itself. The law sets forth measures for increasing capital, reducing expenses, restructuring assets and liabilities, and making changes to staff. If the bank does not undertake any of these measures itself, the CBR is entitled to direct it to do so and to require the submission of a restructuring plan to the CBR. Failure to comply with such a directive can result in the personal liability of the bank's director and in the imposition of regulatory sanctions. Additionally, failure of the bank to comply in a timely manner with a CBR directive can result in the appointment by the CBR of a conservator. A conservator can also be appointed if, despite implementation of the plan, the bank's condition fails to improve. These restructuring measures basically match those of international practice (Hawkins and Turner 1999).

Informal Intervention by a Regulator

In general, the Russian legislation tracks international legislative practice in terms of providing for early implementation of measures to avert bankruptcy. However, international practice also entails informal action on the part of the bank regulator, beyond the formal measures specified by law. For instance, legislation in the United States allows regulators to require formulation of a capital enhancement plan when a bank falls below its capital adequacy ratio. Prior to that point, however, the regulator may enter into an informal agreement with the bank for improvement of its financial condition, based on the bank's failure to meet guidelines founded on a composite rating involving the adequacy of its capital, assets, management, earnings, and liquidity (CAMEL).

In Germany, when a bank falls below a minimum capital adequacy ratio or fails to meet liquidity requirements, the regulator will require it to increase its capital and/or liquidity; if there appear to be sufficient grounds for concern, the regulator can also intervene in the management of the bank (Div. 4, Deutsche Bundesbank Bank Act). In practice, however, rather than simply demand compliance, the German regulator will take an interactive role in the effort to ameliorate the situation. When a bank falls below the regulatory threshold, there begins a process of regular discussion between the bank and the regulator in an effort to ameliorate the bank's situation. The result may be a regulator-directed merger or break-up of the bank for sale to other banks.

Similar rehabilitative intervention by the regulator is found in France, although there it is spelled out more formally. French legislation allows the regulator to require a plan from the bank, including proposals for improvement of the bank's financial condition, changes in management methods, and assurance of the adequacy of the bank's general business plan (Article 43, Law on Activity and Control of Credit Establishments). Informal intervention by the regulator is nonetheless also common.

Regulations for Early Intervention by the CBR

The Russian legislation gives the CBR an apparently passive role in the measures to avert bankruptcy, specifying only that the CBR demand formulation of a plan if a bank does not undertake restructuring measures of its own initiative. In practice and pursuant to CBR regulations, however, there is more interaction between the CBR and the bank than is evident on the face of the statute alone. Although the statute itself does not specify what the CBR does once the plan is submitted by the bank, procedures for this have been promulgated in Instruction 85 (i). Pursuant to this instruction, the CBR should review the bank's plan for adequacy and monitor its implementation. The CBR is, pursuant to this instruction, to be actively engaged in the bank's restructuring efforts even in the initial stages. It is not clear from either the statute or the regulation what criteria are evaluated in the CBR review of a restructuring plan, however.

It is difficult to assess the success of early regulatory intervention in Russia because the Russian bank bankruptcy law, which provides measures for rehabilitation, was enacted in March 1999, subsequent to the August 1998 crisis. By the time the CBR received the statutory ability to intervene for restructuring early, pre-crisis intervention was impossible. Most of the banks requiring the CBR's attention were already in an advanced stage of financial trouble. Under such circumstances, the best that the CBR could hope to contribute was a series of stop-gap efforts to bring troubled banks into temporary regulatory compliance, even though the fundamentals of the banks were insufficient for long-term viability. Many banks were in sufficiently bad shape to justify license revocation and bankruptcy.

Development of Minimum Standards/Use of IAS

A project has been proposed for the development of a set of minimum standards that would establish the threshold requirements for all restructuring plans. This proposal would also include an evaluation of restructured banks according to International Accounting Standards. The objective is to clarify for the banks what is expected of a restructuring plan, and to provide an objective basis to support CBR rejection of inadequate plans. These would be minimum standards only, and each bank's plan would need to be evaluated in the context of its individual circumstances. While this project would be useful, the CBR would nonetheless need to ensure that it exercises judgment in evaluating each plan as a whole for its commercial viability; otherwise, the review of each plan could become a formalistic exercise in which the standards are merely discrete checklist items.

Repeated Restructuring

A problem related to commercial viability is that a restructured bank might soon make a "return visit" to the process of trying to avert bankruptcy. That is, the measures taken during the restructuring may enable the bank to temporarily raise its capital standards and achieve regulatory compliance, but the fundamentals of its business remain flawed and the bank will likely fall again below regulatory standards. A bank that repeatedly implements measures to avert bankruptcy is fundamentally unsound, and further efforts to rehabilitate it only stall its inevitable collapse. It does not appear that the Russian legislation addresses this point. There does not appear to be a provision, for instance, requiring license revocation if a bank has implemented measures to avert bankruptcy more than once in a year. Such a provision is necessary to prevent the CBR from spending time and effort on banks that manage to bring themselves into compliance, only to fall back out of compliance a short time later.

Criteria for Measuring Restructuring Success

Evaluation of a restructuring plan should include consideration of a bank's track record and evidence of any long-term negative trends. For restructuring to make any sense, there must be an ability to conclude, where the circumstances justify it, that a bank is beyond rehabilitation and to liquidate it. The process of restructuring must not be permitted to become an exercise in propping up banks that are fundamentally unsound, simply delaying the inevitable failure of the bank.

It may be that the Russian criteria for measuring success in bank rehabilitation are lax. Part of this is related to the use of Russian Accounting Standards, as noted above. Another part is a focus on the fulfillment of discrete regulatory standards that do not take adequate account of the condition of the bank as whole. For instance, if a bank has been required to undertake restructuring efforts because of a lack of liquidity, it is relatively easy for the bank to enhance its liquidity position—for example, by borrowing funds—without affecting the fundamentals of its operations. There is a need to tighten up the regulatory criteria, or to include within those criteria a consideration of the bank's financial condition as a whole.

Conservatorship

Conservatorship, as set forth in the Russian legislation (Articles 16–31 of the bank bankruptcy law), allows the regulator to become more directly involved in the management of a bank in the attempt to rehabilitate it. A conservator may be appointed by the CBR in the event that a bank fails to comply with the CBR's demand for formulation of a rehabilitation plan. The conservator can be given authority ranging from simple oversight of bank operations to usurpation of total control from bank management. The conservator therefore potentially has the power to effect the same measures for restructuring the bank as the bank has itself, with the proviso that certain measures may require shareholder approval.

From a legislative standpoint, this is generally in accordance with international practice, but it should be noted that in international practice conservators are typically not used even though the legislative framework provides for them—the rationale being that by the time a bank is eligible for a conservator it is probably too far advanced in its trouble to be rehabilitated. Another concern is that announcement of the appointment of a conservator may have the same negative effect on depositor confidence as if the bank were simply closed. In practice, a conservator is not particularly useful for rehabilitation of a bank, but is instead used as a means for gaining control of and preserving the assets of a failing bank in anticipation of a more severe resolution—that is, liquidation.

RESTRUCTURING OF BANKS IN BANKRUPTCY PROCEEDINGS

Prior to enactment of the bank bankruptcy law, it was possible to restructure a bank in the course of bankruptcy proceedings by means of "amicable settlements." These settlements are analogous to Chapter 11 reorganizations in the United States and are fairly common in bankruptcies of commercial enterprises. It is not, however, common international practice to restructure banks in the course of bankruptcy proceedings.

Once in bankruptcy, a bank can no longer legally transact banking business, since its license has been revoked, and from a regulatory standpoint a restructuring at this stage is futile. Early intervention by the regulator, both in restructuring and liquidation, is deemed essential for preservation of the capital necessary to pay depositor claims.

Prohibition of Amicable Settlements

One of the major features of the Russian 1999 bank bankruptcy law was the incorporation of provisions for CBR-directed restructuring and a prohibition of amicable settlements in the course of bank bankruptcy proceedings. Prior to the 1999 law, such settlements were possible because they are allowed by the general commercial bankruptcy code. (Bank bankruptcies are still governed generally by the corporate bankruptcy code, but specific provisions of the bank bankruptcy code override conflicting provisions of the general corporate bankruptcy code.) The legislative intention was to shift the process of bank restructuring from a judicial context to a regulatory, administrative context, with restructuring to be directed by the CBR rather than by a bankruptcy court.

Article 5 of the bank bankruptcy law states that "the external management and amicable settlement specified in the Federal Law on Insolvency (Bankruptcy) shall not be applied to lending organizations." The rationale is that the CBR should intervene early, before the bank is insolvent and its license revoked, to oversee the possible rehabilitation of the bank. If these attempts at preventive action are unsuccessful, then it can be concluded that the bank has no viability and it should be liquidated.

Ad Hoc Settlements

The practice of restructuring amid bankruptcy proceedings has nonetheless continued to be applied to banks, even those whose licenses have been revoked after passage of the bank bankruptcy law. This has commonly been in response to pressure from large creditor groups and stockholders, particularly in the case of larger banks, where a straight liquidation would have given these creditors no repayment on their claim—and a settlement gave them at least something. Another argument used by creditors for amicable settlements has been the absence, up to the point of initiation of the bankruptcy proceedings, of an opportunity for restructuring negotiations. As noted above, the timing of the 1999 bank bankruptcy law may have contributed to this problem, since it was enacted too far in the wake of the 1998 banking crisis to realistically afford much, if any, prebankruptcy rehabilitation.

The arguments for amicable settlements by bank creditors and owners may have had some merit, but a review of the effects of such settlements on depositor interests shows why they have been prohibited. The settlements are not legitimate bank restructurings (i.e., a reorganization with a viable business objective), but are simply exercises in compromise, seeking to afford certain groups of creditors greater repayment than they would receive under a straight liquidation. This is not unique to bank bankruptcies: there is evidence that most general, corporate bankruptcy restructurings in Russia are little more than debt reschedulings, with none of the characteristics of a legitimate restructuring designed for rehabilitation of the enterprise. (This issue is treated in more detail in Chapter 3 on general insolvency law in Russia.) The practice of restructuring during nonbank bankruptcy proceedings in Russia does not generate truly productive results and it should come as no surprise that the country's bank bankruptcy proceedings have the same shortcomings.

Impairment of Depositor Interests in Settlements

Examples of the impairment of depositor interests in the event of amicable settlements are numerous. Uneximbank depositors, for instance, were required to take reduced and/or deferred payment on their claims in the settlement of the bankruptcy proceedings of that bank. Depositors were paid 10 percent cash, with the balance to be paid in the future by way of bonds—the same terms on which commercial creditors were paid. In other bankruptcy proceedings, depositors have for years suffered delayed payment of their claims as creditors and owners have negotiated and challenged delicensing decisions. The settlement discussions in the Inkombank case lasted approximately two years before a decision was made to give depositors an initial payment of 52 percent of their claims, with the balance to be paid after the completion of liquidation proceedings. The liquidation proceedings of the bank Menatep entailed months of initial delay because of a prolonged debate over the issue of liquidation versus restructuring, causing many depositors to take advantage of an opportunity to transfer their deposits to Sberbank, even though this entailed receiving a decreased amount due to the fall in the value of the ruble. Other depositors were later paid directly and in full by Menatep's owners, Yukos Oil and Rosprom. The balance of the depositors—those who neither transferred funds to Sberbank nor took payment from

Yukos/Rosprom—were paid out of the liquidation proceedings. There was also considerable delay in the bankruptcy proceedings of Mezhkombank, as discussions on the "restructuring" of the bank were conducted among its large creditors, including American Express.

According to the law, retail depositors are entitled to expect priority payment of their claims, but under these amicable settlements they typically receive less than they should. In bankruptcy proceedings, the voting rights of each creditor are determined by the amount of the creditor's claim. This means that retail depositors, though perhaps greater in number, are smaller in terms of actual influence. They are also less seasoned in commercial matters and are not unified in their efforts, so it is difficult for them to protect their interests against the claims of larger commercial creditors. The settlement proposals favored by large creditors invariably block full payment of retail depositor claims, because the larger creditors will not agree to a settlement that reduces their payment in order to repay retail depositors 100 percent. Just as inevitably, depositors will agree to the settlement out of frustration with the system, even though it pays them less than their full entitlement under law. To the private depositor, it is better to get something than nothing.

The involvement of retail depositors in the negotiation process, even to the commercial creditors that seek advantage at their expense, is frustrating. Depositors, unable to present a united front and unfamiliar with the process, must individually present their claims, questions, and viewpoints. The delays can be considerable.

Nonjudicial Amicable Settlements

Although not strictly occurring in bankruptcy proceedings, there have also been amicable settlements in some ARCO restructurings that are analogous to the ad hoc settlements described above. ARCO restructurings are initiated at the point at which a bank is essentially insolvent. In some instances the bank may be in a sufficient state of decay to justify liquidation, and ARCO has the right to recommend this if restructuring appears futile. The settlement discussions orchestrated by ARCO are likely the first time that the different parties are brought together to deal with the bank's condition, and invariably there will be a strong, if impractical, desire on the part of creditors to attempt to restructure the bank; if nothing else, they will hope to improve upon the position that liquidation would mean to them.

Though ineffective as restructurings, some settlements orchestrated by ARCO resemble the ad hoc settlements of bank bankruptcy proceedings—from the perspective of retail depositors, at least. For instance, in the restructuring of SBS-Agro, depositors are to be paid 10 percent of their claims in cash, with the balance to be paid in the future by way of bonds. This despite the fact that there are sufficient assets in the bank to pay depositors in full before making any payments to other creditors. A similar restructuring was proposed for Rossiyskiy Credit.

Public Policy Concerns Regarding Amicable Settlements

The problem with these settlements, quite apart from the fact that they are prohibited by statute, is that the purported restructuring of the bank takes place in the context of the "participatory democracy" of the bankruptcy proceedings; that is, the outcome is determined by the votes and power blocs of creditors and shareholders. These parties naturally will want to achieve the result that best favors their own interests, and in any other context this would be acceptable—this process is, after all, fundamental to commercial bankruptcy reorganization in many countries, including Russia. The process will not necessarily take into account the relevant public policies relating to the banking sector, however. Specifically, there is no assurance that the votes of retail depositors will be sufficient to ensure that their interests are represented proportionate to the priority they are given by statute. Furthermore, there have been repeated instances of creditor interests being thwarted by improprieties in the actions of arbitration managers and courts, as discussed below. There is additionally no assurance that the outcome of an amicable settlement will be scrutinized by the court for compliance with public policies or for impact on the banking sector in general.

The CBR participates in the bankruptcy proceedings, but it does not direct them. Pursuant to Article 35, any creditor can initiate a bankruptcy action after the CBR has revoked a bank's license. The CBR participates in the proceedings essentially as another creditor, based upon the existence of debt owed by the bank to the CBR. While the CBR may appoint a temporary administrator, the liquidator is appointed by vote of the creditors' committee, and it is the liquidator and creditors that direct the settlement discussions, not the CBR. The CBR therefore does not have the ability in bank bankruptcy proceedings to direct the outcome of the bank's "rehabilitation," which means that it cannot, as regulator, ensure compliance with the relevant public policies pertaining to the banking sector.

Legislative Proposals for Amicable Settlement

It has been proposed in some quarters that the law be amended to reinstate the amicable settlement into bank bankruptcy legislation. Such a move would contravene the logical and policy underpinnings of the bank bankruptcy framework. If legislators were to pursue such a change, however, they should at a minimum make clear provisions to preclude any dilution of retail depositors' interests. Depositors should receive prompt and full payment of their claims in the same way that they would under a liquidation, and settlement negotiations should not be permitted to delay payment. Depositors, in other words, should essentially be exempted from the process and effects of any settlement discussions.

COMPROMISE OF DEPOSITOR CLAIMS IN RESTRUCTURING

A legitimate bank restructuring must preclude the possibility of any compromise of the claims of depositors, either in an amicable settlement or in measures to avert bankruptcy. To engage depositors in discussions that could diminish their access to their funds would undermine the credibility of the bank as a going concern. Very few countries (among them Malaysia, Uruguay, and Thailand) permit negotiation of depositor claims in the course of restructuring. The Bank for International Settlements has noted that "such action is very uncommon as it leads to many of the same problems as an outright default" (Hawkins and Turner 1999).

Restructuring of a bank's debt is valid as a part of a general rehabilitation plan, but retail depositors should be excluded from this process; they should, in fact, be afforded regular access to their funds during restructuring. There are concerns that affording depositors unlimited access to their funds would spark a run on the bank, and proposals have been made that Russian legislation be amended to allow banks to place a moratorium on depositor access to funds in the event of serious problems. There does not appear to be any analogy in international practice for this. Such a moratorium would, again, have the potential to actually cause the problem it aims to solve. In any event, if a bank reaches the point at which a run on deposits is likely, it should be placed into conservatorship, under which conditions Russian legislation already permits a moratorium on access to deposits. Furthermore, it should be noted that, in international practice, bank restructurings do not generally result in depositor runs. This fact provides another justification for early, informal interaction between the regulator and bank.

JUDICIAL BANK LIQUIDATION

The revocation by the CBR of a bank's license is a clear indication that the bank has no hope of rehabilitation. There are numerous justifications for license revocation, some being sanctions for regulatory noncompliance and others relating to the financial condition of the bank, but in each case revocation follows a series of actions by the bank that demonstrate it is irreversibly unfit for business.

Not all banks that are liquidated have sufficient assets to pay depositors in full. Full repayment, in fact, has been made in just 44 percent of the liquidations that have occurred to date. Had sufficient regulatory measures been taken beforehand, including realistic evaluation of each bank's capital position and early intervention to gain control of assets, this percentage would no doubt have been higher. Even in the cases in which depositors are paid in full, there can be problems of slow and inefficient repayment. This is due largely to the judicial setting in which the liquidation takes place.

Liquidators

In the liquidation process, it is the creditor-appointed liquidator, not the CBR, who has direct control over the process. Though the liquidator is appointed by the creditor's committee and must file reports with the court, and though technically the creditor's committee has the power to remove him, in practice the liquidator is not particularly accountable to the parties involved. The experience with liquidators to date has not been good, with complaints made about their experience and qualifications. While the CBR has promulgated regulations for the licensing of liquidators, there has been some lag in getting qualified, experienced persons into place. Part of the problem stems from the lack of an adequate pool of people from which to choose, and while proposals have been made for the training of liquidators there will inevitably be a significant lag time before the benefits of any training program are felt. There have also been complaints that each CBR license, necessary for appointment as a liquidator, is specific to a single court case rather than being issued as a general license applicable to any case. This delays the processing of license requests and again narrows the field of potential candidates.

More serious than complaints about their credentials are the complaints about the liquidators' integrity. There have been complaints about self-dealing and cronyism, alleging that assets have been sold to liquidators' colleagues for reduced prices; there have been kickbacks to liquidators from the purchasers of assets; and there have been instances of embezzlement, such as the $7 million embezzlement in the Tokobank case. These problems are aggravated by a lack of transparency, with the activities of the liquidator reported only in part to bank creditors.

Complaints about liquidators are not unique to cases of bank bankruptcy. Since bank bankruptcy takes place more or less within the framework of general bankruptcy, the problems it suffers are similar to those endemic within the corporate bankruptcy framework. And within the realm of general corporate bankruptcy there are many complaints about improper liquidator behavior, as detailed elsewhere in this chapter.

Courts

Another weak point in the judicial bank liquidation process may be the judiciary itself. Complaints about the level of training and/or competence of judges are common, with the problem attributed in part to the fact that low pay rates for judges deter better-qualified people from joining the profession. The problem has also been attributed to the experience of the judiciary under the Soviet system, in which judges were uncritical functionaries answerable directly to higher powers. This has created a culture within which judges may see themselves as clerical functionaries rather than arbiters of judicial proceedings, and which discourages the making of bold or controversial decisions. The problem has also been linked to the fact that judges are now expected to interpret a set of new laws for which adequate commentary has not been issued by higher courts or scholarly bodies. There have also been complaints of judicial corruption, alleging the exercise through monetary or other incentives of undue influence on judges by creditors or shareholders.

Another significant problem with judicial bank liquidation is judicial docket congestion. The system is overloaded with bank bankruptcy cases. The CBR has more than 600 delicensed banks that it needs to liquidate, and this is evidently more than the system can handle. Estimates suggest that the court system can adequately process only 12 bank bankruptcy cases per year, and while this may be an understatement, implying that the CBR's backlog of cases would take 50 years to clear, it is broadly acknowledged that there is much delay in court proceedings, there are long periods of inactivity in bank bankruptcy actions, and there are long waits for results.

Procedural Obstacles

One of the problems shared by both the bank bankruptcy framework and the general corporate framework is that there is no special procedural code for bankruptcy, nor are there specialized bankruptcy courts. Judicial proceedings are undertaken in general arbitration courts governed by the general Code of *Arbitrazh* Procedure, as supplemented by the general bankruptcy or bank bankruptcy laws. (This is discussed in detail in Chapter 4.) Gaps and overlaps exist that can give rise to loopholes that impede the progress of bank bankruptcy proceedings. For example, it is possible to challenge the CBR's delicensing determination in one action pursuant to provisions of the Law on Banks and Banking (with a statute of limitations of 10 years), and to challenge it again in the bank bankruptcy action. The recently enacted amendments to the Law on Banks and Banking, limiting the timeframe for challenges to delicensing to 30 days, will hopefully tighten up this area of the law. Furthermore, bank liquidation will in the future not be necessarily dependent on a finding of bankruptcy, thereby eliminating the problem of delicensing challenges in the bankruptcy court (described in more detail below). There should be some further tightening up of the procedures to limit appeal times, and possibly to limit the scope of review of CBR decisions. In the United States and the United Kingdom, for example, the standard of review is whether the regulators abused their discretion in making the delicensing decision.

Proposal for Expedited Payment to Depositors

To address one part of this dilemma, an amendment has recently been made to the bank bankruptcy law. It provides for expedited payment to retail depositors in bankruptcy proceedings. Payment of retail depositors is made at the outset of court proceedings, prior to the complete collection and liquidation of a bank's assets. Payment comes from funds kept by the banks in their CBR correspondent (i.e., reserve) accounts. This proposal makes sense because depositors are distinguishable from other creditors in at least two ways. First, depositors' claims are more easily verifiable. Bank records show the amount of the depositor's claim, and this should prima facie establish the depositor's claim without the need for the filing of proofs of claim or for undue scrutinizing by the liquidator. If the depositor were to dispute the amount, submission, and investigation of a counterclaim, it should certainly be permitted.

Second, depositors are first-priority creditors. The amount paid to depositors is in no way contingent upon the amount paid to other creditor groups (in contrast, for example, to the amount paid to fifth-priority general creditors). This also has the advantage of eliminating depositors from the liquidation proceedings without adversely affecting the interests of the remaining creditors. The viability of the proposal would naturally be contingent in each case on whether the bank in question has sufficient funds in its CBR reserve account to cover the claims of depositors.

Legal Entities as Liquidators

In an attempt to address the evident inefficiency, lack of professionalism, and lack of accountability of individual liquidators, it has been proposed that legal entities be permitted to act in their place. The leading international accounting firms, for example, could currently perform this work, and it will inevitably take some time for the CBR to license enough individual liquidators to break the liquidation bottleneck. The bank bankruptcy law would need to be amended to permit this move, however, and although the Duma is discussing the proposal, realization of any change is not in the immediate future. And even should an amendment be approved, it must be doubted that private firms would be willing to take on the work without various indemnification assurances. In many of the potential liquidations, too, the cost to these firms of performing the liquidation would exceed the amount available in the bankruptcy estate.

Liquidation Agency

There have also been proposals for the creation of an agency to liquidate failing banks, similar to the Resolution Trust Corporation (RTC) in the United States, which was created by Congress for the purpose of liquidating savings and loans in the aftermath of the savings and loan crisis of the late 1980s and early 1990s. These proposals recommend that agency employees serve as liquidators in the court proceedings. The perceived advantages of such a system would be the ability of the agency to set practice standards and uniform procedures to be followed in liquidations; greater accountability, as a result of the involvement of a public entity; and the ability of the agency to rapidly train and oversee the activities of those of its employees appointed as liquidators.

In the United States, the RTC was created more or less out of the framework and with the employees of the FDIC, the federal deposit insurance agency. Since the FDIC had been previously involved in bank liquidations, although not on a comparable scale, it had a base of experience on which to develop the procedures of the RTC. In Russia, it has been suggested that ARCO's mandate be expanded to allow it to function as an administrative bank liquidator.

ADMINISTRATIVE ASPECTS OF BANK LIQUIDATION

The problems that weaknesses in the Russian judicial system incur for bank liquidation will be resolved neither quickly nor easily. This is a complex situation and judicial reform is a long-term proposition. Because Russian bank bankruptcy is an offshoot of general corporate bankruptcy, it is heir to the problems found in general bankruptcy. Resolving the problems of bank bankruptcy will consequently entail resolution of the larger problems of general bankruptcy, unless the niche of bank bankruptcy is further defined so as to distinguish it from general bankruptcy.

A successful effort to distinguish bank bankruptcy from general bankruptcy could both improve the efficiency of the process of resolving failed banks and take account of the public policies uniquely at play in the banking sector. In this regard, it would be beneficial to examine the role that administrative procedures could play in the bank liquidation process. Transferring certain functions away from a judicial and into an administrative setting could improve the efficiency of the process without adversely affecting the rights of the parties involved. Courts do not need to be involved in every detail or decision-making juncture of the liquidation process. Administrative procedures are found in varying degrees in international practice, and it would be useful to determine which aspects of international practice could readily be incorporated into a Russian setting.

International Practice

Administrative procedures in bank liquidation can encompass some or all of the steps of the process, from license revocation to initiation of liquidation to control of the liquidation proceedings. The United States, for example, uses an entirely administrative process. Regulators there make the delicensing decision, and the liquidation takes place in entirely extrajudicial administrative proceedings controlled by the regulators. It is possible to judicially appeal the regulators' actions, but the court does not otherwise enter into the proceedings.

A less extreme model of administrative bank liquidation is used by France, Germany, Japan, and Italy. In these countries, the regulator has the power to determine that a license be revoked, but liquidation of the bank is handled by the court. The determination by the regulator is sufficient for the court to initiate liquidation of the bank without first making its own finding of insolvency. The liquidator, though answerable to the court, is appointed by the regulator.

Bulgaria employs an administratively controlled liquidator in a judicial setting. This process was established through recent legislation, replacing a strictly judicial process similar to that in use in Russia, wherein individual liquidators are essentially independent and overseen primarily by the court. The process was modified so that the liquidators, though still operating in a judicial proceeding with court oversight, are appointed and supervised directly by a newly created deposit insurance fund.

Administrative Developments in Russia

Realistically, it is unlikely that Russia will adopt a completely administrative system such as that found in the United States. There is still a feeling that some determinations are "too important" for the CBR to make; specifically, there is resistance to the notion that any entity other than a court can declare a bank to be bankrupt. This sentiment may or may not be valid, but the larger question is whether a judicial determination of insolvency should be a prerequisite for closing and liquidating a bank.

Banking is a highly regulated industry, subject to specific public policies. Fulfillment of these public policies can require closure and liquidation of a bank even though that bank may not, according to the criteria applied to commercial enterprises, be insolvent. Capital adequacy standards for banks are, of necessity, of greater concern than those for commercial enterprises. While failure to maintain adequate capital may not be sufficient to determine insolvency under the general commercial law, it should be grounds for the closure and liquidation of a bank. If a regulator has made a determination, in accordance with legislative guidelines, that a bank is engaged in unsound practices and that its license should be revoked, it makes no sense to then require an additional finding of the bank's insolvency before the bank can be closed and liquidated.

According to Russian legislation, however, while the CBR has had the ability to delicense a bank based upon a number of different criteria, it was not until recently that a bank could be liquidated without a judicial finding of insolvency. This resulted in the anomalous situation of banks meriting delicensing without a way to wind up their affairs and liquidate them. In such a case, the CBR's discretion as regulator was not being subjected to the checks and balances of judicial review as much as it was being shadowed by a redundant judicial decision-making process.

There has been some progress on the Russian legislative front with respect to this issue. Recently enacted amendments to the law on banks provide for a new procedure for the liquidation of delicensed banks, according to which the banks may be liquidated regardless of whether they are insolvent. If it becomes evident in the course of the liquidation proceedings that a bank is insolvent, it is then referred for bankruptcy proceedings. Should the bankruptcy court determine that the bank is not insolvent, this does not necessarily mean that the liquidation would cease; rather, the case would be sent back to nonbankruptcy liquidation proceedings.

This amendment increases the weight given to the CBR's regulatory decision in delicensing the bank, and so contains an administrative aspect similar to the legislation of the EU and Asian countries mentioned above. This provision will also eliminate one of the opportunities for multiple appeals that has repeatedly been used by bank owners to stymie CBR efforts at bank liquidation. Appeals in the past have been made of both the CBR's delicensing decision and of the bankruptcy court's determination of insolvency. Under the new amendments, a challenge of the insolvency determination will not stop the liquidation proceedings, as is currently the case. The liquidation will continue, regardless of whether the court finds the bank to be insolvent. The only question to be answered is simply whether the liquidation takes place in a bankruptcy setting or in the setting of a nonbankruptcy, judicial liquidation.

Administrative Bank Liquidation

The proposal for the creation of an agency for bank liquidation presents the potential for the addition of another administrative dimension to the Russian legislation. The use of such an agency would be advantageous in that it would ensure greater uniformity and efficiency of procedures and would promote liquidation in a manner consistent with regulatory policies. This would include fulfillment of the policy of expeditious and favored treatment of retail depositor claims and avoidance of the diminution of depositor rights through compromise and settlement negotiations. If such an agency were created that was neither the CBR nor an offshoot of the CBR, it would be necessary to ensure adequate interaction between the CBR and the agency during the course of a liquidation to ensure consistency of the agency's actions with the CBR's regulatory concerns. There is a large number of other details that would need to be worked out if such an agency were to be created, but the proposal sounds like a worthwhile undertaking.

CONCLUSION

The roles of the various bodies that deal with troubled banks need to be examined and evaluated, particularly with a view toward protection of retail depositor interests. Hitherto banks were placed in bankruptcy in exactly the same way as any other commercial enterprise. This process was not sufficiently observant of the special public policies relating to the banking industry. In the future the process of dealing with troubled banks would ideally reflect the following:

1. CBR should be the overseer of bank restructuring and rehabilitation. The current law on bank bankruptcy allows the CBR, as regulator, to intervene early and attempt a salvaging of the bank. However, this new role brings with it the need for the CBR to formulate clear and coherent policies and objectives with respect to restructuring. Standards must be established against which rehabilitation efforts can be realistically measured for success. Additionally the CBR should expand its efforts at early, informal intervention in troubled banks.

2. Prompt liquidation of unsalvageable banks. If a bank cannot be saved, it must be liquidated in a manner that protects the rights of all creditors and recognizes the preeminence of retail depositor interests. After the CBR, as regulator, has determined that rehabilitation is futile, then the bank should promptly be liquidated and the proceeds distributed to creditors in accordance with statutory priorities. There should be no additional "restructuring" efforts by creditors, shareholders, and courts under the guise of "amicable settlements."

3. Reduction of courts' active direction of bank liquidation. Courts should continue to provide checks and balances by being a source of review of bank liquidation activities, but to fulfill this role the courts needn't actively direct all stages of the proceedings. The decision to initiate a closure and liquidation of a bank should be the prerogative of the regulator, not the courts. The courts can effectively protect the rights of the parties by acting in an appellate capacity. The liquidation process in Russia, though improved by recent legislative amendments, still overemphasizes the role of courts and judicial actors (i.e., judges, individual arbitration managers). This emphasis has had negative consequences in light of the disadvantage at which these actors are placed due to lack of training and to an excessive caseload.

4. Greater emphasis on administrative processes in bank liquidation. The problems faced by the courts in the areas of training, inadequate staffing, and docket congestion will not soon be resolved. It would no doubt be easier to develop potential administrative mechanisms for handling the tasks of bank liquidation and allow the court system to focus on review of liquidation actions in an appellate capacity. By "administrative processes" is meant the assignment of bank liquidation tasks to specialized public entities rather than courts or court-related personnel. One particular change that should be considered is the creation of a public agency to act as arbitration manager in bank liquidations. The development of administrative processes should take into account the particulars of the Russian legal system and need not be as extensive as in, say, the United States; but there is considerable potential for developing these processes consistent with the Russian framework, and the result would significantly enhance the effectiveness of the bank liquidation process.

REFERENCE

Hawkins and Turner. 1999. "Bank Restructuring in Practice," Bank for International Settlements, Monetary and Economic Department, Basel, Switzerland.

CHAPTER 12

ARCO

INTRODUCTION

The Agency for Restructuring of Credit Organizations was established in response to the systemic crisis of the Russian banking system in 1998. While recognizing the weak situation of many Russian banks prior to the crisis, the CBR had been considering setting up a separate agency to undertake the task of restructuring banks modeled on the experience of many other countries. Seen from the perspective of the CBR, the purpose of this initiative was to avoid the potential conflict of interest that would arise were the CBR—given its responsibilities as banking supervisor—also to provide banks with financial support to facilitate their restructuring. Thus ARCO's stated purpose was to provide a financing mechanism, governance, and operational structure within which the resolution of troubled banks[1] could be carried out.

ARCO's Peers in Other Transition Countries

As an institution established specifically for the purpose of conducting the "clean up" of a banking system, ARCO falls within a large group of special-purpose state institutions set up in most European transition economies. (Most European transition countries share, to some degree, the same structural problems inherited from the former Communist economic and legal system.) Such special-purpose institutions were given the following: specific but broad mandates to clean up the banking system; access to substantial funding; and the objective of completing their task (generally defined as successful privatization of the restructured banks) in a relatively short period of time—typically three to five years. The banks to be rehabilitated or restructured were generally state-owned banks inherited from the Communist period, although in recent years some countries have made efforts to restructure privately owned banks.

The experience with bank restructuring in transition countries has been varied. Some countries, such as Hungary (after repeated attempts), Poland, and Slovakia (on the second attempt) have completed the process of bank restructuring. In these countries, the restructuring approach combined very large and costly carve-outs of nonperforming assets from the banks with capital injections, replacement of the former management teams, and privatization by means of sale to foreign strategic investors. Other countries, such as Slovenia and Croatia, are still in the process of implementing bank restructuring initiatives. In Slovenia, the final step of privatization was replaced by a long (and continuing) period of state ownership, which poses a challenge as European Union membership approaches and the state banks—while healthy by every measure—face the prospect of competition from EU-based giants. In Croatia, bank restructuring initiatives were successfully applied, but in 1998 and 1999, two private banks were taken into rehabilitation (while many other private banks were allowed to fail), and the costs of bank restructuring rose dramatically. Finally, in some countries bank restructuring initiatives have not met with success. In the Czech Republic, for example, bank restructuring policies were pursued for an extended period of time, but only made systemic problems significantly worse and multiplied the costs of restructuring to previously unseen levels.[2] The types of policies pursued—repeated recapitalizations and carve-outs, constant failures to institute good governance at banks under state control, financial and operational involvement of the central bank in bailing out private banks, resistance to privatization to reputable strategic investors, and hiding the costs of errors in off-budget institutions—provide a useful catalogue of policy errors and their costs.

ARCO's peer institutions all functioned within a broad macroeconomic and institutional framework for systemic bank restructuring. Differences in the macroeconomic environment do not seem to provide a meaningful variable for the relative success of each group. For example, the macroeconomic performance of the Czech Republic in the mid-1990s was among the best in the transition countries, although it failed in its bank restructuring efforts. At the same time Slovenia was moving ahead with successful bank rehabilitation policies in an environment of relatively high inflation and currency depreciation.[3]

However, a key distinction can be observed between groups at the level of institutional framework. In all successful cases, the responsibility for restructuring was highly concentrated, and in most cases (Poland being an exception), the authority was concentrated outside the central bank. The cases of failure all demonstrate a high degree of involvement by the central bank in the restructuring process: in the Czech Republic (until 2000) there was direct operational and financial involvement in the restructuring of medium and small private banks; in Slovakia, the removal of central bank involvement and the transfer of authority to a special unit within the Ministry of Finance marked the beginning of the process that would rapidly lead to success. One conclusion to be drawn from this is that when central banks become the regulators, owners, liquidators, and rehabilitators of significant portions of the banking system, conflicts of interest cannot be successfully reconciled, and no single function can be performed well.

Liquidating Failed Banks

The discussion above does not address ARCO's peers' success in the area of work-out and liquidation of bank assets (see Klingebiel 2000). Most recently, international financial institutions have favored separating the work-out and liquidation function from the bank restructuring function (Democratic People's Republic of Korea, Thailand, and Slovakia are recent examples). Worldwide experience indicates that, as a rule, bank restructuring institutions have not been successful work-out institutions; there is little overlap between the skill sets required for bank restructuring and those required for work-out functions.[4]

Despite the negative implications of this assessment for ARCO, ARCO could be considered for the function of main liquidator of failed banks in Russia. The reasons are twofold: first, once the present portfolio of banks has been sold, ARCO should cease attempting to restructure banks and become a pure liquidator; second, the reality on the ground in Russia must be accepted. There is no other institution with any apparent capacity or inclination to assume the role of general liquidator, and the limited experience gained by ARCO, along with an institutional willingness to undertake a broader role, provides some foundation on which to build a liquidating institution.

The Purpose of ARCO

ARCO does not fit cleanly into any of the groups of peer institutions in transition countries. In terms of operational restructuring objectives, its requirements for bank management after financial assistance is provided are in line with those pursued in the successful and mixed-results groups. In ARCO's approach to governance, it combines the best elements of the successful countries (strong oversight and control) with an acknowledgment of the failures in the less successful countries (the moral and financial hazards in the Czech Republic when former management was left in control of assisted banks). However, because of ARCO's lack of a clear policy in favor of true strategic investor privatization, which presents the possibility that its rehabilitated banks may be returned to the same interest groups that mismanaged them previously, it is in danger of repeating the Czech experience.[5] Similarly, the overall institutional framework within which ARCO operates—where the central bank is simultaneously playing the roles of regulator, owner, creditor, and restructuring institution with respect to the banking system—is similar to the Czech and Slovak frameworks of the mid-1990s.

ARCO is also separated from its peer institutions in the critical area of financing. In marked contrast to its peers, the funding allocated to ARCO (RUR 10 billion equivalent to US$330 million) was completely inadequate for undertaking any large-scale restructuring of the banking system. At the same time, this level of funding was reasonable given the absence of a fully developed legal framework for restructuring and the lack of adequate practices and powers with which to liquidate failed banks. To invest substantial public funds to attempt systemic restructuring in this environment would surely be an error. Table 12.1 provides a list of ARCO's ownership stakes as of the end of 2000.

Under these circumstances it can be argued that achieving success in restructuring the Russian banking system is not feasible at the present time, at least as long as success is defined as the creation of a profitable and prudent system enjoying the trust of depositors. With only weak support in place for enforceable investor and creditor rights and weak bank supervision, creating any viable banking system (in the market economy sense) is not possible. The asset stripping by insiders that followed the 1998 banking crisis and the disregard of minority shareholders' rights as exemplified by the Sberbank share issue in 2001 reveal Russia's lack of readiness. And given this type of environment, reputable investors cannot be expected to risk their capital. Thus it is perhaps best to regard ARCO as a kind of laboratory—unique among institutions of this type—for testing restructuring policies, the effectiveness of bank liquidation as a restructuring tool, the concept of deposit insurance, and the concept of strategic privatization.

ARCO's experience in all of these areas provides useful information that identifies strengths and weaknesses in the current framework for

Table 12.1 Banks in ARCO's Portfolio as of December 31, 2000

Bank Name	Region	ARCO Ownership	Comments
AvtoVAZbank	Samara	88.1%	Sold 2001
Investbank	Kaliningrad	85.15%	Sold 2001
Rossiyskiy Kredit	Moscow	25% + 1 (+ 50% in trust)	
Kuzbassugolbank	Kemerovo	90.9%	Sold 2001
Kemerovo	Kemerovo	—	Merged 2001
Kuzbassocbank	Kemerovo	—	
Kuzbassprombank	Kemerovo	99%	In liquidation
Eurasia	Izhevsk	50% + 1	
RNKB	Moscow	46.09%	Sold 2001
Vyatka	Kirov	73.63%	
Peter the First	Voronezh	96.6%	Sold 2001
Bank Voronezh	Voronezh	99%	Merged 2001
ChelyabComZemBank	Chelyabinsk	74.62%	Sold 2001
Dalrybbank	Vladivostok	99%	
SBS-AGRO	Moscow	99.9%	
Amurpromstroybank	Blagoveshensk	99%	Tendering
Bashprombank	Ufa	97%	
Alfa–Bank	Moscow	25% + 1 in trust	
Vozrozhdenie	Moscow	—	

— None.
Source: ARCO.

bank restructuring, and with this information Russian authorities can design new policies and laws to respond to the challenge of creating a viable banking system. This chapter discusses some of ARCO's key experiences in the areas of bank liquidation, bank rehabilitation, deposit insurance, and privatization. It draws conclusions from these experiences regarding lessons that can be learned and applied to the development of a comprehensive approach to restructuring the Russian banking system.

OVERVIEW OF ARCO'S OPERATIONS

ARCO's experience, although restricted to a relatively small sample of Russian banks, provides useful information—discussed in detail in the following sections—regarding a number of important areas and issues that have systemwide implications. The following specific experiences provided valuable information and data.

ARCO's approach to governance of the restructuring and rehabilitation process provides insights that may be useful in designing a governance scheme for the restructuring and ultimate privatization of state-owned banks.

ARCO introduced the first deposit insurance scheme in Russia, which provides initial data regarding the potential for mobilizing retail deposits through the introduction of a systemwide scheme. This scheme—while interesting as an experiment in determining the importance of an explicit guarantee of deposits to establishing depositor trust—is also troubling. As those ARCO banks that have deposit insurance are being privatized, their deposit insurance coverage is being continued for a period of 18 months, which will create pressures on ARCO to further extend coverage for these banks and to extend the scope of coverage by allowing other private banks to participate in the scheme. These decisions highlight the dangers of starting an ad hoc scheme without first establishing a national policy and legal framework for deposit insurance.

ARCO has begun liquidating one bank in the Kemerovo region. The difficulties it faced in implementing the liquidation process have been useful in identifying weaknesses in the legal framework for bank liquidation and bankruptcy. ARCO has proposed amendments to a number of laws to strengthen the framework and to provide a clear exit mechanism for failed banks. If these amendments are implemented, they would give ARCO a central role in cleaning up the large backlog of delicensed but unliquidated banks that remain a legacy of the 1998 crisis.

ARCO commenced the privatization process for banks in its portfolio in early 2001. While the initial results of this process were disheartening, the process has at least revealed that there is interest from domestic investors in participating in the resolution of the system, and it also has highlighted the informal and formal barriers to entry that exist.

Legal Framework and Funding

ARCO's operations are governed by the Law on Restructuring Credit Organizations (July 1999). ARCO was founded by government decree in November 1998 and commenced operations in March 1999. At that time ARCO was provided with RUR 10 billion from state funds with which to restructure banks transferred to the agency. These funds could be used for equity investments in its banks, for loans to them for liquidity purposes, and for purchases of low-quality assets to strengthen balance sheets. ARCO is entitled to use the proceeds of bank privatizations and earnings from loans to undertake further interventions.

Governance

ARCO's operations are governed by a 13-member Board of Directors with the largest group (5) of members nominated by the CBR. The

Government and the Duma are also represented on the Board. Operational management of the agency is carried out by an Executive Board, which consists of directors of the agency's departments.

This structure does not fully conform to the more flexible and effective governance arrangements seen in similar institutions in other countries (a more typical board for this type of institution would have no more than 7 members). The size of the Board of Directors is inconsistent with the need for it to meet regularly and actively supervise and control the activities of management.

In other—not just transition—countries, the central bank has recognized that there is a fundamental conflict of interest between its monetary and regulatory responsibilities, and its participation in the governance of a state-funded bank restructuring agency. This became clear for two reasons: first, because of the conflict of regulating banks and simultaneously (through the bank restructuring agency) owning and controlling them; and, second, because (and this is true in Russia) the central bank may be a creditor of banks being liquidated by the bank restructuring agency. Other creditors of a bank will naturally question the fairness of a liquidation process where one creditor also has a degree of control over the institution responsible for administering the liquidation process.

ARCO's Portfolio

Banks that have a capital adequacy, by Russian Accounting Standards, of 2 percent or less, *and* that have been unable to make payments, can be referred to ARCO by the CBR.[6] Banks must meet a number of tests to qualify for assistance from ARCO. ARCO can reject, and has rejected, CBR referrals if it determines that the following criteria are not met:
1. The bank must hold more than 1 percent of Russian aggregate household deposits or loans, or 20 percent of its region's household deposits or loans.
2. An ARCO due-diligence process must conclude that the banks can be successfully restructured using ARCO's limited financial resources.
3. Due diligence performed by ARCO must reach the conclusion that there is scope for the bank to be rehabilitated.

As a result of the application of these criteria, the agency has developed a portfolio of small banks with a primarily regional character.

Within the portfolio, there are, however, disturbing exceptions[7] to the criteria established by the law. Prior to implementation of the Law on Restructuring Credit Organizations, ARCO received and accepted a total of 15 applications from troubled banks (notably Alfa-Bank, Vozrozhdenie) for assistance. These banks (all Moscow-based) were not referred to ARCO by the CBR but for unclear reasons were provided with assistance. As a result, there is a perception that the assistance provided to these banks represents another instance of the state bailing out well-connected oligarchs, and ARCO's continued involvement with them tends to undermine the agency's credibility. The criticism directed at ARCO regarding these banks should provide a lesson that ARCO can apply in the future: ARCO cannot expect to be entrusted with a continuing and significant role in restructuring the banking system if its decisions are perceived to be in any way connected to special political or economic interests

ARCO'S EXPERIENCE IN THE REHABILITATION OF BANKS

ARCO follows two basic bank rehabilitation methodologies. The first approach, which applies a conventional mix of measures designed to reduce operating costs, improve governance, and recover bad debts, is in line with the approaches used by other bank restructuring agencies in transition countries. The second approach, however, focuses on amicable settlements with creditors, which is not supported by international experience, and in certain cases, gives rise to questions about the purpose and usefulness of rehabilitation carried out in this way. ARCO argues, however—and the data regarding these settlements seems to support this argument—that given the realities of the bank liquidation process, the amicable settlements have produced much better and faster results for individual depositors than if the banks involved were to have been liquidated.

ARCO's success or failure in restructuring banks will ultimately be determined by its ability to sell banks to reputable strategic investors. (Specific issues related to privatization are discussed in a separate section below.) However, the agency should always bear in mind that there is a temptation to retain ownership of banks that have become profitable (Slovenia's experience bears this out). Experience worldwide shows that the state is rarely a prudent owner of banks over the long term and, in the Russian context where there are political pressures on state banks to direct lending to uncreditworthy borrowers, the need to move ahead as rapidly as possible with privatization is accentuated.

Bank Rehabilitation

ARCO's approach to bank rehabilitation is comparable to the methods used in many other countries, and the agency uses similar tools to control the restructuring process. Banks that were referred to ARCO by the CBR after the ARCO law came in to effect are subject to a quantitative analysis to determine whether they should be rehabilitated using ARCO funds or liquidated (liquidation is seen as a form of resolution). On a bank's referral, ARCO conducts due diligence to determine if rehabilitation is feasible and may reject the referral if it is not. The objective of the rehabilitation process is to privatize the bank concerned.

The mechanism for exerting initial control over banks entering rehabilitation is an ARCO capital (and sometimes debt) injection in exchange for a controlling share position. Existing shareholders' stakes are written down. Once control is established, ARCO works with the bank's management[8] to prepare and then implement a restructuring plan focused on four main areas: operational restructuring to reduce costs and rationalize and improve the bank's network; improvement of governance and controls (particularly on credit[9]); bad-debt recovery; and business development (both attracting new deposits and diversification[10] of the credit portfolio).[11] Progress against objectives established by these plans is closely monitored by ARCO.

During the bank rehabilitation process, ARCO has succeeded in executing some innovations in the Russian regional banking market:

1. In the Kemerovo region, the three steps have been taken to consolidate the regional banking system: (1) branches of Kuzbassprombank were sold to Kuzbassugol Bank in the process of Kuzbassprombank's liquidation; (2) Kemerovo Bank was merged into Kuzbassugol Bank; and (3) some—very limited—success was achieved on retaining retail deposits by using Kuzbassugol Bank as the paying agent for deposits of Kuzbassprombank.
2. In the Voronezh region, ARCO has merged two banks (Pyotr Pervyi and Bank Voronezh) in order to create a larger and more viable bank, which was subsequently privatized.

Of the 10 ARCO banks in rehabilitation, 3 achieved profitability in 2000, while the remaining 7 were operationally (before provisions for credit losses) profitable. By the end of 2000, 7 banks had been identified as ready for privatization. The aggregate profit (under Russian accounting standards) of the regional banks was RUR 21 million at end-2000, and aggregate nonperforming assets were reduced from 22 percent to 10 percent of assets.

Despite these results from the rehabilitation process, the continuing use of Russian Accounting Standards gives rise to skepticism regarding the accuracy of ARCO's claimed success; these accounting standards do not provide any confidence that results conform to reality. Accordingly,

ARCO could consider improvements to its present approach in the following two areas:
1. ARCO could significantly increase its credibility with potential investors and the public by ensuring that International Accounting Standards are used in parallel with Russian standards. IAS audits of the banks would provide assurance that the profits reported by the banks are real and enhance the aggregated reporting of results in the agency's communications with the public.
2. Greater efforts could be applied to replacing the management teams with new people not associated with a bank's failure. This would remove the moral hazard associated with recapitalizing banks without removing management (i.e., rewarding failure). This effort would ease the privatization process by removing the perception that former owners—or their affiliates—have an inside track in privatization tenders through their pre-existing relationships with management.

Amicable Settlements

At end-2000 ARCO had developed or was in the process of implementing a total of six amicable settlements[12] with the creditors of banks in which it had invested. The six banks fall into two groups: (1) four regional banks where ARCO acquired majority ownership and where amicable settlements with creditors can be viewed as a legitimate bank restructuring and rehabilitation technique by requiring private sector creditors to bear some of the costs of rehabilitation (see Table 12.2) and (2) two banks (SBS-Agro and Rossiyskiy Kredit) are the subject of proposed amicable settlements where the purpose and motivation for ARCO's involvement seems extremely unclear. Neither of these banks seems to qualify under the ability-to-rehabilitate standards required for ARCO assistance. If these banks will not be viable even after the amicable settlements (and what depositor or lender would put funds in institutions with such records?) for what purpose are taxpayer funds being used? These two cases suggest that a clear policy of least-cost resolution was not followed, which calls into question whether ARCO is well suited to play a much larger role in the bank restructuring process.

The data on the four amicable settlements where corporate depositors have also benefited support ARCO's argument that, despite the moral hazard inherent in such settlements, the settlements in fact provided individual depositors with a much better result in practice than if the theoretically correct path of liquidation had been followed. ARCO argues that had the banks been placed in liquidation the inefficiencies of the

Table 12.2 ARCO Amicable Settlements in which Corporate Depositors Benefited

Bank	Dalryb Bank	Bashprom Bank	Amurpromstroy Bank	Rossiyskiy-Kredit
Date of Amicable Agreement effectiveness	29.12.00	08.02.01	03.01.01	25.09.00
Total liabilities to individuals (RUR × 000)	128,190	118,266	11,796	1,854,543
Maximum maturity for individuals (years)	1.5	1.0	1.5	1.5
Total liabilities to corporations (RUR × 000)	206,102	153,267	36,599	22,373,085
Prompt repayments to corporations (%)	10	10	5	10
Prompt repayments to corporations (RUR × 000)	20,610	15,327	1,830	2,237,309
Maximum maturity for corporations (years)	20	10	20	10

Notes: Bank "Voronezh"—no prompt repayments to corporations.
Bank "SBS-AGRO"—no prompt repayments to corporations.
Source: ARCO.

process would result in very long delays in repayment and, most likely, at best only partial repayment (the discussion of the significant problems in the bankruptcy and insolvency framework in Chapter 11 also support this argument). This highlights the urgent necessity of reforming the framework for bank insolvency and liquidation to allow efficient liquidation to occur and obviate the need to reach amicable settlements with bank creditors.

ARCO DEPOSIT INSURANCE SCHEME

In 2000 ARCO developed and introduced a deposit insurance scheme for the benefit of banks in its portfolio. As of December 31, 2000, a total of five[13] banks were participating in the scheme (two applications from portfolio banks had been refused due to their failure to meet membership criteria). The ARCO scheme provides slightly higher levels of coverage (as discussed in Chapter 10 of this text) than those proposed by the Government in June 2001.

The deposit insurance scheme is both an interesting source of information regarding depositor attitudes to the use of explicit guarantees as a mechanism to restore trust, and a troubling development from a policy perspective. As discussed more fully in Box 12.1, the scheme—while evidently successful in restoring depositor trust at the banks concerned—

has been introduced ad hoc without assessing its implications for the banking system as a whole or the potential long-term exposure of the taxpayer. The first steps in expanding the ARCO scheme are now being taken as a result of privatization of banks that are members of the scheme. ARCO has decided to continue insurance coverage for a period of 18 months post-privatization (with an increase in premiums). In addition there is a significant danger that this ad hoc scheme will expand further (as other private banks seek membership of the scheme) without first putting in place an adequate legal framework to define and limit the state's liability and to provide the deposit insurer with adequate power to supervise banks that receive insurance coverage.

Box 12.1 ARCO's Deposit Insurance Scheme

The deposit insurance scheme provides individual (physical person) depositors with insurance on a sliding scale according to the total amount of their deposits in an insured bank (see Table 12.3 below).

Criteria for membership in the scheme: ARCO applies membership standards for banks wishing to join the deposit insurance scheme. In order to be eligible to join, banks must (a) be more than 50 percent owned by ARCO, (b) have no overdue liabilities, (c) meet all CBR ratio requirements, and (d) be stable and profitable.

Prior to accepting an application, ARCO undertakes a due-diligence process to ensure that these four criteria are met. The final decision on membership applications is made by the ARCO executive board. As noted above, of the seven ARCO banks to have applied to date, two have been rejected.

An off-site review of the compliance of each bank with the membership criteria is carried out by ARCO; however, no policy is in place to address the issue of what consequences—such as withdrawal of insurance—would be taken against a bank that falls out of compliance (other than use of ARCO's powers to force a bank's management to take corrective action).

Capital and premiums: The deposit insurance fund was capitalized with RUR 500 million from ARCO funds. Member banks pay a quarterly premium of 0.0025 percent of total individual deposits, calculated on a yearly average basis (member banks that are privatized will pay a higher premium of 0.1 percent). According to ARCO, the very low premium for member banks that have not been privatized is explained on the basis that it is the owner of the bank who pays this premium, and therefore has a very high level of control over the risk to the fund posed by its members.

Depositor awareness: The agency has developed a good depositor information program to explain the terms on which insurance is offered. Each member bank is required to display information about the program in each of its branches, and explanatory leaflets are also available to depositors in the branches. In addition, ARCO has developed a "road show" to explain the scheme through the local media when a bank first becomes a member.

(Box continues on next page)

Box 12.1 *(continued)*

Table 12.3 Insurance Coverage of Deposits in the ARCO Scheme

Multiple of the Minimum Monthly Wage (Calculation Basis)	RUR Equivalent at December 31, 2000	Amount Covered
Up to 20 times	2,000	100 percent
More than 20 times and up to 250 times	2,001–25,000	90 percent
More than 250 times and up to 1,000 times	25,001–100,000	50 percent

Source: ARCO.

Impact of the Scheme on Deposit Mobilization

As shown in Figure 12.1 and Table 12.4, the deposit insurance scheme has had a measurable impact on the mobilization of deposits by member banks. This impact indicates that Russian retail depositors are responsive to the introduction of *explicit* guarantees. It can be argued that the

Figure 12.1 Impact of the Introduction of Deposit Insurance on Member Banks
(rubles, thousands)

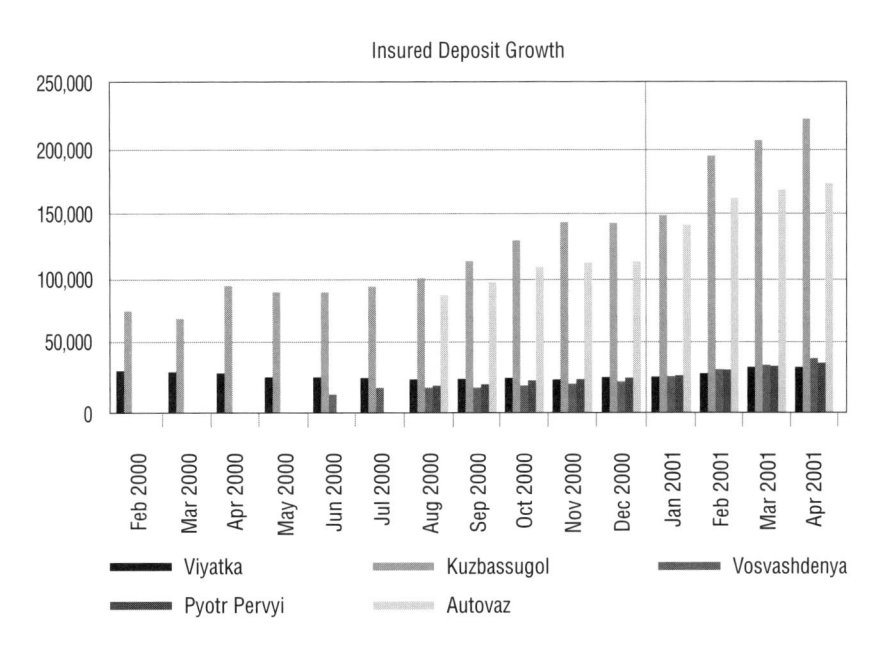

Table 12.4 Deposit Growth per Quarter in Insured Banks Relative to the Region as a Whole
(percent)

Bank/Region	April to July '00	July to Oct '00	Oct '00 to Jan '01
Viyatka Bank	−15.07	−2.05	0.32
Viyatka Region	13.96	8.55	9.96
Kuzbassugol Bank	−1.55	35.46	14.53
Kuzbassugol Region	15.40	4.49	6.24
Vosvashdenya Bank			35.01
Vosvashdenya Region			13.67
Pyotr Pervyi Bank			19.09
Pyotr Pervyi Region			9.89
Autovaz Bank			28.76
Autovaz Region			7.80

Source: ARCO.

ARCO-owned banks in any case operate under an implicit state guarantee (in the same way as Sberbank), but it is clear that depositors have responded positively when this implicit guarantee is structured into a formal guarantee with well explained terms. The strength of this response[14] gives a possible indication of the benefits that could be derived if a systemwide deposit insurance scheme were to be introduced.

Unresolved Issues

While the ARCO deposit insurance scheme has been successful in increasing the volumes of retail deposits mobilized by member banks, the creation of the deposit insurance scheme has been criticized because it occurred ad hoc and outside the framework of a systemwide program. The ARCO scheme is, in effect, a private self-insurance program designed to make explicit the implicit guarantee of state ownership.

ARCO has not established a definitive policy regarding the continuation or discontinuation of deposit insurance scheme membership once its share of ownership falls below 50 percent. Instead an interim decision has been made to extend coverage (with an increase in premiums) for 18 months after a bank has been privatized, ostensibly to allow time for insured deposits to run off and be replaced by uninsured deposits. The data does not make it clear that this is in fact happening, nor is it clear what ARCO's policy will be toward insured deposits that remain at the end of the "run-off" period. The explicit intention of this extension is to allow time for a policy to be developed, or more likely superceded by implementation of the proposed national deposit insurance scheme.

The requirements of the privatization process have thus pushed ARCO to begin extending insurance to non-ARCO, majority-owned banks. Expanding the scheme in this way will also most likely increase the pressure on ARCO to allow completely unrelated private banks to become members, and additional pressure is likely to come from the owners of former ARCO banks to further extend the period of coverage. One option (discussed at the conclusion of this chapter) would be to formalize ARCO's role as the deposit insurer and thus allow for the development and implementation of a scheme that can be applied systemwide. It should be strongly emphasized that the presentation of this option should not be viewed as a recommendation. Our conclusion is an emphatic one: at the present time the condition of the banking system and the quality of bank supervision are in no way conducive to the establishment of any kind of deposit insurance program.

ARCO'S EXPERIENCE OF THE BANK LIQUIDATION PROCESS

The liquidation of Kuzbassprombank (KPB) has provided ARCO with insights into the weaknesses of the present legal framework for bank liquidation, and it helped to clarify how the law can be strengthened. Resolution of the problems raised by the KPB liquidation can provide a basis for ARCO to become the primary vehicle for liquidating the large stock of bankrupt banks in Russia.

In accordance with the Bank Restructuring Law, ARCO attempted to initiate KPB's liquidation by requesting meetings of the bank's board and a general meeting of shareholders. ARCO had become the major creditor of KPB as a result of a payout of retail deposits using funds provided by a loan to the bank. The purpose of calling the meetings of the board and shareholders was to propose the creation of a liquidation committee, which would in turn petition the CBR for removal of the bank's license. Once the license is removed, a bank is able to start self-liquidation (this procedure is essentially voluntary liquidation). Only in the event that the liquidation committee determines that the bank will be unable to pay its creditors in full is a bankruptcy filing necessary.

In KPB's case, the general meeting of shareholders adopted the necessary resolution in favor of liquidation, and ARCO was appointed interim liquidator. However, the board of directors of the bank refused to accede to the shareholders' wishes; once the liquidation committee proposed bankruptcy, the board counterfiled in the local arbitration court to prevent acceptance of the bankruptcy petition. The board's suit was successful at the local level, but on appeal the federal arbitration court upheld the filing and the bank entered bankruptcy.

On January 24, 2001, a receiver for KPB was finally appointed on ARCO's suggestion. The receiver is supervised by a creditor's committee of seven members: two appointed by ARCO, two by the Kemerovo regional authorities, and one each by the CBR, KPB's depositors, and Comerzbank (Germany). The receiver is required to provide monthly status reports and to have major decisions approved by the committee.

Lessons Learned and Remedies Proposed

The KPB case provided two important lessons that ARCO proposes be incorporated into amendments to the Bank Restructuring Law.

First, the KPB experience highlighted the need to create uniformity and predictability in the operation of regional arbitration courts. The ability of parties to a bankruptcy (particularly management and shareholders) to introduce procedural delays or block a bankruptcy filing at the regional court level provides opportunities for asset stripping by insiders. Delays mean that the bank's assets are not "worked" to maximize returns to depositors and creditors, and pressure is placed on depositors and creditors to agree to otherwise unjustified settlements to the benefit of shareholders who would otherwise receive nothing.[15]

Second, the role of ARCO in the liquidation process needs to be clarified, and in particular, the appointment of ARCO as the receiver (arbitration manager) in bank bankruptcy cases should become mandatory in liquidation of any ARCO-controlled banks. While the actions of the ARCO-suggested receiver in the KPB are considered to be satisfactory by ARCO, the legal prohibition on ARCO acting as a receiver opens the way for significant problems in other cases. There is no assurance that an arbitration court will accept ARCO's suggested candidate for receiver in all cases, and the use of unqualified or inexperienced receivers is entirely feasible within the present law.

ARCO's experience in a single case of bank liquidation has, despite the delays, been positive so far, in the sense that at the federal level the rights of the general meeting of shareholders to decide upon liquidation were upheld, and ARCO was able to get its candidate appointed as receiver. However, the experience also highlights the uncertainty of the process; that is, these favorable outcomes could quite well have gone the other way, with negative consequences for the bank's creditors. If the broader problem of bank insolvency in Russia is to be resolved, the path to liquidation must be made certain and quick, and the execution of the liquidation process must be made professional and transparent.

In this context, an amendment to the bank restructuring and bankruptcy laws to create a bank liquidation agency would be desirable, and ARCO could be considered for taking on this role. The development of strong liquidation skills by ARCO as a liquidation agency would assure creditors that their claims would be resolved in a professional and equitable manner.

PRIVATIZATION OF ARCO BANKS

The privatization process for the ARCO banks provides useful lessons for the future regarding the fundamental issue of whether strategic investment can be attracted to the Russian banking system. The privatization of the ARCO banks offers the authorities an opportunity to conduct a privatization process that is transparent, has clear rules, and excludes simply returning these banks to the same owners. On the other hand, there is a real danger that the results of the privatization process could be seen as "more of the same," where legitimate investors are excluded for the benefit of insiders, and where the entire rehabilitation process is seen as one more bail-out of connected private interests by the state. The ARCO bank privatization process is made difficult by three factors:

1. The banks to be privatized are regional and small in absolute terms. These factors may make them unattractive to large strategic investors, and the dispersion of the ARCO portfolio makes the creation of a national network of ARCO banks unfeasible.
2. ARCO management has also made it clear that regardless of strategic investor interest, in certain cases the interest of regional authorities in acquiring banks will significantly reduce the interest of other investors (local authorities have sufficient legal and extra-legal means to ensure that any uninvited investor will have a difficult experience).
3. While ARCO reports that local investors are very interested in some of the banks, the question of whether such investors will be able to provide the governance these banks require once ARCO ceases exercising control is a good one. Also, can these local investors provide the benefits of technology transfer and management skills that strategic investors can provide? There is a real

possibility that one result of the privatization process will be that in the future these banks may become troubled again.

These factors raise the real possibility that ARCO—if it chooses to sell banks only to legitimate investors—could be faced with a situation where the banks are simply not privatizable for the medium term. At that point, the issue of state ownership, and the mechanisms by which governance is exerted, will need to be revisited. A fundamental judgment may have to be made as to whether medium-term state ownership is in fact preferable to privatization under the particular circumstances of the Russian regions.

One further option to address the problem of nonprivatizable ARCO banks might be the creation of some form of state trust to take over ownership and control of banks after a specific period (say three or four years) from the date of ARCO's investment in a bank. If such a trust were to operate under the governance of respected and independent persons and with full transparency, an intermediate mechanism to continue state ownership without continuing the risks posed by state ownership could be successful.

Results of the Privatization Process

The four privatization transactions completed by June 1, 2001, do not provide a basis for a theory that ARCO could provide a useful model for the privatization of other state banks. While in all cases the letter of the law has been applied in the auction process, the ARCO process departs from that seen in other countries, in which the intent of the privatization process is to attract reputable strategic investors by providing adequate opportunities for investors to conduct due diligence; by screening investors to ensure that only those capable of providing good governance, without conflicts of interest, and with the technical skills and financial strength to contribute to the development of the bank are qualified to tender; and to ensure the best price for the state's shareholding by maximizing competition.

A further and very disturbing issue from a supervisory perspective is that in two cases (Autovazbank and Pyotr Pervyi) the bank acquirers were permitted to use an unconsolidated affiliate vehicle to execute their acquisitions. Such a mechanism allows circumvention of accounting and reporting standards for the consolidation of investments by banks, has the potential to allow imprudent violations of loan-to-one-borrower limits, and could result in a situation where the acquired bank in fact provides the financing for its own purchase.[16] ARCO management explained this as standard operating practice in Russia, but this should not justify the knowing participation of a public institution, and it casts doubt on ARCO's understanding of its public responsibilities.

The four initial privatizations completed by ARCO were Chelyabkomzembank (April 2001), Investbank (May 2001), Autovazbank (May 2001) and Pyotr Pervyi (June 2001).

CONCLUSION

The results of ARCO's privatization efforts to date indicate that the process will need to be significantly restructured if there is to be any possibility of attracting reputable strategic investors to the process. The present approach seems designed to actually exclude such investors and, by transferring ownership to investors of opaque origin or using highly questionable indirect and "anonymous" acquisition vehicles, may in fact simply result in the failure of these banks in the future at further cost to the taxpayer and to depositors. The following specific changes to the process could be considered:

1. *Extending the period between announcement of a tender and the auction date:* The legal minimum period of 30 days (ARCO states that up to 60 days is typical) is far too short to allow a reputable strategic investor—without prior inside information regarding upcoming tenders—to conduct appropriate due diligence or, in the case of foreign investors, to even mobilize an acquisition team. A period of six months to one year to complete the privatization process is typical in other transition countries and encourages reputable investors to participate by allowing adequate time for due diligence.
2. *Retaining a reputable financial adviser to market banks and administer the privatization process:* ARCO has relied on its own resources for the tenders conducted so far. This contrasts with the practice in almost all countries of using a reputable financial adviser capable of delivering the widest possible market for each transaction. The participation of a reputable adviser also provides reassurance to investors that the tender process will be administered in a professional and impartial manner, thus fostering competition.
3. *Implementing pre-qualification procedures and criteria designed to exclude investors who do not meet requirements to provide financial strength, good governance, and a lack of conflicts of interest to*

ensure the prudent operation of the bank post-privatization: The present practice, where ARCO either states that it has no knowledge of the business or ownership of the investors purchasing its banks, or allows the use of questionable acquisition designed to circumvent accounting and reporting rules, is indicative of a reckless disregard for well-established principles. Institutions of ARCO's type have a responsibility to the taxpayer to ensure that privatization does not simply return ownership to the types of investors likely to mismanage a bank (and particularly banks with deposit insurance).

The future role of ARCO in the banking system needs to be defined by the Russian authorities. As an institution it presently has a limited mandate; however, it is developing skills in the area of bank liquidation, deposit insurance, and privatization. For the longer term, a strategy for ARCO could take advantage of these skills by providing the institution with a mandate in deposit insurance and bank liquidation (two complementary functions).

In order to implement such a strategy, some basic building blocks must be in place:

1. ARCO should not attempt to restructure or rehabilitate any more banks. As discussed previously, experience of most countries shows that combining the liquidation and restructuring function has not been successful.

2. The process of privatizing ARCO's remaining banks should be halted until it can be redesigned to encourage the participation of reputable strategic investors. The privatizations executed so far encourage a belief that ARCO's banks are being sold in a way that does nothing to ensure the future stability of the system (and may further undermine it) and undermines any confidence that ARCO should be entrusted with a broader role in either bank privatization or the sale of assets in the bank liquidation process.

3. ARCO should not prematurely introduce a system of deposit guarantees. ARCO's limited experience indicates that deposit insurance can have some impact in building trust in the banking system and mobilizing deposits. However, the rules for participation in such a scheme and the powers of the responsible institution to control the risk of deposit insurance by supervising member banks must be established (ARCO's membership requirements and monitoring are useful experiments in this regard). How the scheme would be financed without placing an additional burden on the state must be determined, and the consequences for banks that do not qualify for insurance must be outlined. We emphasize that attempting to

rapidly expand the ARCO deposit insurance scheme under the present circumstances of the Russian banking system would be a mistake. Until the system is restored to solvency under IAS and effective bank supervision is implemented, there is an overwhelming likelihood that the result of introducing deposit insurance will significantly increase costs to the state from bank failures.

4. The laws on bank restructuring and bankruptcy need to be amended to allow the process to become professional and efficient. For ARCO to function effectively as an institution responsible for clearing the backlog of insolvent banks out of the system, and to allow rapid resolution of future bank insolvency, the legal framework for bank liquidation must be amended. The legal framework must remove the ability of shareholders and management to obstruct the liquidation process; it must allow the development and use of ARCO (as a legal entity) as a professional liquidator; and it must ensure that the process is made transparent and accountable to creditors.

5. Criteria should be amended to allow early intervention. The costs of intervention by ARCO are increased, and the proceeds available to pay depositors and creditors are reduced, as a result of the combined capital insolvency and illiquidity threshold necessary for CBR referral to ARCO. The criteria should be amended to allow referral of a bank to ARCO when it becomes either capital-insolvent under IAS *or* becomes illiquid.

6. If ARCO is to be made responsible for liquidating a large number of banks,[17] then it will require additional funding from the state. Under normal circumstances a liquidator is paid from the proceeds of liquidation. However, under the extraordinary circumstances of this type of mass liquidation, it is unlikely that in many cases the costs of liquidation can be recovered from the liquidation of remaining assets. The state will therefore have to provide ARCO with additional funding to cover this one-time cleanup cost.

7. ARCO's governance needs to be reformed. If ARCO is to function effectively as a deposit insurer and bank liquidator, its governance needs to be reformed to remove conflicts of interest and reduce opportunities for political interference. One solution, in conjunction with the expansion of deposit insurance, would be to restructure the ARCO board of directors by making it smaller and more effective in terms of supervising the agency's management; by providing it with a majority of independent professional members;

and by reducing participation by the CBR to observer status. This would remove the inherent conflict of interest in CBR's nomination of members to the ARCO board (discussed above) and help to mitigate the risk of politically influenced decisions.

ARCO remains an experimental institution. As such it has made mistakes—most notably in its approach to bank privatization—but its limited successes should also be recognized. For the Russian authorities the key issue should be how to use the lessons learned from ARCO's experiments to design and implement policies in the areas of bank restructuring, privatization, liquidation, and deposit insurance. ARCO itself, while still a small institution, provides some foundation of skills and experience on which a larger and significantly more powerful institution could be built. The success or failure of this larger institution will be determined by the legal and governance framework that supports it, and this itself provides an opportunity to implement reforms that can eliminate conflicts of interest and build public trust.

ENDNOTES

1. The term "banks" is used throughout to denote credit organizations.

2. Current estimates of the costs incurred in the Czech Republic for bank restructuring are in the 55 to 60 percent of GDP range. The closest competitor in terms of cost is Croatia (about 30 percent of GDP), which incurred exceptional costs from war and the economic consequences of the breakup of the former Yugoslavia.

3. It is often argued (by bankers) that the primary cause of bank failures is dramatic changes in the macroeconomic environment. This argument is used to support the idea that bankers are in some way not responsible for the failure of their institutions and therefore a penalty-free state-sponsored bail-out program is justified. In Russia's case, the change would have been the onset of the currency crisis in 1998 combined with default on state securities. However, this does not explain why some banks survived the same crisis. Research conducted by the U.S. Office of the Comptroller of the Currency in the mid-1980s clearly demonstrated that during periods of macroeconomic stress there was only one significant variable between banks that failed and those that did not: the quality of management and governance.

4. The U.S. Resolution Trust Corporation is often mistakenly cited as an example of an institution that was successful in combining these functions; in fact the vast majority of its assets were performing home mortgages and commercial real estate for which the work-out activities consisted of sale (performed by well

qualified contractors) into pre-existing and highly liquid markets. Similar types of assets requiring liquidation or work out and similarly liquid markets are not a feature of Russia or anywhere else in the region, and the experience is therefore irrelevant.

5. ARCO argues that the reality on the ground is that powerful regional authorities will block the sale of ARCO banks to strategic investors that are not a part of the regional power structure. There seems to be some merit to this argument given the myriad powers (from tax raids to health and safety inspections) available to the authorities to harass any foreign (out of region) investor. This supports the conclusion that real reform of the banking system will have to wait until Russia conforms to the norms of the rule of law and impartial administration required for a functioning market economy.

6. The requirement that banks must meet both of these criteria drives up the cost of intervention by ARCO. Given the lax standards of Russian accounting and supervision, a bank may continue to avoid intervention long after it has become capital insolvent under IAS. This allows insiders additional time to engage in asset stripping and imprudent speculation, and encourages the dissipation of a bank's most valuable assets in order to maintain liquidity. All these factors tend to increase the cost of restructuring and reduce the value of assets remaining to pay depositors and creditors if the bank is placed in liquidation (see Chapter 11 for a further discussion).

7. "Exceptions" may be the wrong term as ARCO accepted 15 banks on a voluntary basis before the enactment of the law and only 6 (out of 9 referred to it by the CBR) after the law became effective.

8. ARCO has generally not followed international practices by appointing new management teams to its banks. Old management teams have generally been retained on the basis of their knowledge of the portfolios, with the addition of a member of each team appointed from the ARCO Anti-Crisis Department.

9. All credits over RUR 10 million require approval by ARCO headquarters. In addition, ARCO has imposed uniform credit policies and procedures on the banks, and conducts regular field inspections of the banks' credit portfolios.

10. Most of the ARCO banks were "pocket banks" of an enterprise or industry in their regions. ARCO establishes targets for diversification away from these enterprises and industries, with an emphasis on SMEs. Geographical diversification remains a significant problem due to the location of the banks in the regions and the lack of opportunities to either sell or purchase loans from out-of-region banks in order to diversify.

11. ARCO might find the corrective action plan and monitoring standards used by the World Bank-funded Bank Review Unit to be of interest in further developing its activities in this area.

12. Settlement proposals that had been approved by the respective arbitration court.

13. Autovazbank, Eurasia, Kuzbassugolbank, Pyotr Pervyi, and Vyatka-bank.

14. An additional—but unquantifiable—point might be that the depositors concerned are located in the regions rather than in the Moscow and St. Petersburg metropolitan areas. The lower levels of financial sophistication found in the regions may be the reason that making the guarantee explicit is important.

15. The same problems arise in the operation of the bank bankruptcy law (see further discussion in Chapter 11).

16. This type of fraudulent financing has been a common factor in many private bank failures in the transition countries.

17. On February 28, 2001, the CBR identified 758 banks as subject to liquidation and 468 as being in receivership with court-appointed interim trustees (Source: *Bulletin of Banking Statistics No. 3* [94]). Given that these numbers are the result of Russian Accounting Standards, the true number of insolvent banks in the system is most likely significantly higher.

REFERENCE

Klingebiel, Daniela. 2000. "The Use of Asset Management Companies in the Resolution of Banking Crises." Policy Research Working Paper 2284. World Bank Financial Sector Strategy and Policy Group, Washington, D.C.

Part IV

Enterprise Financing

Improving trust in market-based intermediation will facilitate access to external financing for those enterprises providing the highest value-added, and thereby the largest, contribution to the growth of the economy. Of particular importance in supporting creditors in assessing and selecting enterprises to be financed are those reforms related to improving creditor rights and insolvency practices, and strengthening transparency and disclosure (Part I). Building on these reforms, Part IV describes current practices in enterprise financing and outlines the agenda for further enhancing enterprise access to financing through the capital markets.

Although the small and medium-size enterprises are usually the "engine of growth" in transition economies, the access of this sector to formal financing in Russia remains highly constrained. Chapter 13 describes the relatively poor access to finance of large segments of the Russian enterprise sector. While a narrow segment of larger raw material– producing and exporting enterprises has access to formal bank or capital market financing, many enterprises continue to rely on barter and tax and payment arrears as their predominant sources of working capital.

Essential as capital markets are to longer-term enterprise financing, instilling trust in the Russian capital market will require the fulfillment of a broad agenda and a concerted medium-term effort. As described in Chapter 14, this agenda includes reforming the market for debt issued by the Government; strengthening corporate governance, especially regarding transparency in ownership and control structures; improving the quality of financial information available to enterprise stakeholders; and strengthening supervision and enforcement of supervisory regulations regarding the capital markets.

CHAPTER 13

Enterprise Access to Financing

During the first decade of transition, major changes took place in the fully state-owned Russian enterprise sector. Today there is a small number of very large enterprises, mostly in the export-oriented oil, gas, and metal industries. There are also thousands of large industrial enterprises, primarily in the manufacturing sector, that have their origins in the pre-transition period. Next are the medium-size businesses, a significant number of which are greenfield projects that were started during the transition. Finally, there are hundreds of thousands of small and micro-size companies, and several million individual entrepreneurs, nearly all of whom emerged during the last decade. Notwithstanding the large absolute numbers, the importance of the Russian small and medium-size enterprises in the economy relative to the large companies in terms of value added and employment is still smaller than in Western economies and their peer transition countries.

SMEs are generally a very diverse set of companies with very different operating environments, goals, and constraints. Their financing requirements and sources differ as well. Chapter 13 provides an overview of the principal methods used by SMEs to raise the funds needed for their operations.

COMMERCIAL CREDIT

The Russian Federation presents a unique case among the emerging economies in terms of their structure of enterprise financing. The access of enterprises to external finance has been very limited; many enterprises have had to rely on trade credits of various kinds—usually referred to as "commercial credit" (see Klepach 1999), This term includes overdue accounts payable as well as wage and tax arrears (see Box 13.1). The use of delayed payments as a source of enterprise financing also occurs in other transition economies, but became pronounced in Russia in the late 1990s. The chain reaction of nonpayments that led to high levels of overdue liabilities could have different origins, but this form of financing is particularly prevalent in countries where the state had a significant role in the economy and ran budget deficits.

Although commercial credit, including conventional trade credit, has been the largest source of financing of large and medium-size Russian enterprises for the duration of the transition period, the importance of this source of financing has declined since 1998. This is a positive trend that

---

Box 13.1 Arrears and Noncash Settlements

Tight monetary policy with soft budget constraints led to an increase in arrears and noncash settlements (NCSs) in the second half of the 1990s (see Pinto, Drebentsov, and Morozov 2000). After 1995, inflation decreased rapidly due to tight monetary policy, but the fiscal deficit was not addressed. Instead, inflationary budget financing was replaced with bond financing. This macroeconomic stabilization policy was combined with soft budget constraints for state-owned and recently privatized but nonviable enterprises. Implicit subsidies came in the form of arrears and NCSs for tax and energy payments. The energy monopolies, in turn, became the largest tax delinquents as well as the most important participants in the tax-offset schemes. At the same time, credit tightening and rising interest rates confronted enterprises with a liquidity squeeze that required even larger subsidies. Tax arrears and offsets resulted in an increasing fiscal deficit and rising interest rates. This inconsistency between macroeconomic stabilization and soft budget constraints led to a vicious cycle of nonpayments and eventually to the crisis of 1998. While initially it was only nonviable enterprises that resorted to arrears and NCSs, over time profitable enterprises linked up with nonviable businesses to profit from the system of nonpayments. Overall, soft budget constraints and the resulting nonpayments decreased the incentives for the enterprises to restructure themselves. NCSs and barter distorted prices and thus impeded efficient resource allocation.

Nonpayments have decreased significantly in the last few years, as shown in Table 13.1 and through anecdotal evidence. This can be explained both by cyclical as well as structural changes. First, macroeconomic developments (commodity price increases and the currency devaluation) have led to a remonetization of the economy. Second, structural reforms have started. Hard budget constraints are enforced by the energy monopolies. Since the vicious nonpayment "chain" started with the energy monopolies, the virtual cycle of eliminating nonpayments has had a positive effect on the whole economy. Tax reform has also resulted in better and larger tax collection (although the issue of tax arrears from pre-crisis years seems to continue to threaten the profitability of many companies). There are no longer any tax offsets at the federal level, and even at the regional level they are less prevalent than before.

Table 13.1 The Role of Commercial Credit

	1995	1996	1997	1998	1999	2000
Bank credit to nonfinancial private sector on banks' balance sheets (billions of dollars)	29	28	38	16	19	31
Overdue liabilities of enterprises (billions of dollars)	54	97	131	62	54	59
Net accounts payable (percent of GDP)	8	14	17	22	16	12
Arrears (percent of GDP)	15	23	29	39	30	23
Noncash settlements/sales (percent)	22	35	42	51	51	43

Sources: Solntsev and Khromov 2001; and Pinto, Drebentsov, and Morozov 2000. Updates by the authors.

reflects a move away from large and widespread nonformal indebtedness. Table 13.1 compares the magnitude of nonformal commercial credit with bank lending to the enterprise sector. Total overdue enterprise liabilities exceeded bank credit to the corporate sector by a factor of three to five from 1995 until August 1998, but then declined sharply after the crisis, reflecting increased payments for cash and increased lending by banks. The same profile is reflected in the data for net accounts payable (accounts payable less accounts receivable), which grew steadily from 1.8 percent of GDP in 1993 to 22 percent in 1998, before declining to 12 percent in the year 2000.

The recourse of enterprises to nonformal credit as alternative forms of working capital finance grew rapidly in the years 1995–98. During this period arrears rose from 15 to 39 percent of GDP, and the ratio of noncash settlements to sales rose from 22 percent to 51 percent. After the crisis both these ratios declined quite sharply due to improved payment discipline and improved access to bank financing (see Commander, Dolinskaya, and Mummsen 2000). This could be explained in part by the banks' improved liquidity reflecting Russia's current account surplus, which was only partially sterilized by the CBR. Banks were also more willing to lend to the corporate sector after the 1998 financial crisis, because other sources of earnings—such as investment in high-yielding government paper—were no longer available.

Another important explanation of the decline in noncash payments was changed behavior on the part of the authorities. The Government was among the largest enterprise creditors through enterprise arrears to the budget and nonbudgetary funds. Efforts by the authorities since the crisis to reduce customer indebtedness by utility companies—in the first instance by electricity suppliers—contributed significantly to the increase of cash payments across the country, and to a corresponding reduction in arrears.[1]

BANK FINANCING

During most of the 1990s, and particularly before the financial crisis of 1998, banks did not have strong incentives to develop a program of lending to the enterprise sector. FOREX operations, investments in GKOs, other high-yield securities, and provision of treasury-like products by insider banks to their financial-industrial group parents were the products of choice for the banking system. Not surprisingly, given the relative ease of earning sizable profits from these activities, banks viewed lending in general, and to the SMEs in particular, as a risky activity that required too much effort and provided uncertain rewards. Since the 1998 crisis, banks have turned more to enterprise lending (as outlined in Chapters 6 and 7), and this recent expansion in bank lending has been dominated by lending to larger, well-established enterprises by the state-owned banks. Bank lending continues to take the form of short-term commitments (up to one year, three months on average) with only a very small volume of loans of longer-maturity (up to three years). As a result only a very small share of enterprise investments in fixed assets is financed by bank credit, and most enterprises continue to rely on financing from internal funds (retained earnings).

Bank credit to the private sector is at about the same level in Russia as it is in other Commonwealth of Independent States (CIS) countries but it is less than in the Baltics, and considerably less than in the more advanced Central European economies (see Table 13.2). The reliance of enterprises on internal funding can be explained in part by the large interest spreads required of Russian banks.

Table 13.3 provides a cross-country comparison of the lending-deposit spread for 1998–2000. In addition to regulatory costs imposed on banks, such as reserve requirements, large interest rate spreads reflect the relative inefficiency of the Russian banking sector and point to the need for both greater competition within the sector—resulting in a reduction of the dominance of state-owned banks—and the need for consolidation (see the discussion in Part II of this book).

Russian Accounting Standards provide banks with limited information on enterprise financials and very little disclosure on key components of the structure of enterprise ownership and control (as discussed in Chapter 4). This reduces the appetite of banks to lend to the enterprise sector. There are also tax-related incentives for enterprises not to show their full financial results on their official books. Many businesses see the tax structure and the intrusion of the tax inspectors as factors that prohibit them from using formal financing arrangements—although the importance of

Table 13.2 Credit to Private Sector
(percent of GDP)

	1998	1999	2000
Central Europe and the Baltics			
Czech Republic	58.7	54.3	49.8
Hungary	23.6	27.8	35.4
Slovak Republic	45.9	37.2	30.7
Poland	19.5	23.6	27.8
Estonia	25.3	26.2	26.8
Latvia	14.9	16.7	18.6
Bulgaria	12.7	14.6	15.6
Lithuania	11.3	13.0	11.6
CIS Countries			
Moldova	12.2	10.6	12.7
Ukraine	7.6	8.4	12.6
Russia	**12.8**	**11.5**	**12.3**

Source: International Financial Statistics (IMF), and national statistics.

Table 13.3 Interest Rate Spreads
(lending rate minus deposit rate)

	1998	1999	2000
Central Europe and the Baltics			
Czech Republic	4.7	4.2	3.7
Hungary	3.1	3.1	3.0
Slovak Republic	4.9	6.7	6.4
Poland	6.3	5.7	5.8
Estonia	8.6	4.5	3.9
Latvia	9.0	9.2	7.5
Bulgaria	10.3	9.6	8.4
Lithuania	6.2	8.1	8.3
CIS Countries			
Moldova	9.1	8.0	8.9
Ukraine	32.2	34.2	27.8
Russia	**24.7**	**26.0**	**17.9**

Source: International Financial Statistics (IMF), and national statistics.

these factors will likely recede following the revision of the tax code implemented in 2001. The accounting, disclosure, and tax environments provide enterprises with incentives to sacrifice access to external financing (first of all, bank loans), and survive by (*a*) using internally generated funds, (*b*) drawing on nonformal sources of funds (such as arrears and noncash settlements) or (*c*) borrowing on the gray market—for example, by using financing provided by related counterparts.[2]

VEKSELS

Veksels (short-term interenterprise debt obligations) have played an increasingly important role in corporate financing. The rapid growth of the veksel market took place in tandem with the growth of nonformal finance in the mid-1990s. While in many ways similar to a commercial paper market, settlement for veksels usually takes the form of offsetting transactions—that is, the transfer of corresponding payment obligations. In many cases, veksels were used to avoid tax and to facilitate asset stripping. The veksel market can be divided into "financial" veksels issued by banks and large enterprises to raise funds, and "commodity" veksels issued by industrial companies to be used for mutual offsets with other holders of such veksels.[3] The market pretty much dried up immediately following August 1998, but started to recover soon thereafter. During the last two years it has transformed itself from a market of mostly illiquid papers (heavy on commodity veksels) used mostly for offsets,[4] to a much more liquid and transparent market of fixed-income financial instruments in which almost all new issues are for the purpose of raising short-term cash (three to six months) for financing current operations of enterprises and banks. In part the growth of the veksel market can be considered a substitute for the government securities market that dried up after the 1998 crisis and is still relatively small (for further discussion, see Chapter 14). The transformation of the veksels market would also appear to be closely related to the growth of cash payments among enterprises for their production and services. Cash payments grew from 30 percent of all interenterprise payments in 1997 to around 50 percent in 1999 to over 70 percent in January 2001 (see Table 13.4).

Estimates of the size of the market vary substantially. The financial veksel market is valued at between US$150 million and US$18 billion (between 0.6 and 7.0 percent of GDP), and the nonfinancial, or commodity, veksel market at about US$36 billion (14 percent of GDP). According to IC Region, a brokerage house and an active veksel market

Table 13.4 Structure of Payments for Goods, Works, and Services in Russia
(percent of total payments)

	November 1999	January 2001
Cash	53	75
Veksels	14	7
Mutual offsets	21	10
Barter	8	5
Other types of payments	4	3

Source: IC Region 2001.

participant, during the last few years the financial veksel market has grown from 3 to 4 liquid issues in mid-1999 to some 20 to 30 liquid issues in 2001. Nonetheless, the market remains highly concentrated. Gazprom's veksels alone account for around 60 percent of all outstanding financial veksels. Bank issues (Gazprombank, Sberbank, Sobin Bank, MDM Bank, etc.) account for another 30 percent, with the remainder divided among large companies, such as Tumen Oil, Mezhregiongas, and Norilsk Nickel. IC Region estimates that there are some US$3.3 billion worth of financial veksels currently outstanding in the over-the-counter (OTC) market. Daily turnover ranges from US$80 million to US$115 million, which is similar or higher than the turnover of treasury paper and corporate stocks.

In terms of their position in the narrow universe of bank and enterprise funding sources in Russia, financial veksels are placed between the interbank market that channels very short-term funds among the banks (90 percent of the volume being overnight loans), and the bond market, where funds can be raised with maturities of over one year. Maturities of veksels range between two weeks and one year, with the most popular being three to six months.[5] As suggested by their maturity, veksels are a source for working capital financing. According to participants, veksels are a cheaper source of finance than bank financing, even though veksels are at a disadvantage compared to bank loans or bonds, because veksel interest payments—in contrast to bond coupon and bank loan interest payments—cannot be expensed by the issuers for tax purposes. Veksels are also more popular with investors than bank deposits because collection is relatively easy to enforce.[6] However, the veksel market is currently accessible only to a handful of large financially strong companies whose credit history allows them to borrow more cheaply through veksels than through bank financing.

The financial veksel market remains an OTC market because only the securities registered with the Federal Commission of Securities (FKCB) can be publicly traded on the organized exchange. However, the Association of Veksel Market Participants (AUVER) is developing an organized veksel information and trading system, which includes a common set of standards, including registration and disclosure of information by issuers. Standardization of the OTC market will contribute to the efficiency of the veksel market by reducing risks and transactions costs. According to the new Tax Code, the 0.8 percent veksel registration fee applied to other securities will also be applied to veksels, thus making veksels similar to other securities in terms of their formal status. Standard & Poor's, the rating agency, has started to work in the Russian market and intends to rate veksel issuers. All these steps work toward promoting a more organized veksel market.

LEASING

Given the continuing expansion of the SME sector, leasing companies have shown increasing interest in covering the deficit of longer-term funding to Russian businesses. The legal and knowledge environment for leasing has been developed during the last six to seven years, with close involvement of foreign know-how and fund suppliers, including the International Finance Corporation (IFC), which is active in providing legal advice in this area. The Law on Leasing, adopted in late 1998, regulates the industry, but needs a number of changes in order to make it internally coherent and to bring it into conformity with the Russian Civil Code and several other laws as well as customs legislation. While leasing provides the financier with additional security compared with conventional bank loans (because the asset ownership remains in the possession of a lessor), enforcement of creditor's rights in the case of a lessee's default is nevertheless problematic. A court decision and order are needed to gain physical repossession of a leased asset. This provides opportunities for a lessee—just like in the case of bank loans—to delay the repossession, thereby prompting lessors to seek additional collateral security from a lessee. If leasing is to cover the vacuum in the market for longer-term, fixed-asset debt-financing, these and other legal/enforcement deficiencies will have to be rectified.

Leasing as a source of asset-based financing is picking up, although it still only provides finance for 3 to 5 percent of total capital goods acquisition in Russia, compared to up to 15 percent in some transition countries, and 20 to 30 percent in OECD countries. There are about 1,500 registered leasing companies, with 75 to 100 of them active in the market. In 1999, only one-fifth of all leasing companies (and an even smaller percentage of the active ones) were owned by the banks, with the majority being owned by private nonbank companies, individuals, and regional governments. As a consequence of this ownership structure and, more generally, the very short horizon of the Russian lenders, the main problem is the lessors' access to long-term sources of funding. At the end of 1999, the leasing industry was estimated to have US$400 million to US$800 million in total assets. The wide range of this estimate is due to differences in the treatment of some leases, which are one-off lease-buyback deals within FIGs. These leasing companies/subsidiaries are established exclusively for one deal.

OTHER FINANCING INSTRUMENTS

Factoring and forfeiting activities are currently almost nonexistent. The popularity of using consignment as the basis for many trade deals among the Russian counterparts and the very short history and uncertain creditworthiness of the majority of Russian enterprises have prevented faster development of factoring in Russia. Warehouse receipts to a very limited extent serve the function of discounting receivables. Warehouse receipts are a new financial instrument, currently trading in a very thin informal market. They are issued by certified warehouses to an owner of the goods kept in the warehouses. The receipts then can be traded as short-term securities. Only the easily marketable goods, such as grain, oil, coal, and similar commodities can be used as a "collateral" for the warehouse receipts. Although efforts were made to strengthen the legal foundation for warehouse receipts, this legislation has not yet been enacted.[7]

Currently bond and equity markets are used as a method of raising funds only by the largest Russian blue-chip companies. In the medium term the growth of the capital market will be crucial to sustained growth in the provision of finance to the enterprise sector. Following the initial facilitation of the privatization process, capital market development in Russia has been slow. Reforms designed to stimulate the development of the capital market are further discussed in Chapter 14.

CONCLUSION

Given the lack of transparency and disclosure related to Russian enterprises, lending to the enterprise sector is still perceived by creditors as a risky endeavor. The lack of long-term funding sources coupled with inadequate longer-term lending and credit analysis skills also contribute to the failure of the financial system to supply the private sector with various lending products. Overdue payables and arrears have been and still are important sources of credit. Only a handful of large, usually exporting companies have relatively easy access to bank and capital market financing (veksels, bonds, and stocks) both in Russia and internationally using syndicate loans, eurocredits, and placement of stocks abroad. The vast majority of larger enterprises continue to rely on internal funds, payables, and arrears, and to a small extent bank (short-) term financing as the primary sources of funds for sustaining and advancing their operations.

In Western economies large banks have been changing their attitude towards SMEs, with the SMEs becoming one of the more important group of clients in their banking operations. This may be due to competition from the rapidly deepening and globalizing capital markets, which allow more and more (typically large) companies to raise funds through bonds, stocks, and similar vehicles rather than the traditional bank loans (for example, securitization). Seeing their interest income, as a proportion of the total income, falling over a number of years, British, Dutch, German, French, and other banks are hard pressed to find new clients for their lending business. This development also reflects the growth of credit-scoring techniques, which have improved the capacity of banks to assess, monitor, and diversify SME credit risks. Thus, challenged by the growth of capital markets, Western banks have developed a wide array of flexible financing products to SMEs, including risk finance (such as convertible subordinated loans), as well as soft loans[8] and lower banking fees for start-ups. Banks also set up special-purpose funds that provide equity (including seed capital) to young enterprises.

It is unrealistic to expect that all large Russian enterprises will graduate soon from bank financing and rely solely on capital markets for their external financing means, which would prompt the banks to look for new clients down the corporate hierarchy line. The large Russian firms will remain desirable clients of the banks for a foreseeable future. Expansion of SME access to bank financing in Russia will thus depend on a number of factors, including the speed of saturation of the large corporate lending market and the growth of the banks' deposit base. It can be expected that even in the medium term, trade finance and internal funds will remain the primary sources of funds for the SME sector.

One of the major reasons for underperformance of the Russian banking sector as an effective channel of private savings to the real sector has been the lack of a proper credit culture throughout the economy. While bigger and financially stronger enterprises may see banks competing for their business, even these successful lenders indicate that the credit they provide is less in volume and worse in terms (higher interest rates, shorter maturities, larger collateral, etc.) than they could otherwise provide, had there been a safer legal and contract enforcement environment. There are positive examples of Russian banks working efficiently and profitably with small businesses and individual entrepreneurs, although this does require astute management of credit risks. Box 13.2 provides some examples of international financial institutions using safeguards to manage credit risks related to on-lending operations through Russian banks.

Absence of a proper credit culture prevents the flow of private savings to financial intermediaries and further to the real sector of the economy.

Box 13.2 Safeguards in Managing Credit Risks

Both the World Bank and the European Bank for Reconstruction and Development have experience in administering credit lines in Russia. On the whole the experience with these credit lines demonstrates that credit risks can be managed with minimal losses, even in an environment where the institutional and legal framework is weak. This does, however, require that certain safeguards are in place. In the case of the micro-credits provided by the EBRD, these safeguards include providing technical assistance in the form of long-term credit advisers. While the World Bank also provided services to the banks to support the upgrading of their institutional capacity, the Bank relied predominantly on close prior technical review of the individual subprojects. This technical review process included clear guidelines, as illustrated below.

- Related/connected party loans should be avoided, unless they are made on an arm's-length basis; otherwise they are losses by definition.
- If local governments are to extend guarantees to the lenders in cases of socially important projects, such loan-securing guarantees must have the appropriate approval of the local legislature and must be supported by clearly assigned assets.
- To properly secure a credit, cash-generating assets should be identified, discounted, and pledged. These assets usually take the form of machinery and equipment or real estate and buildings/constructions, depending on what is being financed. Legislation permits creditors to secure their rights based on the provisions of pledge agreements, and does not require court procedures for foreclosing the collateral—as long as the pledge agreement is fully documented and the bank has undertaken full due diligence regarding the terms of the pledge.
- Cash flow created by a borrower and its affiliates should be "locked" for debt repayment. For this purpose, and in addition to adequate collateral, such instruments as personal guarantees of the major owners and top managers and corporate guarantees of the companies related to the borrower should be provided.

Good practice requires creditors to keep distinct within their organizational structure the responsibilities for proper appraisal, documentation, and sale of collateral, in the case of nonperformance of loans; banks should also ensure, for their self-interest, that collateral is always duly documented in accordance with Russian legislation.

As outlined in Chapter 2, Russian banks would lend more and cheaper funds to enterprises for a longer period of time if they were more certain that, in the case of a borrower's default, their legitimate secured claims would be enforced with minimum headache and possibility of losses to the lenders. The burden of proof should fall on the debtor. Enforcement procedures should be simple and quick to allow creditors to obtain expeditious recoveries of the impaired assets.

ENDNOTES

1. Electricity suppliers were given a clear mandate by the authorities to reduce their accounts receivable and increase cash collections for the electricity by the users, which in turn triggered the business users to increase cash collections from their customers. See also Box 13.1.

2. These can be family and friends for smaller companies; medium-size companies may receive short-term financing from their financially stronger customers or peer enterprises belonging to the loosely organized informal business groupings.

3. For instance, a customer of a company-veksel issuer would purchase the veksels at a discount with an expectation to use them for paying the issuing company for its production.

4. Veksels are used to facilitate offsets when one party trades an obligation (e.g., taxes due) to satisfy a debt owed by another party.

5. Gazprom even issues two-year veksels.

6. According to anecdotal evidence, veksels have to be protested formally through a notary public before they are sent to a judge. Bailiffs then enforce them. Although there are legal ways for the issuer to prevent immediate enforcement, veksels are reported to be more easily enforceable than other credit instruments.

7. A proposed federal law was rejected by the Federation Council in 2001. As of early 2002 a joint Duma and Federation Council commission was on the process of redrafting the law to reflect the changes proposed by the Federation Council.

8. Available through different schemes involving government support, or cooperation among banks and industry associations, chambers of commerce, etc.

REFERENCES

Commander, Simon, Irina Dolinskaya, and Christian Mummsen. 2000 October. "Determinants of Barter in Russia: An Empirical Analysis." Working Paper No. 00/155. IMF European II Department Series, Washington, D.C.

IC Region (Investment Company Region). 2001. Website: www.regnm.ru.

IMF (International Monetary Fund). International Financial Statistics. Website: www.IMF.org.

Klepach, Andrei. 1999. "Russian Economy on the Verge of Growth or Stagnation?" Institute of Economic Forecasting of the Russian Academy of Sciences, Moscow.

Pinto, Brian, Vladimir Drebentsov, and Alexander Morozov. 2000. "Dismantling Russia's Nonpayments System: Creating Conditions for Growth." Technical Paper No. 471. World Bank, Washington, D.C.

Solntsev, O., and M. Khromov 2001. "Banking system in 2000–2001: Trends and Perspectives." Center for Macroeconomic Analysis and Short-Term Forecasting. Institute of Economic Forecasting of the Russian Academy of Sciences. Moscow. Website: www.forecast.ru/_archive/analitics/Banks/ForBanks.asp.

CHAPTER 14

Capital Market Development

Since the beginning of the transition, considerable progress has been made in establishing the foundation for the Russian capital market. While market activity and capitalization suffered from the financial crisis in 1998, the market architecture—institutions and technical infrastructure—have proven to be robust. A network of regional stock exchanges has been established. Trading systems for stock, bonds, and foreign exchange have been established and are well-tested. Share registries and depositories now generally maintain reliable and accessible records. Regulatory authorities with responsibility for supervising various parts of the capital market are in place. More recently the authorities have also turned their attention to the complex tasks of upgrading regulatory enforcement and introducing improved corporate governance practices. Although much has been achieved during the first decade of transition, there still is a considerable outstanding agenda because of the complex nature of capital market transactions. The purpose of this chapter is to describe the major components of this agenda.

THE MASS PRIVATIZATION PROGRAM

Capital market development in Russia originated with the Mass Privatization Program that began in Russia in 1992. Rather than developing the capital market, the primary objective of this program was to facilitate the transfer of ownership in business enterprises from the state to the private sector. It was expected that the new owners would promote restructuring and good governance in ways that would maximize their returns. It was also assumed that the laws and regulations for governing commercial and financial markets would be developed and applied quickly in order to create an enabling environment for a free market economy. As far as development of the capital market was concerned, the Russian privatization experience was a mixed blessing for the following reasons:

1. As a result of the exercise of the second of three privatization options (51 percent to management and worker's collectives), majority control passed to existing insiders, many of whom had no interest in delivering value to anyone but themselves. An average of up to 65 percent of the shares of privatized companies were under insider control, and only 22 percent were in the hands of external shareholders (Pistor and Spicer 1997).
2. The vouchers were in bearer form, enabling large investors with cash to acquire vouchers from citizens, and hence significant stakes in enterprises, at low prices.
3. Many larger enterprises, particularly in the commodity sectors, were held back for strategic reasons, but were later acquired in 1996 by financial and industrial groups via the loans-for-shares scheme. Government still owns more than 25 percent of the equity in more than 2,500 joint stock companies, and a golden share in an additional 580 companies. This may have had a direct effect on the diminution of net worth of these companies (OECD 2001).

Thus although the privatization effort was meant to spread the ownership to many, it actually concentrated the ownership into the hands of management. This concentration has been the source of many of the ills in the Russian economy. The command economy had been dismantled without being replaced by the basic elements of a law-based economy, and the necessary underpinnings of a market economy had not yet been put in place. The following were some of the missing structural elements: an adequate legislative base to define the rights of owners, creditors, and shareholders, and the fiduciary duties of directors; the ability to enforce ownership rights and contracts in the courts, where decisions often went in the direction of the most powerful litigant; effective supervision—that is, the state control mechanisms that previously had been able to insist on compliance within a command economy, were totally unsuited to a market economy; and a fully operational banking and payments system.

Due to lack of an adequate foundation, outside shareholders had no means to insist on good governance; creditors had no means to seize collateral in the event of defaults; and widespread abuses in corporate governance occurred. Some of the salient abuses of corporate governance are asset stripping (sales of assets to companies controlled by family and friends at prices far below current market values); transfer pricing (sales of products at "fire-sale" prices to affiliated intermediaries, who then resold the products worldwide at attractive prices); and share dilution (issuance of new shares to dilute the voting rights of current shareholders).

The new owner-managers had little enthusiasm to restructure their enterprises, and were able to find few sources of outside finance available. Privatized enterprises at best stagnated; at worst, became insolvent.

At the same time, the Government's budget deficit remained at around 7 percent of GDP from 1995 to 1997, with consolidated government expenditure remaining at around 44 percent. Unable to raise adequate revenue from taxes, the Government was forced to turn to borrowing in the market at ever-increasing real rates of interest. Even at their lowest rates, in 1997, yields on government paper averaged 25 percent to 30 percent, despite a fall in inflation to 15 percent. Banks borrowed heavily in foreign markets to finance their speculative activities in the government bond market. The culmination of this process was the default by the Government on its domestic debt in August 1998, which together with a weakening ruble, virtually destroyed the banking system and shattered the confidence of investors in the capital market, both foreign and domestic.

Financing Void

Missteps with the privatization program led to the present financing void; external financing of the Russian private sector is now largely nonexistent. The following are some outcomes of that void:

1. Many of the internally generated earnings were stripped from enterprises by new owners, which left many companies as just husks.
2. Banks did not develop as significant providers of short-term finance, except to the Government and to the enterprises within their circle.
3. The corporate bond markets were initially crowded out by the Government's borrowing program and subsequently by the inability to identify and enforce collateral obligations—only during 2001 did several Russian companies start issuing corporate bonds.
4. The market for government debt has not yet been restored following the 1998 crisis.
5. Equity markets are a complement rather than a substitute for these other forms of finance; they were simply unable to function in isolation following the crisis.

The scale of the financing void is illustrated in Table 14.1, which compares the size of markets for bank finance, debt, and equity in different countries. It demonstrates clearly the sheer lack of scale of the Russian financial markets as a source of finance for both Government and the private sector, even compared with other transition countries. The formal financial sector in Russia is still very small.

As the Russian economy continues to recover from the 1998 crisis, enterprises will have to rely more on outside finance than they have in the past. The failure to create an efficient system of financing enterprises in which lenders and investors will have the confidence to lend to or invest in third parties will severely curtail the ability of entrepreneurial and well-managed companies to grow. Indeed, if Russian enterprises are to expand effectively, they cannot continue to rely on internally generated funds and short-term borrowing (see Figure 14.1).

Due to their reliance on debt financing, Russian enterprises are vulnerable to sudden changes in interest rates, especially as enterprise debt is very short-term. As of December 2000, more than 80 percent of total loans outstanding to enterprises had maturities of less than one year, and

Table 14.1 Financial Market Depth, 2000

Country	M2 (Money and Quasi-Money) US$ billions	% of GDP	Bank Claims on Private Sector US$ billions	% of GDP	Total Bonds* US$ billions	% of GDP	Total Equity US$ billions	% of GDP
Russia	55	22	31	12	9	4	39	16
Czech Republic	37	76	25	50	8	15	11	23
Hungary	20	44	11	26	13	28	12	26
Slovak Republic	18	94	6	31	2	13	1	4
Poland	68	41	41	26	20	12	31	19
France	656	51	942	73	716	55	1,475	114
Germany	1,179	63	2,280	122	1,178	63	1,432	76
Italy	599	56	775	72	941	88	728	68
The Netherlands**	326	89	501	137	197	54	695	190
United Kingdom	1,570	111	1,899	134	565	40	2,933	207
Japan	5,797	126	5,175	112	4,967	108	4,547	99
United States	6,084	61	4,846	49	10,768	108	16,635	168

*Bonds are defined as debt securities with maturities of greater than one year. Total bonds comprise government bonds and corporate bonds. For all developed countries and Russia, bonds data are as of September 2000.
**Data for the Netherlands are for bank claims on the private sector for all residents of the Euro Area.
Sources: IFC Emerging Markets Bonds Electronic Database; IFC Securities Market Development Group Database-2001; IMF—International Financial Statistics (IFS) January 2001; IMF—IFS Electronic Database (SIMA); BIS Quarterly Review, March 2001; IMF—Report on Post Program Monitoring Discussions; Deutsche Bundesbank Monthly Report—April 2001; EIU—Country Profiles—Russia (2000); Central Bank of Russia electronic database.

Figure 14.1 Sources of Corporate Finance in Russia
(percentage of respondents using various financing forms)

[Bar chart showing Equity (~20%), Debt financing (~60%), Internally generated (~90%)]

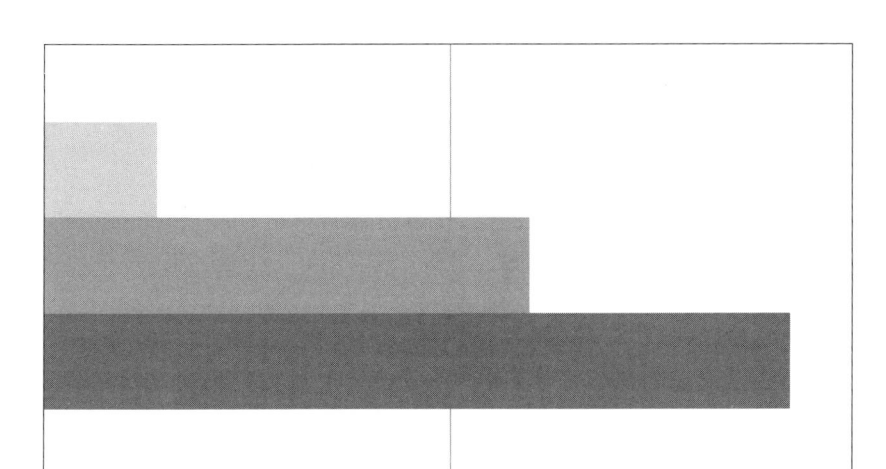

Source: Russian Corporate Governance Round Table 2000.

less than 7 percent had maturities of more than three years. As a result of these developments, a number of directors have more recently shown a willingness to seek outside finance; but of those who were interested, 76 percent said that they could not find ways to raise the capital they needed (see Figure 14.2).

It may be that the respondents were unaware of the complexities of raising money through capital markets or unwilling to entertain the potential dilution of their controlling interests, which usually results from issues of new equity to outsiders. However, there are signs that enterprises are becoming more interested in outside finance, since in 1996 only 19 percent of surveyed companies were interested in raising money through private placement of new issues of shares, and only 17 percent were interested in public offerings.

Much of the supporting technical infrastructure required to support the capital market has been created: banks exist, as do stock exchanges, foreign exchange and commodity markets, together with their associated clearing, settlement, and registration procedures. However, turning the capital market into a reliable financing mechanism for industry and commerce will require implementation of further reforms.

While there is strong evidence of a correlation between economic growth and the development of financial markets in general,[1] there is less strong evidence that a bank-based or market-based financial system produces a better result. In Caprio and Honohan's *Finance for Growth* (2001), the authors comment, "A radical preference in favor either of markets or of banks cannot be justified by the extensive evidence now available. Instead, development of different segments of the financial system challenge the other segments to innovate, to improve efficiency, and to lower prices."

It is noticeable, however, that countries that have had the strongest bank-based systems, Germany and France, are moving increasingly toward more capital market–based systems. This may be influenced by the Anglo-American model, which tends to be more market-based. The Japanese or Korean model, on the other hand, tends to be more capital

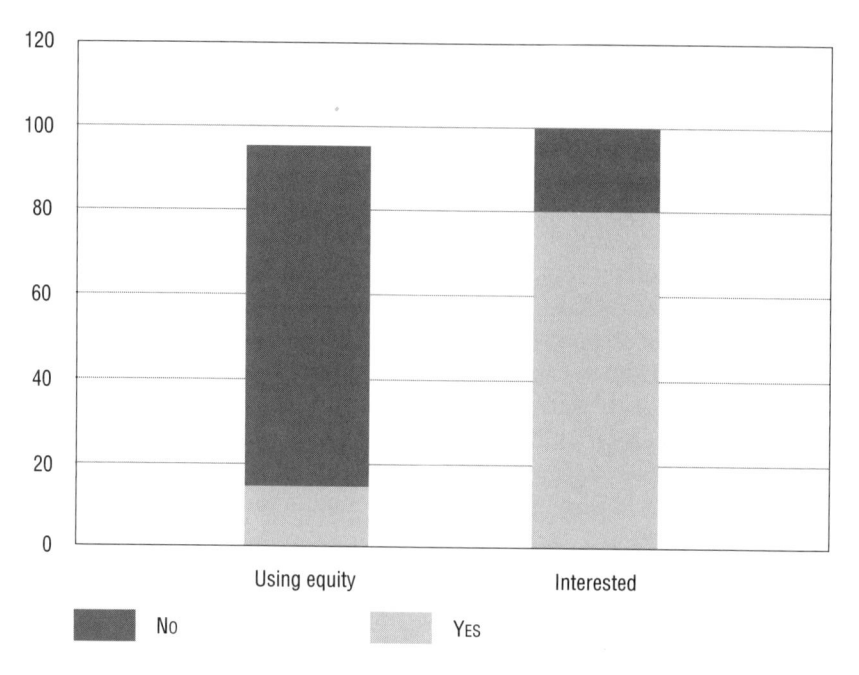

Figure 14.2 Enterprise Use of Equity Finance
(percentage of respondents using equity finance)

Source: Russian Corporate Governance Round Table 2000.

market–based and features a series of cross-ownership of companies within *zaibatsu* or *chaebols* (similar to Russian FIGs). When these systems failed, they left the banking system in both countries virtually insolvent.

Regardless of whether a system is bank-based or capital market–based, there is evidence that "the proportion of firms that grow at rates that cannot be self-financed is positively related to development of both the securities markets and the banking system" (Demirgüç-Kunt and Maksimovic 2000).

Does Russia need to develop its own capital market? It is hard to believe that any country looking to maintain an independent exchange rate can move ahead without a domestic capital market—the void would compel borrowers and issuers, including the Government itself, to seek all their financing abroad. Even though large companies can and do raise money in international markets, medium-size companies will still need a more accessible—and cheaper—domestic market to serve their needs. Equally important, investing institutions will need domestic instruments in which to invest, unless a country adopts the U.S. dollar as its currency and all exchange controls are dismantled.

Weak Corporate Governance and Law Enforcement

One of the most important reasons that investors are hesitant to invest in or lend to enterprises has been Russia's notable failure in the area of corporate governance. The inability to rely on enforcing rights either as shareholders or as lenders has been exacerbated by the opaque structures of many companies and the inadequate disclosure of financial data by them. Table 14.2 illustrates why the Russian enterprises have been unable to attract outside investors.

The lack of trust in Russia's corporate governance has been evidenced by the inability of the courts to enforce commercial contracts, the unwillingness of banks to lend to any but known customers within their affiliated

Table 14.2 Reasons for Inability to Attract Outside Investors

Reason	%
Past violations of shareholder rights	95
Unfriendly attitude of local authorities toward investors	86
Absence of independent directors	67
Close relations with FIGs	57

Source: Russian Corporate Governance Round Table 2000.

group, reluctance (or inability) of investors to engage in the management of the companies in which they might invest, and unwillingness of the small savers to place funds with banks and other savings institutions.

Policy Designed to Restore Trust

There are many signs that the Government and the private sector are becoming more fully aware of the defects that will continue to hamper economic revival if they are not tackled and corrected. These changes need to be far more fundamental than merely tinkering with capital market mechanisms or inventing new instruments.

One of the key indicators of this new awareness is the program prepared by the new Government in 2000, based on the vision provided by the so-called Gref Plan. The Gref Plan recommends that general policy objectives should be as follows:

> Only the rapid development of national capital, the establishment of a favorable business climate, and efforts to ensure economic freedom will make Russia a country that is appealing for investment. Starting conditions for shaping an effective economic system and a favorable business climate include affirmation of the rights of private ownership (primarily of land and real estate), the protection of these rights, the creation of equal terms of competition, and the development of stable and effective financial institutions. The Government must also strike an optimal balance in mutual relations with private enterprise by gradually abandoning the practice of excessive intervention in business affairs. This, in turn, will make it possible to clearly demarcate the sphere of Government regulation and enhance its effectiveness.

REFORM OF THE RUSSIAN BANKING AND PAYMENTS SYSTEM

No capital market can operate efficiently, if at all, without a banking system. The banking system in Russia is small in absolute and relative terms and underdeveloped relative to countries with similar per capita income. Underscoring low public confidence in the financial system is the fact that a large amount of savings is held outside the financial system in hard currency.

Without a functioning banking and payments system, contributions cannot be made to pensions, insurance, or savings schemes; payments of pensions, insurance policy proceeds, dividends, or interest cannot be made; settlements cannot be reliably made for purchases or sales of assets; and temporary liquidity cannot be safely held. Reform of the Russian banking and payments system is critical to the ability of capital markets to function reliably and effectively and to encourage broader participation by the Russian public. Without a functioning banking and payment system, participants in the capital market will lack confidence that investment rewards will be received at a reasonable cost and within a reasonable period.

DEVELOPING THE GOVERNMENT DEBT MARKET

The development of capital markets depends to a large degree on the development of an efficient and trusted market for sovereign debt. Inefficient government debt issuance creates a series of problems for capital markets. First, sovereign debt provides a risk-free asset for banks to invest in. A dearth of such assets lessens confidence in the banking system. Second, a well-functioning sovereign debt market acts as a benchmark for corporate debt issuance and provides a basis for stock exchange and OTC market development. Third, sovereign debt provides a risk-free asset for pension funds and insurance companies to match their liabilities and against which they can measure returns from other asset classes.

While the current fiscal position of the Russian federal Government is strong, institutional and policy problems continue to prevent the Russian Federation from restoring its credit rating (currently B–), according to Standard & Poor's rating agency. Some of these factors are more technical and can be addressed with prompt institutional reform measures. However, a protracted period of good performance, which would allow everybody to forget about past experiences, is the only effective solution. The Government should make visible efforts to enhance its debt management practices and communicate that enhancement to market participants.

Several weaknesses in sovereign debt management, which played an important role in triggering the sovereign default of August 1998, still remain to be addressed. The following are key aspects of improving debt management practices:

1. Closer coordination between monetary, fiscal, and debt management policies
2. Switching from the short-term focus to a strategic focus in sovereign debt management, improving coordination between issuance of external and domestic debt

3. Improving treasury cash management procedures
4. Enhancing transparency in government borrowing policy
5. Strengthening portfolio risk management, improving controls on the borrowing operations of local Governments and state-owned enterprises
6. Installing better data management facilities to support decision-making and investor relations.

During the 1990s, new debt management units were created in response to the emerging need to manage sovereign domestic and foreign debt policies, to manage foreign and domestic debt market sales and redemptions, to manage the Treasury's cash position, etc. However, as a result of this organic growth, the management of the Government's liabilities became fragmented, coordination among the units and agencies involved was inadequate, and their mandates overlapped. State liability management is still organized in the Ministry of Finance by product and not by function, as suggested by best international practice. Scenario analysis suggests that the debt situation in Russia, while tense, is far from catastrophic. It is set to improve in the absence of new shocks. Under the assumption that Russia's export growth slows down after its spectacular performance in 1999–2000, and stabilizes at a modest 2 percent in 2001–04, Russia's debt-to-GDP ratio is projected to decline below 50 percent after 2001, which indicates a fairly stable and improving solvency position. Russia's liquidity situation is also projected to remain stable under this conservative growth scenario. If structural reform progresses faster, and Russia succeeds in diversifying its exports beyond the energy sector, the debt ratios will decline even more quickly. However, should exports decline significantly—were oil prices to drop to $20–$22 per barrel and structural reforms to stall—the debt situation would deteriorate again. Under this scenario the external liquidity problem would reemerge.

In 2000, Russia's external debt stood at 74 percent of its GDP—a high, but not critical level if judged from the long-term solvency perspective. Countries with less abundant and diversified resource bases than Russia have been known to carry debt burdens in excess of 100 percent of GDP without interrupting their debt service payments. However, in the short term, the regularity of debt service payments may be affected by a particularly disadvantageous profile of debt payments ("bunching" of large amounts of payments in a short period of time, which sharply increases the refinancing risk). Even if a country were solvent over the long term, it may experience serious short-term problems with servicing its debts.

In 2000 the MoF started working on a new government debt management strategy, which is built around the idea of creating an independent debt management agency. This project, although still in the design stage, is probably the most important part of the work needed to restore the government debt market. Only by consolidating all the information needed to enable one agency to have a full overview of outstanding debt and the responsibility for managing it can real progress be made to restore Russian sovereign debt as an investment instrument.

From the perspective of private sector issuers, in industrial as well as transition countries, a government debt market is vital for a number of reasons apart from the need for the Government to finance itself:

1. The establishment of a risk-free benchmark rate and a well-defined yield curve against which issuers may price corporate debt issues
2. The credit rating of government debt will affect the rating of corporate issuers
3. The trading and settlement facilities for government debt can also be used for corporate debt
4. The absence of a market for government securities will inhibit the development of institutional investors such as pension funds, insurance companies, and mutual funds, all of which need to be able to invest in a risk-free asset class.

Government debt stands at the top of the asset classes that are available in developed markets, and if the market for government debt is inefficient, it is unlikely that other asset classes will flourish. The choice of domestic securities to be issued should be geared to offer a predictable supply of standardized securities, to facilitate the activities of dealers ready to place securities with nonfinancial investors, and to support some selected points of the yield curve. Contrary to what had been the case in Russia prior to August 1998, the regular issue of a limited number of standardized securities would be advisable. It is also important that the MoF develop refinancing techniques to manage the bunching of maturities and smooth its cash position.

A strategy should be developed to better cope with the eventual recurrence of serious market turbulence. Issuing, for as long as necessary and under a regular schedule, some very short-term T-bills (mainly four-week, but also one-week if necessary) would be one component of such a strategy. Auction procedures should be geared to maximum transparency, leaving as little scope to discretion as possible so that maximum auction participation is encouraged and the Government is perceived to be fully transparent in its efforts to finance its own activities and support the development of financial markets.

Once primary issuance has been improved and confidence has been restored, additional work will be needed to support the development of secondary trading.

Government Debt—Recommendations

There is no doubt that public debt management is a crucial area of public policy. A strategy needs to be developed to address the following points:
1. A clear debt strategy should be formulated and supported by strong analytical capacity and with a requirement that the decision-making process become transparent.
2. Close coordination between internal and external debt management is needed within a single debt management office.
3. The legal foundation for sovereign debt issuance should be strengthened, clearly identifying the rights and obligations of issuers and purchasers.
4. Investment should be made in a computerized and standardized debt information system.
5. A cadre of skilled debt management professionals should be trained and sustained.

MOBILIZING SAVINGS

While there is no lack of savings and investable funds available within the Russian market, the mobilization of these savings is undermined by lack of trust. The challenge facing the Government is to find ways to channel these funds into the formal financial markets, both for banking products and securities.

In trying to stimulate investment in securities, investor compensation schemes have been considered from time to time. These are complex and difficult to devise without exposing the Government or the financial services industry to open-ended commitments. While compensation schemes may help to restore trust, in the long run only the existence of demonstrably honest and competent financial institutions will attract investments.

The Government has also embarked on creating a mandatory "second-pillar" pension fund. Significant volumes of funds would become available to the market if such schemes were organized so that the funds were invested on the domestic market. An important concern here is that the capital market is not yet ready to receive such large flows. The success of such schemes depends on there being a sufficient number of reliable investments in which to place accumulated funds. The danger is that the "elephant in the swimming pool" effect might be created, such as in Kazakhstan, where mandatory second-pillar schemes, introduced in 1998, have reached a value of $1 billion, and there are simply not enough instruments in which the funds can invest. This has had the effect of driving down yields on bonds to unreasonably low levels.

Creating pension schemes requires a great deal of work—actuarial, legislative, and regulatory—and, although the Duma has passed a Law on Mandatory Cumulative Financing of Pensions in the Russian Federation, much more work on detailed regulations and implementation remains to be done. The law stipulates that the state will be the primary administrator of the scheme but outside asset managers and custodians will be used.

As of October 1, 2001, there were 372 licensed nonstate pension funds with a value of around US$970 million.[2] The five largest funds accounted for around 60 percent of total assets.

At the end of March 2001, there were 39 investment funds in operation, of which 22 were open-ended and 17 were of the closed-end type. There were a total of 35 licensed management companies, but only 24 were actually operating funds. The total value of these investment funds is around $212 million.[3]

The Law on Investment Funds, approved in late 2001, is considered very important by the securities industry, as well as the Federal Commission for Securities Markets, as laying the foundation for more widespread savings mobilization.

Recommendations for Mobilizing Savings

While various measures are under discussion presently—such as tax incentives to invest in funds or other assets, and mandatory second-pillar pensions—the problem remains that successful investing in such institutions is dependent upon the availability of good quality assets to buy. These initiatives would contribute significantly to the pool of savings and could stimulate the issuance of new securities. Thus, it is important that the reforms suggested in this chapter be adopted so as to build confidence in the Russian capital market—ensuring that assets acquired by investing institutions are of good quality and that savers earn reasonable and reliable returns.

IMPROVING CORPORATE GOVERNANCE

The result of poor corporate governance practices in Russia has been seen in the reluctance of foreign investors to provide new equity or debt capital to the Russian corporate sector after the crisis of August 1998. For example, as of September 1999, the market capitalization of one major Russian oil company was less than one percent of western competitors (Black 2001). By the end of 2001, the company's market capitalization was almost seven percent of western competitors.

The scorecard in Table 14.3—developed by the World Bank—analyzes the current state of corporate governance in Russia. Despite weak corporate governance practices, there are several recent measures (common business practices and legal and institutional reforms) that have helped to strengthen corporate governance in Russia. The measures include election of independent directors,[4] accessibility to company charters, an initiative by the FCSM to introduce a code of corporate conduct for directors, codification of liability for members of boards of directors as well as company managers, development of private sector–initiated ratings and scoring services on companies' corporate governance practices, and emergence of a corporate bond market. Work already in progress on corporate governance issues includes work on the Joint Stock Companies Law and Securities Law summarized in Table 14.3.

Recommendations for Corporate Governance

The two priority areas under corporate governance are (1) to increase transparency of the ownership and control structures of corporations and (2) to improve the quality of financial information made available to investors and other stakeholders.

Clarification of the ownership position of a company's major shareholders would provide other stakeholders—minority investors, creditors, workers, and even the government tax collectors and FCSM—with the needed information on which to make decisions for investing time and capital in the company. Furthermore, full disclosure of ownership positions would give stakeholders (and particularly investors) the important information needed to understand the motivation of company managers and controlling shareholders as they present their corporate restructuring plans. The Securities Law requires that investors with 20 percent or more of a company's shares must disclose their holdings, and the Law on Joint Stock Companies obliges companies to maintain (and make available to shareholders) lists of affiliated persons. However, even for large

Table 14.3 Corporate Governance Scorecard for Russia

Market and Regulatory Overview		Remarks
Market capitalization (percent of GDP)		$52 billion (20% of GDP)
Number of listed companies on stock exchange	102	246 companies traded on RTS (largest trading system in Russia)
Legal system (origin)		Civil law
Judicial system	Weak	Considered open to corruption and abuse
Publication in English of company laws, listing requirements	Yes	Company laws available through commercial services, listing requirements on internet
Powers of the capital markets regulator	Weak	Can suspend securities issue, delist securities. Limited ability to sanction
Regulator established by special law	Yes	
Stock exchange and other trading floors	Yes	RTS, Micex, other exchanges and trading floors in Moscow
Cross shareholdings by companies and banks restricted	No	No restrictions on cross-holdings, but financial industrial groups are required to register as FIGs
Shareholders' Rights		
One share, one vote	Yes	One-share, one-vote required for all common shares
Proxy (mail-in) voting permitted	Yes	Voting by proxy permitted, including mail-in voting
Cumulative (rather than proportional) voting mandatory for board of directors	Yes	Mandatory for companies with 1,000+ shareholders; optional for others
Quorum requires at least 50% of shares	Yes	But if not achieved, second meeting requires only 30%. Companies with 500,000+ shareholders may set by charter lower quorum for second meeting.
Super-majority shareholder approval to amend company charter	No	Decisions made by 3/4 of shares *participating* at shareholders' meeting i.e., with quorum at 30%, decisions can be made by just 22.5% of shares.
Super-majority approval for asset transfers/increase in charter capital	No	25 to 50% of company's asset book value can be transferred by unanimous decision of board of directors. Larger assets require approval of shareholders' meeting. Capital may be increased by up to 25% by unanimous approval of board of directors, if charter so permits. Larger increases require approval of 3/4 of shares participating at shareholders' meeting.
Right to call extraordinary shareholders' meeting	Yes	Shareholders with 10%+ of voting shares may call extraordinary meeting.
Shareholder right to add to meeting agenda	Yes	2% of shares can propose items for the agenda of shareholders' meeting.
Disclosure of shareholder list	Yes	Available to shareholders with 1% of shares.
Redress against violations on minority	Yes	Derivative suits legally possible but never used. No workable mechanisms of class action to protect interests of unspecified number of shareholders.
Take-over code	Yes	But limited to a single article in Law on Joint Stock Companies.

(Table continues on next page)

Table 14.3 *(continued)*

Market and Regulatory Overview		Remarks
Mandatory tender offer in change of control	No	But must offer to buy remaining shares after purchase of 30% of shares.
Prohibition of deals using insider trading/code of ethics encouraged	No	Law on Securities has general prohibition on deals using insider trading, but no monitoring mechanisms available. No codes of ethics in place.
Preemptive rights	Yes	Only applicable to open share subscriptions. For closed share subscriptions, preemptive rights available to shareholders not voting at meeting or voting against the share issue.
Independent registrars	Yes	Mandatory if company has 50+ registered shareholders.
Oversight of Management		
Clearly defined role for board members	Yes	Some definition in Joint Stock Company Act. Company charter may include more definition.
Independent directors required	No	The law does not require independent directors, but limits executive management to less than 25% of the board of directors.
Disclosure of board members	Yes	Names of board members required under Securities Law to be specified in the prospectus and in quarterly reports.
Periodic election of board members	Yes	At annual shareholders' meeting
Audit committee required	No	Revision commission required but is not part of the board of directors.
Minimum training/experience of board members	No	None required
Disclosure and Transparency		
Disclosure of ownership/control structure	Partial	Shareholders must disclose direct holdings of 20%+ of shares and companies must keep lists of affilated parties. But there is no requirement for disclosure of indirect shareholdings under the securities legislation.
Annual independent audit	Partial	
External auditors approved by shareholders	Yes	But annual compensation approved by board of directors
Public availability of company audits	Yes	
Compliance with ISA	Partial	Auditing law close to ISA
Compliance with IAS	No	Major differences from IAS. No write-off of obsolete inventory or bad debt. Assets listed at cost (not fair market value). No disclosure of guarantees.
Consolidated statements	Yes	
Disclosure of related-party transactions	No	
Company officers–related disclosures	Yes	Disclosed in prospectus and quarterly reports
Disclosure of price-sensitive information	No	
Risk management disclosures	No	
Public availability of company charters	Yes	Companies legally obliged to provide, but sometimes difficult to obtain

publicly listed and actively traded companies, there are no effective requirements for disclosure of ultimate shareholding and control structures, thus requiring that minority shareholders and other stakeholders rely on information available through foreign listings, or on rumors in the marketplace. In particular, the commonly used structure of "floating satellites" allows companies to transfer assets among affiliated firms and transfer profits among the subsidiaries without adequately informing shareholders and other stakeholders who have a keen interest in the future viability and profitability of the corporation.

In Russia some information currently can be obtained by requesting the shareholder list from the share registrar. However, the information often includes only the direct shareholders and not the indirect and ultimate owners. The Transparency Directive of the European Commission requires disclosure to the company and the national authorities when a natural person or legal entity holds (directly or indirectly) more than 10 percent of the voting rights of a publicly listed corporation. The measures described below are designed to improve the quality of corporate financial information. The intention is to define the roles, responsibilities, and obligations of the (supervisory) boards of directors; encourage the creation of audit committees within the (supervisory) boards of directors; increase the liability for auditors; and strengthen the ability of the securities commission to apply sanctions.

The FCSM has developed a Code of Corporate Conduct that would provide useful guidance to directors. The FCSM expects that the Code will provide a set of working guidelines for Russian joint stock companies, as well as for investors, both domestic and foreign. The FCSM also anticipates that as the norms and principles in the Code become part of common business practice, they will become minimum requirements for corporate governance in Russia. In addition, it is expected that the Code will set an industry standard against which the liability of directors can be determined.

In addition, it may be helpful to consider guidelines that are still more detailed than those in the Code of Corporate Conduct. Business advisory task forces ranging from the Dey Commission in Canada to the Cadbury Commission in the United Kingdom have recommended that the stock exchanges develop detailed guidelines for boards of directors. Based on best practices worldwide, the guidelines could provide detailed guidance on such areas as procedures in which board members are selected and removed, the procedures for setting agendas for the board meetings, methods of establishing adequate compensation for board members, and required experience and training for board members. As part of the program, it may be helpful to also provide training for board members (as is planned as part of the emerging institutes of directors), particularly in the important aspects of new accounting and auditing laws. In addition, audit committees should be established for joint stock companies whose shares are publicly traded. The Joint Stock Company Law does provide for the creation of an "audit commission" (also known as a revision commission) but its responsibilities are limited. The proposed type of audit commission would be a committee within the board of directors that would report to the (supervisory) board of directors. The role of the audit committee should be to (*a*) review the financial audits prepared by the independent auditors and (*b*) meet several days a year with the independent auditors to discuss the financial audits, the management letter, and the auditor's recommendations on measures to improve the financial and management information systems used by the company. Generally the members of the audit committee should be taken from outside company management or employees and should represent individuals with a good understanding of the international standards for accounting and auditing.

Even with the introduction of International Accounting Standards and the use of International Standards of Auditing, additional reforms will be needed to ensure that independent audits provide meaningful financial information to shareholders and other stakeholders. Consideration should be given to strengthening the minimum statutory liability of independent auditors, since by common practice the amount of an auditor's liability in Russia may be capped under the auditing contract. In some CIS countries, such as Kazakhstan, the amount of the auditor's liability is set relative to the amount of the company's share capital. However, most auditing firms have a small capital base and their assets are limited to office leases and computer equipment. In light of the crucial importance of the independent audit, international best practice suggests that the amount of the auditor's liability should be a multiple of the auditing company's capital. Training of auditors will also be key, as will the interrelationship of the introduction of IAS with the basis of taxation of companies.

While the Russian legal framework has been amended to strengthen the capacity of the FCSM, the Commission's ability to impose substantial fines is limited, which reduces the effectiveness of the Commission in supervising marketplace behaviors and compliance with the Commission's regulations.

It may be helpful to increase the independence of the Commission from day-to-day political affairs, for example, by removing the legal status of the chairman of the Commission from that of a government minister and by establishing fixed terms for the members of the Commission. Strengthening the ability of the Commission to apply economic sanctions would also help to ensure corporate compliance with the Commission's securities regulations, but there must be checks and balances to ensure that such penalties are not applied for income to the Commission.[5] In addition, it will be necessary to align the penalties that can be applied with the damage caused to investors—the higher the risk to investors, the higher the penalties should be—rather than administrative errors or failures that have no impact on investors.

The Joint Stock Company Law gives some guidance to boards of directors in establishing the price for the sale or transfer of large assets. The law states that the market value of the property should be "the price at which a seller, having full information about the value of the property and not obliged to sell it, would have agreed to sell it, and the purchaser, having full information about the value of the property and not obliged to acquire it, would have agreed to acquire it."

It is proposed that transfers of corporate assets that represent more than 1 percent of company revenues should—on the instigation of minority investors—be made subject to review by a specialist evaluation division of the FCSM. If the decision of the FCSM is disputed, appeal could be made to the proposed independent capital markets tribunal (see below), with directors of boards being personally liable to pay fines and compensation if valuations are found to have been grossly against the interests of shareholders of the company concerned.

LEGISLATIVE INITIATIVES

The recent amendments to the Joint Stock Company Law, which came into effect on January 1st, 2002, are targeted at strengthening the protection of shareholders. They include:

1. Provision of the preemptive rights to *all* shareholders for private placements as well as the public offerings (to prevent dilution of percentage ownership by placement of new equity only to major shareholders and/or their affiliates)
2. Fine-tuning procedures for notifying shareholders of shareholders' meeting and voting procedures at shareholders' meetings so as to improve protection of minority shareholders and reduce costs
3. Strengthening of the safeguards related to large transactions and with interested parties.

The Securities Market Law has also been amended extensively. Amendments important for improving corporate governance include (a) rationalizing provisions regarding title registration for securities and recognition of ownership; (b) strengthening disclosure requirements for large open joint stock companies while relaxing those for small and/or closed companies; (c) enabling holders of depository receipts to participate in decision-making at shareholder meetings, which will be particularly important in encouraging investment by foreigners and introducing corporate governance practices commensurate with international best practice; and (d) clarifying identity and responsibilities of officials signing disclosure and offering documents.

In addition, work is currently under way on the following: amendments to the Security Markets Law to support issuance of secured bonds and stock options; the Law on Investment Schemes, the Law on Regularizing Relationships Connected with Placement of Securities Issued without Government Registration, the Tax Code, the Law on Issued Mortgage Securities, and the Law on Double and Ordinary Warehouse Receipts.

As of January 2002, additional changes to the Securities Market Law were under consideration before the Duma. The changes sort out the problem of bond collateral. Currently a bond, as a security, simply represents the right of a holder to receive repayment of their principal and interest, but not the right to take a borrower's assets, should a borrower default. The right of a holder to claim a borrower's assets is currently specified by a separate contract and is not embodied in the bond itself. This makes outcomes more complicated and unpredictable. Changes to the Securities Market Law will contain all the provisions to ensure that a bondholder has a right to claim the principal, the interest, and assets of a borrower in a case of default.

One important step forward in encouraging the use of collective investment funds in Russia is the enactment of the Law on Investment Funds. This law presents the legal foundation for collective investment vehicles, which previously had been governed only by a presidential decree and regulations of the FCSM.

Recommendations for Legislative Initiatives

It is suggested that focusing on broad measures that would improve trust by reducing the occurrence of abuses and ensuring effective punishment upon their occurrence would be productive interventions. Though such measures may be an extension of the FCSM's mandate, lobbying for such change and demonstrating the need for it would be an appropriate role for the Commission to play.

There is a lack of clarity regarding the responsibility for enforcing particular laws. Establishing greater clarity as to which agency is responsible for enforcement of particular (parts of) the law would strengthen the mandate of the agency and prevent duplication/confusion about initiatives related to enforcement. The following is a broad range of high-priority legislative initiatives:

1. Laws such as the Joint Stock Company Law should clearly identify a body responsible for their enforcement, how that body is accountable for such enforcement, and to whom (usually Parliament or through a ministry to Parliament); and what that body's mandate is and what its powers are. These powers must be sufficient to make compliance an incentive. Responsibility for enforcement of the Joint Stock Company Law may be shared among several agencies, but this responsibility should in any event be clearly designated.

2. The Joint Stock Company Law should introduce a requirement for filing (for public access) all companies' charters, together with annual filing of all companies' reports and accounts, with a list of significant shareholders and directors, and a register of assets over which charges have been granted to lenders (i.e., where collateral has been given against loans). Certain other corporate information should also be required to be filed, upon occurrence of specific events, such as issuance of bonds or equities. Such requirements should be applied to all listed and traded companies by a certain deadline, and all companies, progressively graded by either shareholder capital or by turnover by a subsequent deadline. Penalties should be set for failure to comply with these requirements.

3. The Joint Stock Company Law should make disclosure of ownership, including indirect ownership of companies, mandatory, and it should empower company registrars to identify entities lying behind nominee holders and trusts whether onshore or offshore.

4. The rights of creditors regarding assets they have a claim to should be clarified; this applies both to credits secured in collateral (for further discussion, see Chapter 2) and in mortgage lending, where the lender is registered as the owner until the last mortgage payment is made by the borrower.

ENFORCEMENT OF THE LAW

A number of laws have been enacted in Russia to provide an enabling environment for financial sector and private sector reform. However, many would argue that there is just too much new legislation leading to confusion in the interpretation of laws, given the many challenges faced by Russia's transition to a market economy. The sheer volume of legislation, decrees, and regulations, and the lack of clarity and consistency in many of them make it easier for the devious to find loopholes, and for the Government to impose bureaucratic obstacles. Another problem lies in the inability of law enforcement officers to enforce the law and to be consistent and equitable. Russia's current taxation, judicial, and legal systems simply do not create sufficient incentives for fair and impartial application of the law.

It is imperative that the Government and the private sector financial institutions support the implementation of legislation with actions, and that the rule of law prevails, not just the existence of laws.

As noted in the OECD's publication, *The Investment Environment in the Russian Federation* (2001), "After all, the core element of the rule of law is that it applies in equal measure to the powerful and the non-powerful and that legal institutions have sufficient authority and independence to make meaningful the remedies imposed against the powerful." This is currently one of the greatest problems in the development of capital markets in Russia, and recent comments by President Putin on the need for "a larger role and greater authority" for the judiciary are therefore to be welcomed.

In 2001 the FCSM and its branches considered about 1,700 cases related to breaches of legislation on protection of rights and lawful interests of investors. More than 1,400 fine orders were issued for a total amount of 125 million rubles (see Table 14.4). Among other breaches reviewed in the recent period, the FCSM had to impose sanctions in cases of failure to submit information to the FCSM by registrars, and failure to exclude the words "investment fund" from the names of several former voucher investment funds. For the first time in its practice, the FCSM considered cases where the share registrar illegally refused to record shareholders in the share registers.

The FCSM claims that disciplinary sanctions have contributed to the improvement of information disclosure by company-issuers. So far the companies that have been fined have not repeated breaches, and virtually all fines imposed by the FCSM have been upheld upon appeal.

Effective enforcement requires effective coordination and cooperation between the regulator and the whole range of enforcement authorities.

Table 14.4 Fines for Administrative Offenses in 2001

Registration Office	Number of Cases Considered	Number of Fine Orders	Amount of Fine in Thousand of Rubles
Central Office	216	216	64,790
Moscow	197	146	12,613
St. Petersburg	109	61	2,857
Sverdlovsk	86	49	3,404
Chelyabinsk	50	69	3,718
Omsk	86	59	4,088
Novosibirsk	210	143	3,092
Irkutsk	99	123	1,813
Primorye	78	29	7,438
Rostov	93	165	1,695
Nizhny Novgorod	21	21	2,720
Samara	44	24	4,960
Tatar	190	211	1,076
Saratov	88	47	4,425
Krasnoyarsk	84	65	4,681
Orel	34	33	2,319
Total	**1685**	**1459**	**125,688**

Source: FCSM.

The FCSM has reached an agreement of cooperation with the Federal Service for Financial Recovery and Bankruptcy, which will allow for exchange of information about market participants. Similar agreements will be signed with the ministries for justice, tax authority, tax police, and the interior. The FCSM and the General Prosecutor have sent briefings to prosecutors on the means of cooperation between FCSM and prosecutors in the area of administrative offenses. Cooperation is developing between the FCSM and the Moscow Company Registration office.

Given the size of the corporate sector and the nature of the corporate governance transgressions in Russia, the maximum fines that can be levied (at about $15,000) are not sufficient to encourage compliance with legislative requirements. Furthermore, effective July 2002, changes to the Code of Administrative Violations will reduce the maximum fine to just $5,000.

Recommendations for Enforcing Legislation

Although it will clearly take years to completely reform Russia's judicial system, in the context of capital markets the following recommendations are key:

1. Establish and empower an independent tribunal or arbitration court, properly resourced, to adjudicate capital markets disputes, including disputes between regulators, and between regulators and the regulated.
2. Improve procedures and mechanisms for enforcement of court judgments.
3. Improve the remuneration of the judiciary and enforcers such as bailiffs, and provide the necessary resources to the judicial system for it to operate effectively.
4. Provide training in capital markets law and operations for the judiciary.
5. Improve working relationships and communication between regulators and those responsible for law enforcement through formal liaison structures and communication channels.

Improving the enforcement capability of FCSM, the banking regulator, the police, and the courts of justice remain priority areas for further progress. If enforcement capacity is not strengthened, all other work on corporate governance and legislation will be wasted. There are many other issues on enforcement that require attention, including the following:

1. Consolidation of securities regulation, currently fragmented, into one regulator
2. Regulatory agencies working together to prevent regulatory arbitrage, and having all the necessary powers to investigate and enforce the law
3. Better cooperation with foreign regulatory agencies
4. Improved cooperation among regulatory agencies, the police, and the courts in bringing cases against miscreants
5. Proper and functioning anticorruption legislation, including "whistleblower" protection
6. Improved powers of the courts to enforce their judgments in civil cases
7. Training for the judiciary in financial matters
8. Training for lawyers in capital markets and ethical issues
9. Proper complaints procedures
10. Public education about the rights of depositors, investors, and shareholders.

Expert enforcement advice is already available to the FCSM through the work of the Lantern Corporation, a British-based specialist securities enforcement consultancy, which advises the U.K. regulator (the Financial Supervisory Authority) on enforcement issues, and which is working closely with the police and the judiciary in the area of securities enforcement.

CAPITAL MARKETS SUPERVISION

Supervision is the first level of enforcement. The task of supervisors is to monitor all activities of regulated entities to ensure that they are complying with the provisions of the law and regulations. The main problems in supervision are (*a*) vulnerability of funding, (*b*) lack of resources and skills to effectively fulfill their regulatory mandate, (*c*) high cost in relation to the scale of capital markets (due to small market scale and turnover), (*d*) lack of clear accountability, (*e*) regulatory arbitrage, and (*f*) potential for conflicts of interest.

Supervision of the banking and securities markets is the responsibility of the Central Bank and the Securities Commission, respectively. Supervision of nonstate pension funds is dealt with by a department of the Ministry of Social Protection (with FCSM regulating asset managers of such funds), and a department of the MoF regulates insurance. It is not certain where the responsibility for administering the law on joint stock companies lies, unless with the courts.

Supervision of banks' security market operations has, in the past, proved to be weak. It has concentrated more on form than on substance. Securities supervision by the FCSM has not been much better. Reporting discipline is poor, and the FCSM's analytical capability is weak. One persistent problem is that of nonreporting or late reporting. Both the Securities Commission and the Central Bank can sanction licensed entities with suspension or termination of their licenses, since systematic failure to report or late reporting is generally regarded as a sure sign of deterioration in the business of the company. The reports are filed to standard formats developed by the regulators. The formats of the reports need to be refined further to broaden the list of disclosures and ratios or to make them more targeted. Apart from recording instances of nonreporting, the regulators have difficulty in obtaining accurate information. The accuracy of information often suffers for three main reasons: negligence, failure to understand what exactly should be reported or how exactly various ratios should be calculated, and deliberate suppression or distortion of facts.

It would be useful if software capable of identifying discrepancies in the reporting could be used. Such software would need to be installed at the FCSM department responsible for the regulation of professional participants. Introducing more systematic data processing and analysis methods is crucial; it is also important to identify those areas of risk in companies that are to be analyzed, to develop systems that support the process of identifying abuses, and to require of the systems that they assist the regulator in differentiating between the material and immaterial.

It is clear that the current information technology (IT) infrastructure is inadequate. The FCSM regards the malfunction of the current IT environment as a cause of serious concern and embarrassment inasfar as market participants are aware of the current problems. The installation of new computer-based monitoring systems should assist the FCSM in collecting and processing information and thereby contribute to improved enforcement practices, provided that these systems are fully harmonized with the strengthened and refocused business practices of the FCSM.

The proper financing of the FCSM is a priority. Elsewhere, securities commissions are able to cover many of their costs from contributions made by market participants in ways that include fees for licensing and license renewal; annual establishment charges related to the size of the participant; sale of compendia of rules and regulations; a small percentage levy on issues of securities; and sale of market data to market participants, the media, and information providers.

Fines should not form part of the Commission's retained income, since this encourages excessive penalization for trivial offences. This income should be remitted directly to the state budget and should not be offset against the FCSM's costs. Alternatively, the Government might establish an aggregate limit on the amount to be retained by the FCSM from penalty charges.

Even in mature markets, such as in the United States, annual costs of operation of the Securities and Exchange Commission (SEC) are underwritten by the Federal budget, but are mostly recovered from the fees and charges collected by the SEC. These fees and charges are paid directly to a budgetary account and not to the SEC in order to avoid creating distorted incentives for the securities regulator.

Such a degree of self-financing allows the SEC to set its pay rates above those for government service as a whole, and thus attract high quality professionals, who, while perhaps not earning what they might in the private sector, can regard their work at the SEC as a career opportunity, not a dead end. This may also help reduce the corruption in which civil servants may be tempted to indulge in order to supplement meager incomes. Although it is important to maintain the autonomy of securities regulators in emerging markets, it is unlikely that sufficient funding can be provided by market participants alone—budget support will continue to be needed.

Recommendations for Supervision

The primary recommendations for improved capital markets supervision are the following:

1. Clear standards of public administration should be established and applied to all financial sector regulators; these should include accountability, transparency of decision-making, fairness, competence, honesty, and professionalism.
2. Requirements for the conduct of regulatory personnel, including confidentiality of data, should be explicitly stated in their employment contracts.
3. Financial sector regulators must be reliably financed at a level that is sufficient to enable them to fulfill their mandate effectively; also they must be able to pay salaries that will enable them to attract and keep competent professional staff. It is recommended that the U.S. SEC financing structure be used as a model. This model reduces the potential for government capture of the regulator.
4. Potential for bias or distortion should be eliminated. On the one hand, financial regulators should be made independent from the Government. On the other hand, they should be made specifically accountable for the proper delivery of their mandate, through Parliament and the Government. Also, potential for regulatory arbitrage should be eliminated either through a requirement for regulation only by function, or through a legal requirement that the standards set by the relevant functional regulator (securities regulator for securities markets, banking regulator for banking markets, etc.) must be applied across that function, which introduces the concept of lead regulator.
5. Investment should be made in regulators' IT capacity with the aim of maximizing regulatory effectiveness (for instance, through computer analysis of certain reports and links with regional offices) and improving cost-effectiveness of regulation, together with transparency, ease, and speed of access to information.
6. Government and regulatory officials should be banned from membership on corporate boards and required to hold their assets through blind trusts during the period of their office; clear codes of conduct should be established through employment contracts to identify conflicts of interest that may arise, and how these must be handled (in particular, affiliated transactions). Clear penalties for breaches should also be established.
7. Regulatory penalties should relate to the damage or potential damage caused to those affected by the breach or breaches concerned; presently they relate more to administrative than to investor protection concerns.

THE ROLE OF THE CAPITAL MARKETS SUPERVISOR

It is suggested that in defining its strategic direction for the further work, the FCSM should, as a member of the International Organization of Securities Commissions, use the methods provided by IOSCO for conducting a self-assessment of compliance with its principles.

IOSCO has published self-assessment questionnaires for regulators and other more specialized questionnaires for specific parts of the securities markets—accounting standards, broker/dealers, and collective investments. The purpose of this assessment material is to provide regulators with benchmarks against which to assess their performance. The FCSM has already embarked on completing these self-assessments. The formal assessment of compliance with IOSCO principles is to be undertaken as part of the joint IMF/World Bank Financial Sector Assessment Program being conducted in 2002.

At its 1998 Annual Conference, IOSCO adopted the Objectives and Principles of Securities Regulation, setting forth 30 core principles of securities regulation. As the global forum for securities regulators, IOSCO is committed to establishing and maintaining consistently high standards for the securities industry. The principles are based on three fundamental objectives of securities regulation:

1. *Protecting investors*—regulation of market conduct whose primary aim is to protect both market participants and investors from suffering loss or disadvantage as a result of fraud, theft, or other malpractice
2. *Ensuring that markets are fair, efficient, and transparent*—market efficiency and transparency, which will lead to a broadening and deepening of financial markets
3. *Reducing systemic risk*—prudential regulation, designed to protect the financial system from the systemic risks that may result from failures in any part of it.

The Securities Commission should adopt these fundamental objectives, and measure all changes in legislation, regulation, and organization against them. The 30 core principles give practical effect to these three objectives. Together, the objectives and principles are intended to guide regulators and serve as a yardstick against which to measure progress toward effective regulation.

All IOSCO members are asked to complete the survey to help IOSCO gain a better understanding of the extent to which, and the means by which, the securities regulatory system in each member jurisdiction is consistent with its objectives and principles and to identify areas in which more progress can be made. IOSCO recognizes that the means of implementation will vary across jurisdictions. The survey questions are designed to elicit an explanation of how principles are being implemented, not to imply that a particular method of implementation is mandated by the Objectives and Principles document. IOSCO anticipates that it will update the survey on a regular basis to help track its members' continuing progress in meeting the Objectives and Principles. It is also intended that there should be other, more detailed surveys that would implement specific principles.

When focusing on enforcement, for instance, the FCSM could ask a series of questions as follows, based on IOSCO:

Detect. Does the FCSM have adequate capacity to *detect* abnormal price and/or volume movements in the market, whether through its own system or by effective reporting requirements?

Investigate. When an abnormal transaction takes place on the exchanges or the OTC market, does the FCSM have adequate legal authority to require the directly and indirectly involved parties to swiftly *provide information* about or to explain the transaction?

Enforce. If so justified, does the FCSM have adequate authority and means to *enforce* compliance or initiate court proceedings? Is the penal/court process sufficiently supportive of the securities commission's authority?

Such an approach would assist the FCSM in understanding the impact of particular legal initiatives. The focus of the legal work heretofore has been almost exclusively on legal drafting rather than on developing the capacity of the FCSM as the securities regulatory authority. The following principles should be observed:
1. All capital market regulators, including the Central Bank and self-regulatory organizations, must have sufficient powers to enforce full and timely reporting by entities in their jurisdiction; they also need a system of fines.
2. Standards of reporting must be capable of alerting the regulator to abuses and, as such, help the regulator track down violations with as little effort as possible. A review of the current standards of reporting by capital market players should be undertaken to determine the extent to which they provide adequate information.

3. Since the regulator is supposed to use the reports to diagnose any abuse, the way the reports are dealt with should be systematized by means of a system of automatic alerts. The system needs to rely on ways of analyzing the reports that will differentiate between material abuses and immaterial errors.
4. All market regulators should set up and maintain an advanced relational database and computer systems to monitor the regulated organizations. Ideally, all regulators should have access to each other's systems, or share a single one.

TRANSPARENCY AND DISCLOSURE

Quality of financial information is crucial for investors and other stakeholders to make informed decisions.[6] While Russian accounting rules are slowly moving toward IAS, they remain weak in several key areas. Regarding valuation of assets, Russian standards require no write-offs for bad debts or obsolete inventory. Thus assets are recorded at historical costs and revalued upward at the discretion of management, even when their historical cost has little relation to their fair market value. General and administrative expenses are added to inventory costs so that inventories may show an increase in value despite no increase in the market value for the goods.

In addition, off–balance sheet items include not only guarantees and pledges of assets, but also property belonging to third parties but under the temporary administration of the company. Until 2000, Russian accounting rules did not require disclosure of related party transactions, that is, sales and purchases of assets among companies controlled by each other or by third parties. The new accounting rules will help, but in the absence of reliable disclosure of ownership and control structures, it may be virtually impossible for auditors to verify the nature of transactions among possibly affiliated parties.

A handful of Russian companies file financial statements in accordance with U.S. GAAP or IAS. However, the thousands of remaining large companies in Russia provide information only in accordance with RAS, which fail to provide adequate information for investors. Thus a rapid move toward full adoption of IAS would provide valuable information for shareholders and other stakeholders.

There is an argument that IAS should be adapted to RAS rather than simply translating the international standards into the Russian language. This approach creates a perennial delay and the risk of continued confusion, with difficulties in dissemination of the changes. International Accounting Standards are constantly being changed and modified and with each change, the Russian authorities will be required to sit and review the impact of the changes on the Russian version of International Accounting Standards. Full adoption of IAS, which are already available in Russian, would be much simpler to administer. Adoption of IAS would provide confidence to investors to come through with third party finance for Russian enterprises. Also foreign investors familiar with IAS will find the statements easier to understand and compare with similar companies internationally. Application of IAS may not be suitable for all companies, but it should be required for all large joint stock companies, companies whose shares are publicly traded, and for banks and other financial institutions.

Despite the existence of a register of companies operated through various regional registration chambers, and the FCSM's register of issuers, it is very difficult to find out basic information about Russian companies—unless they are listed, in which case brokers have often compiled such data in order to service potential clients. The information that is made publicly available is very limited and does not assist in the evaluation of a company's equity or bonds; it is also very time consuming to obtain. Lack of access to information about issuers is a key factor in the failure to effectively develop portfolio of investment institutions in Russia. Normally investors in market economies are passive investors needing access to good quality information in order to make investment decisions.

Recommendations for Transparency and Disclosure

It is suggested that a central source for information would be valuable, not unlike the British Companies House, where anybody is entitled to inspect a company's file. This is common practice in all developed and many emerging markets; information registered with the securities regulator is available for public review, except such information that is specifically filed and accepted by the securities regulator as being confidential. These company files contain the whole historical record of the company, including its prospectus for past issues, a register of charges against its assets, the identity of major shareholders (share registers are also available for inspection), the names of directors, the latest financial statements, and other relevant information. Information is also available on companies that are in insolvency, struck off (i.e., no longer registered due to serious transgressions), or dormant.

While Companies House has records of every limited company, it would only initially be necessary for the Russian version to hold the records of open joint stock companies that have made a public issue. There will be no immediate need to include private closed joint stock companies. Quite a lot of this information is already in the hands of the FCSM, and although it is available for inspection, it is not well organized and is difficult to access. The FCSM's current IT project should address this problem.

The Law on State Registration of Legal Entities was approved in 2001, and its enactment is expected to open up access to companies' registration details. The passage of the Law is the trigger to set in motion the use of the Internet to provide access to consolidated company records in all regions. Although there is more work to be done, this would be a highly desirable development.

Partial adoption of IAS is undesirable. The Russian Government should pursue a medium-term plan (over the next three years) to replace RAS with full IAS for all large enterprises. So as to facilitate consolidation on an IAS basis, the Government should also remove barriers that prevent subsidiaries of large companies from using IAS instead of RAS. Publicly traded companies, banks, and other financial institutions should immediately adopt IAS for reporting and preparation of their financial statements. All Russian joint stock companies and Russian subsidiaries of enterprises that prepare consolidated financial statements should have the option to prepare them in full compliance with IAS instead of RAS. All listed enterprises should fully adopt IAS by a specific deadline, such as 2004. International Accounting Standards should be used in the preparation and use of corporate prospectuses for sales of shares of state-owned or state majority-held enterprises. State-owned enterprises should be encouraged to adopt IAS as a basis for financial reporting in place of RAS.

The Institute of Professional Accountants or a suitable alternative body should be developed into an effective, independent, professional association for accounting professionals in Russia. It should promote the integration of IAS into the Russian accounting system. It should also be responsible for training and certifying Russian accounting professionals in IAS, as well as administering an internationally recognized IAS competency examination. An adequate quantity of technical staff resources and funding should be dedicated to developing and implementing the reforms, particularly within official government bodies that will need to develop new IAS-based procedures.

ENDNOTES

1. See also further discussion in Chapter 1.
2. Source: Inspection of Non-state Pension Funds under Russian Ministry of Labor and Social Development.
3. Source: Centre for Collective Investments, Moscow, 2001.
4. By allowing shareholders to consolidate votes for a single member of the board of directors, the introduction of cumulative voting now allows minority shareholders the opportunity to elect at least one board member (see the scorecard in Table 14.3).
5. One model, which might be a point of reference for developing the Commission's financing structure would be the structure adopted by the Securities and Exchange Commission in the United States.
6. See also discussion of these issues in Chapter 4.

REFERENCES

Black, Bernardn 2001. "The Corporate Governance Behavior and Market Value of Russian Firms." *Emerging Markets Review*, vol. 2 (forthcoming 2001).

Caprio, Gerard, and Honohan, Patrick. 2001. *Finance for Growth: Policy Choices in a Volatile World*. Policy Research Report. World Bank, Washington, D.C.

Demirgüç-Kunt, A., and V. Maksimovic. 2000. Funding Growth in Bank-Based and Market-Based Financial Systems. Policy Reseach Working Paper 2432. World Bank, Policy Research Department, Washington D.C.

OECD (Organization for Economic Co-operation and Development). 2001. *The Investment Environment in the Russian Federation*. Paris. Website: http://electradegfi.fr/cgi-bin/OECDBookShop.storefront/.

Pistor, Katharina, and Andrew Spicer. 1997. "Investment Funds in Mass Privatization: Lessons from Russia and the Czech Republic." In I. Lieberman, S. Nestor, and R. Desai, eds. *Between State and Market: Mass Privatization in Transition Economies*. World Bank, Washington, D.C.

Russian Corporate Governance Round Table. 2000. "Survey Role of Independent Directors in Russian Enterprises." Website: http://www.oecd.org/EN/documents/0,EN-documents-28-nodirectorate-no-no-no-28,FF.html.